US Public Opinion since the 1930s

US Public Opinion since the 1930s

Galluping through History

Richard Seltzer

LEXINGTON BOOKS
Lanham • Boulder • New York • London

Published by Lexington Books
An imprint of The Rowman & Littlefield Publishing Group, Inc.
4501 Forbes Boulevard, Suite 200, Lanham, Maryland 20706
www.rowman.com

86-90 Paul Street, London EC2A 4NE

Copyright © 2022 by The Rowman & Littlefield Publishing Group, Inc.

All rights reserved. No part of this book may be reproduced in any form or by any electronic or mechanical means, including information storage and retrieval systems, without written permission from the publisher, except by a reviewer who may quote passages in a review.

British Library Cataloguing in Publication Information Available

Library of Congress Cataloging-in-Publication Data

Names: Seltzer, Richard A., 1951-, author.
Title: US public opinion since the 1930s : Galluping through history / Richard Seltzer.
Description: Lanham : Lexington Books, [2022] | Includes bibliographical references and index.
Identifiers: LCCN 2021047352 (print) | LCCN 2021047353 (ebook) |
  ISBN 9781793653505 (cloth) | ISBN 9781793653529 (paperback) |
  ISBN 9781793653512 (ebook)
Subjects: LCSH: United States—Public opinion—History—20th century. |
  United States—Public opinion—History—21st century. | United States—Politics and government—20th century. | United States—Politics and government—21st century.
Classification: LCC HN90.P8 S45 2022 (print) | LCC HN90.P8 (ebook) | DDC
  303.3/80973—dc23
LC record available at https://lccn.loc.gov/2021047352
LC ebook record available at https://lccn.loc.gov/2021047353

Contents

Acknowledgments   vii

Introduction   1

1   The 1930s: The Great Depression and the Start of World War II   11

2   The 1940s: World War II and the Onset of the Cold War   29

3   The 1950s: Anticommunism, Relative Economic Prosperity at Home, and a Growing Cold War Abroad   49

4   The 1960s: Era of Protest: Civil Rights, Vietnam, and Counterculture   65

5   The 1970s: Watergate, Normalization of Relations with China, Continuing Social and Political Protest, the Growth of International Terrorism, and Stagflation   85

6   The 1980s: Ronald Reagan, the Fall of the Berlin Wall, the Soviet War in Afghanistan, and AIDS   101

7   The 1990s: The Collapse of the Soviet Union and Yugoslavia, the First Gulf War, the Genocide in Rwanda, Bill Clinton, and the Rise of the Internet   119

8   The 2000s: Decade of 9/11, the Iraqi War, the Great Recession, and the Election of Barack Obama   145

9	The 2010s: War against ISIS, the Tea Party, Black Lives Matter, Brexit, and the Election of Donald Trump	167
10	2020: Covid-19, the Killing of George Floyd and Protests, an Attempt to Overthrow an Election	201
Conclusion		213
Appendix 1: Preamble to Gallup History		225
References		237
Index		245
About the Author		257

Acknowledgments

As with any book project, many people deserve a lot of thanks.

I thank Eric Kuntzman, my acquisitions editor at Lexington Books, for his support and many useful suggestions. I also thank Jasper Mislak at Lexington Books for his very skillful editing. The Lexington Books reviewer wrote a detailed analysis of the book with numerous great suggestions. This is why the peer-review process in academics can be so important.

Brenda Foust helped me with general editing and gave me a lot of very good advice on improving the manuscript.

There are several people who read individual chapters and offered me very valuable comments: Russell Canan, Larry Lynn, Gary Roth, Robert Smith, and Charles Turner.

The wonderful people at the Roper Center deserve many kudos for helping me access data and answering my many queries about issues with the data. They were consistently helpful.

My family is always a source of support for my writing projects and giving meaning to my life: Grace, Michael, Mathew, Katie, and Fred.

Introduction

This book combines two deep and enduring interests of mine: survey research and history. I've been conducting surveys for forty years and have loved history since grade school.

When writing a recent book (Smith and Seltzer, 2015), I examined many Gallup surveys ranging from the first one, conducted in 1936, to the present. During that project, I kept getting sidetracked by looking at questions far outside my immediate research topic. I was fascinated by survey questions on the Great Depression, World War II, McCarthyism, race relations, women's equality, sexuality, culture, the Vietnam War, and so on. I would call friends who were history buffs and say, "you wouldn't believe what I came across today!" I then realized that other people would likely also be fascinated by the intersection of survey research and history, so I decided to write a book that uses Gallup survey questions to illustrate history.[1] More importantly, we learn how the public felt about the issues at the time they were topical.

This book should be helpful to historians who want to learn about what the public thought about historical events when they occurred. On the flip side, it should also be helpful to those who study public opinion who might have gaps in their understanding of the relevant historical events. As the pun in the title implies, this is a "gallop through history." In condensing seventy-five years of history and survey research to a couple of hundred pages, I will not satisfy the professional historian or pollster. However, it should provide room for thought as well as become a welcome reference.

GEORGE GALLUP AND THE INCEPTION OF SURVEY RESEARCH

Scientific survey research began in the 1930s arising from two traditions: journalism and market research. Public interest in the results of surveys expanded the readership of newspapers and corporations needed to have reliable information about consumer preferences. Market research in the 1920s had been conducted more by a "rule-of-thumb" approach than by a scientific process and had little concern with sampling or questionnaire design. Most surveys from that early era were based upon convenience samples ("man in the street") or were mail surveys that didn't reach a representative sample. This would all change with the 1936 US presidential election.

The most prominent attempt to predict the outcome of the 1936 election was conducted by the *Literary Digest* (LD). The LD sent out a mail questionnaire to ten million people and got a response rate of 20%. Their survey sample, however, had been mostly generated from among people who owned automobiles or telephones, and since in 1936 you had to be well off to own either of those commodities; the sample was far from representative.[2] George Gallup, sometimes called the "father" of survey research, was openly critical of the LD's methodology and its results, which predicted a victory by Alf Landon, who, they said, would garner 57% of the vote over Franklin Roosevelt's predicted 43%. Gallup, though, was sure he could develop a better survey and even said he would return his subscribers' money if his survey did not more accurately predict the election's outcome. Gallup's poll predicted FDR would get 54% of the vote, which fell short of the 61% of the vote FDR did receive in his landslide victory. Nonetheless, Gallup did not have to return any subscription money.

George Gallup wasn't the only pollster to gain recognition because of the election of 1936: Archibald Crossley and Elmo Roper also developed important survey research techniques, and both also predicted Roosevelt's victory. Only Gallup's, though, would become a household name. Gallup's background in psychology and journalism provided the foundation for his market research career. He received a PhD in applied psychology from the State University of Iowa (1928) and taught journalism at three universities. He left teaching to conduct readership surveys for newspapers and then became director of research at an advertising agency. In 1935, he started his "America Speaks" syndicated column, which reported the results of polls, and went on to become the foremost spokesperson for the science of survey research.[3] Famously, he called polling "democracy in action." His America Speaks column appeared in 60 newspapers in 1936 and 130 in 1944.

FEATURES AND LIMITATIONS OF GALLUP'S SURVEYS

In predicting Roosevelt's victory in 1936, Gallup and the other two pollsters used their experience in marketing research to develop quota samples, that is, samples that are in proportion to characteristics or traits of a population. Quota samples at this time were usually based upon socioeconomic status, region, gender, and age. Often, though, there was no attempt to interview blacks or poor people because these groups were not perceived as potential consumers, or simply because of racism. Of 137 pre-1950 Gallup surveys that I analyzed in a previous book, the average percentage of blacks included in all samples was 3.3% (the population was 9.8% African-American in 1940). In fact, five of these surveys had a sample that was less than 1% black.[4] Quota samples started to come under extensive criticism in the 1940s and a shift began toward probability samples, which employ some form of random selection. This shift was accelerated following the debacle of the 1948 presidential elections (see Erikson and Tedin, 2015; Campbell, 2020: Ch 3). Gallup predicted Dewey would beat Truman 49.5% v. 44.5%, while the reality was 45.1% v. 49.6%. Gallup started using probability samples in 1951.[5] Between 1951 and the end of the decade, the average survey sample was 8.1% black.

Gallup surveys were almost exclusively face-to-face until 1985. From then until 1997 they were conducted both face-to-face and by telephone, at which point they became exclusively telephone surveys.

Many survey questions in the early years were deemed to be taboo—too intrusive to be asked directly. Questions on age, occupation, home ownership, and income were often not asked of the respondent and so the interviewer was told to guess as to the answers. For example, in the 1940s socioeconomic status was coded as wealthy, above-average, average, above poor, or poor, based not on responses but on the interviewer's estimation. Race (white or colored), gender, and age were also based on the interviewer's perception.

There were, of course, some topics not covered by Gallup's surveys. For instance, I could find few useful questions that examined FDR's banking reforms in the 1930s, and there were almost no questions asked about race relations before the mid-1940s. In addition, some questions were difficult to interpret. The Wagner Act of 1935 guaranteed workers the right to engage in collective bargaining and to strike. However, the thirty-five questions about the Act asked in the 1930s surveys do not allow an unambiguous interpretation of whether Americans supported or opposed its premise.

Another challenge with analyzing Gallup surveys concerns the lack of consistency in question phraseology. This was particularly true in the early years, but even today remains an issue. For example, in May 2015, Gallup asked: "Do you think gay or lesbian relations between consenting adults should or should not be legal?" In May 2003, the phraseology had been, "Do you think homosexual relations between consenting adults should or should not be legal?" I understand why the wording was changed. However, did this change affect the answers of respondents?

There were a variety of other reasons to be concerned about the reliability of the survey data used in this book. One issue was that the data was not always cleaned. For example, I found gender codes of 0 and 7 and ages of 3 or M. Another problem was that categories were not always consistent. In some years when asking about education, Gallup allowed codes for business or trade school and not in other years.

Gallup questions were often wonderfully capricious and ranged across politics, religion, fashion, movies, and so on. In recent years, though, the Gallup poll reduced the number of questions it asks and has concentrated on its mainstay topic series: confidence in American institutions, presidential approval, most important problem, etc., although some of these topic series might only be used every several years (i.e., race relations). The Gallup poll came under a lot of criticism following the 2012 presidential election from those in the survey profession because it was such an outlier in its predictions. This caused Gallup to further scale back its range of questions. Therefore, in my analysis starting with the 2010s, I increasingly look to other survey organizations as a source of data.

There is one type of survey question that I avoid: a voting preference. This is the question that many readers are most familiar with as some of us obsessively check polling data to see who is most likely to win an election. However, given the context of this book, I am most concerned with questions about issues.[6]

CROSSTABULAR ANALYSIS

I conducted a simple crosstabular analysis for many of the questions.[7] Because of space limitations, the 164 pages of crosstabs, commentary on the crosstabs, and related wording are placed in an online appendix located at https://rowman.com/ISBN/9781793653505/US-Public-Opinion-since-the-1930s-Galluping-through-History.

I did not want to overwhelm the reader, so I decided to analyze, within each chapter, around half-a-dozen questions in each topic area (this number varied). There is no scientific process for choosing these questions. I picked some because the topic was prominent in current events (Vietnam, Watergate, etc.) and others simply because I was interested (girls asking boys for a date).[8] I also decided to limit the demographic categories to race, gender, age, education, region, and political party. Several caveats concern these categories.

- As discussed above, Gallup interviewed few African Americans before the 1950s. Therefore, extreme caution should be used in analyzing differences between whites and blacks.
- In the 1930s and 1940s, education was not asked in most surveys. When education was not asked, I substituted this with the interviewer's assessment of the respondent's socioeconomic status ranging from wealthy to on relief. These categories often changed and obviously the coding was highly subjective.[9] How I collapsed educational categories changed over time. Few Americans were college graduates before the 1960s so for those years I compared high-school graduates with those who did not graduate. In later years, I added some college and college graduates.
- Respondents were rarely asked to identify their political party in the 1930s and 1940s. In these cases, I often substituted who the respondent voted for in the previous election.
- In looking at the region I decided to divide the sample into South and other. This would capture most of the important regional differences. An issue with the region is that survey organizations differed in determining whether some states were in the South or another region.

With large enough sample sizes, relatively trivial differences can be statistically significant. This is particularly an issue in the early years of Gallup where most sample sizes exceeded 3,000. In previous research (Smith and Seltzer, 2000) I argued that when the percentage difference between demographic categories was less than ten points, this was not substantively significant and was not reported. Therefore, in order to improve readability, I do not display differences that are not statistically significant (p<.05) and the difference is less than nine points (allow for some borderline differences).[10]

I decided not to over-interpret the crosstabs. The result is that my analysis on many of these crosstabs is only surface-deep (sorry, no logistic regressions). Otherwise, attention would be pulled away from the general thrust of the book: the interplay between history and public opinion. This also encourages readers to make their own interpretations.

HISTORICAL ANALYSIS OF ROPER QUESTIONS

Roper provided me with a listing of 17,757 surveys that they had in their collection from 1935 through the end of 2018. I use this listing to describe changes in survey research over the decades. I only analyze surveys that were national in scope (I also excluded exit polls). There were 2,075 distinct entries for the Roper field (sample coverage).[11] I included any political survey that appeared to be national in scope. This included not only the obvious national surveys but also surveys that only included blacks, Jews, Catholics, likely voters, and so on. For each of these surveys, I was also able to determine if the survey was done by telephone, face-to-face, mail, web-based, or multimode.

Caution is needed in analyzing the Roper data. Many survey organizations are either not represented at Roper or sporadically at best: American National Election Survey, Harris, surveys conducted by the US government, and most academic surveys. Nonetheless, the results are fascinating and are mentioned at the beginning of most chapters.

SOURCES OF SURVEY DATA

I looked at every Gallup survey since 1936.[12] To do this, I primarily relied on data accessed from the Roper Center for Public Opinion Research, an archive for public opinion surveys now located at Cornell. Roper allows members to download the raw data and copy of the questionnaire for most Gallup surveys.[13] Roper also has a search facility (IPOLL) for its 700,000 questions. Between looking at over 1,000 survey questionnaires, using IPOLL, and other searches, I was able to enter the results of over 4,000 relevant questions into a database. If I could not find a relevant question asked by Gallup, I would look at questions by other survey organizations: ABC, AP, Bloomberg, CBS, Chicago Council, CNN, Fox, GfK, Harris, Hart, Ipsos, Marist,

Monmouth, NBC, Newsweek, NORC, NSF, *NYT*, Office of Public Research, ORC, Phi Delta Kappa, Pew, Politico, Quinnipiac, Roper, Suffolk, Times Mirror, *USA Today*, *Washington Post*, *WSJ*, Yankelovich, and others.[14]

PROBLEMS WITH THE DATA

Results can be affected by question phraseology, context, mode of interview, and so on (Schuman and Presser, 1996).[15] A more recent problem with surveys is growing non-response rates. In 2017, the average response rate for Gallup (other survey organization's response rates for telephone surveys are similar) was only 7%.[16] Essentially, people who respond to surveys may be different from those who do not.

Above, I discuss the problem that Gallup had with quota samples as well as ignoring people of lower socioeconomic status, women, and blacks. In modern surveys, we usually weigh the data so that the sample reflects the population in terms of race, age, gender, region, education, and so on. The raw Gallup data did not include weights until the late 1960s.[17] I applied weights when they were available.[18]

When I began the crosstabs analysis, it became apparent that results from my analysis of the raw data sometimes differed from those provided by IPOLL. Usually, the difference was no more than a couple of percentage points. For some differences, I contacted Roper to try to help me understand the nature of the problem (they were very helpful). Sometimes the interns or other employees at Roper made an error.[19] In other situations, the difference could be because of issues surrounding weighting the data, how to deal with dirt in the data, or decisions about treating respondents who did not answer the question. Even after accounting for all these issues, sometimes our results disagreed. To avoid confusion, I opted to use my results if there was a difference from the IPOLL data.

ORGANIZATION OF THE BOOK

I have a chapter for each decade (1930s, 1940s, etc.), a short chapter on the singular year of 2020, a "preamble" chapter that discusses some relevant history prior to the first Gallup surveys (which is provided as an appendix), and a conclusion. In each chapter, I subdivided events into the following major categories: world events; US politics; race; sex and gender; the economy; science, technology, and the environment; and popular trends. Crosstabular tables and accompanying analysis for these sections can be found in the online appendix. History, however, does not always fall into neat or exclusive categories. For example, the development of the atomic bomb could fit in a discussion of either science or World War II; I chose to put it in the former.

To avoid redundancy, some survey topics are skipped in some decades. For example, Gallup often asks respondents to identify their favorite sports, what sports they played, and whether they attended sporting events, but since responses to this question typically do not change much over a decade, I might discuss this set of questions in one chapter and skip it in the next. There are a variety of topics that I treat in this way, including labor unions, newspapers, immigration, and gun control. Similarly, an individual topic sometimes spans more than one decade. Lance Armstrong won many of his races in the 2000s, but his scandal arose in the next decade. Therefore, I only discuss Armstrong in the 2010s decade.

This book would be unreadable if I listed the question phraseology for each question. Hence, I usually paraphrase. I will, however, make available upon request the database I created that lists the exact question phraseology, sample size, percentage distribution, and date of the survey.[20] In addition, for each question I analyze in the crosstabs, I provide the full question phraseology in the online appendix.

I report survey results in a standardized manner and, because it is sometimes important to include the percentage of survey respondents who didn't have an opinion, I have included that percentage where appropriate. For example, on the Supreme Court case *Citizens United v. FEC* (which ruled 5-4 that the government could not restrict political expenditures by non-profit or for-profit corporations or by labor unions) I state: "At the time of the Supreme Court decision, only 17% (68%, 15%) favored the decision [2/10-PEW]." This means 68% opposed the decision, 15% did not have an opinion, and the survey was conducted by Pew in February 2010.

In this book, I rarely look at the very complicated question of why certain attitudes were held. For example, immediately after the United States began the March 2003 invasion of Iraq, 72% favored this policy. Was this because most citizens believed, based on a thorough debate of the pros and cons, that the invasion was in the interest of national security? Or does this result reflect that information about WMDs and other issues had been manipulated in a process that Herman and Chomsky labeled Manufactured Consent (2010)? I don't attempt to answer these very important questions.[21]

I also want to caution the reader in over-interpreting any one question. I already discussed the problems with question phraseology and so on. In addition, it is impossible to capture attitudes toward a very complex issue with just one question. For example, in understanding attitudes toward the death penalty, I would want to know respondent attitudes toward aggravating (murder of a police officer) and mitigating (mental health) circumstances, parole, desire for retribution, belief in rehabilitation, and so on. When I have done previous surveys on capital punishment, I used twenty or more questions. In this book, I do not have the space, and most survey organizations ask only a question or two on most topics.

Although I attempt to be as objective as possible, I realize choosing what historical topics to examine and which survey questions to analyze is an extraordinarily subjective exercise. I ended up choosing many historical events that would probably be chosen by any other researcher; I chose other events simply because they interested me. In some ways, I simply wanted to have fun.

OTHER READINGS

There have been a number of very good books on public opinion (Clawson and Oxley, 2016; Glynn et al., 2016; Norrander and Wilcox, 2009; Berinsky, 2020). For the most part, they look at current public opinion. Several books have also looked at public opinion over time. Erikson and Tedin (2011) look at the history of public opinion in the United States. Their chapter 4 has a variety of historical trendlines on civil rights, foreign policy, criminal justice, ideology, partisanship, presidential approval, and so on. They utilize data from many sources: National Opinion Research Center (NORC), American National Election Survey (ANES), Gallup, and others. In chapter 7 they breakdown many of these beliefs by age, political party, gender, and religion.

Page and Shapiro (2010) also look at trendlines starting in 1930. They argue that the American public is rational and hold attitudes that are stable, coherent, and predictable.[22] They present series on foreign policy activism, defense, Russia, Vietnam, Israel, spending preferences, abortion, racial issues, civil liberties, crime, gays, rights of women, birth control, school prayer, pornography, drugs, what to do about the economy, social welfare, regulations, nuclear power, environment, and other issues. They also have a chapter that breaks down some of these questions by race, age, education, and region.

Niemi, Mueller, and Smith (1989) have over 200 tables that show trendlines on questions on a variety of issues: international, economic, confidence in institutions, tolerance, religion, race, gender, sexual morality, work, drugs, crime, and family. Most of their questions come from the NORC-GSS. However, they also have many questions from Gallup, ANES, and other survey organizations.

Rita Simon (1974) provides a fascinating overview of American public opinion through 1971. She examines labor unions, the economy, the role of government, health care, race relations, anti-Semitism, foreign policy, and civil liberties. Most of her tables are trendlines, although she enumerates many questions for single years.

These books are very important and helpful. However, they rarely put the survey questions in the context of history. Given that many of the books discussed above display trend lines of many questions, I did not feel it necessary to duplicate this work.

Other articles and books are cited, when appropriate, in the various chapters.

THEORETICAL QUESTIONS

I would be remiss if I did not mention some of the theoretical debates in examining the extensive survey data discussed in this book. How rational is the public? What affects public attitudes? And what does that mean for the future of democracy?

There is extensive literature purporting to show that the electorate is not competent and is ignorant (Delli, Carpini, and Keeter, 1996; Achen and Bartels, 2017) and ideologically incompetent (Converse, 1964). Essentially, people have little knowledge about political issues and their policy positions are irrational and inconsistent.[23]

Others argue that even though many people may not know the facts surrounding an issue, they still have a rational perspective given their trust in better-informed leaders (Berelson, Lazarsfeld, and McPhee, 1986), ability to focus on the most important issues (Krosnick, 1990), and can combine their pre-existing beliefs with information received from elites (Zaller, 1992). Page and Shapiro (2010) argue that, collectively, the public is rational, and its opinion influences policy.

In Converse's (1964) critique of Americans' understanding of ideology, he noted that many political attitudes are determined by attachment to social groups (race, religion, etc.). Perhaps even more important in recent years is the role of partisanship.[24] In a previous book (Smith and Seltzer, 2015), we showed how political polarization has grown since the election of Ronald Reagan.

Clearly, public opinion influences policy (Page and Shapiro, 1983; Burstein, 2003). However, as I discuss in the concluding chapter, it is crucial to not forget how elites influence public opinion.

NOTES

1. As the reader will soon learn, I also use surveys from other organizations.

2. Lusinchi (2012) argues that this conventional wisdom is wrong. Gallup had a vested interest in attacking the way that the *Literary Digest* pulled their sample. The actual error was because of non-response bias. FDR supporters were less likely to return the mail ballot. Campbell (2020) also notes that Gallup underestimated FDR's vote by 7% points. Campbell further remarks that Gallup still spun this as a victory in electoral polling.

3. Gallup's survey organization was called the American Institute of Public Opinion (AIPO). The Gallup Organization was created in 1958.

4. Robinson (1999) notes that Gallup considered women to be dim-witted and only 34% of the 1936–1937 samples were women and 2% were black. The sample overrepresented professionals and the more highly educated. Sixty percent of the population only had an eighth grade education compared to 39% of Gallup's sample. Robinson believes that much of this discrepancy was due to Gallup's concern for commercial clients. Berinsky (2006, 2009) has an excellent discussion of how Gallup created its quota sample, how the data are not representative, and he discusses how he created post-stratification weights to adjust the data.

5. See Moore (1992) for how Gallup conducted a quota sample. The Roper Center has a detailed analysis of how the Gallup probability sample was created. For example, see the codebook for the January 14–19, 1951 survey (USAIPO-1951-0470). Lusinchi (2018) discusses how the Social Science Research Council (SSRC) went into damage control to explain the problems of 1948 in order that survey research could maintain calling itself a science. The solution was the transition to probability sampling, which was already advocated by many government researchers. Campbell (2020) does a superb analysis of how pre-election surveys still made major errors after the transition to probability sampling. Additional errors occurred because surveys were not conducted immediately before the election, difficulty in determining who is a likely voter, not accounting for enthusiasm factors, issues around how to weight the data, and falling response rates.

6. For two excellent books about pre-election polling see Crespi (1998) and Campbell (2020).

7. The full wording for the questions analyzed in the crosstabs are found in Appendix 3.

8. I was unable to find the raw data for about one quarter of the questions I wanted to analyze.

9. Berinski (2006) notes the correlation between the interviewer assessment of SES and education was only .27.

10. Contact the author if you want a copy of the crosstabular tables that include all differences.

11. For example, there were four surveys labeled: "Adult head of households in Minnesota" and eighteen labeled: "Farmers residing in Iowa—20 years old and over." These are obviously state polls and would be excluded from my analysis.

12. I first looked at every question in date order. I made a second pass after writing my first draft in which I used Roper's grouping by topic—first restricting to Gallup questions and then all survey organizations. I often make a third or fourth pass using key words when I realized some historical topics were missing survey questions.

13. Beginning in 2017, Gallup started restricting members of Roper Center from downloading the raw data of many of its surveys. Gallup is trying to steer users to subscribe to the Gallup portal ($30,000 a year for my university!!).

14. This list can get complicated. For example, often ABC partners with the *Washington Post*. However, they sometimes do their own surveys or partner with someone else.

15. For a good overview of the different sources of error in survey research, see Hillygus (2020).

16. There have been many articles on declining response rates. See Leeper (2019). Response rates for face-to-face surveys are far higher. The response rate for the 2018 NORC-GSS was 59%.

17. Berinsky (2006) developed a method creating weights for these early surveys. His solution is beyond the scope of this book.

18. Applying weights was not always seamless. There were a few times when they made no sense and I opted to simply examine the data without the weights.

19. It was often very difficult to load the data. Gallup (and other organizations) had different forms that had to be combined (or decide not to combine). Furthermore, it was sometimes very difficult to map the data. A record might encompass seven or more lines (cards) in the ASCII file and the documentation was not always easy to decipher. My contact at Roper also noted that the interns they sometimes used made errors.

20. A few of the open-ended questions are not included in the database.

21. For a full discussion of what led Bush to invade Iraq, see Draper (2020).

22. Holsti (2004) also argues that the public is rational and better informed in analyzing foreign policy than previous scholars have advocated.

23. For a good review discussion on citizen competence, see Gilens (2019).

24. For a good review essay on the role of partisanship, see Lyengar et al. (2019).

1

The 1930s

The Great Depression and the Start of World War II

Modern polling was jump-started when three pollsters were relatively accurate in predicting Roosevelt winning the 1936 presidential election: George Gallup, Archibald Crossley, and Elmo Roper. All three surveys used face-to-face interviewing and respondents were selected by a quota.[1] However, there were few criteria on how to fill the quota and, in some respects, the surveys resembled "man in the street" interviews (Converse, 1987: 126).[2] African Americans and poor people were often systematically excluded. By today's standards, there was little attention paid to question phraseology or question order. On the other hand, Gallup often asked different versions of the same question in the same survey (different forms). This allows the modern analyst to compare the effects of changes in question phraseology. Of the 141 surveys from the 1930s in the Roper archive, 89% were fielded by Gallup and the remainder by Roper.

Note to Reader: There are fewer surveys discussed in this chapter compared to other chapters. Gallup's first survey occurred when the decade was half over, and the early surveys often did not ask as many relevant questions.

WORLD EVENTS

The Nazi Rise to Power

In 1930, the National Socialists won 18% of the vote and became the second largest political party in Germany. The following years would see Hitler's ascension to absolute power, the institutionalization of Nazi ideology, and acts of aggression on the part of Germany that would lead to World War II. Hitler was appointed chancellor of Germany in January 1933 by then-president of Germany Paul von Hindenburg. The Nazis blamed the Reichstag fire of 1934 on communists stirring up the anticommunist sentiment that allowed Hitler to pass legislation taking away many of Germany's civil liberties ostensibly to preserve order but effectively to solidify Nazi control of the state. Later in that year, the Reichstag, which was at this point not a true parliament but a puppet body of the Nazi party, passed legislation making Adolf Hitler the dictator of Germany. Labor unions were prohibited, eugenic sterilization was legalized, other political parties were banned, and book burnings took place in university cities across Germany to denounce intellectuals, writers, and artists who were considered "un-German." In 1934, Hitler assumed the title of Fuhrer and the Wehrmacht (the German army) instituted a personal oath of loyalty to him. In 1935, Germany began re-armament in violation of the Treaty of Versailles that ended World War I, and the Nuremberg Laws removed citizenship from German Jews. In 1936, Germany reoccupied the Rhineland and in 1938 annexed Austria. In September 1938, Germany demanded the annexation of the part of Czechoslovakia called the Sudetenland, claiming that ethnic Germans in that area were being persecuted. In reaction, the Soviet Union stated it was willing to go to war to stop the German occupation.

Neville Chamberlain, the British prime minister, met with Hitler in Munich and essentially gave in to Hitler's demands, saying that the Munich Agreement would result in "Peace for our Time," but the treaty had the opposite effect. German troops occupied the Sudetenland leaving the rest of Czechoslovakia vulnerable to invasion and leading the Soviet Union to conclude that the British could not be trusted in any alliance against Germany.

The year 1938 was also the year of Kristallnacht (the night of broken glass). The assassination of a Nazi diplomat in Paris was used by the party to incite large-scale physical violence against Jews in Germany. Across the country, over 7,000 Jewish shops and 1,200 synagogues were destroyed, and 30,000 Jews were sent to concentration camps.

In March 1939, Germany swallowed the rest of Czechoslovakia. Italy, not wanting to be outdone by the Germans, invaded Albania in April. In May, Italy and Germany signed an alliance called the Pact of Steel, connecting Berlin and Rome as the so-called Axis powers. Then, on September 1, 1939, Germany invaded Poland. This was the beginning of World War II, as the United Kingdom and France declared war on Germany.

- *Before Germany's invasion of Poland in September 1939, Americans were critical of Hitler but did not want to get involved. Fifty-two percent thought that England and France made a mistake in agreeing to Hitler's demands over Czechoslovakia; 49% thought the agreement would lead to war and not peace (32%, 19%) [10/38]^3; and only 8% thought that Hitler had no more territorial ambitions. However only 37% thought we would have to fight Hitler in their lifetime [10/38] and 31% felt that Roosevelt should "openly criticize Hitler and Mussolini for their warlike-attitude" [9/38].*
- *Americans were slow to change attitudes on helping France and Germany. In April 1939, only 25% (70%, 5%) thought "the law should be changed so we could lend*

money to England and France in case of war." This had increased slightly to 32% in June of 1940. Although most Americans opposed lending money to France and Germany, 54% favored changing the neutrality law so that they could buy war materials [4/39]. Perhaps reflecting the perceived economic advantages of wartime trade, 42% were also in favor of selling war materials to Germany [10/39].[5]*
- *Americans were not uniformly in favor of preparation for war. Sixty percent thought the United States should increase the size of the army and navy (71%) [9/38]. However, only 42% favored requiring men to serve in the army or navy for one year [5/39].*

FDR, who wanted to support England and France, was constrained by isolationist sentiments in the United States. Many Americans did not want to become involved because of memories of World War I,[6] the belief that because we were separated from Europe by a large ocean we did not have to worry, and the idea that we should concentrate on our own problems. Following Germany's occupation of Czechoslovakia in March 1939, Congress rebuffed FDR's attempt to modify the Neutrality Act and allow arms sales to Great Britain and France. It was only after the invasion of Poland and a fierce debate in Congress that arms sales were allowed on a cash-and-carry basis. In the 1940 presidential election, FDR stated he had no intention of taking the United States into the war. In March 1941, FDR circumvented the prohibition from lending money to England and France by establishing the lend-lease program (the relevant surveys on these topics are discussed in the next chapter).

The Spanish Civil War

Meanwhile, on other European fronts, Italy had, in 1936, annexed Ethiopia and that same year the Spanish Civil War had begun. In Spain, conservative elements of society (the army, the church, monarchists) under the leadership of General Francisco Franco had tried to overthrow the elected government that consisted of liberals and socialists. The coup failed but led to a three-year civil war. Those in support of the elected republic (the Republicans) were a coalition of liberals, anarchists, socialists, and communists that was supported by the Soviet Union. Franco led the Nationalists (also called the Fascists) and was supported by Germany and Italy who provided over 60,000 troops and 1,000 planes. The Spanish Civil War was used as a training ground by German and Italian militaries in which they tried out new combat techniques, such as strafing (using low-flying planes to repeatedly bomb or machine-gun an area) and the use of tanks. The Soviet Union sold the Republicans arms and sent about 2,000 "advisors." Additional support came from approximately 40,000 volunteers from around the world who fought for the Republican side, including 2,800 Americans known as the Abraham Lincoln Brigade. The United States, however, maintained a policy of strict neutrality toward the conflict. Atrocities were perpetrated on both sides, although most historians believe the number of prisoners of war and civilians executed by the Nationalists was far greater than the number killed by Republicans, and that their crimes were more systematically carried out.

The Spanish Civil War had a major impact on art and literature, inspiring Ernest Hemingway's *For Whom the Bell Tolls*, George Orwell's *Homage to Catalonia*, Pablo Picasso's *Guernica* (depicting the bombing of that city), and Joan Miró's mural, *El Segador*.[7] The defeat of the Republicans by 1939 bolstered Germany's and Italy's confidence that the West (France and United Kingdom) would not oppose their expansion, and served as well to underscore the Soviet Union's belief that France and Great Britain could not be relied upon to stand up to Germany and Italy.

- *According to Gallup polls, few Americans wanted the United States to intervene in the Spanish Civil War. Twenty-two percent of Americans said they favored the Loyalists, 12% favored Franco's forces, and the remainder said they favored neither side nor did not have an opinion [1936–1937]. Furthermore, only 19% of Americans wanted "to change the Neutrality Act to permit the shipping of arms to the Loyalists in Spain" [1/39]. Most Americans wanted to avoid any involvement in European wars.*

The Soviet Union and Japan

Joseph Stalin continued to consolidate his role as ruler of the Soviet Union. Between 1936 and 1938 was the era of the Great Purge, during which it is estimated that over 500,000 people were murdered and over five million were arrested for being "enemies of the people," Trotskyites, counter-revolutionaries, and so on, and persecuted groups included intellectuals, dissidents, clergy, land-owners, and members of the military. The purges quashed dissent but also weakened the military before its engagement in World War II. There were a series of military clashes over the Mongolian-Manchurian border between Japan and the Soviet Union between 1932 and 1939. This culminated in a Soviet victory in 1939 (over 40,000 casualties occurred in this one series of battles). This led to Japan pivoting to confront the United States instead of the Soviet Union. In August 1939, the Molotov-Ribbentrop pact was signed in which Germany and the Soviet Union agreed to maintain different spheres of influence. (The Soviet Union agreed to this non-aggression treaty because, as discussed above, the Munich Pact between Chamberlain and Hitler had made them wary of allying with the British.) After Germany's invasion of Poland, the Soviet Union occupied the eastern part of Poland. In November of that year, the Soviet Union also began a war with Finland, called the Winter War.

- *Gallup's survey tells us that Americans at that time were not fond of Russia. More Americans said they would prefer to live under the government in Germany than in Russia (33% v. 22%; 45%) [1936–1937].*
- *Regarding the Soviet Union's decisive 1939 defeat of Japan in a war in Inner Mongolia, 44% said they were more sympathetic to Russia than Japan (4%, 31% said neither and 22% did not know) [8/38].*
- *Most Americans did not agree with the Soviet Union's aggression. Only 11% thought Russia was justified in "marching troops into Poland" [9/39], and 88%*

said they were more sympathetic to Finland than Russia, with 56% saying they were willing to lend Finland $60 million to buy war supplies [12/39].

Gallup asked no questions about Stalin or politics within the Soviet Union. However, one can infer from the above questions the unwillingness to allow arm sales to Loyalists in Spain, and antipathy to communists in the United States (see below), that few Americans supported that government.

It can be argued that the opening salvo of World War II was when Japan invaded Manchuria in 1931 and set up a puppet state called Manchukuo. Despite the League of Nations, the countries of the world did almost nothing in response. Full-scale war between China and Japan began in 1937 with the capture of Shanghai and the capital of the Republic of China, Nanking. The capture of Nanking involved the large-scale massacre of civilians (the reports range from 40,000 to as many as 300,000) and became known as the Rape of Nanking or the Nanking Massacre.

- *Forty-three percent of Americans said they were more sympathetic with China than Japan (2%; 55% neither) [8/37]. However, 49% (42%, 11%) wanted to remove all US troops from China to avoid getting involved in the fighting [1936–1937].*

Public opinion was consistent—no involvement in wars, whether in Europe or Asia.

The 1930s was also an era of increasing anticolonialism. In 1930, Mahatma Gandhi began a civil disobedience campaign, which started with his march to the sea to protest the British monopoly on salt. In 1939, he began a fast to protest British rule in India. Unfortunately, Gallup asked no questions on India, Gandhi, or other issues related to the anticolonial struggle.

US POLITICS

Franklin Delano Roosevelt beat Herbert Hoover in the 1932 Presidential Election (57.4% v. 39.7%). Hoover was blamed for the Great Depression and FDR had garnered a reputation while governor of New York for using state resources to help the poor. Although he was able to get Congress to pass many of his New Deal reforms, the United States Supreme Court ruled some of the reforms were unconstitutional. In particular, the Court believed that too much power was being given to the executive branch. In 1937, Roosevelt proposed, in the name of efficiency, to increase the number of justices in the Supreme Court. This proposal was widely perceived as an attempt by Roosevelt to "pack the Court," that is, fill it with a majority of justices sympathetic to his policies. The proposal backfired; it did not pass, and provoked outrage at his apparent attempt to "rig the system." Ultimately, the Court did rule on his behalf on some legislation (the Social Security Act) and some justices did retire and were replaced by FDR.

- *Only 41% of the public favored what Gallup phrased as "President Roosevelt's plan to increase the size of the Supreme Court to make it more liberal." When the question was worded slightly differently—"Are you in favor of President Roosevelt's proposal regarding the Supreme Court?"—support was still only 44% [1936–1937].*

The 1930s was an era of protest in the United States. In 1932, over 40,000 World War I veterans, the "Bonus Army," came to Washington D.C. demanding the payment of a bonus for their service. Most were unemployed because of the Great Depression. They camped out in "Hooverville" across the Anacostia River from the Capitol. After two of the marchers were killed by police, President Hoover ordered the removal of the encampment, which the army carried out under the supervision of General Douglass MacArthur. George S. Patton, then an army major, was sent in with six tanks and the infantry used fixed bayonets and tear gas. In the confrontation, a twelve-year-old child was killed.

- *In Gallup's 1935 poll, 55% of Americans thought that the veterans should be paid their bonus [11/35].*[8]

The decade was also a time of greater worker militancy. This was caused by increased industrialization and assembly line jobs combined with lower wages and production line speedups. In 1935, a federation of unions, the Congress of Industrial Organizations (CIO), was formed. In 1936, the United Auto Workers Union began its sit-down strike in Flint, Michigan. The strike against General Motors lasted for forty-four days. Rather than simply picketing GM, the UAW had workers occupy the Fisher Body Plant. A series of battles ensued between the police and the strikers, but in February 1937, GM recognized the UAW as the exclusive bargaining agent for its workers and gave the workers a 5% pay increase. The success of the strike gave the UAW momentum and its membership swelled from 30,000 to 500,000.

- *Gallup showed that the American public was not largely in favor of labor unions. Only 33% said their sympathies were with the "group of striking employees" (41% favored GM, 26%); 60% wanted to make sit-wide strikes illegal; 60% wanted the government to "use force in removing sit-down strikers"; and only 26% favored "employers collect[ing] the dues for labor unions by taking the dues out of the workers' pay" [1936–1937].*
- *Sixty-three percent of Americans thought that communists had influence in labor unions and only 12% believed "unions should allow a member of the Communist Party to be an official in that union" [8/38].*

Given the antipathy to militant labor unions, it is somewhat surprising that they had substantial success. The National Industrial Recovery Act of 1933 and the National Labor Relations Act of 1935 gave labor unions the right to collective bargaining and reduced the ability of employers to retaliate. Labor was part of the FDR New Deal coalition and success (and a lot of organizing) begat success. Labor victories caused more workers to join unions and this created greater influence when labor negotiated with government agencies.

The Communist Party of the United States was in fact very active in the 1930s, garnering support for the Republican side in the Spanish Civil War, organizing labor unions, and advocating for civil rights in the black community (this was the period of the United Front). It is estimated that at its height, the CPUSA has approximately 85,000 members; however, support fell between the time Stalin aligned with Germany in 1939 and Germany's invasion of the Soviet Union.

- *According to a February 1939 Gallup survey, communists in the United States were seen as a greater danger than Nazis (33%, 29%, 39%).*

Real-life crime grabbed newspaper headlines and was a major fascination of the American public, such as the kidnapping and murder of the Lindbergh baby in 1932 or the sentencing of Al Capone in 1933 to eleven years in prison for tax evasion.

- *Gallup reported that sixty-seven percent of respondents said it should be a crime to pay ransom to a kidnapper [6/38]; and in July 1945, 80% of Americans could identify Al Capone.*
- *Most respondents in the surveys of this decade would today be labeled "law-and-order": 60% favored capital punishment for murder [1936–1937]; 39% wanted to restore the use of the whipping post [8/37]; only 41% agreed with the parole system [12/37]; and 80% wanted all pistols to be registered with the government [4/38].*[9]

Prohibition ended in 1933, the same year cannabis was outlawed by the federal government. As discussed in the Preamble to Gallup History chapter, prohibition was one of the major factors affecting the growth of the crime rate in this time period.

- *Only 29% of Americans said they would vote for national prohibition if it came up for a vote [1936–1937].*

The 1930's did not have the same levels of political intolerance as exhibited by the Palmer Raids of 1920 or McCarthyism in the early 1950s; however, polls showed support for limiting some civil liberties.

- *Fifty-one percent favored requiring teachers to "take a special oath of loyalty" and 63% thought every American should be finger-printed [1936–1937].*
- *On other questions related to civil liberties: only 14% favored "permitting Nazis who are American citizens to wear uniforms and parade in this country" [9/37]; 24% favored allowing communists to "make speeches to student groups" [12/39]; and just 16% thought that communists should "be allowed to hold public office in the United States" [11/39].*

Immigrants were often disliked because some were seen as radicals, competition in the labor force, or a drag on the economy because they were supposedly using social services and not paying taxes.

- *Sixty-seven percent of Gallup respondents thought that, "aliens on relief should be returned to their own countries" [1936–1937].*

As seen in this section, the anti-democratic impulse of most Americans did not begin with the anticommunist hysteria of the late 1940s and 1950s. In the 1930s, most Americans opposed supporting the loyalists in Spain, were hostile to militant labor unions, could be characterized as "law and order," and were willing to deny civil liberties to controversial groups.

RACE

In March 1931, nine black teenage boys were arrested and falsely accused of raping two white women on a train in Alabama. It required the Alabama National Guard to stop a mob from lynching the boys. All but one (a twelve-year old) were sentenced to death after a trial in Scottsboro, Alabama. The defendants, who came to be known as the Scottsboro Boys, were helped in their appeals by the Communist Party USA. Even though one of the alleged victims later stated that she fabricated the rape story, the defendants were still convicted in a series of retrials. Five of the defendants were found guilty and spent time in jail. Resistance to racism was growing, though. There were national campaigns to free the Scottsboro Boys, and one of the major and continuing demands of the civil rights movement in the 1930s was the passage of a federal anti-lynching bill. In 1935, the National Council of Negro Women was formed by Mary McLeon Bethune.

- *Gallup's survey showed that the bill was favored by 61% of Americans [1936–1937]; however, because of filibusters from Southern Democrats, no anti-lynching bill was ever passed by the Senate.*
- *Sixty percent thought peace officers who don't protect a prisoner from a lynch mob should be punished [11/37].*[10]

In 1939, the Daughters of the American Revolution refused to allow famed singer Marian Anderson to use Constitution Hall for a concert because she was black. Instead, she gave a free concert in April that year to 75,000 people at the Lincoln Memorial. In response to the actions of the DAR, Eleanor Roosevelt resigned in protest.

- *Fifty-nine percent supported Eleanor Roosevelt's "resignation from DAR because of concert cancellation of a Negro singer" [3/39].*

Race was not a major concern for Gallup in the 1930s in terms of either his sample or his topics. For example, in his January 1939 survey, only 15 of the 3,063 respondents were black. Furthermore, only the four questions noted above directly concerned black-white relations.

- *One question that indirectly touched on race found 35% favored (African American) Joe Lewis in the upcoming heavyweight boxing match against (white) Tony Galento (31%; 34%).*
- Many Americans were not immune to the fascist ideology affecting Europe, which is highlighted in Gallup's survey results regarding the political views of Father Coughlin, a Catholic Priest whose radio show during the 1930s reached thirty million people. Coughlin supported a crude populism that denounced capitalists, communists, and Jews and expressed support for the fascist governments of Hitler and Mussolini.
- *Of the 53% who voiced an opinion in Gallup's polls, 47% said they favored what Father Coughlin said [4/38].*
- *In related results, almost half (45%) said that anti-Jewish feelings were increasing in the United States and 21% thought it was likely there would "be a wide-spread campaign against the Jews in this country" [3/39].*
- *When asked whether the persecution of Jews in Europe was their own fault—10% said entirely and 48% said partly [4/38].*
- *Twelve percent said they would support a widespread campaign against Jews in this country and another 10% said they would be sympathetic to such a campaign [5/39].*

That 58% of Americans believed that Jews in Europe were somewhat responsible for their own persecution, 22% would have some support for a similar campaign in the United States, and 47% were favorable toward Father Coughlin indicate an astonishing level of anti-Semitism in this time period.[11] Acts of racial and/or ethnic intolerance were all too frequent in this time period. In June 1939, the United States refused admittance to the ship St. Louis, which held 907 Jewish refugees from Germany. They were forced to go back to Europe and about a quarter of those refugees later died in Nazi death camps. Gallup's polls showed that most Americans had little sympathy for the plight of refugees from Europe.

- *Although only 6% of respondents said they favored Germany's treatment of Jews, only 21% favored allowing more Jewish exiles from Germany to come to the United States and only 39% favored the United States contributing money to help Jews and Catholic exiles from Germany emigrating to South America or Africa [11/38].*

As in Germany, the eugenics movement in the United States of the day promoted actions to "purify" the genetic composition of the population. Some of the positions advocated forced sterilization, restriction on marriage, and even euthanasia. Approximately 60,000 forced sterilizations occurred in the United States of those who were epileptic or considered "feeble minded." The eugenics movement fell into disfavor after World War II when the Holocaust was perceived as the ultimate manifestation of these ideas.[12] But Gallup polls in the 1930s showed widespread support for some policies that would not be tolerated today.

- *Seventy-three percent favored "sterilization of habitual criminals and the hopelessly insane" [1936–1937].*

SEX AND GENDER

Even more than a decade and a half after the passage of the nineteenth amendment granting women the right to vote, many Americans did not believe women should have full rights. Women, seemingly, were also not encouraged to work for pay.

- *Thirty percent of respondents did not favor permitting women to serve as jurors [1936–1937].*
- *Only 33% said they "would vote for a woman for president if she qualified in every other respect" [1936–1937].*[13]
- *Seventy-two percent of respondents said they would favor a bill "prohibiting married women from working in business or industry if their husbands earn more than $1,600 a year ($28,000 in today's dollars)" [7/39].*
- *Other survey questions found that 47% favored firing schoolteachers once they married [8/38] and that only 21% favored a woman "earning money in business or industry if she has a husband capable of supporting her" [10/38].*[14]

As discussed in the "preamble" chapter, the sale of birth control devices was illegal in most jurisdictions. However, most Americans had surprisingly progressive attitudes on some sexual issues, even while a certain amount of prudishness was nonetheless still prevalent.

- *Most Americans favored Congress funding venereal disease controls (68%, 18%, 13%) [1936–1937]; were supporters of the birth control movement (61%, 26%, 13%) [7/37];*[15] *and wanted the government to provide birth control information to married couples (62%, 25%, 13%) [10/38].*
- *Sixty percent thought it was "indecent for women to wear shorts for street wear" and even 30% thought it was "Indecent for men to wear topless bathing suits" [6/39].*[16]

THE ECONOMY

The United States had experienced a long history of economic crashes and depressions before 1929. There had been panics and recessions since the formation of the Republic—in the years 1807, 1815, 1873, 1893, 1896, 1907, 1913, and

1920—with many being quite severe. The Great Depression, however, that began with the stock market crash in October 1929 was far more destructive than previous financial upheavals. Unemployment reached 25%, industrial production fell by 45%, 5,000 banks had failed by 1932, the stock market lost 90% of its value, one million families lost their farms, and the average income of American families fell by 40%.

The causes of the Great Depression are still being debated. Bank failures resulted in depositors withdrawing their savings, which limited the ability of a bank to loan out money and reducing the money supply. Further, because the United States was on the gold standard, interest rates were raised so that international investors would not flee with their gold to countries with higher interest rates. Latter-day conservative economists such as Milton Friedman and Anna Schwartz argue that the Federal Reserve could have done more to increase the money supply. On the other hand, contemporary economist Paul Krugman argues a Keynesian position that there is only so much that monetary policy can do to stop depressions; that is, the main factors creating the Depression were economic inequality causing reduced consumption; farmers, householders, and corporations having too much debt; and rampant speculation by *Wall Street*; and an increase in government spending was needed to take the United States out of the depression.[17]

The Great Depression deepened in the early years of the 1930s. In 1930, Congress passed the Smoot-Hawley Act, the intent of which was to increase import tariffs that would protect United States industries from foreign competition. However, the result was retaliatory tariffs by other countries that actually reduced US exports. Many economists believe this cut US exports and imports by half, thus exacerbating the Great Depression. Economic conditions were made even worse because dust storms on the Great Plains blew away vast quantities of topsoil. This situation had first been caused by a drought, which was then aggravated by farmers plowing up the native deep-rooted grasses to make room for crops. As a result, tens of thousands of farmers had to abandon their homes, events that John Steinbeck's classic 1939 novel *The Grapes of Wrath* chronicles (also see Egan, 2006).

Numerous economic reforms were instituted under the First New Deal when FDR was first elected. In the financial realm, this program put banks under firmer federal supervision, granted loans to sound banks, insured individual bank deposits up to $25,000, suspended the gold standard, with the passage of the Glass-Steagall Act, limited the ability of banks to speculate, and created the Securities and Exchange Commission to regulate *Wall Street*. A variety of public works programs were also created that resulted in the building of roads, dams, bridges, parks, and airports. In agriculture, the Agricultural Adjustment Administration (AAA) set up systems that limited production, leading to scarcity and thus raising prices. The government also established programs to limit soil erosion, convert croplands to parks, curb flooding, and irrigate lands.

- *Despite the success of these measures, polls showed that only 32% of Americans wanted the New Deal Crop Act revived [1936–1937].*

Unfortunately, Gallup asked few questions about these early New Deal programs. Opposition to the New Deal Crop Act (AAA) occurred because of the contrasting images of crops being burned and people starving, general opposition to expanding the role of government, and the Act was declared unconstitutional in January 1936.

The second New Deal, which was implemented from 1935 to 1938, created Social Security for retirement pensions,[18] unemployment insurance, the National Labor Relations Act, guaranteeing the rights of labor unions to organize, and a more progressive tax system that taxed the wealthy and corporations. These policies, created out of the Great Depression, represented a dramatic transformation in the role of the US government. The government was now seen as necessary to regulate the economy and to ensure the basic welfare of the people. A serious challenge to the government having such a powerful role did not emerge until the election of Ronald Reagan in 1980 (Smith and Seltzer, 2016).

There were, based on Gallup polls, substantial divisions and contradictions in American public opinion about what the United States should specifically do to improve the economy.

- *Only 34% thought the government "should start spending again to help get business out of its present slump"; only 24% wanted to increase expenditures for unemployment relief; and 41% wanted the government to fix farm prices. In fact, 53% wanted to reduce relief expenditures; and 70% wanted the government to start balancing the budget [1936–1937].*
- *Only 38% wanted to increase government spending to get out of the current slump [12/37].*
- *Forty-two percent wanted to cut taxes on the wealthy so they could put money into business [5/39].*
- *On the other hand, 56% wanted the Supreme Court to be "more liberal in reviewing New Deal measures [1936–1937]."*

Americans also had mixed views on the role of government in utilities and industry.

- *The majority of Americans favored the government owning electrical power (59%) and the munitions industry (69%) and 64% approved of the Tennessee Valley Authority [4/38].*
- *On the other hand, most Americans did not favor government ownership of railroads (29%) or the banks (42%) [1936–1937].*
- *Only 42% favored the government limiting the size of private fortunes and 32% wanted the government to break up large corporations [7/37].*

What later became known as Social Security had wide support in general, but with important caveats.

- *Ninety percent believed in government pensions, but 72% wanted to limit it to those who "are in need" [11/39].*

- *Only 48% said they "would be willing to pay higher taxes to provide the sixty dollars a month ($1,023 in current dollars) for needy persons 65 and over" [12/38].*

One question best summed up the division of the American public on the issue of government power: "During recent years the trend has been to give the federal government greater power to regulate business, industry and agriculture. Are you in favor of this trend towards centralizing the power in Washington?"

- *Forty-one percent favored the government having greater power (44%, 15%) [1936–1937].*

Attitudes toward FDR himself were also mixed.

- *When asked whether FDR was responsible for the business downturn in 1937, 11% said entirely, 49% partly, and 35% not at all [3/37].*[19]

Clearly, Roosevelt was right to be concerned that the policies of the Second New Deal would face difficulty in the court of public opinion, not to mention the Supreme Court. It is unfortunate that we do not have survey data for Roosevelt's first term.

SCIENCE, TECHNOLOGY, AND THE ENVIRONMENT

Technology continued its upward spiral. Birdseye Frozen foods went on sale in 1930; the first canned beer was sold in Richmond, Virginia, in 1935; Wallace Carothers received a patent for nylon in 1937; Spam was introduced by Hormel in 1938; and in 1939 Hewlett-Packard was founded and General Motors introduced the fully automatic transmission in the Oldsmobile.

Building and infrastructure projects that were completed in this period included: the Empire State Building (1931), the George Washington Bridge (1931), and the Golden Gate Bridge in San Francisco (1937).

In August 1939, Albert Einstein signed a letter penned by Leo Szilard, advising President Roosevelt that Germany was on the road to building an atomic bomb and the United States needed to jump-start its own program. This ultimately led to the Manhattan Project, the fast-track program to beat Germany in developing nuclear weapons.

Consumer technology was spreading, which was partially tracked by Gallup's surveys.

- *Fifty-four percent of Americans had a telephone and 57% had an automobile in the family [1936–1937].*
- *Eighty-seven percent had their home wired for electricity and 58% had homes with natural gas [5/39].*
- *This decade saw the peak of radio's popularity (its "golden age"): 82% of Americans owned a radio [1936–1937].*

In 1930, the first television commercial was aired for Fox Furriers on W1XAV in Boston. (Since TV was in its infancy, Gallup did not ask any questions about it in this decade.)

POPULAR TRENDS OF THE DECADE

Baseball continued to be the most popular American sport. In 1930, the first night game took place in Kansas, and one of the most memorable events in baseball occurred in May 1939 when Lou Gehrig played his 2,130th consecutive game and gave a famous speech announcing that he had amyotrophic lateral sclerosis (later called Lou Gehrig's disease).[20]

- *Forty-one percent of Gallup respondents said they followed Big League Baseball [10/37].*
- *Thirty-four percent said baseball was their favorite sport to watch, followed by football (23%), and basketball (8%) [3/37].*[21]

Radio still dominated the mass media. In 1933, Jack Benny's radio show first aired, as did "The Lone Ranger" show. Also in 1933 (March), FDR broadcast the first of his thirty "Fireside Chats," a revolutionary use of media to bring the ideas of a politician directly to the public. Then toward the end of the decade, the public found out how mass media could actually create mass panic when in 1938, *The War of the Worlds* was broadcast, an Orson Welles radio play about the invasion of space aliens that was believed by some listeners to be describing real events.

- *When asked whether they preferred to get their news from the radio or newspapers, respondents gave radio a slight plurality (50% v. 45%) [4/39].*
- *About a third of Americans said they had listened to one of FDR's fireside chats [4/38].*
- *Fourteen percent of Gallup respondents said they listened to The War of the Worlds broadcast [12/38].*

Movie attendance continued its ascent. The decade of the 1930s brought to the screen some of the most iconic roles in movie history. Bela Lugosi's *Dracula* (1930); Johnny Weissmuller's *Tarzan the Ape Man* (1933); and, courtesy of cutting-edge special effects, *King Kong* and his climb to the top of the Empire State Building clutching actress Fay Wray (1933). In 1934, the first Three Stooges (Moe, Larry, and Curly) short was released, and Donald Duck debuted in the cartoon *Wise Little Hen*. The first feature-length animated movie was released in 1937—Walt Disney's *Snow White and the Seven Dwarfs*. In August 1939, the film *The Wizard of Oz* was released. Other memorable movies of the time included: *Tom Sawyer* (1930); *All Quiet on the Western Front* (1930); *Frankenstein* (1931); *Mutiny on the Bounty* (1935); *Modern Times* (1936); *A Star Is Born* (1937); *The*

Adventures of Robin Hood (1938); *Gone With The Wind* (1939); and *Mr. Smith Goes to Washington* (1939).

- *Sixty-six percent of Americans surveyed said they went to the movies at least once a month [1936–1937].*

Books that were published that decade included: Pearl Buck's *The Good Earth* (1932); Aldous Huxley's *Brave New World* (1932); Sinclair Lewis's *It Can't Happen Here* (1935); and both *Of Mice and Men* (1937) and *The Grapes of Wrath* (1939) by John Steinbeck.

- *Of Gallup's respondents, 27% said they were currently reading a book [7/37].*
- *Indicating the immense popularity of Margaret Mitchell's Gone with the Wind (published in 1936), 23% of respondents said they planned to read it and 23% said they already had read it. Half of the respondents said they intended to see the move [1/39].*[22]

In serial print publications, the first *Dick Tracey* comic strip appeared in 1931 followed by *Superman* in 1936, the same year that *Life Magazine* began publication. Because of a decision to keep its price very low, *Life* had struggled through its first years in business. But its April 1938 edition printed a controversial photo piece, "The Birth of a Baby," which brought the magazine a large readership.

- *Gallup found that 42% of respondents had seen the controversial pictures of "The Birth of a Baby" in Life Magazine, and 61% of the public thought it was an appropriate way to teach the public about childbirth. However, 23% thought it violated the law because "it was obscene, filthy, or indecent" [4/38].*

In 1938, Kate Smith first sang Irving Berlin's "God Bless America" on her weekly radio show. Well-known musicians of this decade included: Bing Crosby, Guy Lombardo, Duke Ellington, Louis Armstrong, Tommy Dorsey, Judy Garland, Glenn Miller, Artie Shaw, Benny Goodman, Billie Holiday, Fred Astaire, and the Andrews Sisters.[23] Folk music, such as Woodie Guthrie's and Leadbelly's songs that often described economic hardship, was a bit more on the fringe of popularity, as was country music, which was then called hillbilly music.

According to Gallup, attitudes toward patriotic music were such that two years before Pearl Harbor, 75% said orchestras and bands should stop playing German music [10/39].

- *In August 1938, 57% (34%, 9%) said they liked swing music.*

In 1935, notably when the United States was still in the midst of the Great Depression, the board game Monopoly came on the market.

CONCLUDING COMMENTS

The 1930s was a decade of contradictions: horrors and progress.

In world affairs, this decade saw the advent of fascism in Germany, Italy, Spain, Japan, and elsewhere. It ushered in, as well, the terror of the Russian Gulag. In response, some countries—particularly England and China—mounted a sustained resistance to the political extremism, and America, prodded by FDR, was beginning to send some aid in that effort. The polls show that most Americans were strongly opposed to any intervention in these matters. However, by the end of the decade, there was an increasing sense that the United States would have to help.

The greatest economic depression in world history encompassed the decade. In the United States, policies were put in place to save the economy, help prevent future economic calamities, and demonstrate that government could help people. In addition, labor unions rose to defend the rights of workers. Many Americans did not support some of the New Deal policies. There was often opposition to government spending to help Americans, and the opposition to labor unions was surprisingly strong. Nevertheless, there was a growing realization that the government had an important role domestically in directing the economy and helping those in need.

Advances in infrastructure (e.g., roads, bridges, tunnels) and technology (e.g., frozen food, nylon, and television) were made that would lead to a post-war boom.

Intolerance toward dissidents was not as forceful as in the 1920s or 1950s. However, most Americans opposed free speech for those not in the mainstream, wanted to deport immigrants, and favored harsh sanctions on criminals.

Blacks continued to live under the harsh conditions of Jim Crow in the South and were legally denied many of the benefits of many New Deal policies that were in place throughout the rest of the country. For example, agricultural and domestic workers, who were mostly black, were not allowed to participate in Social Security; and Federal Housing Administration policy held that incompatible racial groups should not live together. Unfortunately, few survey questions were asked about race in the 1930s, although responses do show there was substantial anti-Semitism, opposition to helping refugees from Hitler's Germany, and support for the eugenics movement. Nonetheless, we also see broad opposition to lynching and support for anti-racist actions such as Eleanor Roosevelt's resignation from the DAR.

Most Americans did not favor women running for political office or working, once they were married. However, although most Americans were extremely prudish by current standards, there was surprising support for birth control

[The reader can find relevant crosstabs and discussion in the online appendix located at https://rowman.com/ISBN/9781793653505/US-Public-Opinion-since-the-1930s-Galluping-through-History.]

NOTES

1. See the introduction for a discussion of the use of quotas.
2. For more on the early years of survey research, see Sudman and Bradburn (1987).

3. A reminder to readers, the numbers in parentheses mean that 32% did not believe that this would lead to war and 19% had no opinion.

4. Question phraseology is important. As discussed in Appendix I, Gallup asked two version of this question in the same April 1939 survey. One had 20% of respondents wanting to loan money to England and France while the other had support at 30%.

5. The question wording for these two questions were very different. On selling war materials to Germany: "If Germany is able to send ships to this country to buy war supplies, including airplanes and arms, should we sell war supplies to them?" Compare this to the question phraseology on selling war materials to England and France: "Our present neutrality law prevents this country from selling any war materials to any countries at war. Do you think the law should be changed so that we could sell war materials to England and France in case of war?" Clearly, caution is warranted in interpreting these questions.

6. Surveys on World War I, League of Nations, etc. are presented in the Preamble to Gallup History chapter.

7. Unfortunately, Gallup asked no questions about these authors or artists.

8. Unfortunately, I could not find any question on whether the military response to the Bonus Army was appropriate.

9. Seventy-three percent wanted to sterilize the "habitual criminals and the hopelessly insane" [1/36]. This is further discussed in the section on race.

10. The 2020 Emmett Till Lynching Bill was passed in the United States House of Representatives and stalled by Senator Rand Paul in the Senate.

11. Sinclair Lewis' 1935 novel, *It Can't Happen Here*, describes how a demagogue could take over the United States.

12. Black (2003) shows that the eugenics movement in the United States had a tremendous influence on the racist ideologies of Nazi Germany.

13. Sixty percent said they would vote for a Catholic and 46% said they would vote for a Jew.

14. Women were somewhat more likely than men to approve of women working (26% v. 18%). The most recent time this question was asked, 73% approved of women working [5/88—NORC-GSS].

15. The question on support for the birth control movement should be interpreted with caution. The "movement" encompassed people who supported eugenics (Margaret Sanger among others). Therefore, some people might oppose this movement because they oppose birth control while others might oppose it because of its link to eugenics and its relation to racism.

16. New York's ban on men appearing shirtless was overturned in 1937.

17. John Maynard Keynes' *The General Theory of Employment, Interest and Money* did not come out until 1936.

18. The Social Security Act of 1935 did not include sickness insurance. FDR was fearful it would have killed the bill.

19. Only 25% said the 1929 downturn should be called the Hoover depression [4/38].

20. Internationally, other sports were also coming into their own. In 1930, FIFA (soccer) had its first World Cup when France beat Mexico.

21. Baseball was also the sports with the most participants (15%), followed by swimming (8%) [3/37].

22. Unfortunately, Gallup asked few questions in the 1930s about what people read or what movies they watched.

23. The lists of musicians in this book are mostly derived from tsort.info.com/music. Many musicians span decades. I usually only list the first decade in which the musician was popular.

2

The 1940s

World War II and the Onset of the Cold War

The National Opinion Research Center (NORC) was founded in 1941 and became a central player in the extension of survey research for government use during the war years (focusing on topics such as labor problems, the morale of the American soldier, how to sell war bonds, etc.). The American Association for Public Opinion Research (AAPOR) was started in 1946. That year also saw the beginning of the Survey Research Center, which eventually begat the American National Election Survey. The decade ended with the 1948 debacle of miscalling the presidential election for Thomas Dewey (Truman won). Of the 491 national surveys in the Roper archive for the 1940s, 55% were designed and conducted by Gallup. Other major survey organizations represented in the archive include NORC (16%), Roper (13%), and Office of Public Research—Harry Cantril (12%). Except for one mail and one telephone, surveys for this decade were face-to-face. The only telephone survey was conducted by Gallup in November 1949.

WORLD EVENTS

Prior to the United States Entering World War II

In September of 1939, Germany invaded Poland, which resulted in France and the United Kingdom declaring war on Germany. The next six months were known as the "phony" war as little military action occurred, but that state of affairs ended abruptly in April and May of 1940 when Germany invaded the neutral countries of Denmark, Norway, the Netherlands, Belgium, and Luxembourg. By attacking and subduing these countries, Germany was able to strike France without having to go through the French defenses known as the Maginot line. Germany's Blitzkrieg—the combined use of tanks, planes, and ground troops in massive surprise attacks—defeated the French and British forces. Over 325,000 retreating British troops had to be evacuated at Dunkirk.

After the fall of France, British Prime Minister Neville Chamberlain (whose policy of "appeasement" toward Germany had in fact led to war) was succeeded by Winston Churchill who was, by contrast, starkly realistic and inspirational. In Churchill's famous first address to Parliament, he said, "I have nothing to offer you but blood, toil, tears, and sweat." By that summer, the Battle of Britain had begun with the German Luftwaffe attacks on the RAF fighter command. In September, the successful defense by the RAF resulted in Germany abandoning plans to invade Britain and instead starting the Blitz, the Germans' large-scale repetitive bombardment of London and other cities that lasted more than a year.

Japan took advantage of the fall of France to take control of French Indochina. FDR responded by seizing all Japanese assets in the United States and embargoing the sale of oil to Japan. Japan estimated at the onset of the embargo that it had only two years of oil reserves.

On June 22, 1941, Germany invaded the Soviet Union (in Operation Barbarossa) with almost four million troops and over 3,000 tanks. Hitler's decision to invade the Soviet Union was motivated by an amalgam of Germany's express colonialist desire to gain "living space" (Lebensraum) for Germans, a detestation of Slavs, and an ideological hatred of communism. By December, the Soviets had suffered about five million casualties and German troops were at the gates of Moscow and Leningrad. The Russian winter in combination with strong Soviet defenses halted the German offense until the Spring.

As German troops took control of areas with large concentrations of Jews, they forced Jews to relocate to ghettos and concentration camps. Concentration camps were used to exploit slave labor as well as for the extermination of prisoners. In September 1941, the first use of the pesticide Zykon B was used to execute Soviet prisoners en masse. This means of extermination was soon extended to Jews and other "un-desirables."

The fall of France had an immediate impact on the United States as well, giving rise to a military buildup. FDR addressed a joint session of Congress on May 16, 1940, asking for immediate financing to build 50,000 aircraft per year, and in September the United States transferred fifty destroyers to Great Britain in return for leases to British bases in the North Atlantic and West Indies. It was also in September that the first peacetime military draft in US history began. In December 1940, FDR set forth the outline of Lend-Lease, which would allow the United States to send materials, food, oil, and armaments to those fighting Germany. FDR promoted this program in a fireside chat, stating the United States must become "the great arsenal of democracy." Lend-Lease became law in March 1941.

There was significant opposition to US involvement in the war before Japan's attack on Pearl Harbor. Charles Lindbergh was the keynote speaker at the first mass rally of the America First Committee in New York City, a group that was against the United States intervening in the war.

- *Eighty-eight percent of survey respondents could identify Lindbergh, but only 10% thought he was "presidential material" [4/42].*
- *The American public was split on supporting France and Britain. Before the fall of France, only 32% favored changing the law so that these countries could borrow money from the United States government [6/40]. Even after the fall of France, only 44% favored lending money to England [8/40].*
- *As for sending war materials, even with a very biased question only 55% favored transferring the 50 US destroyers to England¹ and 40% favored changing the neutrality laws allowing US ships to carry war materials to England. However, 56% agreed to send warplanes to England [8/40].*
- *Despite the fall of France, 62% of Americans believed England would win the war against Germany [9/40]. In October 1940, 52% thought it was more important "for the United States to . . . to keep out of the war ourselves . . ." versus 41% who favored "help[ing] England win, even at the risk of getting into the war." Only 12% favored declaring war on Germany.*
- *By March 1941, the American public turned more favorable toward helping England: 64% favored the Lend-Lease bill and 52% favored leasing an additional 40 US destroyers to England. In fact, 64% said that "if it appeared certain that there was no other way to defeat Germany and Italy except for the United States to go to war against them, . . . they would be in favor of the United States going into the war." However, only 41% favored using US naval ships to guard sending war materials to England.*
- *American support for England increased by October 1941. By then, only 27% said the most important thing for the United States to do was stay out of the war compared to 66% who said it was important to help England. Furthermore, 58% now favored using American ships to send war materials to England.*
- *With Germany's invasion of Russia, only 35% of Americans favored sending war materials to Russia [6/41]. However, 72% said they wanted Russia to win the war, 4% wanted Germany to win, and 24% said it made no difference or they did not know.*
- *Americans were opposed to Japan's aggression. Only 2% favored Japan in its war against China (74% favored China and 24% neither) [5/39].*
- *Two-thirds (67%) of Americans agreed in January 1940 that the United States should "forbid the sale of arms, airplanes, gasoline and other war materials to Japan," and in October, 88% approved of FDR's decision to stop the sale of scrap metal to Japan and 61% said the United States should take steps to make sure Japan does not become more powerful even if that meant risking war.*
- *However, in April 1941 only 41% said the United States should send its navy to help England if Japan attacked Singapore and in July 46% said the United States should go to war if it was the only way to stop Japan from taking British, French, and Dutch possessions in the South Pacific. In fact, in October 1941 only 15% favored "declaring war on Japan now." But Americans believed war was imminent: two weeks before the attack on Pearl Harbor 49% (30%, 21%) thought we would go to war against Japan in the near future [11/41].*

Given the early public opinion against the United States lending support to England and similar opposition to support for Russia, it is clear why FDR moved slowly in trying to get aid to England and later Russia.[2] Without Japan's surprise attack on Pearl Harbor, it might have been years before the United States committed troops. Winston Churchill famously said in his memoirs upon hearing about Pearl Harbor, "I went to bed and slept the sleep of the saved and thankful."

From Pearl Harbor to the End of World War II

On December 7, 1941, Japanese planes from six aircraft carriers conducted a surprise military strike on Pearl Harbor. All eight US battleships in the harbor were destroyed or heavily damaged. Additional damage was sustained by approximately three-quarters of the US planes stationed on the island, ten other ships, and many military installations. A total of 2,403 Americans were killed. On the following day, President Roosevelt delivered his famous "Infamy Speech" to a joint session of Congress and war was declared on Japan.

Japan's attack on Pearl Harbor was not an isolated event. Japan also invaded Hong Kong, British Malaysia, Thailand, Guam, Burma, and the Philippines. The first six months after the United States declared war was, for the allies, one disaster following another. British forces surrendered Singapore (80,000 British, Australian, and Indian troops became POWs) in February and the last US troops surrendered in the Philippines in May (23,000 Americans were killed or captured as well as 100,000 Filipinos). In June 1942, the United States had a decisive victory with the sinking of four Japanese aircraft carriers in the Battle of Midway. In August, 11,000 US marines landed on Guadalcanal Island; however, Japan's control of the water surrounding the island resulted in a hasty retreat of US naval forces, stranding the marines without reinforcements or supplies. Japan reinforced its troops on the island and a series of bloody battles resulted. It was not until February 1943 that the island was secured. After victory in Guadalcanal, a series of horrific battles occurred as other islands were liberated (Tarawa, Saipan, Tinian, Peleliu, Iwo Jima, Okinawa, the Philippines, and many more). The war in the Pacific ended on August 14, 1945, following the deployment of the atomic bomb, and the Soviets starting an offense against Japanese troops in China and Manchuria.

Meetings between FDR and Churchill following Pearl Harbor resulted in the strategy of defeating Germany first. But it was not until November 1942 that US troops first got involved in fighting in the West with the occupation of French North Africa in Operation Torch. Although US troops were defeated at the Battle of Kasserine Pass in February 1943, by May 1943, 275,000 German and Italian troops, under pressure from British and US forces, surrendered in Tunisia thus ending the North Africa campaign. Allied success continued with the invasion of Sicily in July 1943 and Italy in September. On June 6, 1944, 160,000 allied troops landed in Normandy, France and began the process of liberating Western Europe, although many setbacks were to occur on the march to Germany. During the war, 185,924 Americans were killed fighting in the European theater and 106,207 in the Pacific theater.

What a difference a month can make.

- *In November 1941, only 34% of survey respondents thought war against Japan would be difficult. Several days after the attack on Pearl Harbor, this had doubled to 65% and 51% said it would be a long war (36%, 14%).*
- *Despite Pearl Harbor, 64% of Americans agreed with the "defeat Germany first" strategy [12/41].*
- *Right after the atomic bomb was dropped on Japan, 85% of Americans approved the use of the bomb and 69% thought it was a good thing it was developed [8/45]. The navy estimated that between 400,000 and 800,000 Americans would have died if the United States had to invade the Japanese islands. This was clearly a major factor in public support for use of the bomb.*[3]
- *Americans were willing to sacrifice a lot to win the war. As seen below, American morale remained high. This is in sharp contrast with later American attitudes toward Korea and Vietnam. Many said the government had the right to dictate what crops farmers could grow and its price (64%) [12/41]; that the government could regulate car tire sales (81%) [1/42]; and that the government should draft single women for war-related jobs (69%) [2/42].*
- *Seventy-seven percent of Americans bought war bonds [6/42]; 55% said they would plant a Victory Garden [1/43]; 76% thought the draft was being handled fairly [9/42]; 64% thought rationing was being handled fairly [12/42]; 55% agreed that the government should be able to tell workers where to work and at what jobs [12/42]; and even toward the end of the war 61% were satisfied with rationing [8/45]; however, 34% did not believe gas rationing was necessary [6/42].*
- *Twenty-three percent of respondents favored a 10% sales tax to pay for the war [1/43]; 44% supported an increase in income taxes [3/43]; and 66% said most Americans did not take the war seriously enough [4/44].*
- *Most Americans did not see the war as a justification of cultural or racial bias: 19% said they hated the German people and 29% said they hated the Japanese people [6/42]. However, opposition to racial hatred of Japanese is hard to reconcile with the apparent support of the internment of US citizens of Japanese descent that is discussed in the next section.*

It can be argued that the primary adversary facing Germany was the Soviet Union. For example, at the time of the Battle of the Bulge, there were approximately 200 German divisions facing the Soviet Union but only eighty facing allied troops in Western Europe. Approximately thirty million Soviets lost their lives during the war. Although there is some debate about these numbers, the nonetheless enormous Soviet losses had a major impact on Soviet fears following the war which helped prompt Soviet aggression in Eastern Europe and Germany.

- *The Soviet Union was insistent as soon as the United States entered the war that the United States and England land troops in Western Europe to form a second front. Most Americans agreed (45%, 33%, 21%) [7/42]. In the first two years of the war,*

> US troops were neither sufficiently trained nor equipped and any attempt to land troops in France would have resulted in disaster. Most Americans were willing to defer to the US military to make this decision.

In January 1943, Germany had its first major defeat with the Battle of Stalingrad. Around 175,000 German troops were killed and another 137,000 were captured. The Soviets fought many more bloody battles on the march to Berlin, for example, the Kursk battle of July 1943 in which the Soviets suffered 860,000 casualties. In April 1945, Soviet troops began the capture of Berlin. Adolph Hitler committed suicide on April 30[4] and on May 7, 1945, Germany agreed to an unconditional surrender.

In January 1942, Nazi leadership, at a conference in Wannsee (just outside of Berlin), decided upon the "Final Solution" to the "Jewish Problem"—the extermination of the Jews. In the Spring of 1942, the death camps Treblinka and Sobibor opened in Poland. Although it was known that these extermination camps existed, the full extent of the horror did become fully evident until the camps were liberated by allied forces years later. In July 1944, the Soviets liberated the first major camp Majdanek; the Americans liberated Buchenwald in April 1945. Many more camps were later found by allied forces. It is estimated that six million Jews were murdered by the Nazis and their sympathizers. Jews, however, were not the only group targeted by the Nazis; the Nazis also sent to the concentration camps homosexuals, those deemed to be mentally ill, Romany people, Slavs, and political leftists. In addition, over three million Soviet POWs died in German captivity. The Nuremberg trials of 1945 and 1946 tried many Nazi and military leaders for war crimes. Ten of the defendants were eventually hung and many others received lengthy prison terms.

- *Of the 90% of Americans who said they had heard of the trials, 53% thought the verdicts were correct, 5% said they were too severe or unfair, 36% thought they were too lenient, and 6% did not have an opinion [10/46].*
- *In January 1943, 54% said they believed reports that two million Jews had been killed (22%, 24%). After the concentration camps were liberated in May 1945, 84% said the "reports that the Germans have killed many people in concentration camps or let them starve to death" were true.*

During the war and in its immediate aftermath a variety of international institutions were created to create stability and avoid future conflicts. In July 1944, the Bretton Woods Conference ended with agreements to set up the International Monetary Fund (IMF) to foster financial security, the General Agreement on Trade and Tariffs (GATT) to reduce tariffs and expand trade, and the International Bank for Reconstruction and Development (IBRD) to help the development of moderate-income countries, which was later expanded to the World Bank. In October of the same year, the Dumbarton Oaks Conference finalized the framework for the United Nations.

- *Americans did not exhibit an isolationist streak as the war wound down: 58% (29%, 13%) thought that Russia could be trusted to cooperate with us after the war [2/45]; 68% (3%, 29%) favored the upcoming US Senate vote to join the United Nations [6/45]; 41% (13%, 46%) wanted Congress to implement the Bretton Woods Agreement [6/45]; and 71% believed the United States should stay active in world affairs [10/45]. Unlike World War I, the war ended in a total victory, the enemy was unambiguously evil, and Americans came to believe that the US failure to join the League of Nations was one of the causes that resulted in the wars initiated by Germany, Italy, and Japan, combined with the realization that the United States was the most powerful country in the world and could achieve almost any goal led to support for greater involvement.*
- *Furthermore, 74% said they "[w]ould be willing to continue to put up with present shortages of butter, sugar, meat, and other rationed food products in order to give food to people who need it in Europe" [8/45]. In fact, 85% favored keeping our troops in Germany and stationed in other defeated nations [8/46].*
- *On the other hand, relatively few (27%) favored giving England a loan "to help England get back on its feet" or that English Lend-Lease payments should be forgiven (30%) [9/45].*

Three summit meetings among the heads of the United States, the Soviet Union, and Great Britain took place during the war: Tehran in November 1943; Yalta in February 1945;[5] and Potsdam in July 1945. These meetings served to determine the strategy for the war as well as to negotiate many of the thorny political issues that would follow the war (i.e., creating the United Nations, dividing Germany, deciding the status of Poland, and temporarily dividing Korea, among others).

Post-World War II

The global anticolonial struggle was beginning to take shape. The Viet Minh, led by Ho Chi Minh, was formed in May 1941 and in August 1945 took over the Vietnamese capital of Hanoi from Japan. It was also in August 1945 that Indonesian nationalists declared independence from the Dutch; in November 1946 Indonesia was granted independence. In February 1943, Mohandas Gandhi, who was under arrest in India, began another of his famous hunger strikes in protest of British rule. Among the Indian populace, nonviolent protests in combination with armed rebellions led to the British granting independence to India in 1947. Unfortunately, the independence of India also led to religious violence between Muslims and Hindus as Pakistan separated from India. It is estimated that in that conflict fourteen million people were forced to flee their homes and up to three million people were killed.

- *During World War II, 46% of Americans favored giving India independence, 13% were opposed, 6% wanted partial independence, and 34% did not know [8/42]. After the war, there was little consensus on whether England should leave India*

right away or wait until a constitution had been agreed upon (34%, 45%, 21%) [3/46].[6]
- *In a 1942 survey, 69% of respondents could identify India on a map [1/42-OPORWS].*

Following World War II and the Holocaust, many Jewish refugees fled Europe and attempted to migrate to Palestine. The British had control of Palestine since 1920 and their policies dissatisfied both Arabs and Jews. Riots occurred between Jews and Arabs, and both groups attacked the British. In May 1948, the British withdrew from Palestine, and the State of Israel was declared and was subsequently attacked by neighboring Arab states. Around 700,000 Palestinians fled their homes and became refugees. In turn, around 700,000 Jews were expelled from Arab lands and moved to Israel. A 1949 armistice negotiated by the United Nations ended the fighting until 1956.

- *Americans were not in favor of policies allowing the resettlement of Jewish refugees. Only 27% favored "a plan requiring each nation to take in a given number of Jewish and other European refugees, based upon the size and population of each nation" [8/46] and only 40% (54%, 7%) agreed to allow Polish and Jewish refugees into the United States [9/46].[7]*
- *American opinion on Mideast policies was mixed. As the war was winding down in March 1945, 59% (19%, 22% [OPOR]) favored creating a Jewish state in Palestine and immediately after the war, 80% favored allowing Jews to settle in Palestine [12/45]. Before the first Israeli-Arab war, only 30% favored financing Arab development programs in return for their support for independent states for both Israelis and Palestinians [5/47], but 65% supported the UN Resolution calling for two independent states [10/47]. When asked who they favored during the war, 34% favored the Jews, 13% the Arabs, and the remainder said neither or did not know [7/48]. In fact, only 24% wanted to lift the US arms embargo against Israel [3/48].*

The conflict between the Western Bloc (the United States and its NATO allies) and the Eastern Bloc (the Soviet Union and its allies) began directly after World War II and intensified in 1947. Essentially, the Soviet Union wanted to extend its influence over Eastern Europe and Germany. Historians disagree over whether the Soviets were primarily motivated by a desire to spread communist/Russian influence, or by the fear that the United States was building a coalition against them, a fear that was exacerbated given the Soviets' extreme losses during World War II. In March 1946, former British prime minister Winston Churchill gave a speech in Fulton, Missouri, castigating the Soviet Union and stating that "an iron curtain has descended across the continent." In May 1947, President Truman announced what was later known as the Truman Doctrine, pledging to support those nations opposing Soviet expansion. In particular, $400 million in aid was given to Turkey and Greece, whose economic support from Great Britain had been cut off after the war. Later that year, Secretary of State George Marshall outlined the Marshall Plan that eventually led to $12 billion ($120 billion in current dollar value) in aid to Western European countries for economic recovery. It was also in 1947 that Truman signed legislation creating the Central Intelligence Agency and the National Security Council. In August 1949, the Soviets tested their first atomic bomb. This triggered both paranoia and some justified concerns that Soviet spies were stealing atomic secrets. Moreover, this proof of the USSR's possession of atomic weapons gave birth to the nuclear arms race that was the hallmark of the Cold War and that continued until the 1980s. The Cold War intensified in October 1949 when the People's Republic of China was proclaimed and the democratic government of Germany (East Germany) was established.

- *Many Americans were pessimistic about the future international system. Only 23% thought the United States could keep the secret of the bomb to itself and 55% thought the United States would be engaged in another war within twenty-five years [10/45].*
- *Americans wanted to stay prepared. There was strong support (66%) for spending a lot of money for an agency that would spy on other countries, that is, the CIA, and 72% believed that every able-bodied man should undergo military training [11/45]. Few (34%) Americans wanted to reduce military spending [2/47] and 61% favored increasing the size of the army [2/48].*
- *Americans were supportive of the United Nations with only 10% wanting to do away with it [8/47] and 63% wanted a stronger United Nations [2/48].*
- *By February 1946, the belief that the United States could trust Russia had dropped to 35%, and 61% of survey respondents thought the country was too soft on Russia [3/46].*
- *Most Americans thought the Russians were trying to become "the ruling power of the world" and were not "just building up protection against being attacked in another war" (58%, 29%, 13%) [5/46]. Nevertheless, in May 1947, only 32% considered communism to be a "serious" threat.*
- *Most Americans (52%, 37%, 11%) favored the initial declaration of the Truman Doctrine (giving $250 million in economic aid to Greece) [4/47] as well favoring the Marshall Plan when it was announced (57%, 21%, 22%) [7/47]. However, in November 1947, only 47% (41%, 12%) favored a military alliance with France and England and in November 1948, only a third of Americans wanted to spend $2 billion helping Western Europe rearm. By November 1948, 68% favored a defense treaty with countries receiving aid under the Marshall Plan.*
- *Americans were becoming increasingly pessimistic. In January 1949, 49% (38%, 13%) thought it was "just a matter of time" before we got into a war with Russia and only 16% (72%, 12%) thought the Russian leaders wanted peace. In May 1949, 67% favored sending military aid to NATO countries and an equal percentage favored the creation of NATO. This was a substantial change from two years earlier when only 27% [9/45] wanted to give a loan to Great Britain.*
- *The upcoming hostility against China could be foreseen: 65% of respondents believed the Chinese communists were taking orders from Moscow [11/48] and only 25% favored recognizing the new government in China [6/49].*

US POLITICS

FDR defeated Wendell Willkie in the presidential election of 1940 (54.7% v. 44.8%) and in the election of 1944 he defeated Thomas Dewey (53.4% v. 45.9%). (FDR is the only person in US history to win four presidential elections.) Over-reacting to Japan's attack on Pearl Harbor, FDR signed Executive Order 9066 in February 1942, which resulted in approximately 120,000 US citizens of Japanese descent to be interned in camps throughout the Western United States. It was clear that this internment was a result of racism and not because of any legitimate security threat.[8]

FDR died in April 1944 and was succeeded by Harry S. Truman. Harry Truman ran for reelection in 1948 against Thomas Dewey, Southern segregationist Strom Thurmond, and progressive Henry Wallace. In a surprise outcome, Truman defeated Dewey (49.6% v. 45.1%). There were two other consequential candidates. Henry Wallace (Progressive Party) had been vice president under FDR from 1941 to 1945 and became secretary of commerce in 1945. He ran on a platform of civil rights and better relations with the USSR. He was accused of being a communist sympathizer and received 2.4% of the popular vote. Strom Thurmond (Dixiecrat) had served forty-eight years in the Senate and was a staunch segregationist from South Carolina. He opposed Truman's attempt to integrate the military and reduce the effect of Jim Crow laws. He won in four states but also received only 2.4% of the popular vote.

- *Around 49% of Americans believed Henry Wallace's Progressive Party was run by communists [7/48].*
- *During the war, Americans were in favor of FDR's order interning Japanese Americans and its attendant large-scale infringement of civil liberties. Although I could not find any question directly on this topic, only 35% said that those who were interned should be allowed to return to their homes after the war [12/42].*[9]

With the advent of the Cold War, McCarthyism also took hold. McCarthyism went well beyond the accusations of Senator Joseph McCarthy (R-WI). Thousands were accused of being communists or communist sympathizers. Anticommunist fervor in the United States did not reach its full height until the early 1950s; however, in November 1947 the House of Representatives voted to cite ten writers and directors for contempt of Congress when they refused to cooperate with an investigation looking at allegations of communist influence in Hollywood. The so-called Hollywood Ten were later blacklisted (not allowed to work).[10] This repression became a public spectacle when, in August 1948, the first-ever televised congressional hearings occurred as the House Un-American Activities Committee (HUAC) confronted Alger Hiss who was accused of being a spy for the Soviets.

- *Communists were not overly popular among Americans at any time in the 1940s: only 32% thought that Communist Party candidates should be allowed time on*

the radio [9/40];[11] 70% thought that membership in the Communist Party should be illegal [5/41]; and 61% thought that many American labor union leaders were communist [10/41].
- Following World War II but before the beginning of the Cold War, 45% wanted to outlaw the Communist Party [6/46].[12] A year later, with the beginning of the Cold War, 58% (31%, 12%) wanted to forbid membership in the Communist Party; 61% believed that American communists were more loyal to Russia than America; and 67% wanted to forbid communists from holding civil service jobs [3/47].
- By May 1948, 76% favored a law requiring all communists to register with the Justice Department.
- When the Hollywood Ten was cited for contempt and blacklisted, 48% of survey respondents thought that communists frequently "got their propaganda into motion pictures" [10/47] and 47% believed that Hollywood writers who refused to say they were members of the Communist Party should be punished [11/47].

Labor unions had a very important role in the 1940s. The percentage of the labor force that was in a union peaked in 1954 at 28.3% (in 2013 it was 11.3%). Wages were held down during the war and labor strikes were prohibited. However, in 1946, over five million workers were involved in strikes. Congress overrode a veto by President Truman to pass the Taft-Hartley Act of 1947. The Act restricted the rights of union members to strike, have boycotts, donate monies to political candidates, and to have closed shops, and it required labor unions to declare they were not supporters of the Communist Party.

- Labor unions had a somewhat problematic reputation among Americans: 45% believed that communists were behind many of the labor strikes in the United States [6/46] and 82% wanted a law requiring labor union leaders to declare they were not communists.
- Only 32% favored the "union shop—that is, requiring every worker in a company where there is a union to join that union after he is hired" [11/46][13] and 45% believed labor unions should have less power in Washington [11/48].
- Nevertheless, 62% said they approved of labor unions [11/48] and 53% (35%, 12%) believed unions had the right to strike [2/49].
- On Taft-Hartley, 35% believed it was unfair to labor (49%, 26%) [3/49].

RACE

World War II did not produce racial harmony. Race-related riots in Detroit in June 1943 resulted in the deaths of twenty-five African Americans and nine whites. The cause was a competition over jobs and housing given that 400,000 people had moved to Detroit in two years because of the war effort.

There was also substantial discrimination against blacks serving in the armed forces. For example, in July 1, 1944, Lt. Jackie Robinson was arrested at Camp

Hood, Texas, for refusing to move to the back of a segregated US army bus. Jackie Robinson, however, went on to become the first African-American to break the race barrier in Major League Baseball in April 1947.[14]

On other hand, one of the most consequential acts affecting race relations occurred in July 1948 when President Harry Truman signed Executive Order 9981, ending racial segregation in the US army. This had a long-term impact on the military as well as an example of how the US government could be involved in ending racial discrimination.

- *During the war, only 40% of Americans thought that Negro and white soldiers should serve together (22% in the South) [6/42].*
- *Two months before Truman signed Executive Order 9981, only 26% of Americans wanted Negro and white troops living and working together (6% in the South) [5/48]. These findings highlight Truman's courage in signing EO9981 just a few months before the 1948 elections.*
- *In general, there was substantial opposition to federal government intervention to end segregation: only 33% (57%, 11%) believed the federal government should "require employers to hire people without regard to their race, religion, color, or nationality" (9% in the South) [3/48] and less than half (46%) thought the federal government should have the right to deal with lynching's if the state government would not (27% in the South) [3/49]. In fact, a mere 9% wanted Congress to pass Truman's civil rights program [3/48].*[15]
- *Similarly, there was significant support for segregation: 38% (55%, 7%) thought that Negroes should sit in the back of buses or trains when traveling between states (80% in the South) [3/48] and in a May 1946 NORC survey, only 51% (45%, 4%) thought that Negroes should have as good a chance as white people to get a job (40% in the South).*
- *In an interesting contrast, though, only 7% said they approved the Ku Klux Klan (20.0% in the South) [8/46] and 67% wanted poll taxes in the South to be abolished (53% in the South) [3/49].*

Gallup surveys in the 1940s posed only two questions about other racial minorities other than African Americans: 44% thought the United States government had treated Indians fairly (38%, 18%) [11/47] and 42% thought the immigration law banning all Chinese immigrants should be modified [8/43].

SEX AND GENDER

Women's nylon stockings went on sale in May of 1940 and five million pairs were sold on the first day.

- *Fifty-three percent of Americans approved of women going without stockings during the war [8/41].*

Sexuality was still repressed. However, in 1948, Alfred Kinsey published his report on male sexuality.[16] Kinsey and his associates interviewed 6,000 respondents and found that males were sexually active and a sizable proportion were homosexual. He was able to scientifically discuss masturbation, adultery, pre-marital sex, and contraception.

- *Fifty-seven (11%, 32%) percent of survey respondents thought it was a good thing that the information in the Kinsey Report was made available [1/48].*

The well-known image of Rosie the Riveter was based on reality. Around 400,000 women served in the armed forces in World War II and female participation in the economy increased from 27% to 37% and by 1943, 475,000 women were working in airplane factories.

- *In fact, 45% of Americans were in favor of drafting women, ages 21–35, to serve in the WACS or WAVES [7/43]. Furthermore, 60% favored drafting single women over married men [1/44].*
- *However, following the war, only 15% (81%, 4%) approved of married women working if their husband could support her [11/45]; 38% approved of having a capable married woman in the president's cabinet; and only 33% said they would vote for a woman as president even if she was qualified [9/49]. Attitudes toward the role of women reverted to a period of time before Rosie the Riveter.*
- *On the other hand, 77% said that a woman should receive the same pay as men for the same type of work [9/45].*

Americans were not as prudish as is often portrayed.

- *Sixty-eight percent of survey respondents approved of sex education in high schools [5/43] and 61% approved of government health clinics giving out birth control information to married women [12/43].*
- *On the other hand, only 9% thought the divorce laws were too strict [2/45];[17] only 34% approved of women wearing slacks in public [1/48]; and 53% objected to women drinking alcohol in bars and restaurants [10/47].*

THE ECONOMY

One of the effects of the growth in armaments spending because of World War II was helping to pull the United States out of the Great Depression. Clearly, the major fear among economists and Americans was whether depression economics would return following the war.

Glimpses of the post-World War II economic structure could be seen in a number of industrial milestones: the opening of the first section of the Pennsylvania Turnpike—the first long-distance highway in the United States (1940); the opening of the first McDonald's (1940); the introduction of Cheerios (1941); Polaroid's "instant camera" hitting the market (1947); demonstration of the first practical transistor (1947); and Columbia Records' introduction of the 33 1/3 RPM phonograph format (1947).

- *Only half of Americans had access to a telephone [12/43], 58% had a refrigerator [4/46], 95% had electricity [12/49], and 47% had an automobile [6/47].*

Many economists believed the Great Depression was exacerbated by trade restrictions such as the Smoot-Hawley Act of 1930. This Act increased tariffs on 20,000 items in an attempt to reduce competition from imports. Of course, other countries retaliated hurting US exports.

- *Gallup asked in January 1944, if Europeans "can make shoes more cheaply than we can, should we buy more of our shoes from Europe and try to employ our workers in making other things than we can produce more cheaply than Europe?" Americans did not support this basic economic principle (38%, 39%, 23%). However, of the 34% who had heard of the November 1947 international trade agreement lowering tariffs, 63% agreed with it.*

Most Americans wanted less government control in some sectors.

- *Americans did not want the government to own the banks (27%) or the railroads (20%) [6/45].*
- *On the other hand, and perhaps surprisingly, 52% (34%, 13%) wanted the government to require all Americans to participate in a government-run health care system [7/45] and 69% wanted Congress to fund slum clearance and building of low-income housing [11/48].*
- *Not surprising was that, in responding to the following question, 15% favored the government moving toward Socialism:*[18] *"Under Socialism, the government owns and runs many industries and businesses like steel, coal, railroads, and banks—and offers services like medical and dental care, with the people still having the right to elect their government officials. Would you like to see the United States go more in the direction of Socialism or less in the direction of Socialism? [9/49]."*
- *Following the war, only 42% believed that US firms would be able to provide enough jobs without government programs such as the WPA [8/45]. Depression fears began to dissipate and in January 1947, only 31% expected a depression and in June 1948, 32% expected a depression in the next four years.*

Gallup surveys showed major concerns among Americans about rationing, wages, and inflation: 60% wanted to raise the minimum wage [9/45]; 66% wanted rationing to stop on beef, and 73% objected to rationing on shoes [10/45]; and 47% wanted to keep wage and price controls [9/47].

Another major issue revolved around how to pay for the war. The public was almost evenly divided with 48% wanting to cut taxes and 44% wanting to keep taxes relatively high until the debt from the war was paid off [11/46].[19]

SCIENCE, TECHNOLOGY, AND THE ENVIRONMENT

The year 1941 saw the first use of penicillin. However, it was not until 1943 that enough doses became available to have a major impact. In 1947, the first joint replacement surgery occurred.

Of course, many significant scientific advancements were related to the war, the best-known of which was the development of the atomic bomb. As discussed in the previous chapter, the Manhattan Project was the secret US-led effort to develop the bomb. In December 1942, the first self-sustaining nuclear chain reaction occurred in Chicago under the leadership of Enrico Fermi. The bomb was first tested on July 16, 1945, in Alamogordo, New Mexico. On August 6, 1945, the United States dropped an atomic bomb on Hiroshima, Japan, and dropped another one three days later on Nagasaki. The bomb was controversial before and after its use. For example, before the bomb was used, a petition drafted by Leo Szilárd[20] in July 1945 and signed by seventy scientists working on the Manhattan Project asked President Truman to demonstrate to Japan that we had the bomb before using it on a civilian population. After the attacks, many scientists remained outspoken against the military use of nuclear weapons, and an active public anti-bomb movement began.

- *The bomb was central to discussions about science: among Gallup respondents, 59% thought its development was a good thing [2/49], but only 48% wanted to have continued testing of the bomb on Bikini Island [3/46]. Furthermore, 62% wanted international control of atomic energy and 57% were willing to destroy all our bombs on hand to achieve this [10/49-NORC].*

The need for calculating machines in World War II (for use in designing the atomic bomb, deciphering coded messages from Germany [Enigma], and computing artillery firing tables) led to the development of electronic computation machines. By the end of 1945, the first programmable computer (ENIAC) was completed. It covered 1,800 square feet and had about 25 kilobytes of memory.

Other than questions about the atomic bomb, Gallup asked few questions relevant to science in this decade.

- *Forty percent did approve of "test-tube babies" for couples who could not have children [4/49].*
- *Twenty-nine percent thought electrical lights and appliances were the greatest invention ever made (the atomic bomb was second with 17%) [1/47].*
- *Eighty-four percent wanted Congress to spend $200 million to study and treat cancer [5/46] and 78% wanted $200 million to study and cure diseases of the heart [5/48].*

Chapter 2
POPULAR TRENDS

Before the war many cartoons made their debut (*Tom and Jerry, Elmer Fudd, Bugs Bunny, Woody Woodpecker*) as well as comics (*Batman, Captain America,* and *Mighty Mouse*). Memorable movies released in these years included: *The Great Dictator* (1940); *Pinocchio* (1940); *Fantasia* (1940); *Sergeant York* (1941); *Casablanca* (1942); *Yankee Doodle Dandy* (1942); *Bambi* (1942); *This Is the Army* (1943); *For Whom the Bell Tolls* (1943); *Going My Way* (1944); *National Velvet* (1944); *Song of the South* (1946); *It's A Wonderful Life* (1946); *The Best Years of Our Lives* (1946); and *Battleground* (1949).

- *Gallup asked few questions about these movies; however, 72% could correctly identify Walt Disney [6/45] and 90% could identify Charlie Chaplin [7/45].*
- *Movies attendance was high: 44% said they went to the movies in the past week [7/47] and 58% had gone in the previous month [11/46].*
- *Thirty-nine percent had heard of the movie Dive Bomber (1941), and 13% could identify one of the stars—Errol Flynn [10/41].*
- *Seventy-four percent had heard of Citizen Kane (1941), and 14% could name one of the stars—Orson Wells [8/41].*
- *Mrs. Miniver (1942) had been seen by 17% of respondents [8/42].*

Television expanded its reach. The first TV commercial (for Bulova watches) was aired in July 1941 before the start of a baseball game on NBC, and the next day the second game show in US history aired—*Truth or Consequences*, sponsored by Ivory Soap.

- *In December 1945, only 9% of Americans had ever seen a TV. As the decade came to a close, 6% of the population owned television and 54% thought TV would take the place of radio in the home within the next seven years [5/49]. Clearly, the public was primed for the explosion in television that would occur in the next decade.*
- *Radio was the major source of news: 91% listened to the war news on the radio in the weeks after Pearl Harbor [12/41].*

Books that came out in the 1940s included: Richard Wright's *Native Son* (1940); Ernest Hemingway's *For Whom the Bell Tolls* (1940); Betty Smith's *A Tree Grows in Brooklyn* (1943); Norman Mailer's *The Naked and the Dead* (1948); George Orwell's *Animal Farm* (1945); A. C. Kinsey's *Sexual Behavior in the Human Male* (1948); Winston Churchill's *The Gathering Storm* (1948); and Frank Gilberth Jr.'s *Cheaper by the Dozen* (1949).

- *Twenty percent of Gallup respondents said they had heard of or had read the Kinsey report [1/48], and 90% could identify Winston Churchill [7/45]; 18% of*

Americans claimed they had read Shakespeare since leaving school [1/42]; 39% said they had recently read a book [8/45]; and 36% could identify John Steinbeck [7/45].
- When asked about their favorite magazine, the top three choices were: Reader's Digest (11%), Life (10%), and Saturday Evening Post (8%) [5/41].

The 1940s was an era of swing, big band, and the crooners. Popular musicians included: Bing Crosby, Glenn Miller, Jimmy Dorsey, Harry James, Dinah Shore, and Perry Como. Broadway was also booming with popular stage musicals like Rodgers and Hammerstein's *Oklahoma* in 1943 and the war-related yet racially progressive *South Pacific* in 1949.

- *Kate Smith was popular on the radio with 39% hearing her within the last five months [2/45].*
- *Frank Sinatra ruled the music world with 84% able to identify him [7/45].*

In spectator sports, Joe DiMaggio hit in fifty-six consecutive games in 1941. Some consider this to be the greatest feat in the history of baseball. The first NBA game was played in November 1946 with the New York Knicks defeating the Toronto Huskies.

- *During the war, 67% of survey respondents wanted to continue professional sports [2/42].*
- *In September 1949, 45% said they followed baseball and 53% thought Babe Ruth was the greatest baseball player of all time (Ty Cobb was 11% and Lou Gehrig was 10%).*
- *In 1948, more than half of Americans (53%) had attended a football game during the previous year [1/48].*
- *In 1940, survey respondents were given a list and asked what types of games they played in the last year: Checkers (37%), Dominos (17%), Golf (15%), Bridge (38%), Pinochle (27%), Tennis (14%), Poker (30%), Solitaire (33%), Chess (6%), and Charades (4%) [3/40].*
- *And, in a 1948 survey, 42% of Americans said they had heard of Norman Rockwell.*

CONCLUDING COMMENTS

The Depression was over, fascism was vanquished, and the Cold War was on the horizon.

It is estimated that seventy-five million people died in the carnage of World War II. It took a true coalition to defeat the fascists: the United States, the Soviet Union, China, Great Britain, and so many more. With Lend-Lease, the United States began to give real aid to Great Britain and after Pearl Harbor the spigot opened. The horrors of concentration camps and death marches were replaced by a hopeful future reflected by the establishment of international organizations to foster world peace and economic prosperity. However, toward the end of the decade, the Cold War had begun. Much of Eastern Europe fell under the sway of the Soviet Union, the Soviet Union tested its first atomic bomb, and the Chinese Communist Party won the civil war in China.

Pearl Harbor moved American public opinion from isolationism to internationalism. The success of the "Good War" led most Americans wanting the United States to stay engaged in world politics and to be prepared for future conflicts. Although most Americans were hopeful about the future, there was increasing belief that we might end up in a war with the Soviet Union. American public opinion was primed to support NATO and giving military aid to those opposing the Soviet Union.

Domestic politics was relatively quiescent until the end of the war. After the war, the witch hunt against those accused of communist sympathies hit full stride while at the same time labor unions were successful in raising wages, increasing benefits, and instituting the forty-hour workweek. Nonetheless, most Americans were in favor of the communist purge and labor unions were relatively popular.

Jim Crow continued to rule the South and discrimination against blacks in the military continued through World War II. But Jackie Robinson's playing for the Brooklyn Dodgers in 1947 and Harry Truman's 1948 signing of Executive Order 9981 ending racial segregation in the military were harbingers that change was on the horizon. Most Americans opposed blacks and whites serving together in the military and having the federal government intervene to end other forms of discrimination. In fact, there was a surprising level of support for segregation. However, most opposed the Ku Klux Klan and wanted the poll tax abolished.

Women's participation in the economy during World War II proved crucial to the victory. However, following the war most Americans still opposed women's participation in politics and in the economy (except as consumers). Although most supported sex education in high school, prudishness still ruled. It was somewhat surprising to find out how few supported divorce rights for women or even thought women should be allowed to wear slacks in public.

There was little competition to America's economic supremacy at the end of the war. In addition, the future vigor of the economy could be glimpsed with long-distance highways, the opening of the first McDonalds, and the invention of the transistor. Depression and inflation fears were predominant until late in the decade. Americans were contradictory on the role of government. Most wanted government to be in charge of health care and clearing the slums. In other areas, they wanted less government intervention.

[The reader can find relevant crosstabs and discussion in the online appendix located at https://rowman.com/ISBN/9781793653505/US-Public-Opinion-since-the-1930s-Galluping-through-History.]

NOTES

1. The question asked: "General Pershing says the United States should sell to England 50 of our destroyer ships which were built during the last world war and are now being put

back in service. do you approve or disapprove of our government selling these destroyers to England?" using the prominence of General Pershing made the question exceptionally biased.

2. Berinsky (2009) argues in his masterful book on public opinion and American wars from World War II that attitudes toward the war were more of a reflection of partisan attitudes than a reaction to events. Furthermore, much of our understanding of public attitudes during World War II is based upon myth (the good war). In fact, most Americans had little understanding of the reasons for the war.

3. Alperovitz (2010) argues that Japan would have surrendered without the United States dropping the bomb. He believes the bomb was used as a signal to the Soviet Union. Alperovitz initially argued this in a 1965 book that initiated an entire school of revisionist history about the origins of the Cold War.

4. In April 1947, only 47% believed that Hitler was dead!

5. Of the 70% who heard of this Crimean conference, 60% (9%, 42%) favored the results [2/45].

6. I could not find any questions about Gandhi. In fact, there were almost no questions asked about third-world countries.

7. For more on America's view of refugees see: https://news.gallup.com/opinion/polling-matters/186716/historical-review-americans-views-refugees-coming.aspx

8. It was not until 1988 that Ronald Reagan signed a law apologizing for this abuse of civil rights and authorized the payment of $20,000 to each survivor.

9. One other interesting question on civil liberties was that 69% wanted every American to be required to carry an identification card with their fingerprints [1/42]. After the war, only 33% thought it was fair for the government to use wiretaps in court trials [6/49].

10. See the 1976 film *The Front* and the 2015 biographical drama film *Trumbo* for a depiction of the Hollywood Ten.

11. Only 36% thought atheists should be allowed on the radio [12/46].

12. Question order effects might be an issue since the question just before whether the Communist Party should be outlawed was on whether members of the Communist Party were more loyal to the United States or to Russia?

13. One of the major rationales for the union shop is that if a member benefits from the union (wages are higher, better safety conditions, etc.) that person should contribute to the cost of that benefit, otherwise they are receiving a "free ride."

14. No survey organization asked any questions about Jackie Robinson in the 1940s.

15. The United States government actively opposed integration in housing. For example, the FHA would not fund mortgages for black families in white neighborhoods, believing it would lower housing values and endanger other FHA-backed mortgages. For a very important discussion of the role of government in housing segregation, see Rothstein (2017).

16. Kinsey's study on female sexuality would come out in 1953.

17. In 1969, California became the first state to allow for no-fault divorce.

18. IPOLL showed 49% favored socialism whereas the raw data put that figure at 15%. After a series of emails back-and-forth with Roper, it was clear that the IPOLL figure was wrong. Apparently, there was often error by interns, etc. when the IPOLL numbers were posted.

19. Phillips (2012) notes that the United States never really paid off the debt from World War II. The debt simply shrank as the economy grew.

20. Szilard is one of the most fascinating and under-appreciated (by the general public) scientist in the development of the atomic bomb. He did most of his thinking (boinking as he called it) in the bathtub. His biography is a delightful read (Lanouette, 2013).

3

The 1950s

Anticommunism, Relative Economic Prosperity at Home, and a Growing Cold War Abroad

As previously noted, the major scientific pollsters (Crossley, Gallup, and Roper) incorrectly predicted that Dewey would defeat Truman in the 1948 presidential election. As a result of this fiasco (Lusinchi, 2018), the Social Science Research Council prodded the polling industry to start using probability samples.[1] (Gallup moved over to probability samples in 1950.) Gallup was still the primary survey organization, accounting for 65% of the 272 national surveys in the Roper archive that were done in the 1950s. (Twenty-one percent were NORC polls and 11% Roper.) There were three national telephone surveys in this period. In 1957, the Roper Center for Public Opinion Research opened for business. This was before magnetic tapes for data storage were widely available, so scholars had to either visit the center to do basic analysis or request duplicate punch cards.

WORLD EVENTS

Korea, China, and Vietnam

The decade began with a bang as North Korean troops invaded South Korea on June 25, 1950. Korea had been divided into two regions at the 38th Parallel following World War II. Both governments claimed to be the legitimate government of a unified Korea and both massively repressed the opposition. The North Korean military overran South Korea and the American forces stationed there (who were ill-prepared for war) and in two months were close to taking over the entirety of Korea. The United Nations Security Council voted to send United Nations forces to stop the invasion.[2] On September 15, under command of General Douglas MacArthur, UN forces landed behind enemy lines at Inchon and began to occupy parts of North

Korea. China warned the United States that it would intervene if UN forces continued to advance. MacArthur did not believe this threat and UN forces approached the border of China. In late November, Chinese forces entered the war encircling and almost defeating the eighth army. UN forces had to retreat south of the 38th Parallel. MacArthur was sacked by President Truman and a bloody stalemate ensued until an armistice was signed on July 27, 1953. All told, the United States suffered 33,686 battle deaths during the war.

- *A month after the North Korean invasion, 78% of Americans favored Truman sending US military aid to Korea; only 11% wanted to withdraw US troops; and 67% wanted the US economy to go on a war footing [7/50].*
- *While 31% of respondents approved of Truman's decision to remove General MacArthur [5/51], a number of Americans had become disenchanted with the war following the intervention of China: 43% (40%, 17%) now believed the United States made a mistake getting into the war [6/51]; and 32% wanted to pull UN troops out of the country.*
- *On the other hand, 58% wanted to bomb Chinese cities if peace talks failed [8/51] and 50% favored using the atomic bomb in Korea [11/51]. The parallels with the later war in Vietnam are unmistakable: a war with many casualties ending in a stalemate, resulting in declining support for the war.*

The Cold War heated up in other locations as well. In part because of McCarthyism and not wanting to appear soft on communism, the US government refused to recognize the new government in China—the Peoples' Republic of China.

- *Even before the Korean War, only 26% of the American public wanted the government to recognize the PRC [1/50]; only 13% thought the PRC should take over the UN seat for China (decreasing to 7% in July 1954); and 53% wanted the United States to use its veto power in the Security Council to block this [6/50].*
- *Although, only 18% wanted to start an all-out-war with China [5/51], 62% wanted to give the Chinese Nationalists on Formosa ships to blockade China and 63% wanted to give them planes so they could bomb China [2/53].*[3]
- *In July 1954, 47% thought the United States should be friendly to China to woo her away from Russia and 39% thought China does "exactly what Russia tells her" (50%, 11%).*
- *But Americans favored talks with China. Fifty-three percent thought that Secretary of State Dulles should meet with Chou En Lai when Chou suggested such a meeting [2/57] and 57% thought we should allow US newsmen to visit China [6/57].*[4]

The Viet Minh, under the leadership of Ho Chi Minh, fought a war to expel the French from Vietnam. The United States supplied the French with weapons and financial support, but refused the French request for US troops and the use of an atomic bomb. In May 1954, the French surrendered Dien Bien Phu. Approximately, 1,600 French troops were killed during the battle, 1,600 were missing, and 8,000 were captured. The French defeat led to the end of French colonial rule in Vietnam following the 1954 Geneva Peace Accords.

- *Fifty-six percent of survey respondents thought the United States should send war materials to help the French in Indochina but only 12% favored sending troops [5/53]. In May 1954, 29% thought we should drop hydrogen bombs on China if the United States got involved in that war, and 58% thought the United States should use atomic artillery.*

More on the Cold War

Another event that combined the anticolonial struggle and the Cold War was the January 1959 takeover of Havana by Fidel Castro. The Cuban Revolution would have considerable political ramifications in the United States for the next half-century.

- *In July 1959, 20% of Americans had a favorable opinion of Castro (49%, 32%).*

In May 1955, West Germany joined NATO, and the following week eight communist bloc countries formed the Warsaw Pact. Western Europe was recovering from the War and in January 1958 European unity progressed with the formation of the European Economic Community.

- *Americans were generally supportive of helping European allies. Sixty percent (29%, 8%) favored continuing to send troops and aid to Europe in its defense against Russia [3/52] and in September 1954, 70% thought that West Germany should have its own army.*

The arms race intensified between the United States and the Soviet Union. On May 9, 1950, the United States tested its first thermonuclear weapon, and in April 1952 the B-52 bomber flew for the first time. Specifically developed for its ability to drop atomic bombs on Russia, the B-52 could fly more than 8,000 miles without refueling and could carry 70,000 pounds of bombs. In January 1954, the first nuclear submarine—the *USS Nautilus*—was launched. In February 1959, the United States test-fired the first Titan intercontinental missile. The Russians responded in kind. They tested their first thermonuclear bomb in 1955 and, in October 1957, launched Sputnik, the first artificial satellite.

- *Seventy-two percent of respondents favored the development of the hydrogen bomb even when told in the survey question that other countries could develop the bomb and that it would kill many people at one time [1/50]. In the same survey, only 49% wanted to work with Russia to control the bomb before embarking on building an H Bomb.*
- *Americans were more supportive of arms control as the decade progressed. In April 1953, 59% favored international control of atomic energy in which all countries*

would be inspected by the United Nations, and 64% thought we should agree to stop nuclear testing if all other countries, including Russia, also agreed [4/57].
- *Nuclear weapons were not seen as being harmful in these years. Only 41% thought there was danger from fallout after nuclear testing [4/57].*
- *The Russian launching of Sputnik increased the public belief that growth in US armaments was necessary. Fifty percent (32%, 18%) thought the Russians were ahead of us in missile technology [10/57] and only 26% were satisfied with current defense policies [11/57]. This "missile gap" became a prominent theme in the 1960 election, with JFK attacking Nixon for being weak.*

Joseph Stalin died in March 1953 and was replaced by Nikita Khrushchev. On February 25, 1956, Khrushchev made a "secret" speech to the twentieth Party Congress, denouncing the Cult of Stalin and his brutal policies. Khrushchev's stance induced a slow liberalization in the Soviet Union. This move toward reform, though, encouraged massive student activism in Hungary, where, in October 1956, a revolution broke out against Soviet control. Soviet troops invaded and the revolt was put down with an estimated 2,500 Hungarians killed and 200,000 fleeing the country.

- *Only 23% of Americans (62%, 16%) thought the United States should have done more to help Hungary win its freedom [11/56-NORC] and 43% (44%, 14%) thought the United States should allow Hungarians who came to the United States to stay permanently.*
- *In general, Americans were in favor of an aggressive policy toward Russia. Seventy-nine percent favored going to war if Russia attacked US troops in Germany [7/50]; many felt that it was more important to stop Russian expansion compared to keeping out of war (65%, 23%, 6%) [7/50]; and 67% thought we should use the atomic bomb at the outset of a war with Russia [1/51].*
- *On the other hand, only 18% thought there would be an all-out-war with Russia in the next twelve months [5/51].*
- *After the death of Stalin, only 23% thought real change was occurring in Russia [5/53]; only 39% believed that Russia wanted to prevent another war [7/55]; and only 26% thought our relations with Russia were improving [6/57].*
- *But few wanted war. Only 13% said we should go to war with Russia "while we still have the advantage" [8/54] and 66% favored Khrushchev's upcoming visit to the United States in 1959 [8/59].*[5]

Other International Events

The anticolonial struggle was also heating up, in opposition to which the United States orchestrated coups d'état in Guatemala and Iran in 1953, led a failed 1958 coup attempt in Indonesia, and participated in the overthrow of Patrice Lumumba of the Congo in 1959–1960. In February 1955, President Eisenhower sent the first US "advisors" to South Vietnam. However, many colonial countries became independent in this decade (before the wave of independence that was to come in the 1960s): Libya (1951), French Morocco and Tunisia (1956), British Kenya (1957), British Malaya (1957), French Guinea, Chad, and Gabon (1958), and British Nigeria (1959).[6]

One other relevant international event was the October 1956 Israeli invasion of Egypt. The Egyptian president, Gamal Abdel Nasser, had nationalized the Suez Canal and was frustrating British and French policies in other parts of the Mideast. The French and the British encouraged the Israelis to invade Egypt so they would have a pretext to take over the canal. Intense pressure from the United States and the Soviet Union forced all three countries to withdraw. Ultimately, the invasion led to the strengthening of Nasser, the lessening of prestige of the British and French, and the growth of anticolonial struggles elsewhere.

- *Most Americans did not have a strong opinion about the war in the Sinai. When asked who was in the right, 52% did not know, 17% said neither, 11% said Egypt, and 19% said Israel [10/55]. In fact, surveys showed that only 38% wanted to send UN troops to patrol the border [4/56] and 24% wanted to send armaments to Israel [8/56]. Americans were not optimistic about whether Egypt and Israel could peacefully resolve their differences (36%) [4/57].*
- *Americans generally favored an internationalist posture. In the middle of the century, 73% wanted to strengthen the United Nations [12/54] and only 26% wanted to start cutting ground troops [2/55].*

US POLITICS

On November 4, 1952, Dwight D. Eisenhower defeated Illinois governor Adlai Stevenson to become the first Republican president in twenty years (55% v. 44%). Eisenhower also defeated Stevenson in a rematch in 1956 (57% v. 42%). In 1959, both Hawaii and Alaska were admitted as states.

- *Eighty-one percent of respondents favored admitting Alaska to the Union and 78% favored admitting Hawaii [12/53].*

As noted in the previous chapter, anticommunist fervor increased after World War II. On February 9, 1950, Senator Joseph McCarthy of Wisconsin made a speech accusing the State Department of having 205 communists on its staff. There was no proof for this and other accusations that he made. Nonetheless, the "loss of China," the Korean War, and the Soviet testing of an atomic bomb created fertile ground for the anticommunist hysteria in the United States that was to follow. In the 1950s Red Scare, hundreds were imprisoned and over 10,000 lost their jobs. Most of those who were accused were not allowed to confront their accusers and many were forced to testify and invoked the Fifth Amendment in order to avoid being jailed.[7] In March 1954, McCarthy was denounced by American journalists Edward Murrow and Fred Friendly in a half-hour television documentary. In June of that year, McCarthy attacked the US army as having been infiltrated by communists. This caused Joseph Welch, counsel to the army, to lash out during a publicized Senate hearing, asking McCarthy, "Have you at long last, no decency." McCarthy's influence almost immediately began to wane and in December he was censured by the US Senate.

In March 1951, Julius and Ethel Rosenberg were convicted of passing atomic secrets to the Soviets and sentenced to death. Despite the prevailing anticommunist atmosphere in the United States at the time, there was some public support for their innocence and a strong movement to vacate the death sentence.[8] The Rosenbergs were executed in June of 1953.

- *Seventy-three percent of Americans approved of the death penalty for treason [1/53] and 76% favored the death penalty for the Rosenbergs [2/53]. Over half (52%, 30%, 17%) believed McCarthy's assertion that there were communists in the State Department [3/50].*
- *Many wanted to take away rights from both current and former communists. Only 23% thought that former members of the Communist Party should be allowed to teach at colleges even if they denounced the party [3/53]; only 29% thought a communist should be able to make a speech in their town [11/53]; and 51% (34%, 16%) wanted to put admitted communists into jail [5/54].*
- *Given the general hysteria, one of the more interesting beliefs reflected in the survey responses was that 49% (21%, 14%) thought the number of communists in the United States was increasing. However, although 50% of Americans had a positive opinion of McCarthy [12/53] (reduced to 33% in May 1954) only 31% approved of McCarthy's methods [3/53].*
- *Somewhat surprising, only 35% (29%, 36%) wanted the Senate to censure McCarthy. Forty-three percent said they watched the Edward Murrow broadcast and 48% of these said the program had changed their mind about McCarthy [4/54-Roper].*

Gallup surveys in this decade also reflected public opinion on crime, guns, labor unions, and education.

- *According to survey results, crime was not considered a major problem in this decade. When asked whether it was better to punish or rehabilitate prisoners, only 16% of respondents favored punishment over rehabilitation (78%, 6%) [7/55].*
- *Americans were in favor of gun control. Three-quarters were in favor of a law requiring the police to give out a permit before a person could buy a gun and only 41% favored allowing private citizens to have loaded guns at home [7/59].*
- *Labor unions were not very popular in this decade. When asked whom they sympathized with, in labor disputes in the last several years, more respondents were on the side of unions than of corporations (43%, 32%, 26%) [10/52]. However, 47% (23%, 30%) favored the workers in a strike against Ford [6/55] but only 28% (32%, 40%) favored the union in the steel strikes [8/59].*

- *Nevertheless, 43% believed that corruption was widespread in unions [4/57] and 63% were in favor of open-shop laws in which workers could not be required to join a union. However, when asked whether it was unfair for workers who benefit from unions not to pay union dues, 45% agreed that it was (42%, 13%) [7/57]. Most were not in favor of unions for public employees, such as teachers (38%) and policemen (27%). Only 29% favored unions for baseball players [1/59].*
- *Americans became increasingly concerned about education, in part because of the Soviets' successful launch of Sputnik: 71% believed that high-school students must be required to work harder so we could compete with Russia [11/57]. Only 39% thought schools spent enough time teaching reading [8/57]; 89% believed math should be required in high school [11/57]; 70% thought teachers should be able to discipline children more [8/57]; and 53% thought that schools were not asking enough of students (6% too much, 28% about right, 13%-DK) [2/58].*
- *Only 39% wanted to provide tax dollars to make college tuition free, but 81% thought parents should be able to deduct college tuition from their taxes, and 77% thought the government should provide long-term loans for college [1/58].*

RACE

On May 17, 1954, the US Supreme Court unanimously ruled in *Brown v. Board of Education* that segregated schools were unconstitutional. It was also in 1954 that Rosa Parks refused to give up her seat on a bus in Montgomery, Alabama. Her protest led to the successful Montgomery Bus Boycott, which lasted 381 days and helped propel Martin Luther King Jr. to national leadership in the civil rights movement. It took years for *Brown* to reach its full effect. As part of its campaign to force the implementation of *Brown* across the South, the NAACP registered black students at previously segregated schools, including nine students at Little Rock Central High School (LRHC) in Arkansas. In September 1957, in order to block the students from entering the school, Governor Orval Faubus of Arkansas called out the state's National Guard. Violence erupted, and when it escalated President Eisenhower ordered part of the 101st Airborne Division to protect the students as well as federalizing the Arkansas National Guard. The successful integration of the Montgomery bus system as well as LRHC foreshadowed the civil rights struggles of the 1960s. Throughout the decade, however, there was considerable opposition to efforts to promote integration and views on civil rights remained divided.

- *Only 32% (47%, 21%; 14% in the South) of survey respondents favored "a national law requiring employers to hire people without regard to color or race" [1/53].*
- *Only about half (52%; 15% of whites in the South) of Americans supported the Brown decision [12/54] and only 22% thought that the United States should immediately desegregate high schools [10/54].*

- *Support for Brown increased to 63% two years later [12/56]. Most Americans did not support (42% (80% in the South), 47%, 11%) Governor Faubus sending in the National Guard to LRHC. When asked when LRHC should admit the nine students, 51% said now, 27% said wait, 16% volunteered never, and 7% did not know [9/57].*
- *On the other hand, 51% (85% in the South) of Americans favored a constitutional amendment that would allow the states to decide what to do about integration.*
- *Twenty-four percent of those with children said they would object to sending their children to a school at which a few of the children were "colored." An additional 31% opposed their children going to a school where half of the children were colored [9/58].*
- *Over half (55%, 20% in the South) agreed with the Interstate Commerce Commission ruling that "racial segregation on trains, buses, and in public waiting rooms must end" [12/55].*
- *Similarly, in response to more general civil rights issues, survey results showed less than majority support (38%) for a law that would jail or fine those who disobey a court order or one that would deprive someone of the right to vote [7/57].*
- *In one of the most extreme survey outcomes concerning race, only 4% (1% in the South) approved of marriages between "white and colored people" [9/58].*
- *Fifty-six percent said they would not move if a black family moved next door [9/58]. However, only 37% said they would vote for a Negro as president [7/58].*

These survey results show why there needed a robust civil rights movement to change laws, practices, and attitudes. These changes would not come without the struggle and sacrifice of many committed activists in this decade and subsequent decades.

SEX AND GENDER

The 1950s are often viewed as a prudish decade. However, it was in these years that Marilyn Monroe became a cultural icon. *Playboy* came out with its first issue in December 1953 with a centerfold nude of Marilyn Monroe. She married baseball player Joe DiMaggio in 1954 and playwright Arthur Miller in 1956.

- *In a 1957 survey, 88% of Americans could correctly identify Marilyn Monroe [11/57].*

In March 1957, the US Supreme Court ruled that Lawrence Ferlinghetti's work was not obscene. This set up the court battles over pornography of the 1960s and beyond.[9]

- *Only about half of survey respondents (52%) said they would vote for a woman as a president who was nominated by their party [2/55].*

- *A question on sex roles found that only 28% (64%, 8%) thought it was all right for a girl to telephone a boy and ask for a date [6/50]; only 21% thought it was acceptable for women to wear shorts on the street [6/51];[10] and 64% (35%, 1%) believed that "fathers should be the top boss of the family in this country" [1/58].*
- *One telling question was when Gallup asked in June 1950 what profession you would recommend to a girl who came to you for advice. Twenty-eight percent recommended nursing and 16% recommended teaching. Only 2% mentioned being a doctor (combined with dental technician) and no one recommended that women should become lawyers. However, there was strong support (87%) for equal pay for equal work [5/54]. Nevertheless, clearly the 1950s was not a time of enlightened attitudes toward women.*
- *Surprisingly, 67% of Americans approved of having sex education courses in high school [1/51]; 49% (19%, 32%) thought it was a good thing to have the information available that was produced by Kinsey's book on female sexual behavior [7/53]; and 73% thought birth control information should be made available to anyone who wants it [12/59]. But, there was less support for daily newspapers having medical experts discuss the sexual problems (41%, 47%, 12%) [7/53].*
- *The right to divorce was not strongly supported. Only 27% thought people should be permitted to go to another state to obtain a divorce [1/54].*

THE ECONOMY

Shopping was becoming homogenized. Perhaps this trend is best epitomized by the openings of food franchises: Burger King in 1954, McDonalds in 1955, Pizza Hut in 1957, and The International House of Pancakes also in 1957. To round out this list of food firsts, the TV dinner went on the market in 1954.

Americans became increasingly connected. In August 1952, 45% had a TV set (88% in July 1958) and 72% had a telephone (81% in 1956). In 1951, AT&T introduced direct distance dialing.

President Eisenhower was a strong advocate of a national interstate highway system, but, given the stronger role of the states in this time period, the project was championed for reasons of national defense. The National Interstate and Defense Highways Act was passed in 1956 calling for 41,000 miles of interstate highways, with the federal government paying 90% of costs and the establishment of the Highway Trust Fund. In a related development, the highway death toll was on the rise with 36,932 deaths from auto accidents on record for 1957.

- *In March 1953, three years before the passage of the National Interstate and Defense Highways Act, 62% of Americans had favored it. Even though 1930's depression economics was over, many Americans now believed in the power of the federal government to direct parts of the national economy.*
- *In 1957, 84% wanted laws requiring all people to take a driving test before getting a license and 67% wanted to take licenses away for at least thirty days from those convicted of speeding.*

- One of the biggest questions was how to pay for highway construction. Only 39% of respondents (49%, 11%) favored an increase in a tax on gasoline that would fund construction [8/59].

The Korean War created a lot of economic uncertainty. The ability to fight a ground war was limited because American strategic thinking was any future war would be fought with nuclear weapons that resulted in a relatively small number of troops who were prepared for conventional combat. It was not clear how the increase in the military would be funded and how it would affect the rest of the economy.

- At the beginning of the Korean War, 53% of Americans favored a freeze on wages and prices and 67% wanted the US industry to go on a war footing [7/50].
- When asked how to pay for Korean War, 51% favored raising taxes, 26% borrow the money, and 23% did not know or gave some other response [10/50].
- Americans favored a strong role for government in some economic sectors but not in others. For example, few Americans wanted the government to own the electric utilities (18%), banks (14%), or railroads (14%); but, 62% wanted the government to mandate an increase in the minimum wage [9/53].
- There was not a consensus on what to do with any potential budget surplus. Forty-seven percent wanted to use any surplus to reduce debt and 43% wanted to reduce taxes (10%-DK) [1/56].
- For Americans who followed the issue, most favored lowering of tariffs (47%) or keeping them the same (35%). Only 18% favored more protectionism [1/54].

SCIENCE, TECHNOLOGY, AND THE ENVIRONMENT

Many of the inventions that drive our current age came to light in the 1950s. For example, William Shockley, John Bardeen, and Walter Brattain announced the invention of the transistor in 1951; the first transistor radio was announced by Texas Instruments in 1954; IBM released the first Fortran compiler in 1957; the Boeing 707 flew for the first time in 1957; Gordon Gould invented the laser in 1957; James Kilby invented the first integrated circuit in 1958; and the first plain paper copier was introduced by Xerox in 1959.

The first window air conditioner (AC) appeared in the Sears catalog in 1951 and two million units were sold in 1958. This single invention was largely responsible for a burgeoning population in southern and southwestern cities, such as Miami, Las Vegas, Los Angeles, and Houston. The introduction of AC also had a tremendous impact on worker productivity.

Hardly less significant, on February 28, 1952, James Watson and Francis Crick announced that they had discovered the double-helix structure of DNA, which ultimately led to the biological revolutions that have occurred in recent years.

The polio epidemic peaked in 1952 when there were 57,268 cases reported and more than 3,000 deaths caused by the disease. Parents were panicked with stories of children who became paralyzed due to polio and could live only with the aid of an iron lung.[11] Jonas Salk announced a vaccine administered by injection in April 1955 and an oral vaccine developed by Albert Sabin was released in 1962. This was a great success for science and public health as polio was virtually eliminated in the United States. Americans were optimistic about a cure for polio.

- *In February 1954, 86% thought a cure for polio would be found. Eighty-two percent of survey respondents who had children wanted them to be vaccinated for polio [5/54].*

The 1950s was a period in which Americans trusted scientists and advocates for public health. Fluoride was added to the water supply of many American cities to prevent tooth decay (66% of American cities receive fluoridated water now). However, some considered this to be a communist plot and an abridgment of liberties.

- *According to a 1952 survey, 54% (11%, 34%) of respondents favored adding fluoride to the water [1/52].*
- *Other than littering, few environmental issues were of concern to Americans. Only 21% were worried about population growth [12/59] and 45% said fallout from nuclear weapons tests would be a threat to future generations [4/58]. However, 78% thought littering in public spaces was a serious issue [3/56]. The environmental movement was years in the future.*

POPULAR TRENDS

Some of the prominent movies that came out in the 1950s included: *Cinderella* (1950); *Alice in Wonderland* (1951); *Peter Pan* (1952); *From Here to Eternity* (1953); *Godzilla* (1954); *Rebel Without a Cause* (1955); *The Ten Commandments* (1956); *Around the World in 80 Days* (1956); *Giant* (1956); *The Three Faces of Eve* (1957); *The Bridge Over the River Kwai* (1957); *Sleeping Beauty* (1959); and *Ben-Hur* (1959). Unfortunately, no survey questions were asked about which specific movies Americans were seeing in this decade.

- *In January 1951 survey, 19% of respondents said they had gone to the movies in the previous seven days. This number declined to 13% in August 1957. The advent of television was beginning to have a large impact on movie theaters.*

The 1950s is called by some the first Golden Age of Television. The percentage of American households who had a television increased from 9% in 1950 to 87% in 1960. The first color TV went on sale in 1953 for $1,175 ($10,562 in current dollars). TV shows that came out during the decade included: *I Love Lucy* (1951) (69% of TV owners had seen this program in last three weeks [Roper-5/52]); *The $64,000 Question* (1955); *The Honeymooners* (1955); *Gunsmoke* (1955); *Alfred Hitchcock*

Presents (1955); *The Mickey Mouse Club* (1955); *As the World Turns* (1956); *Huntley-Brinkley Reports* (1956); *To Tell the Truth* (1956); and *The Twilight Zone* (1959).

- *In May 1950, only 28% of Americans had seen a television program in the previous seven days. In December 1953, when the 56% who had a television set were asked what their favorite were: Dragnet (26%); I Love Lucy (22%); Arthur Godfrey (20%); and Groucho Marx—You Bet Your Life (19%).*
- *One factoid showing the extraordinary influence of TV on popular culture was that on January 19, 1952, 71% of those who owned a TV watched the episode of I Love Lucy in which Lucy gave birth to Little Ricky. This record remains unbroken.*

New comic strips that were to become classics appeared, counting among them *Beetle Bailey* (1950); *Peanuts* (1950); and *Dennis the Menace* (1951). Broadway premiers included *The King and I* (1951), *My Fair Lady* (1956), and *West Side Story* (1957).

A fascinating breadth of types of books came out (in English) in this decade, ranging from precursors to New Age literature to spy stories to books that reflect the social alienation of the 1950s, including: L. Ron Hubbard's *Dianetics* (1950); J. D. Salinger's *Catcher in the Rye* (1951); Thor Heyerdahl's *Kon Tiki* (1950); Rachel Carson's *The Sea Around Us* (1951); James Jones's *From Here to Eternity* (1951); Herman Wouk's *The Caine Mutiny* (1951); Ian Fleming's first James Bond book *Casino Royale* (1954); J. R. R. Tolkien's *The Lord of the Rings* (1954); William Golding's *Lord of the Flies* (1954); Allen Ginsberg's *Howl and Other Poems* (1956); Patricia Highsmith's *The Talented Mr. Ripley* (1956); Dr. Seuss' *The Cat in the Hat* (1957); Ayn Rand's *Atlas Shrugged* (1957); Boris Pasternak's *Doctor Zhivago* (1958); and Leon Uris's *Exodus* (1959).

- *In May 1952, Gallup asked which magazines the respondents had read in the previous three months, getting these results: Readers' Digest (46%), Life (43%), Saturday Evening Post (29%), Look (28%), Ladies' Home Journal (25%), Better Homes and Gardens (23%), Colliers (22%), Time (21%), Good Housekeeping (18%), McCalls (17%), Newsweek (15%), True Story (10%), and Photoplay (6%).*

The first issue of *Sports Illustrated* came out in August 1954. Newspapers were still popular.

- *Eighty-two percent said they read a daily newspaper [12/56].*
- *Twenty percent said they were currently reading a book. When asked what book they were currently reading, 58% mentioned a novel or current book, 30% the Bible, and 9% a technical book [3/55].*

In music: Bill Haley and His Comets released *Rock Around the Clock* in 1954, an event that is often credited with initiating the rock and roll craze. Elvis Presley released his first hit "Heartbreak Hotel" in February 1956; scandalized the audience of the *Milton Berle Show* three months later with his suggestive hip movements; and appeared on the *Ed Sullivan Show* in September of that year. The television show *American Bandstand* started in 1957, hosted by Dick Clark. Milton Gordy Jr. founded Motown Records in January 1959. As of September 1957, Gallup found only 37% of Americans had a phonograph that could play a long-playing album. Other top musicians of the decade included: Frank Sinatra, Nat King Cole, Miles Davis, Perry Como, Bill Haley and His Comets, Bobby Darin, Doris Day, Kingston Trio, Fats Domino, The Platters, Buddy Holly, Harry Belafonte, Little Richard, Ricky Nelson, and Ella Fitzgerald.

- *In November 1950, 33% said Bing Crosby was their favorite male singer (6% liked Perry Como best), and 11% picked Dinah Shore as their favorite female singer (7% opted for Jeanette McDonald).*

Perhaps the epitome of 1950s culture was the July 1955 opening of Disneyland in Anaheim, California.

- *One other finding was that only 25% of Americans "like[d] modern art" [7/55]. On the other hand, as previously stated, 86% could identify Marilyn Monroe [8/59].*

In May 1957, the Brooklyn Dodgers agreed to move from New York to Los Angeles. Baseball was still the American pastime.

- *When respondents were asked in May 1953 which sports they followed with some regularity the major responses were: Baseball (46%), football (25%), boxing (18%), basketball (14%), and wrestling (11%). Seventy-seven percent could identify Joe DiMaggio [10/51]; Casey Stengel (41% [6/54]); Mickey Mantle (66% [9/56]); and Floyd Patterson (44% [11/57]).*

One other cultural factoid: Barbie Dolls first came out in March 1959 and boys were mesmerized by the coonskin hat popularized by Disney's *Davy Crockett* TV series in 1954 and 1955. Other popular toys were Slinkys, silly putty, frisbees, and hula hoops. Boys traded baseball cards and girls were expected to jump rope and play jacks.

- *Even before the advent of the TV series, 68% could correctly identify Davy Crockett [6/55].*

CONCLUDING COMMENTS

The Cold War hit its full stride and Americans were obsessed with communists at home and abroad. Optimism and traditional roles reigned.

The Cold War turned hot in 1950 with the start of the Korean War. Also, on the global stage in this decade, the French were defeated by the Viet Minh, Fidel Castro took power in Cuba, the anticolonial struggle in Africa and Asia continued to intensify, and Russia launched Sputnik. Military arms competition continued with the launch of the first nuclear submarine, the B52, and thermonuclear weapons. Most Americans were in favor of aggressive policies toward the Soviet Union, particularly in Europe. However, few wanted US military intervention in Vietnam or China.

Anticommunist hysteria in the United States spiked with McCarthyism. But while most Americans supported taking rights away from former or current communists, McCarthy's popularity quickly waned. Crime was not a great concern during the decade. In part because of Sputnik (to better compete with the Russians in the space race), most wanted an increased investment in education. Labor unions came under attack for communist influence and corruption, which led to their decreasing influence in later years.

Events in the 1950s, such as *Brown v. Board of Education* and the successful fight of Rosa Parks, Martin Luther King Jr., and others in the bus boycott in Montgomery, set the stage for the successful civil rights struggles of the 1960s. On the other hand, polls showed that attitudes toward segregation were little changed from the 1940s: most were opposed to equal employment legislation, voting rights legislation, voting for blacks, and interracial marriage.

Traditional sex roles predominated. Few felt it was acceptable for girls to phone a boy or wear shorts on the street, few recommended professional jobs for women, and most believed the father was the top boss of the family. There is a reason why some traditionalists feel nostalgic for the 1950s.

Economic sectors became increasingly integrated, with the rise of national food franchises, wider use of telephones, and the interstate highway system. The first window AC eventually led to the growth of cities in the South and Southwest. Americans supported much of the movement toward an integrated economy and an increase in the minimum wage, but they continued to oppose government owning utilities and banks. There was strong support for science and, following the defeat of polio, most believed that science would lead to better health. Few were concerned about the environment, and the extraordinary growth of television would have long-term consequences in culture and politics. Elvis Presley, the growth of Motown, and the opening of Disneyland were precursors to the explosion of cultural change that would occur in the 1960s.

[The reader can find relevant crosstabs and discussion in the online appendix located at https://rowman.com/ISBN/9781793653505/US-Public-Opinion-since-the-1930s-Galluping-through-History.]

NOTES

1. In a probability sample, every element of the population has a known non-zero probability of selection. The reality is that we rarely have perfect (or even near-perfect) samples of this type.

2. The Soviet Union did not veto this resolution as it was boycotting the UN because the People's Republic of China was not given the seat for China at the UN.

3. Many anticommunists were calling for the United States to "unleash Chiang Kai-shek" on mainland China.

4. Americans were prohibited from visiting China until the ping-pong diplomacy of 1971.

5. Unfortunately, I could not find any questions from any survey organization about Khrushchev's visit after the fact.

6. Other than potential US involvement in Vietnam, I could find no questions on the topics mentioned in this paragraph.

7. Forty-eight percent (16%, 36%) thought a person using the Fifth Amendment was guilty [4/57].

8. After the collapse of the Soviet Union some of the archives that opened up indicated the Rosenbergs were probably guilty.

9. I could not find any question by any survey organization about pornography in this decade.

10. Twenty-seven percent said men should wear jackets when in restaurants and hotels.

11. Oshinksy's (2005) book is a wonderful social, cultural, and scientific history of the polio epidemic in the United States.

4

The 1960s

Era of Protest: Civil Rights, Vietnam, and Counterculture

THE GREAT SOCIETY AND THE MOON LANDING

Surveys became increasingly useful for political purposes. In 1960, Kennedy hired pollster Louis Harris[1] and Nixon hired Claude Robinson to help with their respective campaigns (Sudman and Bradburn, 1987). Training for the profession became more systematized with the founding of the Inter-University Consortium for Political Research in 1962. Polls increasingly began to be used for planning and evaluation of government programs.[2] All but two of the surveys for the 1960s in the Roper archive were face-to-face. The share of Gallup surveys in this decade increased to 84%. One big change to the polling industry was the introduction of exit polls in 1967 by Warren Mitofsky working for CBS.

WORLD EVENTS

Vietnam, Cuba, and China

The 1954 Geneva Peace Accord that ended the First Indochina War temporarily divided Vietnam into two zones (North and South) with the expectation that elections would be held within two years.[3] The president of the South, Ngo Dinh Diem, was a Catholic in a predominately Buddhist country and became known for both corruption and authoritarian rule. It was clear he would lose in an election with the leader of the North, Ho Chi Minh, who had led the liberation struggle against Japan and France. Elections were not allowed and by 1960 an insurgency in the South developed with some support from the North. The Kennedy administration continued to send in "advisors" and Special Forces to South Vietnam. At the beginning of the JFK administration, there were 900 troops in Vietnam, and this had increased to 16,000 by the time of his assassination.

In November 1963, massive protests by Vietnamese citizens against repression led to Diem's assassination in a military coup. In August 1964, the United States alleged that North Vietnam fired upon US destroyers in the Gulf of Tonkin.[4] This led to the Gulf of Tonkin Resolution giving then-president Lyndon Johnson increased power to wage war. The United States began airstrikes against the North and escalated the ground war. As the United States sent in more troops, the North reciprocated. By the end of 1968, there were 536,000 American ground troops in Vietnam and 37,000 Americans had been killed. LBJ's administration claimed the war was being won. However, the media (this was the first televised war) said otherwise. General Westmoreland's assessment that the end of the war was in view was shattered with the Tet Offensive of January 1968.

Both sides in the war exhibited brutality. For example, around 3,000 civilians were killed by the insurgents in Hue during the Tet Offensive and around 500 unarmed civilians were slaughtered by the US army soldiers at My Lai in March 1968.[5] There are no precise numbers, but it is estimated that between 1.5 and 3.5 million Vietnamese, Laotians, and Cambodians died in the war. In the United States, the increasing unpopularity of the war coupled with a growing number of antiwar protests resulted in LBJ on March 31, 1968, declaring a unilateral halt of the bombing of the North, a call for peace talks, and his decision not to run for reelection.

- *Survey results showed that support for the war in Vietnam deteriorated over time. In August 1965, 24% of respondents thought the "U.S. made a mistake sending troops to fight in Vietnam." In subsequent years respondents holding this opinion grew to 35% [9/66], 41% [6/67], 53% [8/68], 58% [9/69], 56% [5/70], and 62% [5/71].*
- *In December 1967, 35% of Americans said they were "doves" (wanting to reduce our military effort in Vietnam). This number increased to 41% [9/68] and 56% [10/69].*
- *At the same time, a significant number of respondents were extreme hawks. Twenty-eight percent thought the United States should go for all-out victory and use the atomic bomb [2/68].*
- *The Vietnam War eroded trust in the government. In March 1967, only 23% thought the administration was telling the truth about the war.*

Opposition to the war increased for a variety of reasons: increased casualty counts, protests, the realization that we were not "winning" and were being lied to, and the daily carnage seen on TV.

Relations between the United States and Cuba deteriorated after Fidel Castro established control, began land reform, and nationalized several US oil refineries after they, at the urging of the US government, refused to process oil from the Soviet Union. In January 1961, Eisenhower had severed diplomatic relations with Cuba. Soon after that, Kennedy approved a plan for the CIA to use 1,400 Cuban exiles to invade the island at the Bay of Pigs in April 1961. The invaders surrendered after three days.

- *Only 21%, favored exchanging tractors for the prisoners from the Bay of Pigs [6/61] and in September 1961 only 23% wanted to send US troops to overthrow Castro.*
- *A year later, only 40% (42%, 18%) thought it likely that Castro would be overthrown in the next two or three years [9/62].*

More on the Cold War

Relations between the United States and the Soviet Union continued to be troublesome. The Soviet Union sent nuclear missiles to Cuba in response to the Bay of Pigs as well as to counter US nuclear missiles in Italy and Turkey. The US overflights of Cuba uncovered the missiles in October 1962, before they were fully deployed. In response, the United States implemented a naval quarantine of Cuba. Events could have spiraled out of control and led to nuclear Armageddon; however, a secret deal was reached in which Soviet missiles would be withdrawn from Cuba and the United States would remove its missiles from Italy and Turkey. The initial public perception was that Khrushchev "blinked."

- *No survey questions were asked specifically about the Cuban missile crisis. However, in February 1963, 56% (27%, 16%) were satisfied with Kennedy's handling of Cuba in recent weeks.*

In August 1961, The German Democratic Republic (East Germany) constructed a wall so that residents of East Berlin could not flee to West Berlin.[6] The United States and Soviet tanks almost started firing at each other over US access to West Berlin in October 1961 and war could have broken out. In June 1963, Kennedy made a historic speech to Berliners declaring "Ich bin ein Berliner." Stating that he was a Berliner symbolized that any attack on West Berlin would be viewed as an attack on the United States.

The United States and Russia signed a treaty banning nuclear weapon tests in the atmosphere in August 1963. Currently, 123 other states have also signed this treaty.

- *Sixty-one percent of respondents (18%, 21%) wanted the US Senate to ratify the treaty and 46% (40%, 14%) wanted more arms reduction treaties with the Russians [8/63].*
- *At the beginning of the decade, only 37% of Americans thought the United States could live peacefully with the Russians [5/60] and 46% (34%, 20%) thought the Russians were ahead of us in rockets [1/61].*
- *Most Americans (82%) supported keeping troops in Berlin, even at the risk of war [6/61] and 64% (19%, 17%) thought the United States should use military force to "fight their way into Berlin" if roads were cut off [8/61].*

- *Several months after JFK's speech in Berlin, 79% said he did an excellent or pretty good job at standing firm over Berlin [10/63-Harris].*

Until the late 1960s, communist countries were perceived as being under the complete domination of the Soviet Union. However, relations between the Soviet Union and China began to fracture because of different national interests as well as different interpretations of Marxism-Leninism. In 1969, the USSR and China engaged in a seven-month border conflict along the Usurri River in which over 100 soldiers were killed.

- *Although, 47% (35%, 17%) believed the United States should buy and sell goods to China and should have better relations with China (53%) [2/61], only 36% (45%, 19%) agreed that China should be allowed into the UN. The portion of respondents who favored admitting the PRC to the UN fell to 33% at the end of the decade [1/69].*

As seen with the above polling data, most Americans supported the concept that the Soviet Union, China, and the various "satellite" states were essentially evil and needed to be opposed. These images began to change in the 1970s.

Other International Events

Another seminal event of the 1960s was the 1967 Six-Day War between Israel and Egypt, Jordan, and Syria. In a decisive military victory, Israel seized the Sinai Peninsula, the Golan Heights, East Jerusalem, and the West Bank. This set the stage for the Israelis to build settlements in the West Bank and the Golan Heights.

- *Forty-five percent favored Israel in the Six-Day War (4% Arabs, 50% neither or DK). However, two weeks after the war, only 24% supported sending arms to Israel in case of a new war [6/67].*

Four other international events require at least passing mention. First, upon taking over the presidency, Kennedy announced the formation of the Peace Corps. From 1961 to 2015, 220,000 Americans served in the Peace Corps. Second, in April 1965, a popular revolt against military rule led LBJ to invade the Dominican Republic. The United States installed Joaquín Balaguer who ruled as a dictator for the next twelve years. Third, in January 1968 the US surveillance ship, the *USS Pueblo*, was seized by North Korea. Its eighty-three crewmen were abused and not released until December 1968, following an apology and payment of reparations from the United States. Fourth, in the 1960s, with the exception of the Portuguese colonies, the remainder of the European colonies in Africa became independent. However, the struggle continued against minority white rule in South Africa and Rhodesia (Zimbabwe).[7]

- *Seventy-one percent of survey respondents favored the formation of the Peace Corps [1/61] and 48% thought that Peace Corps volunteers should be exempt from the draft [3/61].*

- *Somewhat surprising, only 25% of Americans (64%, 11%) initially favored LBJ sending troops into the Dominican Republic [6/65]. This increased to 52% six months later when it was apparent that the situation was not going to become another Vietnam [11/65].*
- *Almost half (47%, 38%, 15%) thought the capture of the Pueblo would lead to war [2/68], but only 22% (57%, 21%-Harris) believed we should go to war if North Korea refused to release the crew.*

US POLITICS

In November 1960, John Kennedy was elected president over Richard Nixon in a very close race (49.7% v. 49.6%). John Kennedy was a Catholic in an era when many thought that a Catholic could not win the presidency.[8] JFK's presidency was often idealized as a "Camelot" era, and he was seen as young and dynamic. On November 22, 1963, Kennedy was assassinated by Lee Harvey Oswald while he was in a motorcade in Dallas, Texas. Lyndon Johnson became president. In 1964, the Republicans nominated Barry Goldwater to run against LBJ. He was pictured as an extremist and LBJ defeated him with 61.1% of the popular vote. In November 1967, Senator Eugene McCarthy declared he would run for president against LBJ on an antiwar platform. In March 1968, Robert F. Kennedy also declared his candidacy and LBJ withdrew from the race.[9] In June 1968, Robert Kennedy was assassinated on the night he won the California primary. At the democratic convention in August 1968, police and antiwar demonstrators fought outside the convention hall[10] as Hubert Humphrey was nominated to run against Richard Nixon. Nixon beat Humphrey in November 1968.[11]

- *Sixty-two percent of Americans said they watched the first-ever televised presidential debate (between Nixon and Kennedy) [8/60].*
- *Sixty-seven percent said they liked "the Jackie Kennedy look" [6/61].*
- *Only 36% (50%, 15%) thought only one man was responsible for JFK's assassination [12/66].*
- *Only 34% (55%, 11%) thought only one man was responsible for RFK's assassination [9/78-Harris].*[12]
- *When asked whether they would vote for a "well-qualified candidate nominated by their party who happened to be a [. . .]," Americans gave the following responses: Jew—82%; Negro—53%; Baptist—95%; Catholic—90%; Mormon—75%; divorced—85%; Quaker—78%; and woman—57% [4/67]. Clearly, these responses should also be noted when reading the sections below on race and gender.*
- *One question asked by Gallup in November 1968 is particularly ironic today. Sixty percent favored limiting presidential campaigns to five weeks. Furthermore, 73% favored limiting political campaign contributions [5/67].*

LBJ became a strong supporter of civil rights (discussed below). It was in his first State of the Union Address in January 1964 that he declared a "War on Poverty," and in his 1965 State of the Union Address he proclaimed the "Great Society." In July 1965, legislation was passed establishing Medicare—health care for the elderly. Medicaid was also established in which the federal government would supply matching funds to states who provided medical care for those with limited income.

- *Sixty-two percent (22%, 15%) favored setting up a domestic version of the Peace Corps [10/62].*
- *Support for Medicare was not universal. Only 50% (43%, 7%) favored the legislation [12/63]. This increased to 57% in October 1964. There are many similarities to how Obamacare was perceived. Both were initially castigated for being socialist, ineffective, and so on. Over time, support grew.*
- *Americans were not supportive of the Great Society. Only 32% (44%, 24%) said they had a favorable attitude to the Great Society Program [10/66].*
- *Americans were split on the causes of poverty and what to do about it. When asked whether too much or too little money was spent on welfare and relief program near where they lived, 20% said too much, 19% not enough, 33% volunteered "about right," and 28% did not know.[13] Later research found that much of the opposition to welfare programs is rooted in racial attitudes (Gilens, 1995). Essentially, many incorrectly see poverty and welfare programs as a "black" thing.*
- *Similarly, when asked who is to blame for people being poor, 31% said lack of effort, 31% circumstances, 34% volunteered both, and 5% did not know.*
- *Sixty-four percent wanted the federal government to provide funds for daycare centers so that poor women could work [6/69].*

The 1960s was the decade in which the student movement took off. The first major student demonstration against the Vietnam War occurred in New York City in May 1964 when about 1,000 people marched. In October 1964, the Berkeley Free Speech Movement occurred when students protested the administration's refusal to allow speakers, political recruitment, and fundraisers on campus. At one point, 800 students were arrested. In January 1965, the university administration backed down. Protests spread across the country. In October 1965, 100,000 protested the war. In April 1968, students occupied the administration building at Columbia University, forcing the university to shut down. Many other universities had similar protests. Parts of the student movement became increasingly radicalized. The Students for a Democratic Society (SDS) splintered in the spring of 1969 when its more radical members formed the Weather Underground.

- *There was a lot of opposition to the protest movement: 58% thought that communists had a lot of involvement in the antiwar demonstrations [10/65]. As of April 1967, only 1% said they had participated in a peace rally; only 25% thought that students should have greater say in running colleges [2/69]; 84% favored taking away federal loans to students who broke the law while protesting [2/69]; and 94% thought college administrators should take a stronger stand against student disorder*

[5/69]. It is remarkable how many policies that were so demonized during this period of time have now become mainstream.
- *One of the demands of the youth movement was that the voting age should be lowered from 21 to 18. This was supported by 64% of respondents [3/67].*[14]
- *In this decade there was considerable debate about education and the culture of schools: 80% favored religious observances in schools [7/62]; 45% (49%, 7%) wanted to require boys to wear ties and jackets and girls to wear blouses and pleated skirts [9/62]; 78% wanted schools to require boys to keep their hair cut short [9/65]; 81% favored a constitutional amendment to allow prayer in public schools [12/63]; 48% (43%, 8%) wanted to require high-school students to pass a national examination to graduate [4/65]; but only 39% wanted students to do more homework each week [4/65].*

One of the more important developments of the 1960s was the output of US Supreme Court decisions resulting in increased civil liberties. Some of these included:

- *Engel v. Vitale* (1962), which rendered mandatory prayers in public schools illegal.
- *Gideon v. Wainwright* (1963), requiring states to provide attorneys to criminal defendants who cannot afford to pay for their own attorney.
- *Miranda v. Arizona (1966)*, requiring law enforcement personnel to inform suspects of their rights before arresting them.
- *New York Times v. Sullivan* (1964), which ruled that speech criticizing political figures cannot be censured.
- *Some of the Court rulings on behalf of Civil Liberties were unpopular. For example, only 27% of Americans approved of the Supreme Court's decision that communists did not have to register with the government [11/65].*
- *In December 1966, 56% (32%, 12%—ORC) said that since Miranda, the police have had too much power taken away.*
- *By June 1968, only 30% of respondents rated the Supreme Court as excellent or good.*

This was the high point of the liberalism of the Warren Court. In 1969, Warren was replaced as Chief Justice by the very conservative William Rehnquist.

RACE

The 1960s was a seminal decade in the struggle for civil rights. In February 1960, four black students started a sit-in at a Woolworth's restaurant counter in Greensboro, North Carolina. They demanded the right to eat at an integrated lunch counter. This tactic rapidly spread to other cities throughout the South and to other segregated public spaces such as museums, pools, beaches, and theaters. These protests led to the creation of the Student Nonviolent Coordinating Committee (SNCC).

In May 1961, the first Freedom Ride occurred to protest the forced segregation of interstate buses and bus terminals throughout the South. The riders were brutally beaten in Montgomery, Anniston, and Birmingham, Alabama[15] and jailed for thirty-nine days in Jackson, Mississippi. Photos of a burning bus and reports of the brutal treatment of the protesters aroused public sympathy, and the Kennedy administration ordered the Interstate Commerce Commission to integrate the buses.

Starting in 1962, a series of voter registration campaigns began throughout the South. Organizers and prospective voters were often met with violence. In the Mississippi Freedom Summer of 1964, around 1,000 activists from other parts of the country came to Mississippi to help register voters.[16] In June 1964, three civil rights workers (Andrew Goodman, Michael Schwerner, and James Chaney) were abducted and murdered in Philadelphia, Mississippi, by members of the Ku Klux Klan working with local law enforcement. It took two months for the bodies to be found buried in an earthen dam. In 1965, the focus of voter registration drive moved to Selma, Alabama, where marchers were attacked on the Edmund Pettus Bridge by law enforcement officials with bullwhips, barbed wire, and other weapons. John Lewis (later a Congressperson) was knocked unconscious. The national broadcast of the carnage prompted a televised address by LBJ condemning the violence and led to the passage of the Voting Rights Act of 1965.

The 1960s were also a decade of racial integration of universities. In June 1963, Governor George Wallace of Alabama tried to block the integration of the University of Alabama by James Meredith, the first black admitted to the University.[17] JFK sent in a military force to force Wallace to step aside and allow the registration of two black students.

On August 28, 1963, about 250,000 people participated in the March on Washington for Jobs and Freedom. In front of the Lincoln Memorial, Martin Luther King Jr. gave his famous "I Have a Dream Speech."[18] It was one month later that the 16th Street Baptist Church in Birmingham, Alabama, was bombed resulting in the death of four children and injuries to twenty-two others. The struggle for integration eventually led to the passage of the Civil Rights Act of 1964 (July) and the Voting Rights Act of 1965. Protests, in fact, had led to major progress.

Two other notable firsts that occurred in the 1960s were the confirmation of Thurgood Marshall as the first African American justice of the US Supreme Court in 1967 and the election of Carl Stokes in November 1967 as mayor of Cleveland, the first African American mayor of a large city in the United States.

The Civil Rights Movement, which initially espoused non-violence and civil disobedience, generated more militant groups such as the supporters of Malcolm X and the Black Panthers. Malcolm X was assassinated in February 1965 by followers of the Nation of Islam. The Black Panther Party fell apart in the late 1960s and early 1970s due in part to infighting and to being targeted by law enforcement officials (e.g., the COINTELPRO Program of the FBI). In December 1969, BPP members Fred Hampton and Mark Clark were shot dead in their sleep in a raid by the Chicago police.

Dr. King increasingly focused on issues around economic equality trying to unite poor blacks and whites. He was assassinated on April 4, 1968, in Memphis, Tennessee, where he had gone to support a sanitation worker's strike.

- *Among blacks, 82% (5%, 13%) believed MLK's assassination was a conspiracy that went beyond the act of one man [5/69].*
- *Only 43% (90% among blacks) had a favorable opinion of King in May 1965.*
- *Also, in a question only asked of blacks, of the 59% who had heard of the Black Panthers, 24% (40%, 37%) approved of them [5/69].*
- *Of the 49% of respondents who had heard of the black Muslims, only 3% had a favorable opinion [5/63].*
- *In a question only asked of blacks, 27% thought that Malcolm X was doing an excellent or good job, 25% said fair or poor, and 38% were not sure [5/69].*

Race riots became an increasing problem. Riots occurred in Watts (Los Angeles, following a traffic stop; thirty-four were killed) in 1965, in Detroit in 1967 (following a raid on a bar; forty-three died), and then nationwide following the assassination of Martin Luther King Jr. in April 1968 (forty-three killed). The riots were used by opponents of the Civil Rights Movement to argue for "law and order" and slowing down the "rush" to integrate. In July 1967, Johnson established the National Commission on Civil Disorders (Kerner Commission) to investigate the causes of the riots that occurred since 1965. The report was issued in February 1968 and immediately sold two million copies. The major conclusion was that the riots resulted from frustration arising from a lack of economic opportunity. Its most famous phrase was, "Our nation is moving toward two societies, one black, one white—separate and unequal."

- *In response to the riots in 1965, 90% (3%–helped, 7%–dk) said it hurt the cause of "Negro rights" [8/65–Harris]. In the same survey, 59% said that most Negroes believe in nonviolent action in demonstrations, 21% in violent action, and 20% volunteered some do and some don't).*
- *In May 1968, 54% thought shooting looters on sight was the best way to deal with the race riots.[19]*
- *Responding to a question about the Kerner Commission, 36% (52%, 13%) agreed with its conclusion that we were moving toward two societies [5/68].*

The Supreme Court made a series of seminal rulings that helped spur the struggle for civil rights:

- *Boynton v. Virginia* (1960), making segregation in public transit illegal;
- *Heart of Atlanta Motel Inc. v. US* and *Katzenbach v. McClung* (1964), which outlawed discrimination in public accommodations such as motels and restaurants;
- *Loving v. Virginia* (1967), which ruled that states could not prohibit interracial marriage;[20] and

- *Jones v. Alfred H. Mayer Co.* (1968), banning discrimination in housing in both private and governmental agencies.

Americans had very mixed opinions about civil rights issues.

- *Regarding civil rights protests, 57% of Americans (28%, 16%; 22% among blacks) thought that the sit-ins and bus rides hurt the chances for integration in the South [5/61]. Of the 67% who had heard of them, only 22% (78% among blacks) approved of the Freedom Riders [5/61].*
- *Just before the March on Washington, only 27% (77% among blacks) thought that protests helped the "Negro cause for racial equality" [6/63] and even fewer (23%; 67% among blacks) supported the march [8/63].*
- *A plurality (46%, 35%, 19%) believed that civil rights groups were infiltrated and dominated by communist troublemakers [9/64].*
- *In March 1965, only 33% said they would approve if their own clergyman marched for civil rights; and 73% said Negroes should stop their demonstrations as they have now made their point [10/64].*
- *On education, 61% of respondents said integration should be gradual, not in the near future [5/61]; 63% favored the integration of schools [5/61]; and 23% said they would object to sending their children to schools with a few blacks (another 29% would object if the schools were half-black) [5/63].*
- *Concerning the integration of public space, 62% approved of the Supreme Court decision integrating buses and trains [5/61]; only 49% (42%, 9%) favored a law requiring hotels, restaurants, and theaters to serve both blacks and whites [6/63]; and 46% thought private clubs should be able to exclude Negroes [6/65].*
- *On integrated housing, 60% thought that houses in their neighborhood should be sold without regard to race [3/66]. However, only 13% thought that a white homeowner or renter should be required to rent to a Negro [7/66] and only 24% wanted Congress to pass an open-housing bill [3/67].*
- *Seventy-eight percent (98% among blacks) approved of the voting rights bill [3/65].*
- *Responding to questions on the reasons for and extent of racism, 14% (51% among Southern whites) believed the Bible to be a basis for segregation [5/62]; 43% (24% among blacks) thought that Negroes have as good a chance at getting a job in their community as whites [6/63]; 53% (19% among blacks) thought Negroes were treated the same way as whites in their community [2/64]; 17% said blacks were to blame for the conditions of blacks, 45% said whites (62% among blacks), 29% both, 10%-DK [6/63]; only 9% (34% among blacks) thought that there was police brutality in their community [4/65]; 48% approved of laws that made interracial marriages a crime [1/65]; and 20% (56% among blacks) would approve of a marriage between whites and non-whites.*[21]
- *And on integration in general, 45% (48%, 7%) thought that states should have the right to decide what to do about integration [5/63]; and only 23% thought civil rights laws should be strictly enforced right from the start (62% said gradual)*

[10/64]. Among blacks, only 10% favored preferential treatment being given to black in hiring or education to make up for past discrimination [5/69].

Compared to the 1950s, attitudes toward race underwent a major set of changes. Clearly, there was a long way to go and these changes would continue in subsequent decades.

SEX AND GENDER

The "pill" was approved by the FDA in the early 1960s. Its effect was epitomized by *Time Magazine* having it on its cover in April 1967. Because of its effectiveness, women had far greater control over their fertility and the economic impact was that women could make long-term plans for education and jobs. Sexual activity could be divorced from procreation. Changes in the law also had a dramatic impact beginning with *Griswold v. Connecticut (1965)*, when the Supreme Court legalized the use of contraceptives by married couples.[22]

The 1950s was not quite as prudish as is often presented: 82% of women who turned fifteen between 1954 and 1963 had premarital sex by age thirty. This increased to 91% for those who turned fifteen between 1964 and 1993 (Finer, 2007). However, even toward the end of the decade, 68% thought sexual relations before marriage was wrong [7/69].

- *In March 1961, 75% thought birth control information should be made available to anyone who wanted it; 54% (31%, 15%) would recommend birth control pills to women who do not want any more children; and 62% would make birth control pills available to women on relief for free [12/66].*
- *Although only 40% wanted to give free birth control to all teenage girls who wanted it, 59% favored birth control information in the public high schools [10/69].*
- *In July 1968, the Pope declared that the pill was an artificial form of birth control and that the use of any artificial birth control was a mortal sin. Only 16% favored the Pope's position on this issue [8/68].*

Before 1967, abortion was illegal in all states. Starting in that year, fourteen states liberalized abortion laws such that abortions were allowed in some circumstances (to save the life of the mother, rape, etc.). New York became the first state to legalize abortion on demand in 1970.

- *In July 1962, Gallup asked whether abortion should be legal based on certain circumstances: 77% said abortion should be legal when a women's health was in danger; 55% approved legal abortion if the child may be born deformed; and only 15% approved if the family did not have enough money to support another child.*

Restrictions on pornography continued to loosen. The courts continued to wrestle with how to define pornography. Supreme Court Justice Potter is famous for pointing the subjective nature of defining obscenity by saying in *Jacobellis v. Ohio* (1964) that "I know it when I see it." The first issue of *Penthouse Magazine* appeared in 1969.

- *Americans were divided on whether pornography was a serious issue (very serious—33%, fairly—24%, not serious—26%, DK—17%) [12/63]; and 75% found nude pictures in magazines to be objectionable [5/69].*
- *Sixty-eight percent of Americans now approved of women wearing slacks in public [10/61]. However, 71% said they would object if their daughter wore a mini skirt [5/67]. During the early years of the decade, it was expected that people would dress up to go on airplanes and many of those over the age of thirty wore suits to go to baseball games.*

The Civil Rights Movement served as a model for the Women's Rights Movement of that era. In 1963, Betty Friedan published *The Feminine Mystique*. Women advocated for equal rights with men in politics, economics, and home life. In other words, women should run for political office, have equal access to jobs, and be paid the same as men for the same work,[23] and men should share in household and childcare chores. The National Organization for Women (NOW) was founded in June 1966.[24]

- *Divorce laws continued to be strict. In January 1966, only 18% of survey respondents said they were too strict, and in fact, 34% said they were not strict enough.*

In 1950, there were just ten women in the US House of Representatives. That number increased to seventeen by 1980, to thirty-one by 1990, to sixty-seven by 2000, and to ninety-six by 2010. It is estimated that in 1960, women earned 61% of the amount paid to their male counterparts. This ratio increased to 80% in 2015. In 1960, 36% of the civilian labor force was women. This increased to 53% by 2012. In 1960, 2% of attorneys were women. In 2015, this had changed to 35%.

- *As noted above, only 57% of Americans said they would vote for a woman for president [4/67].*

It was in June 1969, that the Stonewall riots occurred in New York City. This was the spontaneous demonstration of the gay community against a raid targeting gays at the Stonewall Inn in Greenwich Village. Some believe this was the most important event leading to the gay liberation movement.[25]

THE ECONOMY

The 1960s started as an era of prosperity and great expectations. But in 1962, Michael Harrington's study *The Other America* was published, which detailed poverty throughout the United States. The government funded the War on Poverty as well as the Great Society Programs. However, the Vietnam War also required a large expenditure of money. LBJ wanted both "guns and butter" and this resulted in large government deficits and the ratcheting up of inflation.[26]

In 1962, Kennedy called for tax cuts in order to stimulate the economy. The tax cuts occurred in 1964 and the economy boomed; however, there is considerable controversy today about whether the tax cuts caused the boom.

- *In June 1962, 59% (28%, 13%) of Americans preferred tax cuts over spending for public works to boost the economy. In fact, 73% favored substituting the progressive tax system with a flat tax [12/63]. It is remarkable (to me) how conservative Americans are on some economic policy issues.*
- *As inflation began to pick up because of the war in Vietnam, 46% (43%, 11%) favored wage and price controls until the war was over [1/68].*
- *Nixon's request for a tax surcharge to curb inflation was supported by only 39% (51%, 11%) [6/69].*
- *Somewhat more people favored wage and price controls (48%, 41%, 10%) [6/69]. This level of support was virtually the same throughout Nixon's second term.*

American railroads had entered a period of decline as a result of competition from the automobile, airplanes, government regulatory hurdles, and mismanagement. Several railroads in the Northeast merged in the 1960s to form Penn Central. Penn Central's bankruptcy in 1970 was the largest bankruptcy as of that time.

- *In June 1965, only 39% of Americans favored government financial aid for the railroads.*

Economic milestones of the 1960s included: the opening, in Arkansas, of the first Wal-Mart store (1962); the first Ford Mustang coming on the market (1964); the founding of Nike (1964); the first use of the Sabre reservation system for air travel (1964); production of the first IBM 360 computer (1965); initial government funding for the Corporation for Public Broadcasting (1967); Intel's launch (1968); and the Boeing 747's debut flight (1969).

Consumer protection also became important. Ralph Nader published *Unsafe at Any Speed* in 1965, a critique of the safety of American automobiles. In March 1966, General Motors president, James Roche, before a Senate subcommittee, apologized to Nader for intimidation and harassment.

- *Fifty-nine percent of Americans favored requiring new automobiles to have safety belts. Only 10% had safety belts in their car at this time [10/61].*
- *American economic hegemony was strong. Most respondents did not want to restrict imports: only 11% wanted more import restrictions in general; regarding certain goods, 27% approved restrictions on oil imports, 34% on textiles, 40% on steel, and 51% on automobiles*[27] *[2/62].*

SCIENCE, TECHNOLOGY, AND THE ENVIRONMENT

The first weather satellite was launched in April 1960, and in May 1961, JFK called for putting a man on the moon by the end of the decade. Also in May 1961, Alan Shepard became the first American in space, then in February 1962 John Glenn became the first American to orbit the Earth. JFK's ambition was realized when, in July 1969, Neil Armstrong and Buzz Aldwin became the first humans to step foot on the moon. The space program was not wildly popular.

- *In May 1961, only 33% of Americans wanted to spend the estimated $40 billion to send a man to the moon. In June 1965, 16% favored increasing money spent on space exploration, 33% wanted a decrease, and 50% said the same amount or did not know.*
- *At the time Americans landed on the moon, 39% favored a program to land men on Mars [7/69].*

A seminal event occurred in January 1964 when US Surgeon General Luther Terry released the first Surgeon General's Report on smoking. The report said smoking was a cause of lung cancer. Reports in future years said smoking also caused heart disease and other ailments.

- *In May 1960, 50% of Americans thought that cigarettes were one of the causes of lung cancer. This increased to 70% by July 1970.*
- *At the time of the 1964 Surgeon General's Report, 42.4% of the adult population in the United States smoked cigarettes. This number declined to under 20% by 2010.*

In September 1962, Rachel Carson published *Silent Spring*, a book documenting the indiscriminate use of pesticides, and which became a major impetus to the environmental movement. In 1968, Paul Ehrlich published *The Population Bomb*, which predicted massive environmental and economic upheaval unless population growth was curtailed. Not many survey questions of the 1960s addressed national environmental problems.

- *Seventy-one percent of Americans favored federal government grants to clean up water pollution [12/63].*
- *In May 1963, only 25% of respondents were worried about world population growth.*
- *Few people said that water pollution (13%) or air pollution (10%) was a serious problem where they lived [5/65-ORC].*

POPULAR TRENDS

One of the hallmarks of the 1960s was the countercultural movement. This movement was somewhat apart from the political movements of the 1960s. The expression, "sex, drugs, and rock and roll" helped epitomize this movement. Beyond marijuana, many experimented with LSD, mescaline, and other psychedelic drugs. Timothy Leary advocated the use of LSD to expand the consciousness of mind as well as for personal growth. The sexual revolution challenged the belief that sex should only occur within the constraints of marriage and procreation. Music became more electric, psychedelic, and often associated with the politics of protest. The "hippie" was stereotyped as a young person who had long hair, took drugs, had a lot of sex, did not believe in God,[28] and was trying to drop out of society.

- *Only 12% of Americans favored making marijuana legal and 4% had tried it [10/69]. Sixty-four percent thought American morals were being undermined by sex and nudity in popular culture [8/69] and 74% said there was a major difference between the attitudes of young and older people (the generation gap) [5/69]. Essentially, the counterculture was not widely popular.*

There was an extraordinary range of movies that came out in the 1960s: *Swiss Family Robinson* (1960); *West Side Story* (1961); *101 Dalmatians* (1961); *Raisin in the Sun* (1961); *Lawrence of Arabia* (1962); *Cleopatra* (1963); *It's a Mad, Mad, Mad, Mad World* (1963); *Mary Poppins* (1964); *My Fair Lady* (1964); *Goldfinger* (1964); *Doctor Zhivago* (1965); *The Sound of Music* (1965); *The Jungle Book* (1967); *Guess Who's Coming to Dinner* (1967); *The Graduate* (1967); *Bonnie and Clyde* (1967); *The Dirty Dozen* (1967); *You Only Live Twice* (1967); *Funny Girl* (1968); *2001: A Space Odyssey* (1968); *The Odd Couple* (1968); *Midnight Cowboy* (1969); and *Butch Cassidy and the Sundance Kid* (1969).

- *In December 1968, 18% said they had gone to the movies within the last month, 60% within the last year, and 22% said they never attend.*

Television shows became a little more cutting edge as the decade progressed: *The Andy Griffith Show* (1960); *The Dick Van Dyke Show* (1961); *Wagon Train* (1961); *The Tonight Show with Johnny Carson* (1962); *The Beverley Hillbillies* (1962); *Dr. Who* (1963); *The Fugitive* (1963); *Jeopardy* (1964); *Star Trek* (1966); *60 Minutes* (1968); *Rowan & Martin's Laugh-In* (1968); and *Sesame Street* (1969).

- *Ninety-seven percent of Americans had at least one television set in their house in December 1965, and 12% had a color TV.*
- *The downside of TV was not readily apparent. Only 20% said television was a bad influence on their children [2/62].*
- *TV News was already controversial. Just 40% (42%, 18%) said TV networks were fair in covering all sides on political and social issues [12/69].*

Many of the books that came out in the 1960s had a lasting effect of the political and social landscape, for example: Harper Lee's *To Kill a Mockingbird* (1960); James Michener's *Hawaii* (1960); William Shirer's *The Rise and Fall of the Third*

Reich (1960); Joseph Heller's *Catch 22* (1961); Theodore White's *The Making of the President* (1961); Robert Heinlein's *Stranger in a Strange Land* (1961); Fletcher Knebel's *Seven Days in May* (1962); Rachel Carson's *Silent Spring* (1962); Jessica Mitford's *American Way of Death* (1963); John F. Kennedy's *Profiles in Courage* (1963); John le Carré's *The Spy Who Came in from the Cold* (1964); Saul Bellow's *Herzog* (1964); Frank Herbert's *Dune* (1965); James Michener's *The Source* (1965); Arthur Schlesinger's *A Thousand Days* (1966); Truman Capote's *In Cold Blood* (1966); Jacqueline Suzanne's *Valley of the Dolls* (1966); William Styron's *Confessions of Nat Turner* (1967); Philip Roth's *Portnoy's Complaint* (1969); Mario Puzo's *The Godfather* (1969); and Harrison Salisbury's *The 900 Days* (1969).

- *In February 1969, 21% of Americans said they had read a book within the last week, 14% within the last month, and 16% within the last year. The remaining 49% said long ago, never, or did not remember. When asked the type of book they read, respondents said: fiction (45%), non-fiction (21%), technical (9%), and religious (2%).*

The British invasion refers to the wave of popularity among Americans of British rock groups that started in January 1964 when The Beatles' "I Want to Hold Your Hand" became the number one hit. In February of that year seventy-three million viewers watched the Beatles perform on the Ed Sullivan Show. Other British groups soon followed: The Rolling Stones, The Kinks, Donovan, and others. American psychedelic rock started to become popular in 1966 with the Doors, Jefferson Airplane, The Byrds, Jimi Hendrix, and the Grateful Dead. This music was initially controversial. Many said the Beatles' hair was too long. Over time, other groups were criticized for advocating drugs, sex, and leftist politics. Protest music was popular. Joan Baez released her first album in 1960 and Bob Dylan's first album was released in 1962.

R & B and soul performers were also wildly popular in the 1960s (e.g., The Supremes, The Temptations, The Four Tops, and Otis Redding). The first issue of the *Rolling Stone* came out in November 1967. The decade moved toward its close with the Woodstock Festival in August 1969, where over 400,000 people attended an outdoor rock concert that was billed as "3 days of peace and love."[29] A much darker music festival happened four months later in Altamont, California, where the Hells Angels provided security, there was one stabbing death and three accidental deaths.

Other top musicians during this decade included: Elvis Presley, The Beach Boys, Roy Orbison, Procol Harum, The Monkeys, Chubby Checker, Ray Charles, Bee Gees, The Animals, Simon and Garfunkel, Marvin Gaye, Aretha Franklin, John Coltrane, James Brown, Otis Redding, and Cream.

- *Rock and roll was not widely appreciated. When a Harris poll asked in August 1966 what kind of music they liked best, respondents' favorite genres were: symphony and classical (20%); country music (19%); spirituals (18%); mood music*

(17%); show tunes (17%); mood music (11%); rhythm and blues (8%); opera (4%); rock and roll (4%); Latin-American music (3%); and folk music (2%).
- When asked what kind of music people disliked the most the top choices were: rock n roll (48%); opera (18%); folk rock (11%); symphony and classical (10%); and country music (8%).

Baseball continued to be Americans' most popular sport. In October 1962, Roger Maris of the New York Yankees hit his sixty-first home run of the season, breaking Babe Ruth's record from 1927.

- *Eighty-six percent of respondents could correctly identify Mickey Mantle [8/64].*
- *Baseball (34%) was still the most popular sport to watch, but football was catching up—21% [12/60]. Only 9% mentioned basketball.*

In February 1964, Cassius Clay beat Sonny Liston to become the heavyweight champion of the world. He then converted to Islam and changed his name to Muhammed Ali.[30] In 1966, he antagonized the white boxing establishment, who took away his boxing title when he refused induction into the army, citing his opposition to the Vietnam War.[31] His conviction was overturned in 1970 and he regained his championship in October 1974 when he defeated George Forman in the "Rumble in the Jungle."

The 1968 Summer Olympics in Mexico City became controversial when two black Americans raised their arms in a black power salute upon winning medals in the 200-meter run. They were suspended from the US team for their actions.

The first Super Bowl was played in January 1967, when the Green Bay Packers defeated the Kansas City Chiefs. There were 32,000 empty seats at the Los Angeles Memorial Coliseum and the half-time festivities featured two marching bands.

Marking the end of an era, Marilyn Monroe died in August 1962 from an overdose of barbiturates in what was a probable suicide.

CONCLUDING COMMENTS

This was a decade of change at home and abroad—from Vietnam to civil rights, hippies, and the sexual revolution.

Early in the decade, greatly increased tensions with the Soviet Union revolving around the blockade of West Berlin and the deployment of nuclear missiles in Cuba brought the United States close to war with the Soviet Union. The war in Vietnam intensified through the decade. In addition, a treaty was signed with the Soviets banning nuclear testing in the atmosphere, a rift developed between the People's Republic of China and the Soviet Union, many colonial countries achieved independence, and Israel won a war with several Mideast countries in 1967 resulting in the occupation of the rest of Jerusalem and the West Bank.

In the early years of the war in Vietnam, most Americans supported the role of the United States. Support deteriorated as casualties grew without an end in sight. This antiwar sentiment would affect US foreign policy for decades to come. Americans were generally supportive of Kennedy's handling of the Cuban Missile Crisis and standing up to the Soviets over Berlin. But Americans were open to a détente—most supported the nuclear weapons treaty with the Soviets and opening potential trade with China.

The assassination of JFK in 1963 was a seminal moment. (Everyone of a certain age remembers where they were when they heard the news.) LBJ was able to extend the role of the government with the passage of Medicare, Medicaid, and many antipoverty programs. The student movement and related revolution in music and culture would also have long-term consequences. The Supreme Court added to the revolution with groundbreaking decisions extending civil liberties.

Americans were not universally behind these changes. There was strong opposition to Medicare, the War on Poverty, student protests, the youth movement, and the extension of some civil liberties. Spiro Agnew and Richard Nixon used these divisions to advance their agenda. These clashes were harbingers of the political and cultural divisiveness occurring today.

The 1960s was a pivotal decade for civil rights—sit-ins, Freedom Riders, voter registration campaigns, integration in education, confirmation of Thurgood Marshall on to the Supreme Court, the March on Washington, elimination of laws against interracial marriages, and passages of the 1964 Civil Rights Act and the voting rights and of 1965. It was a decade of racial riots in many cities and the assassinations of Malcolm X and Martin Luther King Jr.

Americans were often critical of the Civil Rights Movement—many believing it was controlled by communists, was too radical, and was moving too fast. Nonetheless, many now approved of integration of public spaces, trains, and buses, integration of public schools, voting rights, and equal access to employment.

The role of women and gender also underwent a radical transformation—the pill became available, more women went to college and joined the workforce, states began to liberalize abortion laws, more women ran for public office, and the National Organization for Women was formed. However, only 57% of survey respondents said they would vote for a woman for president, and few wanted to liberalize divorce laws. On the other hand, the public was more open to abortion, birth control, and liberalizing what women had to wear. The decade ended with the Stonewall riots, which foreshadowed the gay liberation struggle of subsequent decades.

The economic optimism of the 1950s eroded in the 1960s with the realization that poverty was a real problem, cigarettes were dangerous, railroads were collapsing, and cars were unsafe. In addition, the negative economic consequences of the war in Vietnam became apparent. On other fronts, though, economic success continued with the IBM 360 computer, the first flight of the 747, and the first Wal-Mart. Americans remained conservative relative to many economic issues, wanting to eliminate progressive taxes and public assistance programs. The purported link between public assistance and race was used (and developed) by conservatives to attack both issues. Environmental issues were still of little concern.

[The reader can find relevant crosstabs and discussion in the online appendix located at https://rowman.com/ISBN/9781793653505/US-Public-Opinion-since-the-1930s-Galluping-through-History.]

NOTES

1. The Harris Poll began in 1963. Harris and Gallup were fierce competitors.

2. One of the most impressive research projects in the 1960s was the Adult Use of Tobacco Surveys done by the US Department of Health, Education, and Welfare (1964), which set a new standard for questionnaire design and sampling. The 1960s also saw the origins of organizations catering to government research, for example, RAND, Research Triangle Institute, and Westat.

3. The eighteen-hour documentary on Vietnam (2017) by Ken Burns and Lynn Novick is a superb introduction to the war.

4. It was later determined that no such attack occurred.

5. Only 24% (48%, 29%) favored punishing the soldiers involved in the My Lai massacre [12/69]. The massacre was originally covered up. Eighteen months later, Seymour Hersh broke the story. Several heroic army personnel stopped the massacre from getting worse and made sure that the story eventually got out. For a superb book on My Lai, see Jones (2017).

6. The wall was torn down in 1989 with the collapse of the Soviet Union.

7. Only two questions were asked by any survey organization in the 1960s with the word "Africa."

8. Al Smith lost the 1928 presidential election to Herbert Hoover. It is widely believed that one of the factors for Smith's loss was that he was a Catholic.

9. The nomination process was very contested. In May 1968, 25% of democrats said they favored Kennedy, 30% favored McCarthy, 33% favored Humphrey, and 13% did not know.

10. In what was later called a police riot, police beat up many of the demonstrators. Fifty-six (31%, 13%) approved of the way the Chicago police dealt with the protesters.

11. Governor George Wallace of Alabama ran as a third candidate and won 13.5% of the popular vote. Nixon received 43.4% and Humphrey 42.7%.

12. I find it remarkable the extent to which some Americans can adopt conspiracy theories. For more on this, see Hofstadter (2012).

13. Only 31% thought that antipoverty funds were well-spent [3/66].

14. The 26th Amendment to the Constitution, lowering the voting age to eighteen, was ratified in July 1971.

15. For a superb book on the history of race relations in Birmingham and the struggle for freedom, see the Pulitzer Prize-winning book by McWhorter (2001).

16. Only 5% of blacks who were of vote age were registered to vote in Mississippi.

17. Wallace in his inaugural speech as governor said, "Segregation, now, segregation tomorrow, segregation forever!" Seventy percent thought JFK did the right think sending federal marshals to Alabama [5/62].

18. King was awarded the Nobel Peace Prize in 1964.

19. Wasow (2020) argues that reactions to the violent protests of 1968 gave Nixon the edge in the 1968 Presidential Election.

20. Before *Loving*, interracial marriage was prohibited in thirty-eight states.

21. Fifty-nine percent approved of marriages between Jews and non-Jews and 63% between Protestants and Catholics.

22. For an excellent popular article on Griswold, see Bailey (2015).

23. Eight-eight percent thought women should be paid the same as men for the same type of work [6/62].

24. Gallup and other survey organizations asked few questions about women in politics or the economy. They did have a survey of only women in 1962.

25. Gallup asked no questions about gays in this decade. For an excellent documentary on Stonewall, see *American Experience: Stonewall Uprising* (2010).

26. The direct cost of the Vietnam War was about $800 billion in today's dollars and another trillion dollars for VA benefits.

27. The Volkswagen Beetle started its rise to stardom in the early 1960s.

28. Ninety-eight percent believed in God in August 1967 and 43% attended church at least weekly.

29. No survey organization asked any question about the Beatles, the Rolling Stones, Bob Dylan, or Woodstock.

30. No questions were asked by any survey organization in the 1960s about Muhammed Ali. A December 1971 Harris poll found 47% of blacks had a great deal of respect for Ali. Forty-three percent wanted to ban boxing in a June 1965 survey.

31. Muhammed Ali said "I ain't got nothing against no Viet Cong; no Viet Cong never called me Nigger."

5

The 1970s

Watergate, Normalization of Relations with China, Continuing Social and Political Protest, the Growth of International Terrorism, and Stagflation

Telephone surveys started their ascent in the 1970s, accounting for 20% of surveys housed at the Roper Center. Baker (2020) notes that the first national telephone survey occurred in 1964 and the first CATI survey was fielded in 1971.[1] This transition was helped by the introduction of new systems for randomly selecting phone numbers. Gallup began to lose their semi-monopolistic position. They now accounted for 62% of all surveys in the Roper archive compared to 84% in the previous decade. Roper accounted for 17% and Yankelovich, Skelly, and White, 6%. In this decade, joint newspaper/TV-sponsored surveys were launched, with CBS/*New York Times* in 1975, accounting for 7% of all national surveys. Soon, other coalitions were created: ABC/*Washington Post* and NBC/*Wall Street Journal*.

WORLD EVENTS

Vietnam

Nixon began the process of Vietnamization—the slow building up of the Army of Vietnam (ARVN) while withdrawing US troops. In 1970, United States and ARVN troops invaded Cambodia in an attempt to close down communist sanctuaries. The invasion had very limited success. (The massive antiwar protests that occurred in the United States during this decade will be discussed in the next section.) In another military failure, the 1971 ARVN invasion of Laos became a debacle with many ARVN troops deserting. In December 1972, the United States initiated a bombing campaign against Hanoi and Haiphong Harbor using B52s for the first time. The Paris Peace Accords, ending the war, was signed in January 1973. Reacting to strong antiwar public opinion, the Case-Church Amendment of 1973 prohibited the reintroduction of US troops in Indochina without prior congressional approval. Both North and South Vietnam, however, flaunted the peace agreement, and in early 1975, after Nixon had resigned and Gerald Ford had become president, the North began their final offensive against the South. Saigon was captured by the North in April of that year, an event memorialized by the famous photo of an evacuation helicopter on the roof of the US Embassy.[2]

Survey results showed declining support for Nixon's handling of the Vietnam War over time.

- *Whereas 64% of respondents approved of his handling of the war in January 1970, this had declined to 41% in February 1971. Only 21% thought he was telling the public all that they should know [2/71].*
- *In 1971, two-thirds of Americans approved of a proposal to bring home all the troops before the end of the year [2/71].*
- *As the bombing of North Vietnam increased, only 47% were in favor of it (44%, 10%) [4/72].*
- *After the signing of the Paris Accords, 75% now favored Nixon's handling of the war [1/73]. As the governments of South Vietnam and Cambodia began to collapse, only 12% wanted to send them more aid [2/75].*

China

In July 1972, Nixon announced that Henry Kissinger had just returned from a secret mission to Beijing and that he (Nixon) was going to visit China in February 1973. Nixon met with Zhou Enlai and Mao Zedong and the process of normalization between the United States and China began with each opening a liaison office in the other's country.

- *American attitudes were softening on China even before Nixon's trip. In May 1971, 44% (38%, 18%) thought that China should be admitted to the UN. However, just prior to Nixon's trip, only 16% thought it would be very effective in improving world peace (50% fairly, 25% not, 8% DK). By January 1979, 58% approved of establishing diplomatic relations with China.*

The Middle East

When Israel gained control over the West Bank and Gaza in the 1967 war, more Palestinian refugees fled to Jordan, Lebanon, and other countries. South Lebanon was used as a base to launch attacks against Israel as well as airplane hijackings and other actions. Some of the most infamous attacks included: the bombing of SwissAir Flight 330, bound for Tel Aviv, in which forty-seven people were killed; the Munich massacre in which eleven Israeli athletes were killed at the 1972 Summer Olympics; the terrorist organization Black September opening fire at the Athens Airport in

August 1973, killing three and injuring fifty-five; and the June 1976 hijacking of an Air France plane to Entebbe, Uganda, and the subsequent freeing of the passengers and crew in a raid by Israeli commandos.

- *Harris asked what policies should be adopted to stop terrorism: refuse any concessions to hijackers, even if that resulted in the hostages being killed (51%); all those convicted of terrorism should get the death penalty (55%); and airline service should be cut off from any country that harbors terrorists (79%) [11/77]. Furthermore, 60% said terrorism was a serious problem in the United States.*

In October 1973, Egypt and Syria attempted to recapture territories lost in the 1967 war and attacked Israel in what was later called the Yom Kippur War. Although this surprise attack was initially successful, there was some fear that Israel might lose the war, and it took a week before Israeli forces crossed the Suez Canal and approached Damascus. From the Arab perspective, the war showed that they could stand up to Israel and greatly enhanced the reputation of Egypt's president, Anwar Sadat. During the war, the Organization of Arab Petroleum Exporting Countries (OPEC) proclaimed an oil embargo. The price of oil went up fourfold and gave OPEC much greater political and economic power.[3] In November 1977, Anwar Sadat met Menachem Begin in Israel. A peace treaty between Israel and Egypt was negotiated in September 1978 at Camp David, Maryland.

- *Americans were not universally in support of Israel. Following the Yom Kippur War, 37% said their sympathies were with Israel, 8% said the Arabs, 24% said neither, and 31% said they did not know [4/75]. Only 40% (47%, 13%) wanted to send arms to Israel in the middle of the war [10/73] and 28% in March 1978.*
- *In October 1977, 33% (28%, 40%) favored the establishment of a Palestinian state. With the signing of the Camp David Accords, only 24% (55%, 21%) thought the treaty would result in lasting peace [1/79].*

The Shah of Iran's regime had become increasingly corrupt and brutal. Economic shortages in combination with a rejection of western culture by Shia Islamic conservatives led to a popular revolt against the Shah. He was forced to flee Iran in January 1979. Ayatollah Khomeini, an Islamic cleric, came to power in the Iranian Revolution. In November 1979, fifty-two American diplomats and citizens were taken hostage in Tehran. It was one month later that the Soviet Union invaded Afghanistan. Both events will be discussed in greater detail in the next chapter.

- *At the beginning of the Iran crisis, 79% approved of President Jimmy Carter's handling of the situation [12/79].*

Other Important International Events

In 1971 the Indo-Pakistani War resulted in Pakistan forfeiting control over East Pakistan, which became Bangladesh. In May 1974, India detonated its first nuclear bomb.

The civil war intensified in Northern Ireland between Catholics who wanted to unite with the Republic of Ireland and Protestants who wanted to remain in the United Kingdom. (Over time more than 3,500 people died in the so-called Irish "troubles.") In September 1973, the democratically elected socialist government of Salvador Allende of Chile was overthrown in a coup led by Augusto Pinochet. (The United States had set up the conditions for the coup, knew about it in advance, and promptly recognized the junta that took control. Thousands of Chileans were killed and tens of thousands were arrested.) In June 1979, a black-led government took control of Rhodesia (Zimbabwe). And, over the course of the decade, Portugal granted independence to its African colonies of Guinea-Bissau, Angola, Mozambique, and Cape Verde.

- *In December 1971, Harris found 23% favored Pakistan in the war, 14% India, and the remainder said neither or did not know. Later when Nixon gave assistance to Pakistan to build a nuclear reactor, Harris found that only 8% approved of this in February 1977.*
- *In September 1979, Roper found that only 7% said they were supporters of the IRA, 52% said they were critics, 8% volunteered they were supporters but did not like their violence, and 33% did not know.*
- *Harris found 18% said it was right for the United States to try to destabilize the Chilean government, 60% said it was wrong and 22% did not know [9/74]. Furthermore, 7% said it was a proud moment for the United States, 41% a dark moment and 53% said neither or did not know [12/74]. Furthermore, only 12% said it was acceptable to interfere in the internal affairs of Chile [3/74-Yank].*
- *In August 1976, Roper asked what the United States should do about South Africa and Rhodesia, which had black majority populations and minority white governments: 8% of respondents said to support the blacks, 3% favored the whites, 73% said to stay out of it, and 16% did not know.*
- *In September 1977, the United States agreed to transfer control of the Panama Canal to Panama. This transfer was approved by only 43% of survey respondents (38%, 19%) [2/78].*

The above examples indicate that, following the example of Vietnam, most Americans were opposed to additional foreign entanglements in the Third World.

US POLITICS

Richard Nixon won reelection in 1972 (60.7% v. 37.5%) of the vote, beating Senator George McGovern of South Dakota whose platform was focused on an immediate withdrawal from Vietnam. Nixon was forced to resign in August 1974 because of the Watergate scandal. His replacement, Gerald Ford, was beaten in November 1976 by Jimmy Carter (51.1% v. 48.0%).

The seminal political event of the 1970s in the United States was the Watergate scandal. In June 1972, five men were caught breaking into the Democratic National

Committee (DNC) headquarters at the Watergate office complex in Washington D.C. The FBI was eventually able to trace money received by the burglars to the Committee for the Reelection of the President (CRP). Eventually, it was learned that the purpose of the break-in was to repair wiretaps placed on the phones at the DNC. It was also learned that other "dirty tricks," that is, using the FBI, CIA, IRS, and other agencies to harass Nixon's opponents, had been conducted at the behest of Nixon administration members. An attempted cover-up ensued to prevent this information from becoming public knowledge. Investigative reporting by *Washington Post* reporters Bob Woodward and Carl Bernstein (and others) revealed that the dirty tricks and the cover-up were linked to high-level officials at the White House, the FBI, and the Justice Department. Several principals came clean to avoid perjury charges. The Senate Watergate Hearings revealed that the White House often taped conversations in the Oval Office. In October 1973, Nixon ordered the firing (Saturday Night Massacre) of the Attorney General and the Special Prosecutor. In August 1974, the release of a tape showed that days after the break-in, Nixon had approved a plan for a cover-up and this led to further erosion of Nixon's support. As it became clear that the US House of Representatives would vote in favor of impeachment, Nixon resigned. He was replaced by Gerald Ford, who subsequently pardoned Nixon.

- *Seventy percent of Americans said they watched part of the hearings on TV [8/73].*
- *In April 1973, 31% of Americans characterized Watergate as a very serious matter because it revealed corruption in the Nixon administration. This number increased to 46% in June 1973.*
- *Public support for impeaching Nixon increased over time 23% [7/73], 33% [10/73], 46% [4/74], and 64% [8/74]. In fact, by August 1974, 56% wanted him tried on criminal charges. The writing was on the wall. It was time for Nixon to resign before he was removed from office.*
- *Anger toward Nixon had increased to the point that only 35% favored Ford's pardon of Nixon [6/76].*

Spiro Agnew was Nixon's vice president for most of his time in office. He was Nixon's bulldog: attacking antiwar activists, political opponents, and journalists. He was loved by conservatives for his attacks on antiwar activists, famously labeling them effete intellectual snobs and for denouncing the media as being biased toward the left. In October 1973, Agnew was forced to resign when he was found to have received kickbacks for road contracts when he was governor of Maryland. He was replaced as vice president by Gerald Ford, the House Minority Leader.

- *Agnew had a core of strong supporters. Of the 80% who said they heard of his attack on the media, 55% agreed with it [8/70]. However, by the time he was accused of corruption, 62% thought he should resign [10/73].*

The climate of political and social protest persisted in this decade. In February 1970, a jury found the Chicago Seven not guilty of conspiring to incite a riot at the 1968 Chicago Democratic Convention, although five of the defendants were convicted of a lesser charge.

Militant protests occurred in other settings. In September 1971, a revolt broke out at Attica Correctional Facility in New York to protest horrific conditions at the prison. When the maximum-security prison was stormed at the orders of Governor Rockefeller, thirty-two prisoners and ten guards were killed. In February 1973, members of the American Indian Movement occupied the town of Wounded Knee in South Dakota to protest corruption at the Pine Ridge Indian Reservation, and the US government's failure to fulfill treaty obligations. The occupation lasted for seventy-one days. Firefights between protesters and law enforcement officials occurred during the siege. Eventually, an agreement was reached that the protesters would disarm, and they walked through federal lines at night.

When the United States invaded Cambodia in May of 1970, demonstrations closed hundreds of universities as an estimated four million students went on strike. At Kent State University in Ohio, National Guardsmen shot at demonstrators, killing four and wounding nine. At Jackson State University in Mississippi, law enforcement officials killed two demonstrators and injured twelve.[4]

- *Of the 51% who followed the Chicago trial, 75% agreed with the Judge's actions in the courthouse, which included chaining Bobby Seale to a chair and gagging him [Harris, 3/70]. Eighty percent said the defendants were more interested in putting on a sideshow than in justice.*
- *Harris found 51% (21%, 28%) sympathized with the Indians over the Federal Government [3/73] and 35% (35%, 33%) thought that Rockefeller did the right thing in ordering that Attica prisoners be shot [9/74].*

Investigative reporting by the media had a tremendous impact in the 1970s. In addition to the uncovering of the Watergate scandal and the ensuing Senate hearings, the other major media event of the 1970s was the publication of the Pentagon Papers. In 1967, the US secretary of defense Robert McNamara had created a task force to examine the errors that led up to the Vietnam War. Thirty-six analysts created a 1,000-page report that was leaked to the press by one of its members, Daniel Ellsberg. The *New York Times* began publishing sections of the report in June 1970. After the Nixon administration got a court injunction forcing publication to stop, the *Washington Post* continued publication where the *Times* left off. Eventually, the Supreme Court ruled that the government did not meet the heavy burden of proof to prevent publication. Ellsberg was cleared of charges following a mistrial, when it was revealed that FBI agents, at the orders of Richard Nixon, had broken into the office of Ellsberg's psychiatrist.

- *Although Nixon and Agnew accused the media of having a liberal bias and that the media was out to "get them," 58% of survey respondents (29%, 13%) thought the newspapers did the right thing in publishing the Pentagon Papers [6/71].*

- *Surveys also showed considerable agreement with Agnews assessment that the media mistreated the Nixon administration (44%, 27%, 29%).*
- *However, only 33% believed television news was dominated by those looking for ways to criticize the Nixon administration, and when asked whether the television news had a liberal or conservative bias, 8% of respondents said conservative, 26% liberal, 51% equal treatment, and 15% did not know. Similar findings were found when asking about newspapers (13%, 24%, 48%, 15%) and news magazines (9%, 14%, 32%, 46% [8/70]).*

Nixon was an advocate of "law and order," claiming that increasing crime rates required more arrests and harsher prison sentences. In June 1970, he declared the "war on drugs." The result was the beginning of a major trend in which increased numbers of people (most often racial minorities) went to prison.

- *In April 1965, 34% of respondents said there was an area within a mile of their home where they were afraid to walk at night. This had increased to 46% a decade later [6/75].*
- *Similarly, support for the death penalty for people convicted of murder increased from 45% [1/65] to 66% [4/76].*
- *The percentage of respondents who thought that courts in their area did not deal with criminals harshly enough increased from 48% [4/65] to 74% [12/72]. In fact, 67% favored life in prison for anyone convicted of selling hard drugs like heroin [1/73].*

RACE

Twenty years after *Brown v. Board of Education of Topeka*, many school systems were still not integrated. In many areas, because housing was segregated, local schools would also be segregated even if segregation in education was outlawed. Busing of children to different schools was seen as a solution for some school districts. In April 1970, the Supreme Court unanimously ruled *in Swann v. Charlotte-Mecklenburg Board of Education* that busing could be ordered. This set off a debate that is still with us today. In June 1978, the Supreme Court ruled in *University of California Regents v. Bakke* that quotas for college admissions were illegal, but programs could give advantages to minorities. And, in July 1972, the infamous Tuskegee study became public knowledge and was shut down. This study, sponsored by the US Public Health Service and begun in 1932, followed 399 black men who had untreated syphilis. They were never told they had the disease and there was no attempt to cure them. It is estimated that one hundreds of men died from the disease and fifty of them unwittingly transmitted the disease to their wives. The scandal created lasting mistrust toward public health programs among the African American community.[5] The decade ended (November 1979) with five anti-Ku Klux Klan demonstrators from the Communist Workers Party shot to death in Greensboro, North Carolina, by a group of Klansmen and Nazis.[6]

- *Sixty-nine percent of Americans said they would vote for a Negro as president [10/71].*[7] *This increased to 76% toward the end of the decade [7/78].*
- *However, only 14% said they favored busing [3/70] of children for racial integration, and 72% wanted a constitutional amendment against compulsory busing [5/74].*
- *Only 10% thought minorities and women should get preferential treatment in jobs and education to make up for past discrimination [3/77].*[8]
- *Furthermore, only 37% approved of marriages between whites and non-whites [7/78].*[9]
- *A mere 7% (87%, 6%) gave the KKK a positive rating [6/70]. In contrast, 66% (29%, 65%) gave the NAACP a positive rating.*
- *At the same time, surveys showed that most whites did not see discrimination as something real. Eighty-six percent of whites and 47% of blacks said blacks were treated the same in their community and 81% of whites and 41% of blacks thought blacks had an equal chance of getting a job in their community [7/78].*

SEX AND GENDER

In March 1972, the US Congress voted to send the Equal Rights Amendment (ERA) for women to the states for ratification. The ERA would make men and women have full equality of rights. It received only thirty-five of the necessary thirty-eight state ratifications. Perhaps the most important victory for women's rights was the January 1973 Supreme Court case *Roe v. Wade,* which overturned state bans on abortion.

- *Most Americans (74%) approved of the Equal Rights Amendment for women [10/74].*
- *Abortion was divisive. Before Roe v. Wade, 46% (45%, 9%) favored a law allowing a woman to get an abortion at any time [12/72]. When Roe v. Wade was issued, 48% (43%, 9%) favored the ruling [3/74]. However, only 21% favored abortion in all circumstances, 53% in some, and 23% in none [4/75].*

Overall, in this decade, there were a variety of victories for women's rights. The Boston Marathon allowed the first women to compete (1972); the first female rabbi was ordained (1972); first female FBI agent was hired (1972); Title IX was passed that eventually required men and women athletics to receive the same level of support in educational settings (1972); the first female became governor who did not succeed her husband (Ella Grasso of Connecticut in 1975); the first nationally televised women's basketball game occurred (Immaculate University v. Maryland, 1975); women were admitted to the US Military Academy at West Point and the US Naval Academy in Annapolis (1976); and the WAVES were disbanded and women were integrated into the regular navy (1977).

- *There was increasing support for women working. Sixty percent of respondents approved of a woman working even if she had a husband capable of supporting her [6/70].*[10]

- *In addition, 84% said they would vote for a qualified female congressional candidate [7/70] and 73% said they would vote for a woman as president [8/75].*[11]
- *However, 44% did not believe a woman could run a business as well as a man [7/70] and 68% thought women got as good a break as men [7/70].*
- *Only 30% approved of the use of Ms. as an alternative to Miss or Mrs. and 9% preferred to be called Ms. over the more traditional terms [1/73].*

Gays were coming out of the closet. The American Psychiatric Association declassified homosexuality as a disease (1973) and California's sodomy law was repealed (1976). However, a setback occurred in 1977 when an anti-gay campaign led by Anita Bryant resulted in Florida voters repealing the gay-rights ordinance of Miami-Dade County. In turn, protests against this vote in San Francisco led to Harvey Milk becoming the first openly gay elected official of a large US city,[12] and in 1978 San Francisco city council signed the country's most comprehensive homosexual rights bill.

- *In November 1978, 62% thought that homosexual relations between two consenting adults were wrong.*
- *Gallup had a more extensive set of questions on gays in June 1977. Thirty-three percent (53%, 14%) thought it was not possible for homosexuals to be good Christians or Jews; 43% felt that homosexual relations should remain illegal (43%, 14%); and 57% said that homosexuals should have equal rights in job opportunities [6/77]; when asked whether homosexuals should be able to be hired for certain jobs, there was limited support for many categories (elementary school teachers—27%; armed forces—51%; doctors—44%; clergy—36%; and salesperson—68%); and only 14% thought homosexuals should be allowed to adopt children.*

THE ECONOMY

The 1970s was not a good decade for the economy. Because of the Vietnam War and the oil shocks of 1973 and 1979, inflation grew at an annual rate of 7.1%. In August 1971, Nixon stopped the United States from converting dollars to gold. This resulted in floating exchange rates a few years later. Also, in August 1971, in an attempt to control inflation, Nixon imposed a freeze on wages and prices. By 1974, these were abandoned. While the US economy suffered, manufacturing and exports expanded in West Germany and Japan. A combination of factors led to the decline of manufacturing in the United States: inflation, overseas competition, rising interest rates, and automation of manufacturing jobs. It was an era known for stagflation, that is, a combination of high inflation, high unemployment, and high interest rates.

- *Before Nixon imposed price and wage controls, 50% (38%, 12%) of Americans thought controls would be a good idea until the Vietnam War was over [2/71]. Five months after Nixon imposed them, only 33% (55%, 12%) favored the controls [1/72].*

> *However, somewhat surprisingly 50% (11% less, 31% same, 9% DK) wanted to make them stricter.*
> - *Seventy-two percent (10%, 18%) approved of Nixon suspending the conversion of dollars into gold [ORC-8/71].*
> - *After wage and price controls were removed, 50% (39%, 11%) wanted to bring them back [8/74]. In February 1978 (under Carter) a plurality wanted to bring back wage and price controls (44%, 40%, 17%).*
> - *Just before the 1974 election, 57% believed we were heading toward a 1930s-type depression [10/74].*
> - *Fifty-four percent said that American workers were not as productive as they should be [1/72].*
> - *Government was often seen as a problem. Fifty-one percent thought that the government was most responsible for inflation rather than labor (20%) or business (14%) [9/78]. Furthermore, more said the government was the biggest threat to the future (46%) compared to labor (20%) or business (20%). However, only 27% wanted to privatize some government functions such as garbage collection and street cleaning [8/78].*

The growth in federal debt was also becoming a concern in some circles. Because interest rates were so high, so was the amount that the government had to spend to service its debt.

> - *Eighty-one percent favored a Constitutional Amendment requiring a balanced budget [6/78]. When asked whether it was more important to balance the budget or to cut taxes 43% (45%, 12%) gave priority to balancing the budget [4/78].*

The energy crises of 1973 (caused by the oil embargo associated with the Yom Kippur War) and 1979 (caused in part by the Iranian Revolution) resulted in rapid price increases, shortages, and very long lines at gas stations. Jimmy Carter is remembered for encouraging people to lower the thermostats and for installing solar panels at the White House. Reagan removed the solar panels upon moving into the White House.

> - *With the 1973 energy crisis, 62% of survey respondents said it would be a good idea to lower the highway speed by 10 miles per hour to save gas [6/73]; only 33% (53%, 14%) favored gas rationing [1/74]; and even less (10%) favored an increase in the gas tax [10/74].*
> - *After a 55-mph speed limit was set for highway driving, 72% wanted to keep it [5/74].*
> - *Americans were very cynical about the energy crisis. Seventy-four percent thought it was "a phony crisis to force prices up" [4/74]. When the energy crisis of 1979 kicked in only 43% thought it was serious [2/79].*
> - *Furthermore, only 16% were in favor of letting gas prices rise to encourage production [6/79] and 49% (28%, 23%) wanted to impose a windfall tax on energy companies to pay for Carter's energy program [8/79].*

Other economic highlights of the decade included: the opening of the World Trade Center in New York City (1973); the start of Federal Express (1973); Miller Lite's market release (1973); Volkswagen opening the first large non-American automobile maker factory in the United States (1978); and McDonald's introduction of the Happy Meal (1979).

SCIENCE, TECHNOLOGY, AND THE ENVIRONMENT

The decade of the 1970s included these major milestones of technological innovation and growth:[13] Intel released the first microprocessor, the Intel 4004 (1971); HP released the first handheld calculator (HP-35) (1972); Atari released Pong for home use (1972); the CT scan and mammogram were introduced (1973); Lexis-Nexus began (1973); the first handheld mobile phone call was made (1973); a patent was awarded for the first ATM (1973); Bill Gates and Paul Allen founded Microsoft (1975); the first Apple II computer went on sale (1977); and Phillips demonstrated the first compact disc (1979).

The 1970s was the decade in which environmental concerns first came to the forefront. In April 1970, the first Earth Day was celebrated. It was in December 1970 that the Environmental Protection Agency, which was proposed by Richard Nixon, was established. The National Resources Defense Council was founded in 1970 and Greenpeace in the following year. The ban on DDT became effective in 1972 and the Endangered Species Act was passed by Congress in December 1973. In general, the below survey results show that Americans were beginning to develop some environmental consciousness in the 1970s. However, the economy was deemed far more important.

- *Only 43% of Americans surveyed thought that public utilities were doing an excellent or good job controlling pollution, and 52% (30%, 18%) said they would be willing to pay more on their utility bills to reduce pollution [7/73].*
- *However, most Americans were not willing to give up economic growth to curb pollution (27%, 58%, 15%) [5/72].*
- *The public was split on spending more to curb pollution. Just 46% wanted to increase government spending to reduce air pollution (48%, 6%). With the energy crisis, 55% (30%, 15%) favored reducing environmental protections to produce more energy [7/79].*

In March 1979, a serious nuclear accident occurred in a reactor at the Three Mile Island Nuclear Generating Station, Pennsylvania. The partial meltdown contributed to the decline of new reactor construction in the United States.

- *Even before Three Mile Island (TMI), only 34% thought that nuclear power plants were safe enough [6/76]. After TMI, only 23% thought these plants were safe enough. However, only 24% wanted to shut down all nuclear power plants and only 41% were willing to pay more to move away from nuclear power [4/79].*

In October 1972, modern molecular biology was jumpstarted with the first publication by Boyer and Cohen describing recombinant DNA. In July 1978, the first "test-tube baby" was born; that is, the egg was fertilized by the sperm outside the body. Since then, approximately, 65,000 babies have been born in the United States using in vitro fertilization (IVF).

- *In August 1978, only 28% (60%, 13%) opposed artificial insemination.*

"Lucy," a skeleton of a female hominid estimated to have lived 3.2 million years ago, was discovered in Ethiopia in November 1974.

The last case of smallpox was diagnosed (1975). This was the first time a disease affecting humans was eradicated worldwide.

- *Americans were skeptical of some science. Only 37% had a great deal of confidence in the people running science [Harris-10/72] and only 38% wanted to adopt the metric system [1/77].*[14]
- *At the same time, scientists had an excellent (59%) or good (27%) reputation; and 70% said science and technology had changed life for the better; [NSF-5/72].*
- *Fifty-seven percent of respondents believed that UFOs were real [3/78].*

POPULAR TRENDS

Some of the more prominent movies released in this decade included: *M*A*S*H* (1970); *Love Story* (1970); *The Godfather* (1972); *The Exorcist* (1973); *Blazing Saddles* (1974); *The Towering Inferno* (1974); *Young Frankenstein* (1974); *One Flew Over the Cuckoo's Nest* (1975); *Jaws* (1975-seen by 21%); *The Rocky Horror Picture Show* (1975); *Rocky* (1976); *Close Encounters of the Third Kind* (1977); *Smokey and the Bandit* (1977); *Saturday Night Fever* (1977); *Star Wars* (1977); *Grease* (1978); *National Lampoon's Animal House* (1978); *Superman* (1978); *Apocalypse Now* (1979); *Star Trek: The Motion Picture* (1979); and *Alien* (1979).

TV shows that debuted in the 1970s included: *All My Children* (1970); *Monday Night Football* (1970); *All in the Family* (1971); *The Price is Right* (1972); *M*A*S*H* (1972); *Wheel of Fortune* (1975); *Saturday Night Live* (1975); *Roots* (1977-seen or heard about by 73% [3/77]); *E.R.* (1978); *Taxi* (1978); and *The Holocaust* (1978-seen by 48% [4/78]). It was in November 1972 that HBO was launched followed by ESPN in 1979.

- *Violence was more prevalent on TV shows and 70% of respondents thought there was a relation between TV violence and the crime rate [1/77].*
- *Most Americans did not place a lot of trust in television; only 37% of survey respondents said they had a great deal or quite a lot of confidence in the institution of television [5/73]. The somewhat uncritical acceptance of TV in the 1950s was now gone.*

- *When asked to rate specific types of programming the following said excellent or good: sports events (73%); discussion shows (46%); serious drama (36%); situation comedies (45%); news coverage and documentaries (79%); adventure series (56%); and cultural specials (46%).*

Notable publication events included: Erich Segal, *Love Story* (1970); J. (Joan Terry Garrity), *The Sensuous Woman* (1970); Charles Reich, *The Greening of America* (1970); William Peter Blatty, *The Exorcist* (1971); Dee Brown, *Bury My Heart at Wounded Knee* (1971); Germaine Greer, *The Female Eunuch* (1971); Frederick Forsyth, *Day of the Jackal* (1971); Herman Wouk, *Winds of War* (1972); Gore Vidal, *Burr* (1973); David Halberstam, *The Best and the Brightest* (1973); Alex Comfort, *The Joy of Sex* (1973); Bob Woodward and Carl Bernstein, *All the President's Men* (1974); Alex Haley, *Roots* (1976); Wayne Dwyer, *Your Erogenous Zones* (1977); and William Styron, *Sophie's Choice* (1979). The first issue of *People Magazine* appeared in 1974.

In music: The rock opera *Tommy* was first performed (1970); Jimi Hendrix died from an overdose (1970); Jim Morrison of the Doors died from a probable overdose (1971); Pink Floyd released *Dark Side of the Moon*; and U2 was formed (1976). It was an era of disco, country rock (Eagles), soft rock (The Carpenters and The Jackson Five), southern rock (Allman Brothers), and outlaw country (Willie Nelson). Other notable musicians of the decade were: Elton John, Pink Floyd, Abba, Led Zeppelin, John Lennon, Paul McCartney, Village People, Queen, Eagles, Chicago, Roberta Flack, Donna Summers, Rod Stewart, Wings, Carpenters, Barbara Streisand, Carole King, and Stevie Wonder.

- *In January 1973, the Harris poll asked about the type of music people listened to most often with these results: popular songs (65%); country and western (53%); folk music (49%); religious (47%); Broadway musicals (41%); symphony, chamber, or other classical music (40%); rock (37%); jazz (33%); and opera (19%).*
- *Furthermore, 37% said they attend musical events on a regular basis.*

Sports and fitness trends were changing.

- *Baseball was no longer America's most popular sport. Harris found that 34% thought that baseball was too slow moving and took too long to play [3/71]. However, 56% said it was a great sport because it involved more skills and talent than other sports.*
- *The most popular sports to watch were football (38%), baseball (19%), and basketball (10%) [1/72].*
- *A fitness boom was also under way: 25% of Americans said they were jogging [9/77].*
- *Support for women in competitive sports was increasing. Sixty-one percent of survey respondents said they favored a proposed law requiring the same amount of money be spent on girls' sports in high school as on boys [5/79]. Furthermore, 59% thought that girls should be able to play noncontact sports with boys.*

Legalized gambling became more mainstream. Scratch-off lottery tickets became available in the 1970s and casinos on Native American reservations began to open. Casinos also began to operate in other locations: Atlantic City in 1978.

- *Most Americans opposed legalized casino gambling (52%, 39%, 9%) [6/78]. Thirty-six percent had been to a gambling casino in 1978 and 23% said they were interested in going to Las Vegas.*

For comic strip fans, there were two major debuts: *Doonesbury* (1970) and *Garfield* (1978). Finally, Walt Disney World opened in Orlando, Florida, in 1971.

CONCLUDING COMMENTS

Optimism was over. America was defeated in Vietnam, a president resigned in disgrace, riots raged in the cities, and stagflation plagued the economy.

Richard Nixon went from invading Cambodia and Laos and bombing Hanoi and Haiphong with B52s, to signing a peace treaty in 1973. His successor, Gerald Ford, saw the collapse of the Saigon regime. Nixon also began the normalization of relations with China while at the same time orchestrating a bloody coup in Chile. There were several terrorist actions against Israel and other nations and another Mideast War in 1973. The decade ended with a momentous event that still affects us today—the takeover of Iran by Islamic fundamentalists.

Americans were tired of adventures abroad—they increasingly opposed the war in Vietnam, did not want to send arms to Israel, and were in favor of normalization of relations with China. But they also wanted to aggressively attack terrorism.

The Watergate scandal was the pivotal domestic event of the decade, leading Nixon who, in any case, was not well liked or trusted, to resign in the face of impeachment and almost certain removal from office. It was also an era of protests—antiwar, civil rights, Attica, Wounded Knee, and hundreds of demonstrations against Nixon's invasion of Cambodia leading to the death of four students protesting at Kent State and two at Jackson State University. Following the investigative reporting on Watergate and the release of the Pentagon Papers, conservatives, led by Nixon and Agnew, began a concerted attack on the media, accusing it of having a liberal bias. Similar attacks on the media continue to this day.

Initially, few saw Watergate as a serious problem. But, over time, as more information became available, most wanted Nixon removed from office. On the other hand, many agreed with Nixon and Agnew's attack on the press and supported the harsh treatment of protesters. Nevertheless, most still believed the media was not biased and supported the publication of the Pentagon Papers.

Backlash against racial integration centered around opposition to busing and affirmative action. Most still opposed the interracial marriage and did not see discrimination as real. Nixon's slogan of "law and order" was a not-very-subtle appeal to white fear of blacks. However, the percent of Americans who said they would vote for a black president increased.

The equal rights for women failed to be enacted. On the other hand, abortion was legalized with *Roe v. Wade*, women were allowed to compete in the Boston Marathon, and the military academies admitted women. There was increased support for women working and voter support for women politicians. Many still believed a woman could not run a business as well as a man. Gays were increasingly coming out of the closet and the American Psychiatric Association declassified homosexuality as a disease. Forty-three percent still believed that homosexual relations should be illegal and that questions on gay marriage were not relevant. But there was increased support for homosexuals having equal job rights.

Because of Vietnam and two severe oil/energy crises, unemployment and inflation combined to become recognized as the economic scourge of stagflation. Americans had to wait in huge lines to buy gas and the American automobile industry and other heavy industries went into decline. American opinion vacillated on supporting price and wage controls. Government was often seen as the cause of the economic problems. Similarly, there was a concerted campaign against government deficits—which was often an excuse to reduce the role of government. Microsoft was founded, Apple computers went on sale for the first time, and the first mobile phone became available.

The environment became a notable concern, the first Earth Day was observed, and the Environmental Protective Agency and Greenpeace were founded. The public was split on increasing money to curb pollution, and few were willing to give up economic growth to protect the environment.

[The reader can find relevant crosstabs and discussion in the online appendix located at https://rowman.com/ISBN/9781793653505/US-Public-Opinion-since-the-1930s-Galluping-through-History.]

NOTES

1. For an excellent history of the use of technology in survey research from 1960 to 2020, see Baker (2020). He discusses landline telephones, cell phones, CATI surveys, web-based surveys, and so on.

2. The tragedy of Indochina did not end in 1975. In April 1975, the Khmer Rouge took the capital of Cambodia—Phnom Penh. Pol Pot ordered the evacuation of the capital. Thus, began the Killing Fields, in which an estimated two million Cambodians died: half from starvation and half from executions. In a very complicated history, border skirmishes as well as a war occurred between Vietnam and Cambodia from 1975 to 1998. There was also a border war between Vietnam and China in early 1979, when China invaded Vietnam in response to Vietnam's occupation of Cambodia.

3. Thirty-six percent favored sending in US troops if Arabs cut off oil shipments to the United States [11/78].

4. I found no questions on who was at fault in these two shootings.

5. I could not find any questions on the Tuskegee study.

6. Despite video footage of the killings, the Klansmen and Nazis accused of killing the demonstrators were acquitted in criminal cases.

7. It was 48% in August 1963.

8. The question asked by Gallup was biased in asking respondents to choose between preferential treatment and ability and test scores.

9. The Supreme Court ended any state law that prohibited interracial marriage in the *Loving* case in 1967. (This is discussed further in chapter 4.)

10. Remember, it was 18% in 1945.

11. Fifty-two percent had said they would vote for a woman candidate in February 1955.

12. Harvey Milk was assassinated in November 1978.

13. Sixty percent (28%, 13%) believed computers improved the quality of life in society [Harris-11/78].

14. Currently, only the United States, Liberia, and Myanmar have not adopted the metric system.

6

The 1980s

Ronald Reagan, the Fall of the Berlin Wall, the Soviet War in Afghanistan, and AIDS

Telephone surveys now dominated. The share of surveys conducted by telephone increased from 20% in the 1970s to 76%. With the availability of national long-distance calling, telephone surveys were far cheaper and easier to conduct than face-to-face surveys. Gallup now accounted for only 26% of surveys. Media sponsored surveys (ABC, CBS, NBC, *WPost, NYT, LAT,* AP, *USA Today, WSJ*) came into their own, accounting for at least 47% of all surveys conducted.

WORLD EVENTS

Iran, Iraq, Afghanistan

The taking of fifty-two American hostages by Iran dominated the last year of the Carter presidency. There was a failed rescue attempt in April 1980 when one of the rescue helicopters crashed and eight US troops were killed. In September 1980 Iraq invaded Iran. This invasion and the death of the shah of Iran from cancer prompted Iran to negotiate a resolution of the hostage crisis. The Algiers Accords provided the release of the American hostages, the unfreezing of $7.9 billion in Iranian assets, and a pledge by the United States not to intervene in Iranian domestic politics. The hostages were released on the day that Ronald Reagan was sworn in as president in January 1981. The Iranian hostage crisis was one of the contributing factors in the defeat of Carter by Reagan in the November 1980 presidential election.

- *In February 1980, 58% of Americans approved of how Carter was handling the Iranian hostage crisis. By May, support for Carter's handling of the crisis fell to 42%. After the hostage deal was announced, 67% (24%, 10%) said we should go along with the deal [1/80].*

- *Most Americans were not in favor of a military solution. When asked what the United States should do if hostages were harmed, 36% (54%, 10%) said using military force [1/80].*

Saddam Hussein had become president of Iraq in 1979. His invasion of Iran the following year was precipitated by a history of border disputes, a desire to take over Iranian oil fields, and fear of the Iranian Islamic revolution spreading. The United States provided limited assistance to Iraq in the war. Iraq used chemical weapons during the war that directly caused close to 50,000 Iranian casualties. The war ended in July 1988 with the acceptance of a UN resolution. Approximately, half a million people died in the war and neither side gained from it.

- *When asked who they favored in the war, 25% of respondents said Iraq, 6% Iran, 47% neither, and 22% did not know [11/80]. In fact, 84% (10%, 6%) agreed with Carter's position that it was wise not to get involved in this war [10/80].*

In December 1979, the Soviet Union instigated a coup in Afghanistan, in which Afghan president Amin was killed and Babrak Karmal was installed in his place. Soviet forces entered Afghanistan with 1,800 tanks and 80,000 troops. In January 1980, President Carter proclaimed a grain embargo against the Soviet Union and in March announced that the United States would boycott the 1980 Summer Olympics in Moscow. Funded by the United States, the United Kingdom, Pakistan, and other Muslim countries, Afghan insurgents (the Islamic Mujahideen) fought a war against the Soviets. Eventually, the United States provided Stinger missiles that were used to shoot down 350 Soviet aircraft. The Soviet occupation was brutal, and it is estimated that well over one million civilian casualties occurred. About 15,000 Soviets died in the war.[1] The Soviets began to withdraw their troops in 1988. The withdrawal was initiated by the large number of Soviet casualties, unrest at home, and the realization that the war could not be won. Many believe that the Soviet-Afghan War was one of the contributing factors to the collapse of the Soviet Union.

- *Sixty-one percent of Americans did not want the United States to participate in the Moscow Olympics (2/80).*
- *But few wanted direct United States involvement in Afghanistan. Only 9% wanted to send US troops to Afghanistan although an additional 21% were willing to send arms (1/80). However, with a slightly differently worded question, Yankelovich in the very same month found that 56% wanted to send military aid to the rebels who are fighting Soviet troops.[2]*
- *Under Reagan, 30% wanted the United States to have a more active policy in Afghanistan (10/82).*

The Caribbean and Central America

In April 1980, protests in Havana and asylum requests by 10,000 Cubans at the Peruvian embassy (and other embassies) induced the Castro government to declare the port of Mariel open to anyone who wished to leave. By October 1980, around 125,000 Cuban refugees had reached Florida. This resulted in a considerable debate about immigration policies as many of those leaving Cuba had been released from jails and mental institutions.

- *Only a minority (33%) of Americans supported allowing Cuban refugees to stay in the United States [5/80].*
- *At the point that 40,000 Cuban refugees had arrived in the United States, Gallup asked whether more should be allowed to come in. Survey responses were: 13% saying all or most should be allowed in, 12% saying some, 28% saying only if they have relatives in United States, and 46% saying that no additional refugees should be accepted.*

At the same time as the exodus from Cuba, many Haitians were fleeing their island for economic reasons. Some accused the United States government of hypocrisy for allowing Cubans in but not Haitians, who were mostly black.

- *Only 39% of Americans (46%, 15%) wanted to allow the Haitian refugees into the United States [5/80]. It is interesting that this percentage is similar to that when asked about Cuban refugees (33%).*

Reagan wanted a more aggressive US foreign policy. The military budget increased by 43% during his tenure as president. In October 1983, the United States invaded the island nation of Grenada following a coup against the socialist government of Maurice Bishop by a faction that was more hard-lined.

- *As Reagan took office, 51% (22% too much, 22% right amount, 12%-DK) thought we were spending too little money on the military [1/81]. However, in September 1982, only 42% wanted to spend more money on the military.*
- *In 1983, 60% (32%, 9%) favored Reagan sending troops to Grenada [11/83] and in a differently worded question, 63% said it was not a mistake.*
- *However, by April 1987, 48% (44%, 6%) wanted to cut military expenditures.*

A twelve-year civil war was fought in El Salvador between a very brutal military regime and a Marxist insurgency (the FMLN). The El Salvadorian government used death squads against opponents and forced a million people to be displaced (many fleeing to the United States). The United States provided substantial military aid to the government under Carter, Reagan, and Bush. A peace accord was finally reached in January 1992.

- *In March 1983, only 23% (67%, 10%) of survey respondents favored Reagan's request to Congress for an additional $60 million in US aid to El Salvador. Similarly, only 24% wanted to send more US military advisors.*

Ronald Reagan also aimed at overthrowing the government of Nicaragua, which was under the leadership of the Sandinista National Liberation Front (FSLN),[3] by fomenting and backing right-wing rebel groups (Contras). Even though Congress passed legislation (the Boland Amendments) prohibiting the United States from funding the Contra insurgency, the US military continued to illegally fund and train the Contras by selling arms to Iran (to obtain the release of seven American hostages held in Lebanon) and then funneling those proceeds to the Contras. This became known as the Iran-Contra affair. Numerous investigations and trials occurred after the story broke in November 1986. Oliver North, a Reagan appointee to the National Security Council, who oversaw the program, destroyed many of the documents associated with the program. Eventually, eleven government officials were indicted, including Caspar Weinberger, secretary of defense; Robert C. McFarlane, national security adviser; and Elliott Abrams, assistant secretary of state. Some took a plea bargain and some were convicted, but most were pardoned by President George H. W. Bush. The Tower Commission concluded that Reagan did not have full knowledge of the extent of the affair.

- *In 1983, most Americans did not want to be involved in Nicaragua. Only 33% (43%, 24%) favored ongoing military assistance to overthrow the government [11/83].*
- *In March 1985, 26% (44%, 31%) approved of Reagan's policies in that country and 42% (50%, 8%) thought we should help the rebels.*
- *Then, in January 1987, only 22% favored the $100 million aid package to the Contras. Just over a third (35%) of Americans thought that Reagan was lying when he said he did not know that money from the sales of arms to Iran was going to fund the Contras [1/87] and only 9% thought he should be impeached or resign if he did know [12/86]. However, only 13% approved of the aid to the Contras using weapon sales to Iran [12/86].*
- *After the Contra hearings, only 30% (58%, 12%) thought that Oliver North should be tried on criminal charges [7/87]. Furthermore, 49% (41%, 10%) thought that Reagan should pardon North if he was indicted [1/88].*

Although most Americans did not want military aid being sent to the Contras, they were unwilling to prosecute those who broke the law sending that aid. As long as many Americans were not dying, the principle could be overlooked.

The Soviet Union and Eastern Europe

The Soviet Union was in crisis because of the debacle of the Afghan War and an economy that was doing poorly. Mikhail Gorbachev became general secretary of the Politburo in March 1985 and began implementing reforms. Liberalization of the economy (perestroika), increased political openness (glasnost), and some troop withdrawals from Warsaw Pact countries encouraged increased political protests in Eastern Europe. Semi-free elections in Poland in 1989 ended with the solidarity[4]-led opposition taking the majority of seats. East Germans began fleeing through Hungary and Czechoslovakia to Austria. Increased protests in East Germany led to the collapse of the Honecker government. Finally, in November 1989, the Berlin Wall came down and the government of East Germany collapsed.[5] Czechoslovakia also became free in that month with the Velvet Revolution. Other countries soon followed.

- *Americans understood and supported the changes in Russia and Eastern Europe. Sixty percent thought Bush should do more to help Russia (29%, 10%) [11/89]; 68% thought that the reforms in Eastern Europe would continue and there would not be a hard-line crackdown [12/89]; 77% had a favorable opinion of Gorbachev [12/89]; and 46% (47%, 7%) thought it was the beginning of the end for communism [12/89].*

The Middle East

Israel invaded South Lebanon in June 1982 in an attempt to defeat the PLO. The invasion ended up as a debacle for Israel when its allies, the Christian Militia, massacred up to 3,000 civilians at two refugee camps (Sabra and Shatila). Israel suffered over 1,200 deaths before they left Lebanon in May 2000. Ultimately, 850,000 Christians left Lebanon and the PLO was replaced by Hezbollah.

- *Only 25% (48%, 27%) of survey respondents approved of Israel's invasion of Lebanon [7/82]. Nevertheless, more Americans (50%) said they were more likely to sympathize with the Israelis instead of the Palestinians (14%, 36%). Furthermore, only 30% (27%, 43%) favored the establishment of a Palestinian state [5/88].*
- *Americans were divided on military aid to Israel: 41% wanted to reduce or eliminate military aid and 50% wanted to increase it or keep the same [1/87].*

In August 1982, French, Italian, and American military forces were sent to Beirut as part of a peacekeeping force to oversee the evacuation of PLO forces. A truck bomb, probably orchestrated by Iran, resulted in the death of 241 US marines at the US embassy in Beirut in October 1983. Ronald Reagan withdrew the remaining US troops.

- *Before the truck bombing, only 41% (50%, 9%) wanted to keep the marines in Lebanon [9/83]. After the bombing, 45% said it was a mistake to send in the marines [11/83]; 57% (34%, 9%) wanted to withdraw US troops from Lebanon [1/84]; and only 28% approved of Reagan's policies in Lebanon [2/84].*

The polling data above show that American attitudes toward Iraq and Iran, Afghanistan, El Salvador, Nicaragua, and Lebanon were very similar—stay away.

Other World Events

Political reforms in China came to a screeching halt in June 1989 with the Tiananmen Square crackdown. Demonstration for political reforms had spread to 400 cities. Martial law was proclaimed and perhaps a couple of thousand protesters were killed (estimates vary widely).

- *Some Americans wanted to recall the US ambassador to China (42%) and restrict American investments in China (60%), but only 22% wanted to suspend diplomatic relations [6/89].*

In 1982, war broke out between the United Kingdom and Argentina over who owned the Falkland Islands (called Islas Malvinas by Argentina). The ten-week war began when Argentina occupied the islands and the United Kingdom sent a naval task force to contest this. A total of 255 British military personnel and 649 Argentine military personnel died in the war, which ended when the United Kingdom successfully assaulted the islands.

- *Sixty-six percent of those who knew about the war thought that Great Britain had the better case. However, fifty-four percent thought we should not take sides (4% favored Argentina and 38% the British).*

US POLITICS

In November 1980, Ronald Reagan defeated Jimmy Carter in the US presidential election. Reagan received 50.7% of the vote, Carter 41.0%, and third-party candidate John Anderson 6.6%. Reagan was reelected in 1984, defeating Walter Mondale (58.8% v. 40.6%), who won only in his home state of Minnesota. In the 1988 presidential election, George H. W. Bush defeated Michael Dukakis (53.4% v. 45.6%). Dukakis' defeat was largely due to his being labeled "liberal" and soft on crime.

Ronald Reagan, a former Hollywood actor, past two-term governor of California, and staunch anticommunist, became the most conservative president since before FDR. He was an ideologically driven conservative who wanted to severely reduce the role of government. In his first inaugural speech he said, "in this present crisis, government is not the solution to our problems, it is the problem."

- *This Reaganesque view of the government was mirrored when 55% (34%, 11%-LAT) of survey respondents said the government regulation of business did more harm than good [4/87]; 58% agreed the government was too big [1/88]; 66% said*

that government programs were wasteful and inefficient [5/88]; and 61% said the government controls too much of our daily lives [5/88].
- *However, only 36% said they would support the policy of a presidential candidate who wanted to replace Social Security with a tax-free saving program; 78% wanted to increase public works [1/88]; and 53% said that government is really run for the benefit of all the people [1/88].*

Reagan had strong support from religious evangelicals and conservative religious political organizations such as the Moral Majority, founded by Jerry Falwell in 1979. The Moral Majority had a lot of influence, but little popular support.

- *Of the 55% who had heard of the Moral Majority, only 22% (51%, 27%) approved of the organization [12/81].*
- *Nevertheless, 59% favored requiring prayer in public schools [8/80] and 79% favored a Constitutional Amendment allowing prayer in public schools [5/82]; 39% believed "The Bible is the actual word of God and is to be taken literally"; 10% believed "The Bible is an ancient book of fables, legends, history and moral precepts recorded by men" [8/80]; and 38% said they were "born again," that is, a turning point in your life when you committed yourself to Christ [8/80].*
- *Fifty-three percent agreed with the theory of creationism, compared with 18% who supported the theory of evolution [4/82]. Reagan was able to bring people who advocated these evangelical positions into his coalition.[6]*
- *Fifty percent wanted to ban "dangerous books" from public school libraries [4/87].*

An assassination attack on Ronald Reagan by John Hinckley Jr. in March 1981 also wounded his press secretary, James Brady, and two police officers. Brady subsequently became an advocate for restrictions on the sale of handguns and assault rifles.

- *Before the assassination attempt on Reagan, 58% favored federal registration of all firearms [8/80] and 59% wanted to make handgun laws mores strict [1/80]. After the assassination attempt, 44% wanted a total ban on handguns [9/82] and 72% wanted a ban on assault rifles [8/89].*

In 1984, the use of crack cocaine began spreading throughout the United States. The Anti-Drug Abuse Act of 1986 created mandatory minimum sentencing for many drug offenses. A five-year mandatory minimum sentence was enacted for possession of 5 grams of crack cocaine compared to 500 milligrams for powder (100 to 1 disparity).[7] The prison population increased by 78% under Reagan. African Americans were much more likely than whites to be targeted by the "war on drugs." For example, although the percentage of whites and blacks who use illegal drugs was about the same, in 1999, 58% of those serving time in prison for drug offenses were African American.

- *Fear of crime was such that 57% believed their state needed more prisons [1/82]; and 48% said they were afraid to walk at night a mile from their homes [1/82].*
- *Only 29% favored the legalization of marijuana [9/82] and 67% wanted even possession of small amounts of marijuana to be a criminal offense [7/86].*
- *Ninety-two percent approved of Bernhardt Goetz's type of vigilantism when he shot four teenagers who demanded money from him on a New York City subway; 72% favored mandatory death penalties [4/87]; and 51% thought that the police should be able to search the houses of well-known drug dealers without a court order [4/87].*

Labor unions continued their long decline. In August 1981, the Professional Air Traffic Controllers Organization (PATCO) went on strike. Reagan ordered them back to work and fired over 11,000 controllers who ignored his order. This destroyed the union.

- *Forty-two percent (44%, 14%) thought the government should not rehire the controllers even if it took more than a year to bring air traffic back to normal [7/81]; 59% thought that labor unions had too much power; but 67% believed unions were necessary to protect workers [4/87].*

Reagan supported amnesty for illegal immigrants who put down roots. In November 1986, he signed a law that gave amnesty to many illegal immigrants in return for stronger laws. Many of the new laws targeted employers who employed illegal immigration.

- *Forty-one percent (51%, 7%) approved of illegal immigrants obtaining residency status if they had been here for more than seven years and 79% wanted to make it against the law to hire someone who came into the United States illegally [10/83].*

RACE

A lot of the racial politics of the 1980s revolved around Jesse Jackson's run for the 1984 and 1988 democratic presidential nominations. Jackson tried to mobilize racial minorities and progressives into the Rainbow Coalition. He received 18% of the primary votes in 1984 and won eleven states in 1988 with 21% of the vote. His running galvanized the African American community, and many became active in electoral politics.

- *In March 1988, 53% of Americans had a favorable opinion of Jesse Jackson; 60% thought of him as a champion of social justice; 49% that he would represent all Americans; 72% that he is honest and sincere; 39% that he could improve economic conditions for people like me; 39% that he could deal effectively with foreign leaders like Gorbachev; 34% that he can manage the federal government; and 41% that his attitudes are too extreme.*

- *A series of survey questions showed how support for racial equality, at least in the abstract, continued to grow. However, there was little support for the implementation of some concrete policies to implement these principles.[8] Only 15% thought that private clubs should be able to exclude prospective members because of their race; 91% agreed that everyone should have equal opportunity to succeed; only 25% said they have little in common with people of other races [5/88]; and 50% now believed it was OK for blacks and whites to date each other [1/89]. However, 45% thought we had gone too far in pushing for equality [5/88]; only 24% agreed that in order to make up for past discrimination, blacks should be given preferential treatment [4/87]; and 26% supported busing for racial integration [9/82].*

SEX AND GENDER

In June 1981, five homosexual men were diagnosed with a rare form of pneumonia, which was later found out to be AIDS. It was initially called gay-related immune deficiency (GRID), which parts of the media characterized as the "gay disease." In 1982, the CDC renamed it AIDS and in 1983 Robert Gallo and Luc Montagnier isolated the HIV virus. In 1981, there were 234 known deaths from AIDS in the United States. This had increased to 18,447 in 1990 and 41,920 in 1993. By 2000, the number of annual deaths had declined to 14,499. The first effective drug against HIV (AZT) was approved by the FDA in March 1987.

Many in the gay community initially discounted the epidemic, stating it was a conspiracy to stop gay culture. However, a gay-led political movement soon coalesced to educate their own community and to pressure the government for more research and expanded medical care.[9] Many Republicans initially opposed government help, believing HIV/AIDS was an immoral disease. Reagan barely mentioned the disease until 1987 after his Hollywood friend, Rock Hudson, died from AIDS and several other Hollywood celebrities such as Elizabeth Taylor and Joan Rivers spoke out. His surgeon general, C. Everett Koop, went against Reagan by publicly speaking out, advocating the use of condoms, rejecting mandatory testing, and sending out an information packet to every household.

Attitudes toward HIV and gays affected one another. There was substantial fear and misinformation about AIDS which went hand-in-hand with the anti-gay attitudes held by many. Jerry Falwell, of the Moral Majority, said, "AIDS is not just God's punishment for homosexuals, it is God's punishment for the society that tolerates homosexuals."

- *Gallup first asked about AIDS in June 1983: 77% of the sample had heard of the disease and 43% of those said they thought it would reach epidemic proportions.*
- *In August 1985, only 4% said they knew someone who had AIDS, but 42% said they were worried that they or someone they knew would come down with the disease.*
- *Fear of AIDS was such that, if there was a student with AIDS in their child's school, 17% said they would fight to have the child removed from the school, 8% said they*

would keep their children home, and another 26% said they would instruct their child not to have contact with the infected child. Only 30% said they would not worry [8/85].
- In November 1986, 49% believed that AIDS was causing unfair discrimination against gays [11/86].
- In April 1987, 40% wanted to limit people with AIDS from public spaces and 44% thought AIDS was God's punishment for immoral sexual behavior.
- In October 1987, most people knew that you could get AIDS from: sharing hypodermic needles (97%); sexual contact with same sex (96%); sexual contact with opposite sex (88%); and blood transfusions (86%). However, 26% thought you could get AIDS from a drinking glass or toilet seat (18%).
- In January 1989, 51% said we were spending too little money (6% too much, 33% about right, 10% DK) on AIDS and in October 1989, 58% said they would be willing to pay $100 a year more in taxes for research on AIDS.
- Sixty-three percent said they had received Surgeon General Koop's brochure on AIDS and 32% said they had read it [7/88].
- Many did not support gays having rights. Fifty-one percent (42%, 7%) thought that school boards should "have the right to fire teachers who are known homosexuals" [4/87]; only 44% thought that homosexual relations between two consenting adults should be legal [11/85]; and only 29% would vote for a homosexual for president [4/83].
- In July 1983, 24% said they had a friend who was homosexual, and 65% thought homosexuals should have equal job opportunities.

In July 1981, President Reagan nominated the first woman to the US Supreme Court, Sandra Day O'Connor, and Sally Ride became the first woman in space aboard the space shuttle Challenger (1983).[10] Additionally, girls' participation in sports continued to grow.

- There were mixed opinions about which high-school sports teams should allow girls to join the boy's teams (tennis—85%; swimming—79%; track—68%; baseball—48%; basketball—40%; football—16%; and wrestling—11%) [5/85].
- Eighty-six percent of Americans approved of O'Connor's appointment to the Supreme Court [7/81].

THE ECONOMY

Reagan's economic policies (known as Reaganomics or supply-side economics) were centered on reducing taxes (especially for the wealthy and corporations) and government regulations. His stated desire to reduce government expenditures and debt went by the wayside when military expenditures increased from $267 billion in 1980 to $383 billion in 1988. Public debt increased from $712 billion in 1980 to $2.05 trillion in 1988. Also, during his presidency there was a major recession in

1982, a modest increase in median family income, and an increased growth of income inequality.

- *Reagan's economic policies were not initially popular. Sixty-nine percent believed that Reagan's tax cuts would mostly benefit the upper class [8/81]; only 41% approved of his handling of the economy [1/82]; and in April 1982, 50% thought the recession was getting worse (30% recovery, 16% the same).*
- *On policy issues: Americans were divided over whether greater attention should be paid to curbing inflation or dealing with unemployment (49% v. 44% [1/82]); 74% wanted a constitutional amendment requiring a balanced budget [9/82]; and only 18% wanted to raise taxes in order to reduce the deficit [1/83]. However, 53% were willing to have an increase in the gas tax of 5 cents a gallon to repair the roads [11/82].*
- *As the United States came out of the recession, 51% approved of Reagan on the economy [3/85], but 61% said the federal deficits were a "serious" problem [11/85].*

Ronald Reagan was famous for denouncing welfare and "welfare queens." Many Americans were sympathetic with his perspective.

- *Sixty-nine percent wanted their state to enact legislation requiring people on welfare who cannot find work to have some type of public service or non-profit job without additional pay [11/85]; and 63% said "welfare benefits make poor people dependent and encourage them to stay poor" [8/89].*
- *On the other hand, 53% agreed that the government should help needy people, even if the government went deeper into debt and 62% agreed that "the government should guarantee every citizen enough to eat and a place to sleep" [4/87].*

One of the effects of deregulation was the savings and loan crisis. Many saving and loans associations were losing money because they were paying a higher rate for deposits than they were charging for loans. Many turned to speculation. The best-known instance involved the 1989 failure of Lincoln Savings and Loans (S&L). Charles Keating, its president, was eventually convicted of fraud, racketeering, and conspiracy. Three US senators (part of the Keating five) received formal reprimands from the Senate for improperly interfering in the investigation by the Federal Home Loan Bank Board (FHLBB). The bailouts of the S&Ls cost US taxpayers around $200 billion.

- *Most Americans (73%) identified S&L institutions for being in the news because of bankruptcy issues and 63% said they had less confidence in the financial stability of banks compared to a year ago [1/89]. However, 63% believed the government would step in to guarantee the depositors of these banks.*

In the 1980s the first minivan was introduced (Dodge Caravan—1983), McDonalds introduced the McNugget (1983), the Bell System was broken up into seven independent companies (1984), and the first Starbuck's opened (1987), as well as the first Walmart store (1989).

SCIENCE, TECHNOLOGY, AND THE ENVIRONMENT

The 1980s was a decade of the personal computer, seeing the launches of the IBM PC (1981), IBM XT (with a 10 MG hard drive 1983), Lotus 1-2-3 (1983), Apple Macintosh (1984), and Windows 1.0 (1985). The first Internet virus also arrived— the Morris worm—in 1988. Other electronics that were introduced included the Sony Walkman Radio (1980), Pacman for arcades (1982), GPS systems were made available for civilian use (1983), the first transatlantic fiber optic cable was completed (1988), and Nintendo released the Gameboy (1989).

- *Seventy-two percent said the good effects of computers outweigh the bad effects (3/85-Roper). However, only 35% (45%, 20%) thought that new industries would find enough jobs for those displaced by the disruption in technology [1/86—Cambridge].*
- *Roper asked about the dangers of people at home hacking of computers at corporations and government. Only 25% said it would grow and become a danger, 27% said it would only happen in rare instances, and 35% said it would quickly stop (13% did not know) [9/83].*
- *In June 1987, 16% of Americans used a personal computer at home and 33% at work.*
- *Americans were still optimistic about science. In January 1981, 58% said that science would generally help mankind and not harm (16%, 22% both, 4% [CARA]) and 32% wanted to have the government spend more on scientific research and 55% said the same amount (9%, 4% [1/89]).*

In January 1986, the space shuttle Challenger disintegrated after launch, killing all seven astronauts. This resulted in a thirty-two-month suspension of shuttle flights. The Rogers Commission (1987) found that NASA had a culture of complacency and had ignored warnings.

- *Eighty percent said they had followed the disaster very closely and 38% said they were very confident (41% fair amount) that accidents like this could be prevented in the future [7/86].*
- *Market Opinion Research found 89% wanted to continue with manned space shuttle flights [8/86] and NBC/Wall Street Journal reported only 11% advocated discontinuing the program [6/86].*

Several environmental crises became evident in the 1980s. In the late 1970s, a variety of studies came out which showed that the release of chlorofluorocarbons (CFCs), which are most used in air conditioning and aerosol sprays, was depleting the ozone layer in the Antarctic. Scientists said that this would result in increased ultraviolet lights exposure and hence more skin cancers and other negative environmental effects. After a 1986 EPA report, under the Reagan administration, stated that there could be 800,000 cancer deaths in the United States in the next eighty-eight years, an international agreement to reduce CFC production 50% by 1999 was approved by most nations of the world. In June 1988, James Hansen from NASA testified in the senate that man-made global warming had begun because of the release of CO_2 and other greenhouse gases. His testimony was seminal in that it was the first Congressional testimony on this issue and was widely publicized.

- *Eighty-four percent of Americans said they were aware of scientists' concerns about the ozone layer [4/88]. Cambridge Energy Research Associates found 86% favored "banning all spray cans using fluorocarbons that hurt the ozone layer" [12/89].*[11]
- *In November 1989, 61% expected major changes in the Earth's climate by the year 2000.*

Another disaster in technology was the meltdown of a nuclear reactor at the Chernobyl power plant in Ukraine (at that time part of the USSR). The April 1986 catastrophe resulted in thirty-one immediate deaths and an estimated 4,000 deaths over time because of radiation poisoning. Some 350,000 people were forced to relocate. The last undamaged reactor at the complex was shut down in 2000 when a deal was reached with the international community. Many other nuclear reactors around the world increased their safety standards and others were shut down or not built.

- *Gallup found 80% were closely following the Chernobyl story [7/86] and 54% said they were worried a great deal (24% a fair amount) about radioactive contamination of soil [5/89].*
- *ABC News found 58% said the Chernobyl accident made them more fearful about other similar accidents happening [4/86].*
- *Most Americans were supportive of efforts to clean the environment.*[12] *Less than half (45%) wanted to reduce environmental regulations [9/82].*
- *In August 1980, 42% wanted to build more nuclear power plants and only about one-third (34%) wanted to relax pollution controls to reduce costs to industry [9/84]. In fact, 62% (28%, 10%) said they favored prioritizing the environment over economic growth [9/84]; 73% said we should use fewer pesticides and chemicals on food even if that caused prices to rise [3/89]; and 79% favored a ban on chlorofluorocarbons to protect the ozone layer even if that resulted in higher prices [5/89].*
- *On the other hand, 48% (39%, 13%) favored easing restrictions on strip mining to get more coal [6/81] and allowing more oil exploration on federal lands (76%). Clearly, there was a disconnect between awareness of the problem and the policies necessary to fix it.*

Finally, in March 1989, the Exxon Valdez supertanker struck a reef and over ten million gallons of crude oil spilled into Prince William Sound, Alaska. The environmental impact was devastating for birds, fish, and other wildlife. A jury said Exxon had to pay $5 billion in punitive damages. Over a series of appeals, this was reduced to about $500 million.

- *A large number (89%) said they had been closely following the Exxon Valdez story and 48% of those said they would be willing to boycott Exxon because of Exxon's record on the environment [3/89]. In a Harris survey, 84% said the accident was very serious, but 42% gave Exxon good grades on paying for the cost of the cleanup [5/89].*

POPULAR TRENDS

Movies that came out in the 1980s included: *Indiana Jones and the Raiders of the Lost Ark* (1981); *Tootsie* (1982); *E.T.: The Extra-Terrestrial* (1982-seen by 24%); *Ghostbusters* (1984); *Beverly Hills Cop* (1984); *Indiana Jones and the Temple of Doom* (1984); *Back to the Future* (1985); *Top Gun* (1986); *Crocodile Dundee* (1986); *Three Men and a Baby* (1987); *Fatal Attraction* (1987); *Rain Man* (1988); *The Little Mermaid* (1989); and *Batman* (1989).

Cable TV continued to grow. CNN was launched in 1980 followed by MTV and the Weather Channel in 1982. Memorable TV events included the last episode of *M*A*S*H*, the most-watched television episode in history (1983); the first episode of *Wheel of Fortune* (1983); the syndication of *The Oprah Winfrey Show* (1986); and the first *Seinfeld* and *The Simpsons* episodes (1989). Other TV programs that premiered were: *Hill Street Blues* (1981); *Cheers* (1982); *Late Night with David Letterman* (1982); *The Cosby Show* (1984); and *The Golden Girls* (1985).

- *Americans watched a lot of television (median of 3.0 hours) [5/83].*
- *In February 1989, 63% of households had a video cassette recorder.*
- *In 1980, 28% of households that had televisions used cable. By the end of the decade this had increased to 57%.*

Some of the more important books that came out in the 1980s were: Carl Sagan, *Cosmos* (1980); Robert Ludlum, *The Bourne Identity* (1980); Jane Fonda, *The Jane Fonda Workout Book* (1982); Umberto Eco, *The Name of the Rose* (1983); Stephen King, *Pet Sematary* (1983); Lee Iacocca, *Iacocca* (1984); Garrison Keller, *Lake Wobegon Days* (1985); Tom Clancy, *Red Storm Rising* (1986); Scott Turow, *Presumed Innocent* (1987); Tom Wolfe, *Bonfire of the Vanities* (1988); Donald Trump, *The Art of the Deal* (1988); and Stephen Hawking, *A Brief History of Time* (1988).

- *Americans claimed to be readers. Seventy percent said they read a book all the way through in the previous month [2/89].*

There were a lot of memorable events in the music industry. Michael Jackson released *Thriller* in 1982, the biggest selling album of all time. Rock and roll began to show some philanthropic tendencies, with Live Aid concerts in 1985 raising around $100 million for famine relief in Ethiopia. In December 1980, former Beatle John Lennon was assassinated outside his apartment in New York City by Mark David Chapman. New musical genres include hip-hop, electronic rock, and new wave. Other musicians who came to prominence were: Prince, Madonna (who used music videos as a marketing tool and was the more successful female star of the 1980s), U2, Bruce Springsteen, Phil Collins, Elton John, Billy Joel, Lionel Richie, Tina Turner, John Cougar Mellencamp, Bon Jovie, Foreigner, Talking Heads, and Guns & Roses.

- *In a Roper survey, 93% could identify Michael Jackson [5/84]. Roper found that 28% had closely followed the assassination of John Lennon [1/81].*
- *Seventy-three percent had heard of the Live Aid Concert and 90% said its impact would be positive [USA Today 7/85].*
- *Americans were eclectic in their music tastes. When asked in June 1983 (Roper) what music they often listened to, the responses were: country/Western (48%); easy listening music (44%); soft rock (33%); popular vocalists (28%); big band music (26%); jazz (23%); gospel music (23%); country rock (23%); hymns, other religious music (22%); symphony (20%); folk music (19%); show tunes (17%); hard rock (16%); disco (14%); soul (13%); chamber music (9%); new wave (9%); opera (7%); reggae (6%); and Latin music (6%).*
- *Harris [3/87] asked whether people participated in cultural activities (once in a while), such as: going to live theater performances—not counting those of your own children (65%); attending popular musical performances (57%); doing photography (51%); doing needlepoint, weaving, or other handwork (41%); playing a musical instrument (30%); going to live opera or classical musical performances (27%); writing stories or poems (24%); performing one's own dance or ballet (23%); singing in a choir or other choral group (22%); attending live concerts (19%); making sculpture or working with clay (8%); or working with a local theater group (6%).*
- *In another question, Roper asked about other cultural activities respondents had engaged in within the previous twelve months, such as visiting a science or natural history museum (44%); or an art museum (55%); or a history museum or historical site (54%).*

Perhaps the most memorable sports moment in the 1980s was the US Olympic hockey team defeating the Soviet Union in the Winter Olympics (February 1980).[13]

- *Football continued to grow in popularity as 41% said it was their favorite sport to watch on TV compared to 17% for baseball and 9% for basketball [1/81].*
- *Americans participated in a variety of sports within a one-year period (swimming 41%; bicycling 33%; fishing 30%; camping 23%; jogging 22%; bowling 21%; aerobics-dancercise 20%; weight training 19%; billards 18%; softball 18%;*

calisthenics 15%; motorboating 14%; volleyball 14%; baseball 13%; hunting 13%; basketball 13%; golf 12%; ping-pong 12%; tennis 11%; and canoing-rowing 10%) [11/84].

Newspapers continued to lose influence, and distrust of the media was growing.

- *Only 27% said newspapers were their main source of news compared to 53% who mentioned TV [7/84]. In fact, 71% of respondents said they regularly watched the network news [4/87].*
- *Nevertheless, newspapers were still a big part of Americans' lives, with 66% saying they read a newspaper every day [4/87].*
- *When asked whether news organizations generally got their facts straight or were often inaccurate, a plurality thought the news was inaccurate (48%, 44%, 8% [1/88]).*
- *Furthermore, when asked whether "news organizations deal fairly with all sides or [if] they tend to favor one side," only 30% (59%, 11%) thought the news organizations were unbiased [1/88].*
- *Only 32% rated the honesty and ethical standards of TV reporters and commentators as high or very high; newspaper reporters fared even worse, receiving only 26% of respondents' trust [5/83].*

CONCLUDING COMMENTS

Military spending increased, Reagan tried to undo the New Deal, AIDS emerged, and personal electronics ruled.

The American hostages held by Iran were freed on Carter's last day in office. The Iran-Iraq War, the Soviet-instigated coup in Afghanistan, Israel's invasion of Lebanon, and the forced American evacuation from Lebanon guaranteed that the Mideast would remain in the spotlight over the course of the decade. With US involvement in El Salvador and Nicaragua, Latin America became a political hotspot. The decade ended with the start of reforms in Eastern Europe and the fall of the Berlin Wall.

After Vietnam, Americans were wary of foreign interventions abroad, but were in favor of increased military spending. Most opposed military aid to El Salvador, involvement in Nicaragua, or using US troops as peacekeepers in Lebanon. Most were supportive and optimistic of reforms in Russia under Gorbachev.

Ronald Reagan tried to undo the New Deal ideology of the 1930s. He wanted to reduce the role of government, and his administration radically reduced taxes on corporations and wealthy individuals. Crime and crack cocaine were high on his agenda and the prison population increased by 78% under his administration.

Most Americans supported reducing the role of government and favored many of the conservative talking points ranging from prayer in the public schools to creationism. Fear of crime helped advance the Reagan agenda. Reagan used antiwelfare attitudes (often linked with race) to argue for reductions in nonmilitary government spending.

Jesse Jackson's political campaigns created a transition from civil rights protest to electoral politics as a perceived means of change. This would have long-term consequences in the elections of thousands of minorities to local offices and eventually into the White House. Support for racial equality continued to rise. There was now little support for private clubs excluding blacks, and there was more support for equality in employment, as well as support for interracial marriage.

AIDS was the dominant concern among the gay community in this decade. Protests over lack of resources dedicated to research and treatment had a big impact and educated future LGBT activists on how to demand their rights. Early in the epidemic, there was tremendous fear and misinformation about HIV/AIDS and gays. Over the course of the decade, anti-gay sentiment and irrational fear of HIV slowly declined.

The structure of the economy continued to change with the introduction of minivans, McNuggets, the IBM PC, and the Sony Walkman. Americans were beginning to use personal computers and were excited about the forthcoming computer revolution.

Disasters and almost-disasters also occurred: the crash of the space shuttle Challenger, the sinking of the supertanker Exxon Valdez off the coast of Alaska, the meltdown of a nuclear reactor at Chernobyl, and the effect of CFCs on the ozone layer. Most Americans now favored phasing out CFCs, were more wary of nuclear reactors, and became more supportive of efforts to clean up the environment. However, most opposed restrictions on coal.

[The reader can find relevant crosstabs and discussion in the online appendix located at https://rowman.com/ISBN/9781793653505/US-Public-Opinion-since-the-1930s-Galluping-through-History.]

NOTES

1. See Aleksievich (1992) for a disturbing collection of oral interviews with Soviet soldiers (and their relatives) who fought in Afghanistan.

2. When I later run crosstabs on the United States' aid to Afghan rebels, I use the Yankelovich data since the Gallup data was not available.

3. The FSLN had overthrown the Somoza regime in July 1979.

4. Solidarity was a nationalist, pro-Western trade union led by Lech Wałęsa.

5. On June 12, 1987, Reagan made a speech in West Berlin, stating: "Mr. Gorbachev, open this gate. Mr. Gorbachev, tear down this wall!"

6. Frank (2007) argues that conservatives were able to get many Americans to vote against their own economic interests by focusing on these cultural issues.

7. Crack cocaine was mostly used by blacks (79% of those convicted for crack cocaine offenses were black compared to 28% for powder cocaine offenses). Blacks received far harsher sentences for drugs that were equally dangerous. This disparity in sentencing was not eliminated until the Fair Sentencing Act of 2010.

8. Kinder and Sears (1981) discuss how principles and policies can disagree in their discussion of symbolic racism.

9. For a wonderful cultural/political history of this era, see Shilts (2011).

10. Eighty-one percent said Sally Ride proved that women could do as well as men (was not an exception) in jobs requiring complex skills [6/83-Merit].

11. For a wonderful PBS documentary on how scientists convinced politicians to treat the ozone layer issue as a priority, see *Ozone Hole: How We Saved the Planet* (2019).

12. Upon becoming president, Reagan tore out the solar panels at the White House installed by Jimmy Carter and cut solar research by 2/3. NBC found of the 78% who heard of Reagan's economic proposals, only 31% (56%, 13%) supported Reagan's cut to solar research [4/81].

13. I was not able to find any question that asked about this victory by any survey organization. The movie, *Miracle*, came out in 2004.

7

The 1990s

The Collapse of the Soviet Union and Yugoslavia, the First Gulf War, the Genocide in Rwanda, Bill Clinton, and the Rise of the Internet

In the 1990s, telephone surveys eclipsed other modes of surveys (94%); however, the increasing nonresponse rates associated with these surveys may have affected their quality (Curtin, Presser, and Singer, 2005).[1] The increasing nonresponse was driven by new technology such as answering machines and caller ID as well as the growth of telemarketing. Gallup still accounted for about one-quarter (28%) of all national surveys archived at the Roper Center. Survey centers (PSRA, Chilton, ICR, Hart-Teeter, Gordon Black) started to take more market share.

WORLD EVENTS

The USSR (Russia) and Europe

Gaining momentum from the fall of the Berlin Wall and major dissent in other Soviet republics, the disintegration of the Soviet Union continued apace. Virtually all of the republics of the Soviet Union (Ukraine, Tajikistan, Belarus, Estonia, etc.) had rebellions in 1990 and 1991. In December 1991, 90% of the Ukraine voted for independence, and by the end of that month, Moscow had granted independence to all fifteen republics, Mikhail Gorbachev had resigned, and Boris Yeltsin had become president of the Russian Federation. For Russia, the 1990s were marked by widespread corruption and economic and social upheaval, with a small number of oligarchs taking control of most of the economy. Vladimir Putin became acting president in 1999.[2]

- *Support for NATO fell, with 54% (34%, 12%) of respondents favoring a 50% reduction of US troops in NATO [5/91].*

- *In fact, 62% of respondents thought relations with the Soviet Union were getting better and 54% approved of giving food aid to Russia [7/91]. Furthermore, 74% had a favorable opinion of Gorbachev [7/91] and 53% thought the Cold War was over [8/91].*

European integration accelerated during this decade. East and West Germany merged in October 1990.

- *Given World War II, 33% of Americans said they were very fearful of the reunification of Germany, 50% said fairly fearful, and just 10% said they were not worried [2/90].*

Yugoslavia, under the leadership of Josip Tito, had been aligned with the Soviet Union following World War II, but by 1948 a major split occurred between Tito and Stalin after which Yugoslavia became a nonaligned socialist country. Yugoslavia consisted of a federation of groups and ethnicities that had either been countries in the past or wanted now to gain statehood: Croatia, Serbia, Bosnia and Herzegovina, Macedonia, Montenegro, and Slovenia. With the death of Tito in 1980, the federation began to break up.[3] A complicated series of wars began in 1991, lasting until 2001. War crimes were committed by many of the participants and an estimated 140,000 people died. Serbia was accused of committing most of the massacres. NATO forces (mostly the United States) bombed Serbian forces in 1995 following massacres in Bosnia and Herzegovina, and again in 1999 after atrocities against the Albanian population in Kosovo. A peace treaty was negotiated under US auspices in Dayton, Ohio, in December 1995 ending the fighting in Bosnia and Herzegovina; another agreement was signed in March 1990 ending the fighting in Kosovo (the Rambouillet Accords).

- *Americans were, at best, ambivalent about US intervention in the wars in the old Yugoslavia. In August 1992, when asked what should be done to stop the fighting in Bosnia, 13% favored supporting UN air attacks on Serbian forces, 6% supported ground offensives, 34% said both, 35% neither, and 12% did not know. Forty-three percent (43%, 14%) agreed that the United States "cannot stand by and let rival ethnic forces eradicate one another."*
- *As peace agreements were discussed, only 40% of Americans favored sending up to 20,000 US troops as part of a UN peace-keeping force [10/93].*
- *After air strikes began, 65% said they favored the strikes and 41% favored sending in US troops if air strikes did not work [4/94].*
- *When Clinton finally agreed to send US troops to Bosnia as part of the international peace-keeping force following the 1995 Dayton treaty, only 33% of Americans were in favor of sending the troops and another 27% wanted to provide other types of support instead [12/95].*
- *By January 1998, 53% (43%, 5%) supported the presence of US troops in Bosnia. Following Serbian atrocities in Kosovo, 53% favored US air strikes against Serbia*

as part of the NATO reaction, but only 39% wanted to use US ground troops [3/99].
- When the 1999 Rambouillet Accords were signed, 65% (14%, 21%) favored the agreement and 69% favored keeping US troops as peacekeepers in Kosovo [6/99].
- When asked whether US troops should be used more to stop human rights atrocities such as ethnic cleansing, 24% said use more, 43% the same amount, 29% less, and 4% did not know [6/99].

Following World War II, many believed the best way to avoid another war in Europe as well as how to counter the influence of the Soviet Union was to foster the integration of all the countries in Europe. Many steps were taken toward integration and in 1957 the Treaty of Rome set up the European Economic Community (EEC), which worked to bring about economic integration in Europe. The European Union (EU) was formally established in 1993 following the Maastricht Treaty of 1991. The EU allowed for the free movement of goods, capital, and people across the fifteen countries and had a common external tariff. The EU also began the process of political integration with common practices for agriculture, transportation, and economic standards. One indicator of the success of European integration was the opening of the Chunnel in 1993—a tunnel linking France and England. In January 1999, the Euro was established, replacing almost all European currencies.

- *To the extent that Americans paid attention to Western European economic integration, most thought it would be good for the United States (48%, 28%, 24%) [10/90]. Furthermore, 52% believed Common Market trade policies were fair toward the United States [6/93].*

Rwanda and South Africa

Other, even more brutal atrocities occurred in Rwanda during the civil war (1990–1994) between the Hutu-led government and a rebel force of mostly Tutsi refugees—the Rwandan Patriotic Front (RPF). A ceasefire and power-sharing arrangement was signed in 1993 but was opposed by many in the Hutu Government. President Juvénal Habyarimana, who negotiated the agreement, was killed when his plane was shot down in April 1994. Genocidal killings began the next day against Tutsi and Hutu moderates. Approximately 800,000 Rwandans (mostly Tutsi) were killed in 100 days. Western countries were criticized for doing nothing to try to stop this genocide (especially when compared to reacting to atrocities committed by Serbia).[4] The RPF fought back and by July had defeated the Hutu-led government.

- *Gallup asked no questions about what to do about Rwanda. A Time/CNN poll found 45% (41%, 14%) favored using US troops as part of a UN mission to stop the violence and only 34% said the United States should do more to stop the violence [5/94]. It is clear why Clinton was reluctant to intervene.*

South Africa had instituted apartheid in 1948, a system under which the minority whites (19%) had the complete economic and political control. Blacks were forcibly moved to "tribal lands" or other segregated areas, non-whites were not allowed to vote, and marriage, education, and economic life was segregated. Resistance movements at home and international condemnation abroad led to the 1990 release of Nelson Mandela from prison, the repeal of apartheid, and Nelson Mandela winning the presidency in 1994 at the head of the African National Congress (ANC).

- *In February 1990, 65% of Americans said their sympathies were with blacks in South Africa and 15% sympathized with the whites (20% said both, neither, or did not know).*[5]
- *Only 38% wanted the United States to apply more pressure on South Africa to end apartheid.*[6] *However, 57% supported the divestment campaign to pressure South Africa [2/90-Harris].*
- *Mandela visited the United States in June of 1990 and 64% (27%, 9%) had a positive view of him; although 50% said they were concerned about his radical past [6/90-Harris].*

The Gulf War

In August 1990, Iraq, under the leadership of Saddam Hussein, invaded and occupied Kuwait. Iraq was heavily in debt following its war with Iran and accused Kuwait of exceeding its OPEC quota—thus lowering worldwide oil prices. Iraq also claimed that some of Kuwait's land was actually Iraqi. President George H. W. Bush mounted a coalition of 28 countries and 670,000 troops to forestall an Iraqi invasion of Saudi Arabia and to eventually force Iraq out of Kuwait. The coalition was under the auspices of the UN. The air war began in January 1991 and was followed by a ground war in February. Iraqi forces were decimated, and Iraq accepted a UN ceasefire on March 3. The US suffered 148 combat deaths and it is estimated that over 20,000 Iraqi soldiers died. There was some controversy as the coalition forces did not try to remove Hussein from power. There was further controversy when coalition forces did nothing to stop Hussein from squashing a popular uprising in Southern Iraq that ended with over 10,000 people being killed and over a million displaced.

- *United States involvement with the Gulf War was fairly popular.*[7] *Seventy-eight percent approved of sending troops to Saudi Arabia [8/90] immediately after the invasion. Although this had declined to 64% just before the air war began [1/91], 81% favored the decision to go to war once hostilities began [1/91].*
- *Two noteworthy findings were that 45% (45%, 10%) of Americans favored using nuclear weapons against Iraq if it would save US lives [1/91], and that 31% wanted to outlaw peaceful demonstrations in the United States while the troops were fighting [1/91].*
- *After the war ended, 72% thought it was worth going to war and 56% said we should have continued until Saddam Hussein was removed from power [4/91].*

US Military Involvement Elsewhere

The United States invaded Panama in December 1989 to depose General Manuel Noriega, who was accused of corruption and stealing the election of 1989. His supporters said he was deposed for standing up to the United States. He was captured, flown to the United States, and convicted of drug trafficking and money laundering. Twenty-three US servicemen were killed during the invasion and around 1,000 Panamanians.

- *Eighty-two percent of respondents approved of the invasion [1/90-ABC/WPost], and forty-nine percent rated the actual invasion as excellent or good (40%, 11%) [10/90].*

In 1976, a military coup in Somalia led to a socialist government there led by Mohamed Siad Barre. Somalia deteriorated because of a war with Ethiopia and economic mismanagement, resulting in the collapse of the Barre Government in 1991. The UN sent troops to prevent a civil war between warring factions. In the Battle of Mogadishu (1993), Somali militia shot down two UH-60 Black Hawk helicopters and in the ongoing battle, eighteen American soldiers were killed and seventy-three were wounded.[8] UN troops withdrew in March 1995 as the country descended into anarchy.

- *Most (74%) Americans supported the use of US troops to help deliver UN relief supplies in Somalia [12/92]; however, only 31% also wanted troops to attempt to bring a permanent end to the fighting in Somalia.*
- *When US troops were used in a UN military operation against a Somali warlord, 65% (23%, 12%) approved [6/93].*
- *In September 1993, only 39% (57%, 5%) wanted US troops to remain in Somalia as part of the UN peace-keeping mission. But, when Clinton proposed doubling the number of US troops in Somalia (supposedly to protect other US troops) 55% supported this decision [10/93].*

Following the Soviet Union evacuating its troops from Afghanistan in 1989, the country slid into chaos. In September 1996, the Taliban captured the capital city of Kabul. The Taliban was extreme in its interpretation of Sharia law. For example, most sports were outlawed, men were required to wear beards, thieves had their hands amputated, and women were prohibited from working or wearing Western clothes. The Taliban allied with Al Qaeda and Osama bin Laden moved to Afghanistan in 1996. In August 1998, Al Qaeda sponsored suicide truck bombings at two US embassies, killing over 200 people, including 12 Americans, in Nairobi, Kenya, and in Dar es Salaam, Tanzania. In retaliation, Clinton ordered cruise missile attacks against targets in Sudan and Afghanistan. In retrospect, the missile attack in Afghanistan had very limited effectiveness and the target of the strike in Sudan was a supposed chemical weapons factory, but, in fact, turned out to be a factory for pharmaceutical drugs.

- *Three-quarters of Americans supported these retaliatory strikes immediately after they occurred [8/98]. One interesting finding was that 45% (38%, 17%) believed the United States had a vital interest in Afghanistan [10/98].*

Americans were ambivalent about the use of US troops in other situations, such as the military coup in Haiti against the democratically elected government of Jean-Bertrand Aristide, or the ongoing tensions between North and South Korea.

- *Following the military coup in Haiti only 27% wanted to send US troops if economic sanctions did not work [10/93].*
- *Attitudes of Americans on North Korea were confusing. Only 31% favored using US troops if North Korea invaded the South. However, 59% were in favor of US military action if it appeared that North Korea was developing an atomic bomb [11/93].*

The Mideast

Optimism about peace in the Mideast was rampant in September 1993 when Israel and the Palestinian Liberation Organization signed what became known as the Oslo Accords. Secret negotiation in Oslo led to an accord being signed under the auspices of Bill Clinton that called for the Palestinian National Authority to govern the West Bank and Gaza and the PLO renouncing violence. Furthermore, the Israelis would withdraw from Gaza and parts of the West Bank. It was expected that further negotiations would lead to a Palestinian state following agreement on what to do about Jerusalem, refugees, borders, and settlements. In July 1994, Israel signed a peace treaty with Jordan. The Israeli Prime Minister at the time the Accords were signed, Yitzhak Rabin,[9] was assassinated in November 1995 by an Israeli opponent of the Oslo Accords. His death made it far more difficult for Israel and the Palestinians to negotiate further agreements. The Likud Party, led by Benjamin Netanyahu, came to power following elections in May 1996.

- *Before the Olso Accords, 59% of Americans said they favored Israel in the conflict (17% Palestinians, 23% both or neither) and 46% favored the formation of a Palestinian state (31%, 23%) [3/91].*
- *However, 47% thought Israel had too much power over US policy (with 6% saying not enough, 36% about right, and 11% having no opinion) [9/91].*
- *Eighty percent (12%, 9%) supported the peace agreement in the Oslo Accords, but only 49% thought it was likely it would lead to a permanent peace [9/93].*

India conducted its first nuclear weapons test in 1974. In May 1998, they conducted a series of five tests. In the same month, several weeks after India's test, Pakistan also tested five nuclear weapons. Since Pakistan and India had wars in 1947, 1965, 1971 and has skirmished numerous times in recent years, some believe that their conflict is the world's most likely to trigger a nuclear war.

- *In June 1998, 43% believed that Pakistan's possession of nuclear weapons posed a serious threat to the United States and 47% said this about India.*

US POLITICS

In November 1992, Governor Bill Clinton of Arkansas defeated George H. W. Bush to become the 42nd President of the United States. Clinton received 43.0% of the vote, Bush 37.5%, and 3rd party candidate Ross Perot 18.9% In 1996, with 49.2% of the vote, Clinton won reelection in 1996 against Republican Bob Dole with 40.7% and Ross Perot with 8.4%.

In the mid-term elections of 1994, Republicans captured both the House and Senate under the leadership of Newt Gingrich of Georgia. Gingrich's "Contract with America" became the blueprint for conservative ideals and led to an ongoing set of battles between congressional Republicans and Clinton. Gingrich was censured by the House and fined $300,000 for ethics violations concerning money he took for teaching a college course. He resigned following the 1998 mid-term elections after the Republicans did worse than expected.

- *In November 1994, respondents were asked whether they supported individual proposals within the Republican Contract with America: 85% wanted a balanced budget Constitutional Amendment; 77% a line-item veto; 88% tougher anti-crime legislation; 79% legislation limiting welfare payments; 42% an increase in defense spending; 83% a cut in taxes for most Americans; 41% legislation preventing US troops from serving under commanders of the UN; and 58% a cut in the capital gains tax.*
- *Overall, of the 34% who had heard of the contract, 56% (24%, 21%) supported it [11/94]. However, in January 1997, 57% thought that Gingrich's ethical violations were important indicators of his character.*

Clinton made the decision to appear as a "centrist." He supported the death penalty, increased incarceration, which resulted in many more people of color going to prison, and curtailing welfare. During his 1992 candidacy, he famously criticized rap singer Sister Souljah about comments she made about the LA riots. The polling data below provide the context of why Clinton felt the need to "tack to the right" on these issues.

- *Fifty percent of Americans (26%, 25%) favored Clinton's making this criticism [6/92].*
- *Fear of crime was a real issue and Americans were becoming increasingly punitive. Eighty-four percent of survey respondents said there was more crime in the United States than a year ago [9/90]; 86% thought the courts were not harsh enough [10/93]; 50% (40%, 8%) wanted to treat juvenile offenders the same as adults [9/94]; 61% favored the death penalty for teens [9/94]; and 57% thought defendants should be required to testify [3/95].*

- On the other hand, 85% supported the Brady Bill which required a five-day waiting period before the purchase of handguns in order to conduct a background check [6/97]; 77% wanted the laws concerning the sale of firearms to be stricter [3/93]; and 68% supported a ban on the sale of semiautomatic rifles [2/99].

During Clinton's presidency, several real and not-so-real scandals occurred. When Clinton was governor of Arkansas, the Clintons invested and lost money in the Whitewater Development Corporation (WDC). It was alleged that the Clintons pressured an individual to make illegal loans to one of Clinton's partners in WDC. Congress, under control of Republicans, held 300 hours of hearings to investigate the allegations and an independent counsel was appointed, but ultimately no charges were filed.

- *At first, few people seemed to care about Whitewater (a sex scandal is always more interesting). Only 12% thought Clinton did something wrong and 73% did not know [1/94]. Two months later, though, 51% thought the Clintons were hiding something [3/94], and one month after that, 12% thought Hillary Clinton had done something illegal, 38% thought she had done something unethical, 25% said she had done nothing wrong, and 37% did not know [4/94].*

Hillary Clinton was frequently in the spotlight. She was disliked by many Republicans because she used her maiden as her middle name (Hillary Rodham Clinton), was outspoken, much more outspoken than previous first ladies, and took the point position on health care.

- *Eighteen percent of survey respondents in 1994 thought Hillary Clinton was highly principled, 53% said she had the same level of principles as others, 27% saw her as hypocritical, and 2% had no opinion [4/94].*
- *In fact, 49% thought Hillary Clinton should play a more traditional role of first lady [1/95] and 44% thought she had too much influence [1/97].*

Paula Jones, represented by a conservative legal organization, filed a sexual harassment suit against Bill Clinton in May 1994, alleging that Clinton propositioned her in May 1991. Jones' lawsuit was initially dismissed by a judge in 1998. Jones accepted a $850,000 settlement in return for dropping any appeal. Clinton continued to maintain his innocence and said he wanted to move on with his life.

- *In May 1994, only 27% of respondents (57%, 17%) thought that Paula Jones was telling the truth. This had increased to 45% (38%, 18%) by May 1997 and to 58% (29%, 13%) in January 1998.*

Jennifer Flowers, during the 1992 presidential race, purported having a twelve-year relationship with Clinton. A tape by Flowers was alleged to be doctored. During a January 1998 deposition, Clinton admitted that he had a single sexual encounter with Flowers. A related sexual accusation was that Clinton used Arkansas state troopers to enable Clinton to have affairs so that his wife would not find out (Troopergate). There was little to back up the Troopergate claims.

- *In 1992, 31% of respondents believed Flowers, 38% believed Clinton, and the rest did not know or said neither [1/92].*
- *Later, of those who followed the Troopergate allegations, 19% thought they were true [1/94].*
- *Even with all these sex scandal allegations, but prior to the Monica Lewinsky affair becoming public, only 27% said Bill Clinton was more corrupt than previous presidents, 19% the same amount, 52% less corrupt, and 2% did not know [1/97].*

The biggest scandal for Bill Clinton involved a twenty-two-year-old White House intern Monica Lewinsky. Clinton had several sexual encounters with Lewinsky in the Oval Office, including fellatio, but not sexual intercourse. The scandal broke in January 1998 after Lewinsky spoke of the encounters to a confidant, Linda Tripp, who secretly recorded their conversations. Clinton initially denied the allegations and it was not until August that he admitted having an improper physical relationship with Lewinsky in a taped grand jury testimony. In December 1998, the Republican-controlled House voted articles of impeachment stating that Clinton had committed perjury and obstruction of justice. Clinton was acquitted in the Senate following a twenty-one-day trial.

- *Immediately after the Monica Lewinsky scandal broke, 56% (39%, 6%) of Americans thought the allegations of the affair were true [1/98].*[10]
- *Although much of the public was riveted by the affair, 54% said Bill Clinton's personal life doesn't matter to you, as long as he does a good job of running the country [3/98].*
- *In fact, only 24% thought Clinton had done something illegal; although 47% thought he had acted unethically [4/98], and only 19% favored his impeachment [6/98].*
- *Even after a formal inquiry, only 34% favored impeachment [10/98] and 36% wanted to remove him from office [1/99].*

Thurgood Marshall, the first African American Supreme Court Justice, died in January 1993, and President H. W. Bush nominated Clarence Thomas as his replacement. Thomas, an archconservative, was accused of unsolicited sexual advances by Anita Hill while she was a subordinate of his at the Equal Employment Opportunity Commission (EEOC). After a very contentious appointment hearing, Thomas was confirmed by a 52-48 vote in the Senate. The hearings raised public consciousness about sexual harassment in the workplace and eventually led to Congress passing new legislation on sexual harassment,[11] inspired more women to run for public office, and prompted many companies to start training programs on the issue.[12]

- *Following the televised hearings, 58% (30%, 12%) favored Thomas serving on the Supreme Court [10/91]. In addition, 58% said they believed Thomas over Hill (24%, 18% [10/91-CBS/NYT]).*

Extreme antigovernment groups garnered support in the wake of two events. In August 1992, there was an eleven-day siege in Ruby Ridge, Idaho, against Randy Weaver and his family. A shoot-out occurred when US marshalls attempted to arrest Weaver for weapons violations. In the shoot-out, a marshall was killed as well as Weaver's fourteen-year-old son. Several days later, Weaver's wife was killed by a sniper and Weaver was wounded. After Weaver surrendered, he was acquitted of all the major charges and subsequently received $3.1 million in an out-of-court settlement.[13]

In February of the following year (1993), the Bureau of Alcohol, Tobacco, Firearms and Explosives (ATF) attempted to raid the Branch Davidian compound outside of Waco, Texas, because of weapons violations. The Branch Davidians, led by David Koresh, were an offshoot of the Seventh-Day Adventist Church and believed that society was about to collapse bringing in the Second Coming. Four ATF agents were killed in the initial raid and sixteen were wounded. A fifty-one-day standoff ensued. The ATF stormed the compound using tear gas, a fire was started, and seventy-six Branch Davidians (including eighteen children) died.

These two events also led to the growth of conspiracy theories and an increase in the number of right-wing antigovernment groups. In April 1995, Timothy McVeigh, who said he was motivated by these incidents, set off a truck bomb at the Alfred P. Murrah Federal Building, in Oklahoma City, killing 168 people (including 11 children). McVeigh was executed in June 2011.

- *In April 1993, 23% of respondents said Janet Reno (the Attorney General) had a great deal or a moderate amount of responsibility for what happened in Waco (with 33% saying the same of the FBI, and 93% seeing David Koresh as being at fault).*
- *By July 1995, 43% thought that federal officials were irresponsible in their handling of the crisis and 57% thought the FBI had a great deal or moderate amount of responsibility.*
- *Eighty-six percent (5%, 10%) thought the charges against McVeigh were true [5/97].*

Domestic terrorism took another turn when a bomb exploded in the garage of the US World Trade Center in February 1993. Six people were killed. Four terrorists, from the Mideast, were eventually convicted for the bombing, which was semi-linked to Al Qaeda.

- *Thirty-two percent thought the bombing was the work of a few terrorists (33%, 35%) and only 22% (55%, 24%) said it would negatively impact their view of Muslims [3/93].*

Another example of domestic terrorism was the Unabomber.[14] Ted Kaczynski was a mathematician who had taught at UC Berkeley, became a recluse living in a cabin in Montana, and over seventeen years sent sixteen mail bombs that killed three and injured twenty-three. He issued a variety of messages critiquing modern technology. He was turned in by his brother (who recognized his writing), was arrested in April 1996, and eventually sentenced to life in prison.

- *Eighty-six percent thought that the charges against Kaczynski were true [11/97] and 61% wanted him to receive the death penalty if he was guilty [1/98-NBC/WSJ].*

In March 1993, Dr. David Gunn, who performed abortions in Florida, was assassinated as he was getting out of his car. His assassin was sentenced to life in prison. Ten other people were killed in attacks on abortion clinics from 1993 to the present.

- *Twenty-two percent said the assassination of Gunn was a direct consequence of the confrontation style of antiabortion activists and 52% said it was the work of a lone fanatical assassin [3/93]. Only 33% had a favorable opinion of people active in the antiabortion movement [3/93].*

And before the decade was over, domestic terrorism took yet another form with the April 1999 Columbine High School massacre. Two teenagers in Littleton, Colorado, killed twelve students, one teacher, and injured twenty-one others. The two assailants committed suicide. The massacre set off a wide-ranging debate about gun control, antidepressants, bullying, and high-school cliques.

- *Twenty-five percent thought that the parents of the gunmen should be charged (26%, 49%) [4/99].*

RACE

In March 1992, a videotape was made of four Los Angeles police officers severely beating with their batons a motorist who had been stopped—Rodney King. King suffered a fractured facial bone, a broken ankle, and other bruises. The four officers were charged with the use of excessive force and were acquitted by a jury in May.[15] A six-day riot ensued in Los Angeles in which fifty-three people were killed and that resulted in $1 billion in fire damages.

- *Ninety-two percent of Americans had heard of or seen the Rodney King video immediately after the beating [3/91]. However, only 44% (27%, 29%) thought the beating was racially motivated [4/92-Time/CNN].*
- *But, there were large racial differences in perceptions of how frequently such beating occurred nationally: 19% of whites said very frequently compared to 51% of African Americans. In fact, 17% of whites and 40% of blacks said they knew someone who*

had been mistreated by the police [3/91]. Only 17% of respondents (2% of blacks) thought that justice was served when the jury acquitted the four police officers [2/93].

Across the country, New York City had its own example of police excessive use of force in February 1999, when Amadou Diallo, an immigrant from Guinea, was shot forty-one times by four police officers when he reached into his jacket to show his wallet. The police officers said they mistook him for a rape suspect. The four police officers were acquitted of second-degree murder. Diallo's family eventually accepted a $3 million settlement from the city of New York.[16]

In June 1994, Nicole Brown Simpson and Ronald Goldman were found murdered in her home in Los Angeles. Nicole Simpson was the former wife of O. J. Simpson, who was accused of the murders. O. J. Simpson had been the star running back for the Buffalo Bills and later became an actor and a commentator for *Monday Night Football*. Simpson's criminal trial lasted eleven months, was televised, and widely watched. The high-profile defense team was able to show that the LAPD mishandled evidence[17] and that racism in the LAPD may have played a role. Simpson was acquitted in October 1995. In February 1997, jurors awarded the Goldman and Simpson family $33 million in a civil suit.[18] The trial was called by some the "Trial of the Century" and several movies and documentaries about Simpson, the trial, and race relations were later released. Gallup has asked over 200 questions about O. J. Simpson since the murder of Nicole Simpson and Ronald Goldman.

- *Until the verdict, 63% believed Simpson was guilty (68% of whites and 29% of blacks) [9/95]. After the not guilty verdict, 47% believed the jury made the right decision [10/95], and following the civil case, 68% thought the jury did the right thing [2/97].*

The Million Man March was held in Washington, D.C. in October 1995. The March was originated by Nation of Islam leader Louis Farrakhan. It was highly publicized and well-attended.

- *Of the 88% of respondents who had heard of the march, 62% (85% of blacks) said it was a good event for blacks to take part in but few felt that Farrakhan himself had positively influenced their view of the march (3% of whites and 19% of blacks) [10/95]. Fifty-eight percent (63% among whites and 41% among blacks) had an unfavorable opinion of Farrakhan [10/95-Newsweek].*

One other notable event concerning race was that in March 1995, Mississippi became the last state to ratify the 13th Amendment to the United States Constitution—that is, outlawing slavery.

SEX AND GENDER

Conservatives wanted to punish any organization that either provided abortion or advice on abortions. Congress passed legislation prohibiting employees at federally funded family planning sites to counsel any patient about abortion (i.e., Planned Parenthood). In May 1991, the Supreme Court ruled in *Rust v. Sullivan* that the government could restrict government funding for any agency that promoted or advised women about abortions. The first major legal challenge to *Roe v. Wade* was decided in June 1992 in *Planned Parenthood v. Casey*. Casey essentially affirmed a women's right to obtain an abortion up to the point of viability of the fetus. Furthermore, the state cannot place undue burdens on women wanting an abortion. In particular, Pennsylvania's requirement of spousal consent was overturned.

- *Only 25% of Americans supported the Rust v. Sullivan decision [5/91].*
- *Just prior to Casey, 50% (42%, 8%) favored using federal funds to enable poor women to have abortions and less than half (42%, 52%, 6%) wanted to overturn Roe v. Wade.*
- *However, attitudes toward abortion were complicated with only 32% favored allowing abortions under all circumstances (52% certain circumstances and 17% none) [5/91].*
- *In July 1996, Gallup found 71% would favor a law making it illegal to perform an abortion after the third month unless the mother's life was in danger.*

Other advances for women's rights included an April 1993 executive order requiring the US Air Force to allow women to fly warplanes; however, as reflected in Gallup polls, attitudes toward many women's issues were mixed.

- *Fifty-five percent favored allowing women to have combat jobs [11/92].*
- *Forty-three percent (56%, 2%) thought it was best if the man was the achiever outside the home [8/93], but only 29% thought that women were making unfair gains at the expense of men [5/91].*
- *One interesting question found that 35% agreed "with the following statement taken from the Bible? A wife should submit graciously to the servant leadership of her husband" [6/98].*

Attitudes toward gay rights were also complicated.

- *Only 36% (54%, 10%) said that homosexual relations between consenting adults should be legal [8/91] and only 38% thought homosexuality was an acceptable lifestyle [6/92].*
- *However, in June 1992, 74% of survey respondents thought that homosexual men and women should have equal job opportunities, and four years later the number went up to 84% [11/96].*
- *Less than half (39%) thought that the same civil rights laws protecting blacks and women should be extended to homosexuals [9/94].*
- *Gallup asked its first question about gay marriage in March 1996 and found only 27% thought such marriages should be valid. On the other hand, only 28% supported a law prohibiting recognition of gay marriages in their state [4/96].*

In July 1993, Bill Clinton introduced "Don't Ask, Don't Tell (DADT)" policy concerning gays in the military. The law prohibited the military from discriminating against *closeted* gays and lesbians, but prohibited open gays and lesbians from serving. Although this policy allowed gays to serve, and was deemed at the time a compromise, it was widely attacked by both sides. Large numbers of gays and lesbians continued to be thrown out of the military for being open.[19] Numerous lawsuits occurred, and in December 2010, congressional legislation overturned DADT and allowed gays to openly serve in the military. Hate crimes against gays continued, most notably in October 1998, when Matthew Shepard was beaten and left to die outside of Laramie, Wyoming.

- *Prior to Clinton's announcement about DADT, 49% (42%, 9%) thought that homosexuals should be able to serve in the military [9/92]. However, only 43% wanted to end the ban on homosexuals in the military [1/93]. The country was evenly divided about DADT after it was released (48%, 49%, 3%) [7/93] and only 33% thought it did not go far enough [1/94]. Although Clinton was widely criticized by gay rights advocates, it is clear why he believed that he needed to compromise.*

Attitudes toward sexuality in general were changing.

- *Only 40% (57%, 6%) thought that sex before marriage was wrong (it was 68% in 1969), and 53% (32%, 13%) said they would more likely support a presidential candidate who favored giving condoms to high-school students [1/92].*
- *Viagra was approved by the FDA for use in erectile dysfunction in March 1998. Fifty-nine percent thought that was a good thing for society [5/98].*
- *As for pornography: 33% wanted a total ban on the sale or rental of x-rated videos and 42% wanted a ban on the showing of x-rated movies in movie houses. Twelve percent had seen an x-rated movie in the last year [8/91].*

THE ECONOMY

The 1990s was the longest recorded economic expansion (ten years) hitherto in US history.[20] There was strong economic growth, low inflation, a surging stock market, and even a government surplus.[21] Much of this growth was caused by rapid changes in technology. In fact, 83% of Americans were using email by November 1998. Economic growth was accompanied by economic fraud. In the 1990s, there was continued fallout from the S&L crisis that began in the late 1980s.

- *Fifty-nine percent of respondents said the S&L crisis was a serious scandal, but the public was divided over whether selling off the troubled banks continued the problem or was the best that could be done given the circumstances (42%, 48%, 11% [7/90]).*

- *Furthermore, there was debate over who was responsible for the scandal: 29% said Reagan, 32% government regulators, and 25% Congress [7/90]. Economics was often confusing to people (as well as many economists!). Only 15% said they had a good understanding of the S&L crisis [6/90].*

In April 1990, Michael Milken, the Junk Bond King, pled guilty to securities fraud and insider trading. He was fined $600 million and served two years in prison. The Glass-Steagall legislation of 1933 had separated commercial and investment banking. Essentially, banks that took deposits were not allowed to speculate. This restriction was relaxed beginning in the 1960s and eliminated in 1989. Many argue that this getting rid of Glass-Steagall was one of the major reasons for the 2008 Great Recession.

Economic inequality was growing.[22]

- *Eighty percent favored increasing taxes for those earning over $200,000 a year [11/92].*
- *Forty-one percent thought it was more difficult to get rich than it used to be (31% thought it was easier, 28% the same or didn't know); 51% (36% some, 12% little/none) thought that if a person worked hard they had a good chance of getting rich; and only 31% thought the current income and wealth distribution was fair [5/90].*

In August 1992, the United States, Canada, and Mexico reached an agreement on the North American Free Trade Association (NAFTA), which eliminated most tariffs among the three countries. There is considerable debate about its effect, particularly vis-à-vis Mexico. US exports to Mexico expanded but job losses in the rust belt also increased. There continues to be tremendous contention on whether the loss of jobs was because of NAFTA or because of increased automation.[23]

- *Prior to NAFTA being signed, 72% said a free trading zone including the United States, Mexico, and Canada would be good for the United States [3/91].*
- *Furthermore, only 39% favored more trade restrictions if it increased jobs and consumer prices [2/92].*
- *However, support for NAFTA was at 54% (24%, 21%) a month after NAFTA was signed [9/92] and fell to 38% in November 1993.*
- *Immigration was also an ongoing debate. Sixty-one percent believed immigration improved our country as it brought in people with different talents and cultures [2/92].*
- *However, 65% wanted to reduce immigration [7/93]; 50% wanted to stop all legal immigration for the next five years [4/96]; but only 27% wanted to erect a wall along the border with Mexico [7/93].*

Another controversial law, passed in August 1996, prescribed welfare reform. The Clinton-led law required recipients to begin working after two years, placed a lifetime limit of five years on welfare benefits, banned food stamps for felons, limited funds for unmarried parents, and restricted funding for all immigrants. Proponents of the law argued that it reasserted America's work ethic and limited dependency of people on welfare. Critics argued that it did not deal with the major causes of poverty—lack of jobs and low wages—and effectively destroyed the social policy safety nets for poor people.

- *In January 1992, 80% said they would favor a presidential candidate who would require all able-bodied (including women with small children) to work, and in September 1992, 89% said they wanted welfare payments cut off after two years, but that the government should continue to help people find employment.*
- *Most Americans had tremendous disdain for those who received welfare benefits. Respondents were much more likely to say that people on welfare were taking advantage of the system instead of genuinely needing help (68%, 28%, 4%) [4/94]. This is another example of how public opinion "forced" Clinton to shift right.*

Bill Clinton's major legislative defeat was on health care. In September 1993, he delivered a speech on health care to a joint session of Congress. He appointed his wife, Hillary Clinton, to head a task force to come up with a comprehensive policy for universal health care. The effort was strongly opposed by conservatives, and insurance and pharmaceutical companies.[24] The legislation died by August 1994. The initiative was controversial for both its scope and the central role Hillary Clinton was given.

- *Prior to Clinton's election, 60% (28%, 8%) said they would more likely support a presidential candidate who "advocated a national health care system administered by the federal government and paid for through new payroll taxes" [1/92].*
- *When the health care initiative was first announced 54% (31%, 14%) favored it [9/93]. By April 1994, support had fallen to 43%.*

SCIENCE, TECHNOLOGY, AND THE ENVIRONMENT

There were rapid changes in science.

The Human Genome Project began in 1990, which by 2003 succeeded in mapping all of the human genes. Dolly the sheep was cloned from an adult cell (1996).[25] There was some skepticism about progress in the biological sciences.

- *Twenty-seven percent thought that foods using biotechnology posed a serious health risk and 20% were unsure [9/99].*
- *However, only 6% thought that cloning humans would be a good thing and 88% said it would be morally wrong [2/97].*

Science and religion were sometimes at odds, especially over the Darwinian theory of evolution. The Supreme Court ruled in *Epperson v. Arkansas* (1968) that states could not prohibit the teaching of evolution. Religious fundamentalists responded by passing laws mandating that the theory of creationism have equal time with the theory of evolution. Various courts ruled that "creation science" has no basis in science, was simply a religion, and should not be given equal time. In the mid-1990s, some fundamentalists argued for teaching "intelligent design" in schools, which was the same theory as creationism but with the religious references taken out. The courts ruled that intelligent design was also religion masquerading as science.

- *Fifty-eight percent supported a law requiring the teaching of creationism in schools [4/96] and 46% thought that God created man in his present form in the last 10,000 years [10/91].*

The Hubble Space Telescope was launched in April 1990. A flawed mirror degraded its ability to perform its primary mission until the problem was corrected by a space shuttle mission in December 1993. Other space achievements included the discovery of the first extra-solar planets (1992); NASA's Galileo probe entering Jupiter's atmosphere (1995); and the launch of the first segment of the International Space Station (1999).

- *The public gave lukewarm support to space sciences. Forty-seven percent said the cost of the moon landing was justified [7/94]; 40% said investment in space research was worthwhile [5/91]; and 56% supported funding sending unmanned missions to Mars [12/99].*

In the 1990s, there was continued implementation of antismoking policies: smoking was banned on domestic airline flights (1990); Los Angeles banned smoking in restaurants (1992); the EPA classified second-hand smoke as a carcinogen (1992); New York City banned smoking in most workplaces (1995); Clinton ordered smoke-free environments for federal employees (1997); and attorney generals of forty-six states signed the Master Settlement Agreement (MSA) with four tobacco companies, which restricted tobacco advertising and requiring the firms to pay $206 billion to the states over twenty-five years (1998).

- *Public opinion on antismoking policies was mixed: 48% of Americans thought that second-hand smoke was very harmful to adults and 36% said somewhat harmful [5/96]; 94% believed cigarette smoking was one of the causes of lung cancer; and 49% wanted to ban cigarette advertising [7/90].*
- *Thirty-four percent wanted to ban smoking in the workplace and 18% in hotels (61% and 73% advocated set-aside areas) [9/99].*
- *Sixty-six percent supported the ban on cigarette machines [6/97].*
- *Fifty-one percent supported the Justice Department's lawsuit (MSA) against the tobacco industry seeking to recover billions in health care costs [9/99].*
- *And few (25%) thought that tobacco companies should be held legally responsible when sued by families of smokers who died from smoking [5/96].*

The prospects for people with HIV began to improve. In November 1991, Los Angeles Lakers basketball player, Magic Johnson, announced he was HIV positive. Johnson was very active in combating HIV, in part, by being one of the first to stress that HIV was not just a "gay" disease. In 1996, AZT was made available and HIV was no longer an automatic sentence of death.

- *By this time there was somewhat greater tolerance among Americans of those with AIDS. Only 10% thought that landlords should be able to evict tenants with AIDS [5/91].*
- *Seventy percent said they were more likely to practice safe sex because of Magic Johnson's announcement that he had HIV [11/91].*
- *But, 40% thought if people got AIDS, it was their own fault, and 47% said that people with AIDS should be required to carry an identity card stating they had AIDS [10/97].*

In the year 1990, Tim Berners-Lee created the first web server at CERN. When it was released the following year, it became the basis for World Wide Web. In 1993, Mosaic became the first popular browser, the optical DVD was announced, and eBay was formed. In 1995, America Online offered general access to the internet, Amazon was founded, and the first full-length computer-animated movie—*Toy Story*—came out. The chess computer "Deep Blue" defeated world chess champion Gary Kasparov in 1996. In 1998, Google was founded, and Mozilla was released, and in 1999, Napster debuted. This was also the decade that cell phone use exploded in the United States, growing from 5.2 million in 1990 to 86 million in 1999.

In October 1998, the Justice Department sued Microsoft for using unfair practices to protect its monopoly. Microsoft lost its case in front of a judge, the case was overturned on appeal, and Microsoft settled in November 2001. The settlement was considered by many to be just a "slap on the wrist."

- *Most respondents sided with Microsoft instead of the Department of Justice (45%, 28%, 27%) even though most believed Microsoft to be a monopoly (49%, 38%, 13%) [2/99].*
- *Regarding Microsoft and computers in general: 58% of respondents had a favorable opinion of Microsoft (13%, 16% mixed, 13% don't know); and of Bill Gates (55%, 17%, 20%) [3/98]; and 81% (8%, 12%) thought Microsoft had a positive impact on the computer industry [2/99].*
- *However, only 50% had a great deal or quite a lot of confidence in the computer industry (34% had some or very little confidence, and 6% didn't know), and 35% thought the ethical standards of computer executives were very high or high (with 48% saying they were average, 9% low, and 8% not knowing [11/99]).*

Of course, along with the growth of the computer industry, attendant problems with computers were also surfacing. Because many software programs stored only the last two digits of the year, it was predicted that many programs (including those used for air traffic control, nuclear power plants, banking, and even VCRs) would fail on the first day of the new century, since "00" could be interpreted as the year 1900 or 2000. (This glitch was known as the Y2K bug.) A lot of resources went into upgrading software and, consequently, little disruption occurred.

- *In 1998, only 34% of respondents thought Y2K would be a major problem [12/98].*
- *As the new century approached, 51% said they would not travel on an airline on January 1, 21% said they would put aside a large amount of cash, 24% planned to stock up on gasoline, and 53% would make sure they had hard copy documentation of their financial accounts [12/99].*
- *By February 1995, there was a computer in 40% of households and 30% of those who had a computer used an online service such as Prodigy or CompuServe. In August 1999, these numbers had increased to 60% and 74%, respectively.*
- *As the internet began to develop, a majority (57%, 28%, 16%) thought it would have a positive impact on society [3/98].*
- *In April 1999, 74% predicted that the internet would change society more than the introduction of television or the telephone.*
- *Most people thought that scientific advancements helped people (62%), compared to 15% who said they were harmful, with 23% saying some of each [5/90].*

In February 1992, the US Senate approved a measure calling for a faster phaseout of CF2 omissions, which was depleting the ozone layer, than was called for by the Montreal Protocol. This legislation (enacted when George H. W. Bush was president) is a reminder of a time when there was a bipartisan effort to clean up the environment. After twelve years of Republican presidents, Clinton put forward a somewhat more positive role for the government.[26] There was a renewed stress that the environment was as important as economic growth. The EPA budget was increased, and Clinton signed the Kyoto Protocol of 1997, which called for the international community to reduce greenhouse gases. The treaty was never submitted to the Senate as it would not have been ratified.

- *Harris found 74% of the 55% who had heard of the Kyoto Protocol approved of it [12/97].*
- *Seventy-nine percent favored the ban on CF2 omissions [4/91]; 71% said "protection of the environment should be given priority, even at the risk of curbing economic growth" [4/91]; and only 24% said the Endangered Species Act went too far [8/95]. In fact, only 15% thought Clinton's plans on global warming went too far [10/97].*
- *Americans wanted businesses to spend more to reduce pollution. When told that current antipollution laws cost businesses $33 billion per year, 78% favored a new Clean Air Act that would increase costs by another $20 billion per year [4/90].*

POPULAR TRENDS

Movies that came out in the 1990s included: *Ghost* (1990); *Dances With Wolves* (1990); *Home Alone* (1990); *Beauty and the Beast* (1991); *Aladdin* (1992); *Mrs. Doubtfire* (1993); *Jurassic Park* (1993); *The Lion King* (1994); *Forrest Gump* (1994); *Toy Story* (1995); *Independence Day* (1996); *Men in Black* (1997); *Titanic* (1997); *Saving Private Ryan* (1998); *The Sixth Sense* (1999); and *Austin Powers: The Spy Who Shagged Me* (1999).

- *In a 1993 Gallup poll 51% or respondents said they intended to see Jurassic Park [6/93].*

Television continued to undergo massive changes in the array of programming and channels. Television shows and networks that debuted included: Comedy Central (1990); *Law and Order* (1990); *The Larry Sanders Show* (1992); *Barney & Friends* (1992); Cartoon Network (1992); *E.R.* (1994); *The Daily Show* (1996); Fox News (1996); *Southpark* (1997); *Sex and the City* (1998); *Sopranos* (1999); *The West Wing* (1999); and *Family Guy* (1999).

- *Seventy-one percent of families owned more than one TV [8/90] and 66% subscribed to cable [11/93].*
- *In August 1990, 39% said they watched four or more hours of TV on a weekday; 58% said watching TV was a good use of their time; and only 13% said they were addicted to TV.*
- *Television content was controversial: 80% said there was too much violence on TV and 76% believed TV violence was related to the crime rate in the United States [7/93].*

In the world of publishing, these were some of the major new books: Bryan Burrough's and John Helyer's *Barbarians at the Gate* (1990); Michael Crichton's *Jurassic Park* (1990); Steven Hawking's *A Brief History of Time* (1993); Anonymous (Joe Klein's) *Primary Colors* (1996); John Grisham's *Runaway Jury* (1996); Hillary Rodham Clinton's *It Takes a Village* (1996); Scott Adams' *The Dilbert Principle* (1996); J. K. Rowling's *Harry Potter and the Philosopher's Stone* (1997); Jon Krakauer's *Into Thin Air* (1997); and Tom Brokaw's *The Greatest Generation* (1998).

- *By July 2000, 71% of respondents had heard of the Harry Potter books.*
- *Eighty-one percent said they had read a book during the previous year. The types of book respondents had most recently read were: novels (54%); biographies (7%); other nonfiction (10%); textbooks (5%); the Bible (2%); and how-to books (5%) [12/90].*
- *Of the 39% who said they had a favorite author, the only author mentioned by more than 10% was Stephen King (18%).*

Some important events in the world of music included: the suicide of Kurt Cobain of Nirvana in 1994; the death of Queen's Freddie Mercury of AIDS in 1991; and the rise of rap music. It was a decade of alternative rock or grunge (Nirvana, Pearl Jam, and Red Hot Chili Peppers), contemporary R & B (Whitney Houston), urban adult (Mariah Carey), country music (Garth Brooks), and hip-hop (Dr. Dre, 2Pac, Snoop Dogg, and Lauryn Hill). Other musicians whose careers began in this decade included: Celine Dion, REM, U2, Spice Girls, Aerosmith, and Alanis Morrissette.

- *Only 14% said they liked rap music a lot compared to 42% for rock, and 13% for heavy metal [1/90].*

In sports, boxer Mike Tyson, the heavyweight champion of the world, was found guilty of rape in 1992 and released on parole in 1994. Tyson's conviction was somewhat controversial as he claimed the sex was consensual. After his release, there was some controversy over whether he should be allowed to box again. He ended up regaining the championship in March 1996 in a fight that grossed over $96 million.[27]

- *As Tyson was about to be released from prison, 59% of respondents (33%, 8%) said Tyson was guilty of rape [3/95].*
- *Seventy-five percent said they thought Tyson should be allowed to box again after his release from prison [7/95].*

In 1994, figure skater (and Olympic hopeful) Nancy Kerrigan was clubbed on her leg by an accomplice of the husband of her main rival, Tonya Harding.[28]

- *Thirty-two percent thought Harding was involved in the attack and an additional 41% thought she had prior knowledge [1/94].*

That same year (1994), baseball players went on strike for 232 days over owner demands for a salary cap. The post-season was canceled, replacement players were used, and attendance dropped because many fans were upset. In May of 1996, in one of the biggest disasters in mountaineering history, eight climbers were killed climbing Mount Everest.

- *Forty percent believed that baseball players were most responsible for the strike, 31% said the owners, and 25% blamed them both [12/94-NBC]. On a related issue, 75% believed that baseball players were overpaid (hockey-27%, football-62%, basketball-59%) [2/90].*
- *The most popular sport as measured by those attending a game in the previous year was baseball (26%). Other attendance rates were: football (20%), basketball (17%), auto racing (8%), and soccer (3%) [2/90]. When asked what their favorite sport to follow was, the sports followed by more than 10% of respondents were: football (32%), baseball (16%), and basketball (15%) [4/95].*

Perhaps the biggest celebrity story of the decade concerned the ongoing saga of Prince Charles and Princess Diana of the United Kingdom. They were married in July 1981, but it is generally accepted as a fact that Charles at that time was in love with Camilla Parker Bowles and did not want to marry Diana. Charles and Diana were divorced in August 1996 and she died in a car crash in Paris the following year. The marriage, their two children, separation, divorce, and her death became media sensations.

- *When asked who was responsible for the separation, 46% blamed Charles, 11% Diana, 22% said neither or both, and 21% did not know [12/92].*
- *One indicator of this enormous celebrity of the story was that 45% of Americans (43%, 12%) thought that President Clinton should have attended the funeral for Diana [9/97].*

CONCLUDING COMMENTS

The Soviet Union was replaced by Russia, the United States, and its allies were victorious in the Gulf War, sex in the White House became an everyday topic worldwide, and the tech economy boomed.

The collapse of the Soviet Union that began in the 1980s continued and by end of the 1990s Vladimir Putin achieved power in post-Soviet Russia. Yugoslavia also collapsed leading to several wars (coupled with war crimes) between the ex-provinces. In contrast, integration among nations occurred in Western Europe with the founding of the EU. In Africa, there was liberation in South Africa and war crimes in Rwanda. Elsewhere, the Gulf War forced Iraq out of Kuwait, the United States deposed Noriega in Panama, Afghanistan continued to deteriorate as a country, and Israel signed a peace accord with the PLO.

Most Americans viewed the collapse of the Soviet Union very positively, were supportive of the US role in the Gulf War and Panama, grudgingly supported efforts to prevent massacres in the Balkans, were reluctant to help in Rwanda, Somalia, or promote freedom in South Africa, and were supportive, but doubtful, about the peace agreement between Israel and the PLO. In short, Americans were more supportive of interventions abroad when compared with the 1970s and 1980s, following the cynicism arising from Vietnam.

The 1990s were dominated by Clinton as president and the Republicans opposed to his administration. Clinton's real scandal (his sexual involvement with Monica Lewinsky) and not-so-real scandals (Whitewater) curtailed his ability to govern. The right gained influence because of the intransigence of Newt Gingrich, the portrayal of the government's actions at Ruby Ridge and Waco, and the rise of political Evangelicalism as exemplified by the Moral Majority. Reacting to the public's concern over crime, Clinton pivoted to the right on criminal justice policies and he countered right-wing attacks on government by restricting public assistance.

Clinton was buoyed by a robust economy and few of the scandals, except for Monica Lewinski, had any effect on his image. Even with that scandal, few favored his removal from office. Many, though, were upset by Ruby Ridge and Waco, and this would lead to growth in the future of conspiracy theories about the role of government.

Police brutality became a major issue with the beating of Rodney King, the subsequent riots in Los Angeles, and the killing of Amadou Diallo. O. J. Simpson was acquitted of the murder of Nicole Brown Simpson and Ronald Goldman in a trial that had obvious racial overtones. The public was divided, along racial lines, in their reactions toward Rodney King and O. J. Simpson.

It was becoming more accepted for women to take on combat roles in the military. Attempts to end and/or restrict abortion led to many protests and Court challenges. Restriction of abortion funding was enacted, and pro-choice Republican politicians became an endangered species. On the issue of gays in the military, Clinton tried a compromise with Don't Ask, Don't Tell policy.

Most Americans continued to support abortion rights, albeit with mixed attitudes. Only about one-third thought homosexual relations between two adults should be legal, but there was increased support for equal opportunity related to jobs. The country was divided on Don't Ask, Don't Tell.

The economy boomed with the rise of tech, but the reduction of oversight on banking would be a key factor in causing the 2008 Great Recession. The passage of NAFTA would lead to lost jobs in the rust belt, later negatively affecting Hillary Clinton's presidential campaign in 2016. Clinton's major legislative defeat concerned his health care initiative.

Americans originally supported both NAFTA and the health care initiative, but support for both quickly declined. Despite all the issues Clinton had to face during his two terms in the 1990s, his popularity remained high. He benefited from a robust economy and was able to avoid a major war.

[The reader can find relevant crosstabs and discussion in the online appendix located at https://rowman.com/ISBN/9781793653505/US-Public-Opinion-since-the-1930s-Galluping-through-History.]

NOTES

1. There are few more acrimonious topics discussed among survey research practitioners than whether nonresponse rate affects the quality of the data. See Groves et al. (2006).

2. Russia felt slighted by the US treatment of Russia as a second-rate power. American understanding of Russian history was often deplorable. When asked which country contributed the most to Germany's defeat in 1945, only 11% said the Soviets and 65% said the United States [5/94].

3. Remember: it was the June 1914 assassination of Archduke Franz Ferdinand by a Serbian agent in Sarajevo (Bosnia and Herzegovina) that precipitated World War I.

4. The 2004 movie, *Hotel Rwanda*, on the Rwanda genocide was nominated for three Academy Awards.

5. Eight percent said they supported Apartheid [6/90-Harris].

6. In September 1986, 46% (34%, 20%) favored a trade embargo and ending US investments in South Africa.

7. General Colin Powell enunciated a doctrine (later known as the Powell Doctrine) in which military force could be used: vital US interests were at stake, the objective was clear and attainable, nonviolent measures had been exhausted, there was broad international support, an exit strategy existed, and there was support from the public. This doctrine was created to avoid future Vietnams. The Gulf War met these criteria, and the United States could quickly get in and out.

8. The movie *Black Hawk Down* was based upon this incident.

9. Rabin was awarded the Nobel Peace Prize in 1994 along with Yasser Arafat and Shimon Peres.

10. Eighty-five percent said that Kennedy had affairs while he was president [1/98].

11. Thirty-seven percent said sexual harassment was a big problem in the work place, 51% somewhat, and 10% not a problem [10/91—Yankelovich].

12. Joe Biden was chairman of the Senate Judiciary Committee and was criticized for how he handled the hearings by being insensitive and not fully investigating Hills' accusation. In April 2019 Biden apologized to Hill. She said she was not satisfied with the apology. However, Hill later said she would vote for Biden in 2020.

13. The only question I could find on Ruby Ridge was a difficult-to-interpret question asked by the *Los Angeles Times* over whether congressional hearings made respondents more (10%) or less favorable (33%) toward the FBI (51%-no change) [9/95].

14. In 2017, Discovery Channel had an eight-episode mini-drama titled *Manhunt: Unabomber*.

15. The trial had been moved to a mostly white jurisdiction—Simi Valley. In May 1993, three of the officers were convicted in federal court of violating King's civil rights. They received light sentences. King won a $3.8 million judgment against the city in April 1994.

16. In response to Diallo's killing, Bruce Springsteen wrote *American Skin (41 Shots)*. The NYC Police Benevolent Association called for a boycott of Springsteen. He also played the song after the shootings of Trayvon Martin in 2012 and after similar shootings. The only survey question I could find on Diallo was that 63% said they closely followed the trial [3/00-Pew].

17. Most famously when O. J. Simpson could not put on the bloody glove that was left at the crime scene.

18. In September 2007, Simpson was arrested for stealing sports memorabilia at gun point, which he said had been stolen from him. In December 2009, Simpson was sentenced to thirty-three years in prison and was released on parole in July 2017.

19. The Service Members Legal Defense Network reported that over 13,000 military discharges occurred under DADT.

20. At the beginning of this economic expansion, Donald Trump was in financial difficulty and was put on an allowance by his creditors. Thirteen percent of Americans said they felt sorry for Trump [7/90].

21. Gallup even had a question on what to do with the surplus. Thirty-one percent wanted to reduce taxes, 50% wanted increased aid for schools, and 20% did not know or said both [7/98]. Nevertheless, 83% favored a constitutional amendment requiring a balanced budget [4/96].

22. For more on the growth of economic inequality, see Piketty (2017).

23. In May 1993, only 5% could foresee automation eliminating their job in five to ten years.

24. The Harry and Louise advertisements opposing the Clinton Bill was particularly effective. They were funded by a health insurance industry lobbying organization.

25. Eventually the fertility business became multibillion dollar. The Centers for Disease Control states 12% of American women have used assisted-reproductive technologies. The number of attempted pregnancies using donor eggs was 21,200 in 2015.

26. Only 33% said they trusted the government to do what is right all or most of the time [5/97].

27. Only 32% said they were a fan of boxing [9/91].

28. *I, Tonya*, the movie starring Margot Robbie and Allison Janney, came out in 2017.

8

The 2000s

Decade of 9/11, the Iraqi War, the Great Recession, and the Election of Barack Obama

The decade began with the debacle of Voter News Service miscalling the state of Florida in the exit poll.[1] The first web-based survey archived in the Roper Center occurred in February 2001—a CBS News Survey conducted by Knowledge Networks. By the end of the decade, eighty-three national web surveys had been conducted (2% of all surveys), one of which was multimode (combined with a telephone sample). Roper has only seven face-to-face surveys for the 2000s in its archive; Gallup now accounts for only 18% of all archived surveys. In 2008, Nate Silver (538.com) accurately predicted the outcome in forty-nine states—thus starting the rise of data journalists. Silver combined the weighted results from many different surveys to come up with his projections.

WORLD EVENTS

Decade of 9/11

On September 11, 2001, four passenger airliners were hijacked by nineteen al-Qaeda terrorists.[2] Two of the planes crashed into the twin towers of the World Trade Center in New York, one crashed into the Pentagon, and the fourth crashed in a field in Pennsylvania after passengers tried to overcome the hijackers. Almost 3,000 people were killed in these attacks. The attacks were authorized by Osama bin Laden who was living in Afghanistan after receiving protection by the Taliban, who ruled Afghanistan.

The immediate reaction from world powers was overwhelmingly support for the United States. In France, the headline in *Le Monde* was "We are all Americans," and "The Star-Spangled Banner" was played at the Changing of the Guard in London.

More importantly, Article 5 was invoked by NATO for the first time signifying the 9/11 attack was an attack against all, and even Iran began sharing intelligence with the United States.

Over the course of the decade, the United States would not be the only victim of terrorism: 202 were killed in bombing of two night clubs in Bali in 2002; 116 were killed in the Philippines in an attack in 2004 on a ferry; 191 were killed in an attack on four trains in Madrid in 2004; 4 different attacks on London's transportation system resulted in 52 deaths in 2005; and 195 were killed in a series of attacks in Mumbai, India, in 2008.

After the Taliban refused to extradite Osama bin Laden, the United States, supported by its allies, invaded Afghanistan in October, and by December Al-Qaeda and the Taliban had fled to Pakistan and remote areas of Afghanistan. US troops began to withdraw from Afghanistan in preparation for the invasion of Iraq. The Taliban then took advantage of both the reduction in US troop strength and the corruption and mismanagement by the new Afghan government to begin an insurgency. To date, the war in Afghanistan has resulted in over 2,300 US combat deaths and has cost over $1 trillion. At the end of the decade, there were almost 15,000 US troops in Afghanistan and the Taliban still controlled substantial areas in Afghanistan.

- *In the immediate aftermath of 9/11, Americans were strongly behind a military response: 82% favored sending troops to Afghanistan; 76% said to continue to campaign against terrorism even if 5,000 troops were killed; 77% supported a military draft if necessary; and 77% wanted to allow the United States to assassinate known terrorists [9/01].*

In March 2003, a US-led coalition invaded Iraq. The rationale for the invasion was that Iraq possessed weapons of mass destruction (WMDs), and that the Iraqi regime, led by Saddam Hussein, was repressive and undemocratic. At the time of the invasion, many Americans questioned this rationale and it was later determined that Iraq in fact did not possess WMDs.[3] The US-led coalition troops entered Baghdad in April and Saddam Hussein was captured in December. All told, 139 US troops were killed during the invasion as well as 9,200 Iraqi combatants.[4]

An insurgency soon developed that was hastened by two major US errors: disbanding the Iraqi army and excluding members of the Baathist Party (which had ruled Iraq) from any government position.[5] Essentially, the two major influences that could stabilize Iraqi society were no longer a coherent power within the country. Furthermore, disbanded members of the military and members of the Baathist Party no longer had jobs and therefore had more incentive to join the insurgency. The insurgency received an additional boost, given that the new government was essentially Shiite and was not willing to share power with the Sunni or other groups (Kurds, etc.) in Iraq.

It can be argued that the invasion of Iraq was the worst foreign policy decision ever made by the United States. As of the end of 2018, 4,572 American military personnel had died in the war and the financial cost of the war was over $2 trillion.

In addition, the veteran expenses would eventually cost another $4 trillion. Approximately, 500,000 Iraqis died in the war and another two million fled the country. The US invasion of Iraq led to long-term instability in Iraq and Syria, greater influence on the part of Iran, and the diminution of American power and prestige. The international good will toward the United States that had followed 9/11 was quickly lost.

- *In the aftermath of 9/11, 74% of Americans were in favor of sending troops to remove Saddam Hussein from power [11/01]. As the Bush administration began to accuse Iraq of having WMDs, 82% said Iraq was evil and 55% said they believed Iraq had WMDs, and another 40% said they thought Iraq was trying to obtain such weapons [2/02]. Furthermore, even with no one in the administration alleging this, 47% (37%, 16%) believed that Saddam Hussein and Iraq had a major role in 9/11 [9/03-PRSI].*
- *In June of 2002, however, war fever was in some decline as support for sending ground troops fell to 59%. Just prior to the invasion, support for the Bush administration position was not overwhelming: 52% thought the United States had done all it could diplomatically; 52% said they would support Bush's word about Iraq having WMDs over the position of the UN [12/02].*
- *By early 2003, just prior to the invasion, only 27% wanted a return to the draft and only 41% were certain that Iraq had WMDs [1/03].*
- *Americans were divided over whether a war would be justified if Iraq did not have WMDs. In March 2003, 41% said war would only be justified if WMDs were found, 38% said it would be justified anyway, and 15% said the war was not justified even if WMDs were found.*
- *Following the defeat of the Iraqi military, 70% said the war was going well [5/03], and only a minority (31%) believed that Bush deliberately misled the public about Iraq having WMDs [6/03].*[6]
- *Support for US policy in Iraq slowly began to erode. In October 2003, only 47% (50%, 3%) approved of how the United States was handling post-war Iraq and only 14% wanted to send more troops.*[7]
- *By June 2005, only 44% wanted to keep US troops in Iraq if it would take years to stabilize, and by January 2006, 50% said the war was a mistake and 49% said it was time to set a timeline to withdraw US troops.*
- *The US role in Afghanistan did not come under the same criticism as that of Iraq (after all, the Taliban did harbor Osama bin Laden). In August 2007, 57% said the invasion of Iraq was a mistake compared to 25% who said the same about the invasion of Afghanistan. In fact, in February 2009, 65% approved of Obama's decision to send 17,000 additional troops to Afghanistan.*

A major issue following 9/11 and the Iraqi invasion was the treatment and detainment of prisoners suspected of terrorism in Iraq and elsewhere, and at the US military base in Guantanamo, Cuba, that the Bush administration established in 2002. Two hundred forty-five prisoners were initially housed at Guantanamo, few of whom were ever charged with a crime and several of whom were severely tortured.

Obama made it one of his priorities to close the prison, but Congress would not allow the transfer of Guantanamo prisoners to US soil. By the end of his presidency, the prison remained in operation and still held forty-one prisoners, with the rest having been freed or transferred to other countries.

In 2003, there were widespread reports of prisoner abuse committed by US military personnel at Abu Ghraib, a detention facility holding around 8,000 prisoners in Iraq. In April 2004, *60 Minutes* broadcast photos of prisoners being tortured and humiliated. An investigation by the Pentagon reported many incidents of torture.

In addition, following 9/11, hundreds of prisoners were subject to rendition. This was the policy of sending prisoners (either captured or kidnapped[8]) to the so-called black sites throughout the world (secret CIA-operated prisons) or handed over to governments friendly to the Bush administration. Many of those rendered were tortured in an attempt to gain information.

- *Americans were largely not in agreement with "enhanced interrogation" techniques, that is, torture. Gallup asked whether it was right or wrong for the US government to use them on prisoners suspected of having information about possible terrorist attacks against the United States. Only 18% said it was right to force prisoners to remain naked and chained in uncomfortable positions in cold rooms for several hours; 49% thought it was acceptable to deprive prisoners of sleep for several days; 35% said it was right to threaten to transfer prisoners to a country known for using torture; 29% thought threatening prisoners with dogs was acceptable; only 16% agreed with waterboarding (strapping prisoners on boards and forcing their heads under water until they think they are drowning); and only 12% said that having female interrogators make physical contact with Muslim men during religious observances that prohibit such contact was "right" [1/05].*
- *Nonetheless, 49% believed that the reporting of these abuses was a major setback in the war against Iraq [5/04].*
- *Americans were also divided about operations at Guantanamo: 72% thought that the treatment of Taliban prisoners at Guantanamo was acceptable [1/02]; 58% wanted to continue operating the prison [6/05]; and in July 2007, 34% wanted to close the facility and 30% in November 2009.*

Other International Events

In March 2000, Vladimir Putin was elected president of Russia. A potential ally following the collapse of the Soviet Union, Russia, started to become an enemy. The Russian economy was in shambles and once Putin was in power, he won a power struggle with the Russian oligarchs and put his own allies in economic power. The economy became even more dominated by the oil industry,[9] freedom of the press eroded as papers were closed and journalists assassinated, political opponents were jailed, and a swing toward right-wing nationalism developed, which included the repression of gays and reestablishing the stature of the Russian Orthodox Church. George W. Bush received a lot of ridicule for stating, after he met with Putin, that he had found him to be trustworthy after looking into his eyes and getting a sense of his soul.

- *In October 2003, 38% of Americans had a favorable opinion of Putin (28%, 34%).*
- *At the end of the decade, only 12% considered Russia to be a serious threat to the United States (41% somewhat, 42% not, 5% DK), but only 40% had a favorable opinion of Russia [2/09].*
- *Sixty-two percent (30%, 8%) looked at Bush's comments as a good thing [7/01].*

One of the most covered news stories of the decade involved Elián González. His mother had drowned in November 1999 when fleeing Cuba with Elián, and he was placed with relatives living in Miami while his father, who lived in Cuba, sued to have him returned. The US courts ruled that Elián should be returned to Cuba, which occurred in June 2000. The case polarized political opinion, especially in Florida, and may have had a role in Al Gore losing the state of Florida in the 2000 presidential election.

- *Anti-Castro sentiment was no longer monolithic. Sixty-seven percent (25%, 8%) approved of sending Elián González back to Cuba [4/00] and 56% (35%, 9%) wanted to establish diplomatic relations with Cuba [10/00].*

In 2003, the International Atomic Energy Agency (IAEA) reported that Iran was not reporting its enrichment of nuclear materials. The UN demanded that Iran stop the enrichment. Iran claimed that its enrichment program had nothing to do with nuclear weapons.

- *In January 2006, 80% of respondents believed that Iran was trying to develop nuclear weapons.*
- *Only 9% favored military actions against Iran to stop its nuclear programs, and 68% favored economic sanctions (18% said take no actions and 5% did not know) [2/06].*

North Korea announced in February 2005 that it possessed nuclear weapons, and its first weapons test occurred in October 2006. Agreement was reached in March 2007 that North Korea would close its nuclear facility in return for fuel aid and normalization of relations with the United States. The agreement fell apart in 2009 when North Korea began a series of missile tests following congressional failure to fund economic aid to North Korea, which was part of the agreement.

- *Americans were sharply divided about what to do about North Korea. Forty-seven percent (48%, 5%) wanted to use military force if economic and diplomatic efforts were unsuccessful [1/03].*
- *At the end of the decade, 52% said they were very concerned about North Korea's nuclear capability [4/09].*

Yasser Arafat died in November 2004. Palestinian elections in January 2006 led to the fundamentalist Hamas organization taking control of Gaza, withdrawal of most international aid to Gaza, a blockade of Gaza by Israel, and a split between the Palestinian National Authority in the West Bank and Hamas in Gaza. Also, in 2006, Israel invaded Lebanon for thirty-two days following Hezbollah's firing rockets at Israel, killing three Israeli soldiers, and the kidnapping of two others in an attempt to obtain the release of Hezbollah prisoners held by Israel. The invasion displaced 1 million Lebanese, 1,200 Lebanese people were killed, as well as 165 Israelis. In December 2008, in response to rocket attacks from Gaza, Israel carried out a 3-week-long invasion of Gaza, during which over 1,000 residents of Gaza were killed as well as 13 Israelis.

- *Americans had become disenchanted with the US role vis-à-vis Israel. Only 32% wanted the United States to be involved in finding a diplomatic solution to the ongoing violence between Israel and the Palestinians [8/01].*
- *In April 2002, 71% approved of Bush's demand that Israel start withdrawing from the West Bank and only 24% said we should take Israel's side.*
- *Only 41% favored Israel's invasion of Lebanon [7/06]. In fact, 38% believed we supported Israel too much (44% about right, 11% too little, 8% no opinion) [7/06].*

One of the most disturbing stories of the decade involved the war in Darfur, a region of Sudan. The residents of Darfur felt discriminated against by the Arab-dominated government in Northern Sudan. Armed rebellion, which began in February 2003, was soon met by attacks on the civilian population resulting in over 100,000 deaths and over a million people fleeing to refugee camps in neighboring countries. There was a very active "Save Darfur" movement in the United States and elsewhere.[10]

US POLITICS

In November 2000, George W. Bush defeated Al Gore in a very controversial presidential election. Only 537 votes separated the two candidates in Florida.[11] Gore requested a recount in four counties and there was substantial debate over validating voting cards that were not properly punched. ("Chads"—the paper remaining after a card is incompletely punched—became a hot topic). The Supreme Court, in a highly contentious 5-4 ruling, stopped the recount and gave Florida and the election to Bush. Subsequent analysis by a consortium of news organizations determined that in a statewide recount, Gore would have won.[12]

- *Not surprisingly, Americans were divided about the outcome of the election: 48% thought Bush won the election fair and square; 32% thought he won on a technicality; and 18% said he stole the election. Forty-nine percent agreed with the Supreme*

Court's decision to stop the recount; 34% (30% of whites and 65% of blacks) thought that black voters were not counted fairly in Florida; and 83% said they would accept Bush as the legitimate president [12/00].
- *A year later, only 21% said they had a great deal of confidence in how votes were counted in the United States (20% lot; 32% some, and 26% little) [11/01].*

In another very close election, George W. Bush defeated John Kerry in the 2004 presidential election (50.7% v. 48.3%).

Throughout Bush's eight-year presidency, there was substantial controversy about his vice president, Dick Cheney. He was often portrayed as the power behind the throne—masterminding the war in Iraq; arguing for "enhanced interrogation techniques"; and expanding the power of the presidency.

- *In May 2001, only 13% thought Cheney had too much power. Seven years later, Cheney's approval rating was only 32% (and Bush's was 34%) [1/09].*

The third presidential election in the decade had Senator Barack Obama defeating Senator John McCain in November 2008 (52.9% v. 45.7%). The election was memorable as Obama was the first African American to become president. Obama had defeated Hillary Clinton in a very tight Democratic nomination battle. The campaign season was also marked by McCain's dubious choice of Governor Sarah Palin of Alaska as a running mate.

- *The electorate was polarized during the Bush presidency and this polarization increased after Obama became president. Two years after Bush became president, 57% of survey respondents thought he was making a sincere effort to bring civility back to DC [11/02].*
- *Three months into his presidency, 66% thought Obama made a sincere effort to work with Republicans [4/09].*
- *However, civility began to seriously erode as the Affordable Care Act (Obamacare) began to work its way through Congress (to be discussed in the next chapter). At one point, Congressman Joe Wilson of South Carolina yelled out at Obama—"You lie" during a speech before Congress (21% supported his yelling [9/09]).*

Following 9/11, there was a substantial controversy about the trade-off between civil liberties and protecting the public from future acts of terrorism. The Patriot Act was signed into law in October 2001, which allowed for indefinite detention of immigrants and greater surveillance of individuals and groups by security agencies. The Department of Homeland Security was established in November 2002.

- *Seventy-two percent of Americans approved of establishing the Department of Homeland Security [6/02].*

- However, only 29% (67%, 4%) agreed that the government should take all steps necessary to prevent additional acts of terrorism in the United States if that meant violating one's basic civil liberties [8/03].
- When asked about support for a variety of acts preventing terrorist attacks in the United States the following data indicate the extent to which Americans were willing to restrict certain civil liberties:
  - allowing police to enter a person's home at any time without a search warrant (6%);
  - allowing police to stop people on the street at random and ask them to show their ID (48%);
  - requiring Arabs, including those who are US citizens, to carry a special ID (46%);
  - requiring Arabs, including those who are US citizens, to undergo special, more intensive security checks before boarding airplanes in the United States (53%);
  - requiring every person going into an office building or public place to show ID (70%);
  - requiring every person going into an office building or public place to go through a metal detector (81%);
  - allowing police to stop people on the street at random to search their possessions (29%);
  - making it easier for legal authorities to read mail, e-mail, or tap phones without the person's knowledge (25%);
  - requiring mass transit systems like subways, buses, and trains to institute security systems similar to what is found in airports (78%);
  - requiring all Americans to carry a national ID card (66%);
  - allowing the government to search a list of books people have checked out of the library (37%);
  - allowing the government to imprison US citizens who are suspected of terrorism without putting them on trial for years (21%) [7/05].
- More specifically, 51% approved of the Patriot Act's provisions that banks are required to tell federal agents, without a court order, if a person has an account; that agents can secretly search a home (26%); and that organizations (including libraries) have to turn over lists of their users and not notify the user of the fact (45%) [2/04].

Hurricane Katrina made landfall in Louisiana and Mississippi on August 29, 2005. It ended up being the costliest natural disaster in US history. Over 1,800 people died, and property damage exceeded $100 billion. The greatest destruction was in New Orleans when various levies were breached. The Federal Emergency Management Agency (FEMA) and other segments of the US government came under strong criticism for mismanagement by not preparing for the storm and not responding adequately in the days and months after. George Bush came under particularly harsh criticism for not paying attention to the storm (he was on vacation) and not being an effective crisis manager.

- Ninety-three percent of Americans said Katrina was the worst natural disaster in their lifetime and that the government should have been better prepared. In rating

who handled the aftermath of the storm as very good or good: 57% said state and local government; 59% said the residents of New Orleans; 44% said George W. Bush; and 36% said FEMA and other federal government agencies responsible for handling emergencies. However, only 27% said the government responded slowly because the people affected were poor or black [9/05].
- *Six months after the hurricane struck, 51% thought the government was not doing enough to help rebuild [2/06].*

Stories of child sexual abuse committed by Catholic priests exploded in 2002 following an investigation by the *Boston Globe*.[13] Since 2002, over 3,000 civil suits have been filed against the Catholic Church in the United States and it is estimated that the Church paid approximately $3 billion in settlements. Eight Catholic dioceses declared bankruptcy.

- *In April 2002, 74% said the Catholic Church has done a bad job in dealing with the problem of sexual abuse committed by its priests, and 77% said the priests should immediately be removed instead of being given therapy and being more closely supervised.*

Another big news story concerned Terry Schiavo of Florida, who in 1990, at the age of twenty-seven, had a heart attack and ended up in an irreversible persistent vegetative state. Her husband wanted to remove her feeding tubes after two years and this was challenged in court by her parents and various Republican officials. After fourteen separate appeals and despite intervention by Florida Governor Jeb Bush and President Bush, the tubes were removed, and she died in March 2005.

- *At the time the feeding tubes were removed, 57% (32%, 12%) thought they should be removed [3/05].*

Mass shootings continued. In April 2007, Seung-Hui Cho killed thirty-two people at Virginia Polytechnic Institute and then committed suicide. In April 2009, Liverly Wong killed fourteen at an immigration center in Binghamton New York and then committed suicide. In November 2009, Army Psychiatrist Nidal Malik Hasan killed thirteen at Fort Hood Texas.[14]

- *Even before these mass shootings, Americans were generally in favor of gun control measures: in 2000, 73% of respondents supported registering all handguns [1/00]; 79% were in favor of requiring all handguns to be sold with trigger locks; and 93% supported requiring a five-day waiting period to allow for background checks (93%) [4/00].*
- *And in 2004, 60% supported making the laws surround the sale of firearms stricter [1/04].*

RACE

The election of Barack Obama was a seminal moment in the history of race relations. In July 1958, only 37% of Americans had said they would vote for a well-qualified man nominated by their party if he happened to be a "Negro."[15] In 2008, there were many examples of racists stating they were going to "vote for the N..." Questioning the power structure and issues surrounding the economy (the Great Recession of 2008) became more important than race.

- *In fact, 59% of respondents (73% among blacks) said the election of Obama was one of the most important advances in race relations in the last 100 years [10/09]. Furthermore, 59% of whites and 79% of blacks expected race relations to get better because of the election [10/09].*
- *On other general racial attitudes: 39% of whites and 57% of blacks believed that relations between blacks and whites would always be a problem; 84% of whites and 59% of blacks said blacks had just as good a chance as whites getting a job in their community if they were qualified; 51% of whites and 72% of blacks said racism against blacks was widespread in the United States; and, conversely, 47% of whites and 40% of blacks said racism against whites was widespread [10/09].*

Another racial controversy was whether Confederate flags should be taken down from flying over state capitol buildings in the South.

- *Forty-seven percent (44%, 10%; 20% of blacks said it was OK) thought it was okay for these flags to fly and 56% said the flag was more a symbol of pride than of racism (59%, 28%, 5%) [5/00].*
- *Reparations for slavery were advocated by some civil rights leaders.[16] Only 41% thought that corporations that had made a profit from slavery prior to the civil war should apologize; 20% (64% among blacks) said these corporations should make cash payments to descendants of slaves, and 43% said they should set up scholarship programs [1/02].*

The other big story affecting blacks and Hispanics was the Great Recession, which is discussed in greater detail below. Blacks fared far worse than whites during the economic crisis. The net worth of blacks fell by 32.8% as compared to 11.5% for whites. Black and Latino homeowners were twice as likely as whites to have their mortgages foreclosed on. In 2000, HUD found that "In predominantly Black neighborhoods subprime lending accounted for 51 percent of refinance loans in 1998—compared with only 9 percent in predominately white areas." Harney (2006) discusses a study by the National Community Reinvestment Corporation using paired testers in six cities and found brokers discussed fixed rate loan options with 90% of white applicants and only 56% of blacks. Similarly, whites were shown twice as many loan options, and only 9% of whites were pressed for credit problem information compared with 40% of blacks.[17]

- *Twelve percent of respondents believed the 2008 recession hurt blacks worse than whites, 8% said whites hurt worse than blacks, and 80% said both hurt equally. Surprising to me, there were no differences between the white and black respondents [12/09-CNN].*

SEX AND GENDER

It was an extraordinary decade for gay rights. In January 2000, California started registering domestic partners, giving them benefits such as the right to hospital visitations and health insurance. On the other hand, in March 2000, 63% of Californians voted in favor of marriage being reserved only for couples of the opposite sex, and in May, Colorado became the thirty-third state prohibiting same-sex unions. The battles intensified. In June 2003, the Supreme Court ruled in *Lawrence v. Texas* that sodomy laws were unconstitutional. In November of the same year, the Massachusetts Supreme Court became the first state court to legalize same-sex marriage. However, in February 2004, Ohio approved a gay marriage ban, blocking adoptions by same-sex couples, and prohibiting state employees from sharing benefits with domestic partners.

In the 2004 presidential campaign, Bush called for a constitutional amendment defining marriage as being between a man and a woman. Some cities (San Francisco and Multnomah County, Oregon) began issuing marriage licenses for same-sex couples though these were often overturned in the courts. Some states (New Jersey, Oregon, and Washington State) began to allow civil unions which often had the same rights as marriages. On the other hand, in November 2008, with a 52% majority vote on Proposition 8, California banned gay marriage.

- *At the beginning of the decade, only 31% of respondents thought that the Boy Scouts should be required to allow openly gay scout leaders [6/00], and 42% would support civic unions for homosexual relations [10/00].*
- *At the end of the decade, only 40% said that same-sex marriage should be recognized under the law as valid [5/09]. However, 70% favored allowing openly gay men and women to serve in the military [5/09]; and 68% said that gay and lesbian domestic partners should have health and other employer benefits, inheritance rights (73%), and be able to adopt (54%) [5/09].*
- *Support for women's rights continued to grow. When asked how long it would take before a woman became president, 40% thought in the next ten years [1/01].*[18] *However, only 46% said that if a draft were necessary, women should be drafted similarly to men [12/01].*
- *Most (77%) favored allowing women to fly combat aircraft and serving in combat jobs (52%) [12/01].*
- *Sexual mores continued to liberalize. Over half (55%, 27%, 18%) approved of unmarried men and women living together [9/07] and 54% said it was morally acceptable to have a baby outside of marriage [5/05]. However, only 9% thought having an extramarital affair was morally acceptable [5/05].*

THE ECONOMY

The decade opened with a promising forecast by the Congressional Budget Office of a $5.6 trillion budget surplus over the next ten years. Alas, this did not occur given Bush's tax cuts in 2001 and 2003 (mostly benefiting the wealthy), the cost of the Iraqi and Afghani wars, and, of course, the Great Recession. In the year Bush was elected (2000) the federal budget had a surplus of $236 billion. In 2002, there was a deficit of $158 billion.

- *Sixty-one percent favored the 2001 Bush tax cuts, but 75% preferred that fewer of the benefits go to the rich [3/01].*
- *After the cuts were initiated, 46% said they had worsened the federal budget deficit [7/03].*

Bush's other major attempt at economic policy reform concerned social security. In February 2005, he advocated partial privatization of the system by allowing people to divert retirement money from the social security system to private investments. This was not widely supported and was tabled in the House.

- *In October 2000, 66% thought people should be able to invest part of their social security taxes in the market. Four months after Bush proposed partial privatization, only 45% (50%, 5%) thought it was a good idea [6/05, CBS/NYT].*

The biggest economic story of the decade was the Great Recession. Unemployment doubled from 5.0% in December 2008 to 10.0% in October 2009. During the time of the Great Recession, housing prices fell by 30%; over 3.1 million houses were foreclosed; the net worth of US households and non-profit organizations declined from $67 trillion to $52 trillion; and stock market prices fell by 57%. It was the worst economic downturn since the Great Depression of the 1930s.

There were two major factors that triggered the Great Recession. The first was the collapse of the housing bubble. Prices of housing expanded at an unsustainable rate, increasing 124% between 1997 and 2006. Many people were buying homes with little savings and insufficient incomes. Twenty percent of those purchasing homes were given sub-prime mortgages, loans with much higher interest rates.[19] When the bubble began to collapse, those with sub-prime mortgages were unable to keep up given their high mortgage payments and the value of their house was now less than what was owed.

A second factor triggering the Great Recession was financial speculation. The repeal of the Glass-Steagall Act in 1990 gave banks greater ability to make riskier investments. Furthermore, new financial products (e.g., CDOs) were complex and not fully understood, and therefore their risks were not obvious to many in the market. These financial products were often used to fund sub-prime mortgages, thus compounding both problems.

On September 15, 2008, Lehman Brothers, with over $600 billion in assets, filed for bankruptcy, causing the Dow Jones to drop by 500 points and acting as the immediate trigger for the Great Recession. This was seven weeks before the 2008 election. A bipartisan effort led to Bush signing a $152 billion stimulus bill; other legislation allowed the government to purchase $700 billion in troubled assets; the Federal Reserve lowered interest rates to banks; and the Federal Reserve started to purchase $1.2 trillion in other troubled assets.

After Obama came to power, Congress passed another stimulus bill in February 2009, amounting to $831 billion. The bill supported lower tax rates, increased spending for infrastructure, alternative energy, education, health care, and scientific research, and more aid for the unemployed. The Obama administration also supported the bailout of General Motors and Chrysler (who had both filed for bankruptcy) and proposed legislation (Dodd-Frank) to expand financial regulation, which was passed in July 2010 and will be discussed at greater length in the next chapter.

- *Economic problems linked to the recession had been perceived well in advance. In December 2007, 62% said the mortgage companies were completely or mostly to blame for the problems in the mortgage market, including foreclosures. Furthermore, 71% said the economy was getting worse [12/07] and 54% predicted a recession in the next twelve months [11/07]. Even before the full onslaught of the Great Recession, 73% favored a stimulus bill to grow the economy [1/08].*
- *However, the $700 billion signed by Bush was supported by only 48% (46%, 7%) of the public, and 47% supported giving the automobile companies major financial assistance if they were close to bankruptcy [11/08]. In December 2008, 35% said it was very likely we would have a depression and another 39% said somewhat likely. Although most feared a depression, there was not an overwhelming output of support during the end of the Bush Presidency or the beginning of the Obama Presidency for the drastic measures most economists advocated.*
- *In Obama's first year, many of his economic policies lacked wholesale support: 46% thought his home mortgage plan would be helpful and 51% said it was unfair to those who were paying their mortgages; only 39% wanted to help the banks[20] and 41% wanted to help the auto companies [2/09]. On the other hand, 83% wanted to give aid to state governments that were in trouble; 65% wanted to give aid to homeowners who were facing foreclosure; and 83% favored a government program to create jobs [2/09].*
- *When Congress passed the $831 billion stimulus bill, 48% (22%, 25%) said it would make the economy better [2/09]. Fifty-three percent approved of the government's actions on the economy [3/09], but only 28% said Obama's economic policies would work in the short term [7/09].*

Beyond the economic fraud discussed above concerning the sub-prime market and financial speculation, there were other egregious examples of fraud. In December 2001, Enron was forced to file for bankruptcy protection. Enron bought and sold energy products and by 1992 was the largest seller of natural gas in North America. Enron used misleading and fraudulent accounting practices to misstate its earnings. Its downfall also led to the collapse of Arthur Andersen, one of the five largest accounting partnerships in the world. The Bush administration was tainted by the bankruptcy. Enron and its president Kenneth Lay had donated over $2 million to Bush over the years, many members of the Bush administration had stock in Enron, Bush had lobbied for Enron, and, as the scandal broke, Lay and others had many meetings with members of the Bush administration.

- *Forty-three percent of Americans (47%, 10%) thought that the Bush administrators were trying to cover-up their contacts with Enron, and in another question, 15% said the Bush administration officials acted illegally or unethically (43%) [2/02]. Furthermore, 20% said Enron-type misconduct was a crisis and another 57% said it was a major problem [6/02].*

The other major economic scandal of the decade concerned Bernard Madoff. He was arrested in 2008 for operating a decades-old Ponzi scheme. Approximately, 4,800 investors were defrauded of $65 billion. Madoff was sentenced to 150 years in prison and his son Peter received a 10-year sentence. His son Mark committed suicide because of the scandal.

- *Gallup asked no questions about Madoff. CNN/Opinion Research found that 74% thought his behavior was common among financial advisors and institutions [12/08] and Fox News found that 11% said they had lost money to unscrupulous advisors like Madoff [1/09].*
- *Before the beginning of the Great Recession, most Americans had a positive view of the economic system: 60% wanted to eliminate all inheritance taxes (even if over $1 million in assets) [6/00]; but only 38% thought it was correct to characterize American society as divided into haves and have-nots.*
- *However, 38% thought money and wealth should be more evenly divided [9/00].*
- *After the advent of the Great Recession, most Americans wanted the government to regulate business and industries. Only 28% said the government was doing too much regulation, while 30% wanted more regulation, and 39% said there was the right amount [2/02].*

Americans were buffeted by high energy prices. The price of a gallon of gas increased from $1.51 in 2000 to $3.27 in 2008. By 2017, it had fallen to $2.49 a gallon. In February 2000, 40% said the increase in gasoline and home fuel prices had caused them financial hardship. This number had increased to 63% by March 2008.

- *When asked who was to blame for the energy problems, the following entities were assigned a great deal of blame: US oil companies (60%), Congress (44%), the current Bush administration (49%), foreign countries that produce oil (46%),*

environmental laws and regulations (25%), American consumers (31%), and US automobile companies (31%) [5/08].
- *Anger toward oil companies was such that 58% (31%, 11%) said they were more likely to vote for a candidate who advocated a windfall profit tax on oil companies and 62% wanted price controls on gasoline. Furthermore, respondents also said they were more likely to vote for a candidate who supported: easing restrictions on offshore domestic drilling (57%); building more nuclear power plants (47%); authorizing a $150 billion investment by the federal government in research on biofuels and clean energy sources (64%); and raising fuel mileage standards on vehicles (68%) [7/08].*

SCIENCE, TECHNOLOGY, AND THE ENVIRONMENT

The space program had major ups and downs. The International Space Station had its first residents in 2000. Then, in 2004, the space shuttle Columbia disintegrated upon reentry, killing all seven astronauts aboard. NASA landed two large robotic explorers (rovers) on Mars in 2004, and in 2008, Space X became the first privately developed space craft to launch.

- *Seventy percent said the Mars landing was a major scientific achievement [1/04].*
- *Despite the Columbia disaster, 74% wanted to continue the manned space program [6/05].*

Other major scientific or technological advances included the advent of: PlayStation 2 in 2000; the iPod in 2001; the first self-contained artificial heart implant in 2001; Facebook's web page in 2004; Gmail, also in 2004; YouTube in 2005; Twitter in 2006;[21] the iPhone in 2007; Kindle in 2007; and circulation of a proton beam for the first time at CERN's Large Hadron Collider in 2008.

- *The internet continued to grow. At the beginning of the decade, 54% had internet access, and of those: 89% were using e-mail, 21% had visited a chat room, 95% were finding information, 30% had used the internet to track the presidential campaign, and 48% had purchased something on the internet [2/00].*
- *Five years later [12/05], 73% were using the internet, and of those: 52% were using it for shopping, 28% were instant messaging, 87% were using it to read emails, 28% to play games, 72% to check news and weather, 40% to pay bills, 41% to find medical advice, and 22% to watching video clips.*
- *In August 2005, 81% of Americans had a cellphone, 91% a DVD player, 56% high-speed internet, and 85% cable or satellite TV.*

The internet created problems for many segments of the economy. Napster and other peer-to-peer file sharing systems allowed people to share songs encoded in MP3 format. In 2001, Napster had over ten million users and in 2002 record sales

160   Chapter 8

had declined by 8.9% from the previous year. The Record Industry Association of America (RIAA) sued and was able to shut down many of these sites.

- *Forty-three percent of respondents (46%, 11%) thought that trading songs on the internet should be legal [3/02], and 18% said they had downloaded songs that were not authorized [5/02].*

Another problem with the internet concerned security. Individual computers, networks, and websites were increasingly being maliciously attacked for financial gain, political causes, national security, and sometimes just as a prank.

- *In February 2000, of the 54% who said they had used the internet in the thirty days previous to the survey, 46% said they were not confident that using a credit card would be secure.*
- *DNA evidence was being used in more legal trials, with 20% of respondents saying it was completely reliable and 57% saying very reliable [3/00].*[22]
- *But, people were also skeptical of some new scientific research. Thirty percent thought that using biotechnology in food was safe [3/00]; only 9% approved of cloning humans [11/01], and only 15% approved of cloning pets, and 38% of cloning endangered species to keep them from going extinct [5/02].*
- *Eight percent wanted parents to have the ability to choose genetic traits for their children such as intelligence or height [1/03].*

Science was becoming more politicized. Scientists became more capable of extracting embryotic stem cells that could be used in medical research for new treatments. Stem cell research was, though, opposed by some who wanted to make abortions illegal, and in August 2001, Bush announced that no new stem cell lines would be allowed. This policy was reversed when Obama became president and reversed again when Trump became president.

- *Fifty-four percent (39%, 7%) wanted stem cell research to continue [7/01].*
- *Only 36% supported Bush's veto of legislation expanding funding for stem cell research [7/06].*

In December 2004, approximately 250,000 people died in tsunamis in countries bordering the Indian Ocean following a 9.1 earthquake off Indonesia.

- *One-third of Americans said they gave money to tsunami relief funds, and 91% said the United States has given its fair share or more than its fair share in disaster relief [1/05].*
- *Most Americans were not worried about their family coming down with new diseases that were appearing. Fifteen percent were concerned about West Nile Virus*

[9/02]; 43% about Severe Acute Respiratory Syndrome, or SARS [4/03];[23] *16% about Mad Cow Disease [1/04]; and 29% about Bird Flu [3/06].*

However, extensive controversy erupted following a 1989 article that appeared in *Lancet* linking autism with MMR (measles, mumps, and rubella) vaccinations. *Lancet* retracted the article in 2010 after determining that the main author, Andrew Wakefield, committed deliberate fraud and did not disclose financial ties to attorneys suing the vaccine maker. But the damage had been done. Many parents stopped vaccinating their children, which led to outbreaks of measles in the United Kingdom, the United States, and elsewhere. Some say it was one of the most serious frauds in the medical history. Celebrities such as Jenny McCarthy promoted these false claims and became known as anti-vaxxers.

- *Of the 54% who heard of McCarthy's claims, 42% said they were now more likely to question the safety of vaccines [11/09].*

The Intergovernmental Panel on Climate Change published its fourth assessment report in 2007. It stated that global warming is unequivocal and is caused by human actions. The scientists predicted, among other findings, global temperatures to rise between 3.2 and 11.5 °F and sea levels to rise between 7 and 23 inches by the twenty-first century. Many Americans became educated about global warming after the release of *An Inconvenient Truth* in 2006 (which won two Academy Awards). This documentary featured Al Gore's lecture and slide show about global warming. The movie mobilized many environmentalists. Unfortunately, a conservative backlash also developed, and the issue became increasingly polarized.[24]

- *According to a 2001 survey, public attitudes on climate change, even though mixed, were generally in assent with the report. Only 30% said the threat of global warming was exaggerated; 61% said the increase in global temperatures were due to human activity; 63% were willing to pay $500 a more per year so industry would reduce pollution; 75% wanted higher emission standards for automobiles; and 79% wanted the government to spend more on developing solar and wind power [03/01].*
- *Furthermore, only 40% approved of George Bush's decision not to adhere to the Kyoto Agreement that would limit global warming [6/01] and in March 2005, a plurality said the United States should still adhere to the agreement (42%, 23%, 35%).*
- *When asked whether protecting the environment should be given priority over the economy, even if economic growth was curbed, 54% (36%, 10%) chose the environment [5/02]. However, 53% wanted to increase tax incentives to drill more oil and gas [3/01].*
- *Contradictory views continued at the end of the decade. Sixty percent of Americans said the effects of global warming were already happening and that the government should require government office building to use renewable energy resources even if*

that caused taxes to rise. However, only 38% supported very strict restrictions on businesses and utilities if that caused some to go out of business [3/07], and 57% said they were more willing to vote for a candidate who advocated easing restrictions on offshore domestic oil drilling [7/08].
- *In 2007, Al Gore and the IPCC won the Nobel Peace Prize for their work on global warming. Forty-three percent of Americans (26%, 31%) thought Gore's prize was well-deserved [3/07].*

POPULAR TRENDS

Top movies of the decade included: *How the Grinch Stole Christmas* (2000); *The Lord of the Rings: The Fellowship of the Ring* (2001); *Harry Potter and the Sorcerer's Stone* (2001); *Spider-Man* (2002); *Finding Nemo* (2003); *Transformers* (2007); *The Dark Knight* (2008); *Iron Man* (2008); and *Avatar* (2009).

More and more television programming came from nontraditional outlets such as HBO, Comedy Central, and Showtime. Some of the new TV programs were: *Survivor* (2000—84% had heard of the series and 45% had seen it [7/00]); *Curb Your Enthusiasm* (2000); *American Idol* (2001); *The Wire* (2002); *Chappelle's Show* (2003); *Deadwood* (2004); *Lost* (2004); *The Colbert Report* (2005); *The Office* (2005); *30 Rock* (2006); *Breaking Bad* (2008); and *Mad Men* (2007).

Books that came out in the 2000s included: James Bradley with Ron Powers, *Flag of Our Fathers* (2000); Laura Hillenbrand, *Sea Biscuit* (2001); Michael Moore, *Dude, Where's My Country* (2004); Bill Clinton, *My Life* (2004); Malcolm Gladwell, *Blink* (2005); and Barack Obama, *The Audacity of Hope* (2006).

The release of the iPod and iTunes in 2001 had a dramatic impact on the music industry. Teen rock remained popular (*NSYNC, Backstreet Boys, Britney Spears), but hip-hop and contemporary R & B (Usher, Rihanna, and Beyoncé) and country (Carrie Underwood and Shania Twain) dominated. Other popular musicians included: Eminem, Coldplay, U2, Black Eyed Peas, Pink, Alicia Keys, Jay-Z, Kanye West, Shakira, Justin Timberlake, Destiny's Child, and Taylor Swift.

In February 2005, Jose Canseco appearing in *60 Minutes* and credited the use of steroids for his successful baseball career and said as many as 80% of players used steroids. Over the course of the decade, Mark McGwire admitted to using banned substances during the season when he hit seventy home runs (1998); Alex Rodriquez admitted using steroids between 2001 and 2003, when he was the American League MVP; and Ken Caminiti said he had been using steroids in 1996, the year he was named the National League MVP. Barry Bonds, who won seven National League MVP awards, was indicted for perjury in 2007 when, in the course of the federal government's investigation of the issue, he denied using steroids.

- *Ninety-two percent of Americans wanted to test baseball players for steroids and 11% said they thought all or most players used steroids, while another 22% said half [10/03].*

- *Regarding Barry Bonds, only 19% thought he was telling the truth [2/05] and 52% thought his batting record should be taken away if he was found to take steroids [3/06]. Nevertheless, only 23% said steroids were ruining baseball [3/05].*
- *When asked in which sports they thought most or all athletes used enhancement drugs, 33% of respondents identified football, 27% professional baseball, 20% professional cycling, 9% swimming, and 21% track and field [6/07].*

Bob Knight, head coach of the University of Indiana's men's basketball team, was seen on television grabbing a player by the throat. Consequently, Knight was forced to retire, but at the time of his retirement he had won more NCAA Division 1 games than any other coach in basketball history.

- *Forty percent of respondents had seen the video and another 29% had heard of it. Thirty-nine percent of those who had seen the video thought Knight should be fired for his actions [4/00].*

Tiger Woods became a major celebrity as the dominant professional golfer from 1997 to 2010. In November 2009, he was involved in a car accident and news soon leaked of his having many extramarital affairs. He and his wife divorced in 2010.

- *In his prime, Woods had extraordinarily high approval ratings of 85% [6/05].*
- *In December 2009, 68% of respondents wanted him to continue playing golf and not retire. However, his approval rating had plummeted to 33%.*

Michael Phelps won eight Olympic medals in the 2008 Summer Olympic Games in swimming. In February 2009, Phelps was photographed smoking marijuana using a bong.

- *An NBC/WSJ survey found that 57% had a favorable opinion of Phelps, 3% a negative opinion, 13% were neutral, and 27% had not heard of him [8/08]. Pew found that 67% believed that too much coverage was given to his smoking marijuana [2/09].*

The most covered event in celebrity news was the death of entertainer Michael Jackson in 2009. Jackson had hit songs such as "Billy Jean," "Beat It," and "Thriller," and his album *Thriller* was the best-selling album of all time (sixty-five million copies). But he was also vilified by many for apparently changing the color of his skin to look whiter, and because of accusations of child sexual abuse, on which charges Jackson was acquitted by a jury in June 2005. Jackson died after his personal physician administered a lethal dose of Propofol, an anesthesia, to treat his insomnia. (Jackson's doctor was later convicted of involuntary manslaughter.)

- *After Jackson was arrested, only 1% of Americans said they had never heard of him, and 65% had an unfavorable attitude toward the entertainer [12/03].*

- *Seventy-seven percent thought that the charges that Michael Jackson sexually abused a child were true [2/06]. After the jury reached a not guilty verdict, only 34% (48%, 18%) agreed with the verdict.*

CONCLUDING COMMENTS

This was the decade of 9/11, the invasion of Iraq, the Great Recession, and the election of America's first black president.

Immediately after the horrific events of 9/11, Americans were united and our allies and many of our supposed enemies offered aid. But the invasion of Iraq reversed both trends and may have been the worst foreign policy mistake in US history, leading to an unwinnable twenty-year war and creating instability throughout a large part of the world. Elsewhere, Putin consolidated power in Russia, Hamas took power in Gaza, North Korea acquired nuclear weapons, and the slaughter in Darfur was ignored.

As with the Vietnam War, American public opinion was initially supportive of the invasion of Iraq. Attitudes turned negative as it became apparent that this was another quagmire that would cost trillions of dollars, and that there would be many casualties and long-term negative effects on our prestige. Also similar to reactions to the Vietnam War, Americans were now less likely—for good or for bad—to support other interventions abroad.

Bush's controversial defeat of Gore in 2000 had far-reaching consequences. If Gore had won, it is unlikely that Iraq would have been invaded and it is likely that we would have kick-started the fight against global warming. The 9/11 also led to the United States using torture on prisoners and limiting the civil liberties of its citizens. Hurricane Katrina happened toward the end of the Bush presidency, perhaps symbolizing the systematic neglect of urban areas. The election of Barack Obama in 2008 was a different type of symbol: the first black president. The symbolic impact was different among racial minorities as compared to many white Americans.

Americans were not supportive of the use of torture and some of the more extreme measures of the Patriot Act. Cultural and ideological polarization increased because of the war in Iraq and was notched up to an even higher level with the election of Obama.

Obama's election did not end racial controversies and in some ways, because of the reactions of white nationalists, accentuated tensions. This will be discussed at greater length in the next chapter.

Sexual mores continued to change with over half of Americans now approving of unmarried partners living together and seeing it as acceptable to have a baby outside of marriage. The Supreme Court in 2003 ruled that laws against sodomy were unconstitutional and the struggle for LGBT rights rose to a new level with the fight over gay marriage. In 2008, California's Proposition 8 outlawed gay marriage. However, public opinion was turning. At the end of the decade, almost half of survey respondents supported gay marriage and more than that approved of gay partners having employer benefits and inheritance rights.

When Bush became president, the United States had a budget surplus. When he left, there was a substantial deficit, and the country was engulfed in the Great Recession. As with public opinion during the Great Depression, opinion was greatly divided on many of the policies needed to produce recovery, such as financial assistance to the automobile companies and help for those who would otherwise default on their mortgages. However, in other areas the pendulum has shifted, more Americans were concerned about income inequality and most wanted greater regulation of corporations and financial institutions.

Changes in technology in this decade provided the foundation for new industries and new ways of conducting one's personal life (e.g., the growth of online shopping and the ascendency of social media), and, by the same token, remarkable opportunities for high tech and retail entrepreneurs. It was in this decade that public awareness grew about climate change and the battle over environmental policies became even more protracted.

[The reader can find relevant crosstabs and discussion in the online appendix located at https://rowman.com/ISBN/9781793653505/US-Public-Opinion-since-the-1930s-Galluping-through-History.]

NOTES

1. Exit polls were becoming increasing problematic as response rates dropped, early and absentee voting gained an increasing role, Republicans were less willing to participate in the exit polls, many precincts kept interviewers at a distance, and many selected precincts were not covered or were covered by poorly trained interviewers (Campbell, 2020). The debacle in Florida was further driven by data entry errors.

2. This was not Al-Qaeda's first act of terrorism in the decade. For example, in October 2000, the *USS Cole*, a navy destroyer, was badly damaged in Aden, Yemen, by a small boat filled with explosives, killing seventeen crew members.

3. In February 2002, the CIA sent Joseph Wilson to Niger to look into allegations that Niger was sending Uranium cake to Iraq. Wilson reported this was not happening. Following the invasion of Iraq, he wrote an op-ed article in the *New York Times* questioning the WMD rationale for the invasion. Following his op-ed article, a conservative columnist "outed" his wife, Valerie Plame, as a CIA operative. In March 2007, Lewis (Scooter) Libby, who was chief of staff to Vice President Cheney, was convicted of perjury in lying about his role in "outing" Plame. President Bush commuted his thirtieth-month sentence in March 2008 (66% opposed this commutation [7/07]). Fifty-one percent said they were closely following Karl Rove's role in this story. Of those, 25% said the leaking was illegal, 37% unethical, 15% nothing wrong, and 23% did not know [7/05]. Of those who followed Libby's role, 55% thought that Cheney was aware of Libby's actions and 45% thought Libby acted illegally or unethically (31%) [10/05].

4. There is substantial controversy over why the Bush administration initiated the Iraqi War: gain access to oil, show other regimes that we could change the world order, retaliation for a supposed assassination attempt against George H. W. Bush, belief that we could export democracy, putting pressure on Saudi Arabia, etc.

5. One had to be a member of the Baathist Party to hold a government position. Approximately 100,000 Iraqis were thrown out of their jobs, including 40,000 schoolteachers.

6. By February 2008, 53% thought Bush had purposely misled the public about Iraq having WMDs.

7. A compilation of Gallup and CNN polls that show how support for the war deteriorated over time can be found in CNN (2007). The data shows that the percent who believed that the war was morally justified dropped from 73% in 2003 to 47% in 2006. Similarly, the percent who favored the war dropped from 72% to 40% in the same time.

8. It is estimated that 100 people living in Europe were kidnapped by the CIA.

9. For a fascinating account of the role of the oil industry in Russia, see Maddow (2019).

10. Gallup asked no questions on Darfur. CNN/Opinion Research found 61% favored sending US troops to Darfur as part of an international peacekeeping force [10/07].

11. Nationwide, Gore received 540,000 more votes than Bush. In addition, Ralph Nader, the Green Party candidate, received 2.9 million votes.

12. Furthermore, a poorly designed ballot (the butterfly) in Palm Beach County, Florida, resulted in over 6,000 ballots being disqualified for people voting for both Al Gore and Pat Buchannan (a right-wing fringe candidate). Subsequent analysis showed that almost all of these were actual votes for Al Gore. Having an even greater impact was Florida's purging of suspected felons from the voter lists. It is estimated that 12,000 were incorrectly purged (they were not felons) and if they were allowed to vote, Gore would have easily won the state of Florida.

13. The 2015 movie *Spotlight* looks at the role of the *Boston Globe* in uncovering the scandal.

14. For a database on mass shootings, see http://www.motherjones.com/politics/2012/12/mass-shootings-mother-jones-full-data.

15. The word "Negro" seems antiquated at best. In December 2000, 19% of blacks said they preferred African American, 14% black, and 63% said it did not matter.

16. One of the best arguments for reparations can be found in Coates (2014).

17. Paired testers are identical on paper (same income, marital status, etc.). The only difference is their race. Therefore, any racial differences are due to racial discrimination (not differences in income, etc.).

18. Thirty-six percent thought a black would become president within the next ten years.

19. Mortgage lenders that originated the sub-prime loans often did not care that the borrower had a high probability of a default. They were selling the mortgages to others and would not be affected by the default. Money was made in the initial financing. There was a tremendous amount of fraud in this process.

20. Fifty-four percent wanted the government to temporarily take over banks that were in danger of failing [2/09].

21. Peter Thiel famously said, "We wanted flying cars, instead we got 140 characters."

22. The TV show—*CSI: Crime Scene Investigation*—began to air in 2000 and presented an overly optimistic view on the efficacy of forensic evidence.

23. Covid-19 is also called SARS-Cov-2 (discussed in a later chapter). They are closely related. SARS-Cov-2 is more contagious than SARS, but less deadly.

24. See Michael Mann, *The New Climate War* (2021) for an excellent discussion of how fossil fuel companies generated "doubts" about climate change.

9

The 2010s

War against ISIS, the Tea Party, Black Lives Matter, Brexit, and the Election of Donald Trump

There were 253 web-based surveys (6% of the total) in the Roper archive. Eighty-seven of these were supplemented by some other form of data collection (mostly telephone). The move to web-based surveys was necessitated by the rising cost and declining response rate of telephone surveys. Furthermore, web-based panels allowed for easier reinterviewing of respondents. The widespread use of cell phones accelerated the need to develop special cell phone samples, which is difficult to accomplish as people frequently do not live in the area code of their telephone number. Most major telephone surveys used dual frames (landline and cell phone). Gallup was still the largest single survey organization in Roper; albeit much smaller (14%). PSRA (mostly Pew), Langer (mostly ABC/*WPost*), and CBS accounted for another 24% of the surveys. Gallup got out of electoral predictions when Nate Silver rated Gallup as being the least accurate of any major survey firm.

WORLD EVENTS

ISIS and Terrorism

President Bush had begun withdrawing US troops from Iraq in December 2007 due to a decrease in violence in Iraq and an increase in the public's desire to end US involvement. The US–Iraq Status of Forces Agreement, negotiated by the Bush administration, called for withdrawing all US troops by the end of 2011. Neither the Bush nor the Obama administration was willing to keep US troops in Iraq without an agreement giving these troops immunity from Iraqi courts.[1] The Iraqi government refused to grant this immunity given concern about its sovereignty and fear of potential repercussions from Arab Spring protesters. Furthermore, Obama campaigned on removing all combat troops (not Special Forces) from Iraq. This policy differed from that of John McCain who argued for giving American generals increased flexibility. The survey data displayed below show how Obama benefited from his proposals.

- *In August of 2010, most Americans had little stomach for staying in Iraq. Only 34% thought that the Iraqi government would be able to limit insurgent attacks if US troops left and 54% (43%, 4%)[2] wanted the United States to withdraw all its troops regardless of what would happen in Iraq.*
- *There was also little support for staying in Afghanistan. Only 38% (57%, 5%) wanted to keep a significant number of troops in that country. In fact, in May 2011, 60% said the United States had completed its mission in Afghanistan and the troops should be brought home (36%, 5%).*

Sparked by the self-immolation of Tunisian street vendor Mohamed Bouazizi in December 2010, public demonstrations intensified in Tunisia to protest corruption, unemployment, and lack of civil liberties. The president of Tunisia, Zine El Abidine Ben, was forced to flee to Saudi Arabia in January. The success of the Tunisian revolt inspired similar demonstrations in Libya, Egypt, Yemen, Syria, Iraq, and many other countries, the collective event becoming known as the Arab Spring. In Libya, the civil war led to the overthrow of Muammar Gaddafi, who was killed in October 2011. Libyan rebels were helped by NATO's (mostly American) 14,000+ air strikes. Egypt underwent a quick series of government shifts: President Hosni Mubarak was forced to resign in February 2011 following the killing of protesters by Egyptian security forces; the Muslim Brotherhood took control of the country in June 2012 after Islamist Mohamed Morsi was elected president; then in July 2013, Morsi was deposed in a military coup. In Syria, peaceful protests led to a brutal crackdown by the government of Bashar al-Assad; civil war soon resulted.[3] In Tunisia, the protests gave rise to a semi-stable democratic government that was still in existence as of the time of this writing. In other countries, chaos resulted.

- *Pew asked who would provide the best leadership for Egypt: 11% of respondents said the Muslim Brotherhood, and 45% the military. Nineteen percent volunteered neither, and 25% did not know [8/13].*
- *In another survey, only 16% (78%, 6%) said the United States should try to influence events in Egypt and promote an end to the violence [7/13-United Technologies/ National Journal].*
- *Most Americans were sympathetic to the protesters in Egypt: 82% supported them; 66% said the protests were good for Egypt; and 61% said they were good for the United States [2/11].*
- *On the Arab Spring in general, 34% said it was mostly good for the United States, 24% mostly bad, and 37% said it would have no impact [5/12-Chicago Council].*

Unrest in Libya had a major impact on politics in the United States. In September 2012, members of an Islamic group assaulted the US government compound in

Benghazi, resulting in the deaths of US Ambassador Christopher Stevens and three of his security detail. Republicans in the United States blamed Secretary of State Hillary Clinton, stating that the State Department had not provided adequate security. There were eight separate Congressional investigations on Benghazi. Clinton supporters said there was no substance to any of the accusations and the hearings were meant to discredit Clinton in any way possible. In the last hearing, Clinton testified for eleven hours before the House Select Committee on Benghazi in October 2015. Most neutral observers declared Clinton the victor in these hearings. However, in the process of these investigations, it was learned that Clinton had a private email server.

- *Even if most commentators thought Clinton was the victor in these exchanges, the public was unsure. On some of the earlier hearings, 43% (38%, 18%) said they approved of the hearings and 43% said they were following it closely [6/14].*
- *Gallup did not ask any relevant questions about the 2015 hearings. However, NBC/WSJ [10/15] found only 30% (38%, 32%) were satisfied with her responses, and Fox [11/15] found that only 37% (57%, 7%) said they thought she was being honest.*[4]

A fundamentalist Islamist group, the Islamic State of Iraq and the Levant (ISIS or ISIL), took advantage of the withdrawal of US troops in Iraq, the corruption of the Iraqi government and military, and the repression of the Sunni by the Shiite, to move into Sunni-opposition strongholds in Iraq. The group also took advantage of the Syrian civil war to establish itself in parts of Syria. In June 2014, they proclaimed themselves to be a worldwide caliphate—an Islamic state. Their rule was especially brutal: they videotaped their beheadings of soldiers and civilians, destroyed cultural heritage sites, practiced sexual slavery, and carried out ethnic cleansing. By the middle of 2014, they had taken control of extensive areas in Syria and Iraq, including Raqqa in Syria and Mosul in Iraq. Mosul was the third largest city in Iraq with a population estimated at two million and Raqqa was the sixth largest city in Syria with a population of around 250,000. At its height, ISIS controlled approximately 30,000 square miles (the size of Belgium).

The capture of Mosul was particularly unnerving, as an ISIS force of 1,500 defeated a force of 60,000 soldiers and police officers. ISIS captured $500 million worth of gold bullion, hundreds of vehicles, including tanks, and a tremendous amount of ammunition and other arms. ISIS executed approximately 4,000 captured security personnel.

At the invitation of the Iraqi government, the United States began air strikes against ISIS positions in August 2014. Special Forces were soon introduced, and other countries also contributed to the campaign. In September, President Obama announced the United States would also intervene with ground troops in Syria. The Syrian intervention was particularly complicated, as different groups of rebels were fighting among themselves as well as with the government of Bashar al-Assad, and against ISIS as well.[5] By the end of 2016, the combined effects of better training of Iraqi troops, the use of Shiite and Kurdish militia, intensified aerial bombing by the United States and others, and the revulsion felt by Iraqis and Syrians toward the brutality of ISIS rule, all led to a slow reconquest of most of the territory taken by ISIS. Mosul was declared liberated in July 2017 and Raqqa three months later.

Obama faced many challenges concerning how best to fight the spread of ISIS, Al-Qaeda, and other similar groups. In addition, there was substantial debate within the administration on the extent to which the United States should try to pressure governments in the Mideast to foster democracy and civil liberties, and to reduce tensions between various countries. In May 2011, Obama announced that Osama Bin Laden had been killed in Pakistan in an operation carried out by Navy Seals.[6] In general, when Obama had to choose between more involvement or less involvement in conflicts in the Arab world, he usually chose the latter. For example, the complexities of the civil war in Syria did not allow for easy answers. It was not clear whether the opponents to Assad were credible, were aligned with Al-Qaeda or ISIS, or what they would do with money or sophisticated military equipment. Therefore, Obama generally gave the least amount of support to such groups. Events became even more complicated in September 2015, when Russia began air strikes against opponents of Assad in Syria.

Since the Obama administration, the erratic foreign policy of Donald Trump has further complicated matters. In November 2019, Trump agreed to a US pullout from the Syrian border with Turkey where the Kurds held power. Subsequently, Turkey invaded, forcing the Kurds, who had been our allies against ISIS, to withdraw. This resulted in ISIS taking over some of these lands and reduced the ability of the Kurds to fight ISIS.

- *Americans were very reluctant to intervene in Syria before ISIS took over large parts of the country. Only 24% (68%, 8%) wanted to use military action to intervene in the civil war if diplomatic and economic sanctions failed. In fact, only 37% favored arming the Syrian rebels [6/13].*
- *After ISIS conquered Mosul and Raqqa, 50% said ISIS was a critical threat to the United States and another 31% said it was an important threat [9/14]. However, only 40% wanted to send in ground troops to fight ISIS.*
- *In 2016, Americans were divided over what to do about Syria. Thirty-four percent wanted more involvement, 30% less and 29% said the same amount [2/16].*
- *In 2019, only 30% of respondents favored Trump's decision to remove support from the Kurds [10/19—Quinnipiac].*[7]

Other acts of terrorism linked to ISIS or Al-Qaeda occurred throughout the decade: the Boston Marathon bombing killed 3 (2013); the shooting at the Jewish Museum of Belgium killed 4 (2014); 2 gunmen killed 12 people at the Paris office of the satirical magazine *Charlie Hebdo* (2015); 130 Parisians were killed when coordinated attacks were made on the same night at a concert venue, various restaurants, and a football stadium (2015); the bombing of a Russian airliner over Egypt killed 224 (2015); a shooting at a San Bernardino, California civic center killed 14 (2015); a truck attack in Berlin killed 12 (2016); a truck attack in Nice, France, killed 86 (2016); the shooting at an Orlando, Florida, nightclub killed 49 (2016); a bombing in the St. Petersburg Metro killed 15 (2017); two car attacks in London killing 4 and 8, respectively (2017); a bombing at a concert by Ariana Grande in Manchester, England, killing 23 (2017); an attack on a mosque in Sinai, Egypt, killing 305 (November 2017); and a shooting at two mosques in Christchurch, New Zealand, killing 51 (March 2019).

- *Just before his sentencing, 53% of respondents favored the death penalty for Dzhokhar Tsarnaev, who was convicted of the Boston bombing [4/15-CNN].*
- *Forty-eight percent said the Pulse nightclub shooting in Orlando was an act of Islamic terrorism compared to 41% who said it was mostly related to domestic gun violence [6/16].*
- *Forty-seven percent said they were worried about a member of their family becoming a victim of terrorism [12/15].*
- *In December 2015, Gallup asked respondents whether they thought the following policies would be effective in fighting terrorism:*[8]
  - *Send more US special operations forces to fight the Islamic State or ISIS (70%).*
  - *Ban gun sales to people on the federal no-fly watch list (71%).*
  - *Overhaul the federal visa waiver program to provide tighter screening for people who come to the US temporarily for travel or business (79%).*
  - *Enact a new law that would impose a religious test for entering the United States, banning those who identify their religion as Muslim (29%).*
  - *Require Muslims, including those who are US citizens, to carry a special ID (32%).*
  - *Provide more US training and equipment to Iraqi and Syrian forces fighting the Islamic State or ISIS (55%).*
  - *Enact a new law that would prevent any Muslim from entering the United States (38%).*
  - *Intensify diplomatic efforts to pursue ceasefires and a political resolution to the Syrian war (57%).*
  - *Send large numbers of US ground troops to Syria and Iraq to fight the Islamic State or ISIS (59%).*
  - *Pass new laws making it harder to buy assault weapons (55%).*

Other International Events

The relationship between Israel and the Palestinians remained problematic. Israeli settlements continued to expand in the West Bank (17,400 total settlers in 1980; 111,600 in 1993; 234,500 in 2004; and 400,000 in 2014). The blockade of Gaza continued. In 2010, nine activists were killed when Israeli Navy forces stopped several ships trying to bring in humanitarian supplies. The raid brought about deteriorating relations with Turkey as well as eliciting worldwide denouncements.

In November 2012, Israel invaded Gaza for a week resulting in the death of 140 Palestinians, including the Hamas military chief, and five Israelis. Following the kidnapping of three Israeli teenagers, Israel invaded Gaza again in June 2014, and, in the course of seven weeks, 2,100 Palestinians and 71 Israelis were killed.

The Trump administration has closely allied itself with Evangelical Christians who believe in a Biblical prophecy that for Jesus to return, Israel and Jerusalem must remain under Israeli control. Along with offering unmitigated support for Israeli Prime Minister, Benjamin Netanyahu, the Trump administration, in December 2017, officially recognized Jerusalem as Israel's capital. A majority of world leaders condemned this decision.

- *Americans continued to favor the establishment of a Palestinian state on the West Bank and Gaza Strip (51%, 37%,12%) [2/12]. However, 62% said their sympathies were with Israel and only 16% said the Palestinians (22% said neither or both) [2/15].*
- *On the settlements in the West Bank—17% said they helped the security of Israel, 44% hurt, 29% no difference, and 11% did not know [2/13-Pew].*
- *On moving the US embassy to Jerusalem, Americans were divided with 45% (44%, 11%) [12/17-CNN] approving the move.*

In July 2015, the Iran nuclear deal was signed by Iran, the United States, the United Kingdom, China, Russia, France, Germany, and the European Union. Essentially, the treaty provided that Iran agree to dismantle its nuclear program in return for an end to economic sanctions. Israel and many conservatives in the United States opposed the deal, stating it would still be too easy for Iran to develop nuclear weapons in the future and that the deal did not address Iran's aggressive foreign policy. In May 2018, despite affirmation from the International Atomic Energy Agency (IAEA) that Iran was fully complying with the deal, President Trump unilaterally withdrew from the Iran nuclear deal and reimposed harsh economic sanctions against Iran. Iran reacted by beginning again to enrich uranium.

- *In February 2016, only 30% of survey respondents (57%, 13%) favored the Iran nuclear agreement. Since then, Americans seem to have become accustomed to the deal and as of May 2018 (just before Trump withdrew from the deal) only 29% (63%, 8%-CNN) wanted the United States to withdraw from the deal. A year after the United States withdrew, only 40% (55%, 5%) [5/19-Pew] favored this action.*

Saudi Arabia was much in the news following the election of Donald Trump. In 2015, a civil war between the Saudi-backed Yemeni government and Iran-backed Houthi rebels escalated, with large-scale bombing and troop intervention by Saudi Arabia and its allies. It is estimated that over 70,000 civilians have died in this conflict. The United States has supplied most of the bombs used by Saudi Arabia; however, in March 2019, the United States Senate voted (54-46) to end US military support for this war. This resulted in Trump's first veto, which the Senate upheld. In addition, a diplomatic crisis for Saudi Arabia was triggered in October 2018 when

Washington Post journalist Jamal Khashoggi was murdered inside the Saudi consulate in Istanbul. This murder was likely ordered by the Saudi Crown Prince Mohammed bin Salman.

- *Only 24% of Americans thought we were sufficiently tough on Saudi Arabia for the killing of Khashoggi (58% not tough enough) [12/18-CNN]. Furthermore, only 29% had a favorable opinion of Saudi Arabia [2/19].*[9]

North Korea continued its progress toward the development of nuclear weapons. Between 2013 and 2017, they carried out three nuclear weapons tests (earlier tests were done in 2006 and 2009). Furthermore, in February 2017 they tested a solid-fueled intermediate-range missile that could hit Japan, and in July tested an intercontinental ballistic missile (ICBM) that could hit the mainland of the United States. The United States is constrained in what it can do because North Korean artillery and rockets are within easy range of Seoul with its population of around twenty-five million. Relations between the United States and North Korea worsened in June 2017 when an American student, Otto Warmbier, was returned to the United States in coma after spending seventeen months in a North Korean prison for the petty offense of attempting to steal a propaganda poster. He died a week after his return.

In a surprise move, President Trump met with North Korean leader Kim Jong-un in June 2018 in Singapore. A subsequent meeting occurred in Hanoi in February 2019 and a third, short meeting took place in the demilitarized zone between North and South Korea in June 2019. No substantial breakthroughs concerning North Korea's nuclear arsenal came out of these meetings.[10] Nonetheless, following the meeting in Singapore, Trump declared, "There is no longer a nuclear threat from North Korea."[11]

- *In April 2013, 55% (34%, 10%) said the United States should help defend South Korea if it was attacked.*
- *In September 2017, 50% (45%, 5%) still believed the situation with North Korea could be resolved with diplomacy, but 58% (39%, 4%) said they would approve of military action if economic and diplomatic efforts failed.*
- *In June 2018, 49% (33%, 17%) [Quinnipiac] of Americans said the meeting in Singapore between Trump and Kim was a success and 41% believed it was likely that the talks would lead to North Korea getting rid of its nuclear weapons [6/18-ABC-WPost]. However, only 22% agreed with Trump that North Korea was no longer a nuclear threat [6/18-Quinnipiac].*

Relations with Russia continued to deteriorate. In November 2013, President Viktor Yanukovych of Ukraine suspended an agreement that would have linked Ukraine closer to the European community.[12] He was forced to flee to Russia following mass protests. In the Crimea and some parts of eastern Ukraine, ethnic Russians are a majority of the population. Russia sent in troops dressed as Ukrainians to fight for separating parts of eastern Ukraine. Following a referendum, Russia annexed Crimea in March 2014, an area of geopolitical and economic significance. In May 2019, Volodymyr Zelensky became president of Ukraine. A case of truth being stranger than fiction, he had starred in a comedy show from 2015 to 2019 in which he played the president of Ukraine. In reaction to the history of extreme corruption among leaders of Ukraine, voters elected Zelensky, who was running on an anticorruption platform, with a 73% majority.

Trump's relationship with Vladimir Putin has been extraordinarily controversial. (This is discussed in far greater detail in the section on US politics.) Often, Trump has been obsequious toward Putin. In July 2017 at the G20 meeting in Germany and again in November 2018 at the G20 meeting in Argentina, Trump met with Putin without an aide or translator. On the other hand, in February 2019 Trump "terminated" the Intermediate-Range Nuclear Forces Treaty over alleged Russian violations.

- *Only 45% of Americans wanted to send more US weapons to Ukraine to fight pro-Russian rebels [2/15]. Less than a third (30%) had a favorable opinion of Russia [2/16], and only 22% had a favorable opinion of Putin [2/17].*
- *As for Trump, 47% were concerned that he was too friendly with Russia and 48% believed his behavior presented a national security threat to the United States [7/17-Mommouth].*

In Myanmar (formerly Burma), a military operation began in 2017 targeting the Rohingya minority population of Muslims. It is estimated that over 10,000 Rohingya people were killed and 700,000 were forced to flee to the neighboring country of Bangladesh. This violence on the part of the Burmese military has been decried as "ethnic cleansing" and/or genocide.[13]

In June 2016, the British passed a referendum (with a 51.9% majority) that called for the United Kingdom to withdraw from the European Union (Brexit). Prime Minister David Cameron initiated the referendum in order to garner more control over the Tory Party, not expecting it to pass. Supporters of Brexit were generally older, working class, anti-immigration, and nationalistic. Given the vote, Cameron was forced to resign. There was substantial debate within the United Kingdom over whether to go forward with Brexit, and if so, how "hard" the exit should be. Negotiations with the EU on the nature of the exit were not easy. After Parliament rejected the agreement, Prime Minister Theresa May was forced to resign in June 2019 and Boris Johnson became prime minister in July. Johnson's Party won a majority in the December elections and the United Kingdom officially withdrew from the EU on January 31, 2020.

- *No US survey firm asked a question about support for Brexit, but 34% claimed it was personally very important to them [12/16—AP].*

There were two major earthquakes in this decade. In January 2010, a 7.0 magnitude earthquake struck Haiti, killing over 316,000 people; in the aftermath, close to 60,000 Haitians were allowed to come to the United States. (In February 2017, Trump announced he would end their legal immigration status within eighteen months.[14]) In February of the following year, an earthquake and subsequent tsunami killed over 15,000 people in Japan. The tsunami destroyed the backup diesel generators at the Fukushima nuclear power plant, resulting in the failure of the cooling systems and meltdowns at three of the nuclear reactors. Almost a quarter of a million people were evacuated from their homes. Nuclear power had generated about 30% of Japan's electricity at the time of the disaster. In the wake of the disaster, Japan shut down all its nuclear plants and only a few have subsequently restarted.

- *Seventy-six percent of Americans said the United States was doing enough to help the victims of the Haiti earthquake [1/10].*
- *Twenty-five percent said they were now much more concerned about an earthquake or tsunami occurring in the United States because of the events in Japan [3/11].*

US POLITICS

In the 2010 midterm congressional elections, Republicans took control of the House and gained seats in the Senate. In election campaigns, Republicans gained leverage by attacking Obama on the issues of health care and a slow economic recovery.

Barack Obama was elected to his second term in November 2012 by defeating Governor Mitt Romney of Massachusetts with 51.1% of the popular vote.[15] However, the Republicans kept control of the House and made gains in the Senate. One of Romney's major gaffes was getting caught on camera in a speech to wealthy donors saying, without basis in fact, that 47% of the public was dependent upon the government, pay no taxes, and would vote for Obama no matter what. Romney was a Mormon, which caused some to be uncomfortable.

- *In reference to Romney's remark, 34% of respondents said that comment would make it less likely they would vote for Romney and 18% said more likely [9/12].*
- *Seventy-six percent said they would vote for a Mormon. When asked about candidates who might belong to other groups, respondents said they would vote for: a gay or lesbian—67%; a woman—93%; a black person—94%; a Baptist—92%; a Jew—89%; an atheist—49%; a Hispanic—89%; or a Catholic—92% [6/11].*

The biggest election surprise in modern times was Donald Trump's win over Hillary Clinton in the November 2016 presidential election. Trump, a businessman and host of *The Apprentice* reality TV series, defeated sixteen other Republican candidates in the primaries, including the presumed frontrunner—Jeb Bush. Trump appealed to right-wing populist voters by advocating building a wall along the Mexican border (to try to halt illegal immigration), repealing and replacing the Affordable Care Act (Obamacare), and deporting illegal immigrants. He was severely criticized for attacking the media, allowing violence at some of his rallies, and obscene statements he had made about women earlier in his career in what became known as the "Access Hollywood Tape."

Hillary Clinton, a former first lady, US senator, and US secretary of state, came under severe criticism for using her private email server when she was secretary of state, receiving over $250,000 per speech to Wall Street groups like Goldman-Sachs, and making ill-considered statements about supporters of Trump (calling them "deplorables"). Support for Clinton turned when 20,000 pages of emails stolen from John Podesta, the chair of Clinton's election campaign, as well as stolen emails from the Democratic National Committee, were slowly released by WikiLeaks. The emails, stolen by Russian intelligence services,[16] had some embarrassing content. Furthermore, James Comey, director of the FBI, announced ten days before the election that the FBI was investigating the laptop of Anthony Weiner, the disgraced husband of Clinton's closest aid, for emails relevant to the Clinton's server. Although, nothing was found, it raised enough suspicion to have a marked influence on the vote.[17] It is widely thought, though, that Clinton's principal strategic errors were attacking Trump on personnel issues and not sufficiently stressing the battle for economic equality and the needs of the working class. The election campaign was extremely ugly on both sides, and Clinton lost despite that fact that she had almost three million more votes than Trump (48.2% v. 46.4%).

There were a variety of issues specific to the campaign. In the "birther conspiracy," Trump and his allies claimed that Obama was not a US citizen and that he was a citizen of Kenya. Beginning in 2011, Trump started promoting that claim, and asserting that Obama's birth certificate was a fraud, which was probably the first major issue that endeared Trump to his political supporters. It was only in September 2016 that Trump reluctantly admitted that Obama was a US citizen, but in typical Trump style he falsely blamed Clinton for starting the conspiracy.

- *Sixty-one percent of Americans said Trump had some responsibility for the violence at his rallies [3/16-FOX].*
- *Forty-eight percent said Clinton's use of an email server was very important to their vote [11/16—NBC/WSJ]. Furthermore, many said the use of the email server was illegal (19%) or improper (28%) [10/16-CBS/NYT].*
- *Twenty-six percent said Clinton's "deplorables" remark would help her campaign, 31% said it would hurt, and 41% said it would have no impact [10/16-GfK].*
- *Around the time Trump first jumped on the birther movement, 67% of survey respondents said Obama was born in the United States (13%, 20%) [5/11].*
- *When asked about the Access Hollywood Tape, 40% said the video made them think worse of Trump [10/16-CBS]. Twenty-seven percent said it was a "deal breaker" [10/16-Quinnipiac].*
- *Immediately following the election, 48% (47%, 4%) wanted presidential elections to be decided by popular vote instead of by the Electoral College [11/16]. On the other hand, Trump claimed he won the popular vote when he stated, without any*

evidence, that 3–5 million people voted illegally. Twenty-nine percent said Trump was correct in this claim [3/17-Quinnipiac].[18]

The Russia story did not go away after the election. American intelligence agencies unanimously concluded that Russia tried helping Trump during the campaign by: leaking emails; using thousands of fake social media accounts on Facebook, Twitter, etc., to advocate for Trump and create general dissension; and intruding into state voter registration systems. After the election it became apparent that one of Trump's campaign managers (Paul Manafort) and Trump's first National Security Advisor (Michael Flynn) had financial ties to Russia. Furthermore, it appeared that Trump, his family, and his business organization may also have had links to Russia.

Trump fired the director of the FBI (James Comey) who was investigating Trump's ties to Russia. Then, in May 2017, the Department of Justice appointed Robert Mueller as special counsel to investigate matters relevant to Russia and the 2016 campaign. Mueller uncovered several secret meetings that occurred between Trump's campaign officials, family, and advisors with individuals linked to the Russian government. A total of thirty-four individuals were indicted by the Mueller investigators and eight pled guilty or were convicted of felonies (most prominent: Michael Flynn Paul Manafort, Michael Cohen, and Roger Stone).[19]

Mueller released his report to Attorney General William Barr in March 2018. Barr put out a four-page summary essentially stating—incorrectly—that the Mueller Report exonerated Trump. A 448-page redacted version of the actual report was released in April. The report concluded that Mueller did not have the legal authority to indict Trump because a sitting president cannot be charged with a crime. However, the report did find that the Russians had intervened in the election to the benefit of Trump, described ten incidents in which Trump may have obstructed justice and pointedly said the report did not exonerate Trump.

- *In August 2017, when asked about Trump and his involvement with Russian interference in the 2016 campaign, 25% of Americans believed that Trump had done something illegal, 37% thought he had done something unethical, and 35% said he had done nothing wrong.*

In September 2019, because of a whistleblower complaint, it became a public knowledge that Trump ordered withholding around $400 million in military aid to Ukraine unless they helped investigate one of Trump's political enemies, Democrat Joe Biden. In the House impeachment hearings, the Trump administration did not allow any witnesses who worked for the administration to testify or allow the release of any documents. Through the testimony of others, though, it became apparent that Trump's attorney, Rudolph Giuliani, at Trump's behest, had worked to remove Ambassador Marie Yovanovitch from her position because she opposed the pressure on Ukraine. On December 18, the House voted to impeach President Trump (230-197). The Senate failed to remove Trump on a 52-48 vote on February 5, 2020. The data below show that the American public was not clamoring for Trump's impeachment or removal from office.

- *Only 42% believed that Trump had done something illegal, while another 32% said his actions were unethical (25% said nothing wrong) [1/20-AP/NORC].*
- *The American public was divided on impeachment (47% in support and 48% opposed [12/19-Marist]). After the House impeachment vote, the percentage who favored removing Trump from office was similar (46%, 49%, 5%) [1/20-NBC/WSJ].*

Two competing populist organizations had a large impact in the early years of the decade. The Tea Party Movement (TPM) was initially a 2009 conservative reaction to an Obama proposal to give financial aid to bankrupt homeowners. The TPM received much of its funding from a Koch brothers advocacy group, had many visible protests, and advocated for the dismantling of Obamacare and the reduction of taxes. Toward the other side of the political spectrum, Occupy Wall Street (OWS), a protest movement from the left, held a number of highly visible long-term protests in cities across the country that raised the issue of income and wealth inequality and the growing political influence of corporations.

- *Support for the Tea Party hovered in the 25% realm. For example, in September 2011, 21% of respondents said they supported the Tea Party, 26% opposed it, and the remainder said neither or did not know.*
- *Similar percentages also resulted when respondents were asked about the Occupy Wall Street Movement (26%, 19%, 56%) [5/11].*

After Trump was elected, protests against him and his policies expanded. An estimated 2.5 million attended the Women's March protests in the United States on the day after Trump's inauguration,[20] as well as in places around the globe. Large protests also occurred over climate change (March 2017) and protecting science (April 2017), and there were numerous ongoing demonstrations against (among other issues): restricting immigration from predominately Muslim countries; attempts to revoke DACA; gun violence; attempts to repeal Obamacare; and lowering of taxes on corporations and wealthier individuals.

- *Trump has been historically unpopular (Skelly, 2019). In March of the second year of his presidency, his approval rating was 40%. The comparable figures for other presidents in March of their second year were: Barack Obama (49%), George W. Bush (79%), Bill Clinton (51%), George H. W. Bush (71%), and Ronald Reagan (46%).*
- *Despite Trump's unpopularity and allegations that he only became president because of help from Russia, 66% of Americans [4/17] said he was the legitimate president.*

Trump's unpopularity in conjunction with dissatisfaction with Republican policies on health care resulted in the Republicans losing control of the House in the 2018 midterm elections. With the highest voter turnout in midterm elections since 1914, the Democrats had a net gain of forty-one seats.

The leaking of information became a big issue in this decade. In June 2013, Edward Snowden, a computer contractor assigned to the National Security Agency (NSA), leaked documents to several journalists about secret US government surveillance programs. The revelations included that: phone companies were providing most of their records to the NSA; the NSA could access most commercial servers; the NSA was spying on foreign leaders, including Angela Merkel; the NSA had a program that could search all internet access by users; and the NSA was collecting all text messages. Some hailed Snowden as a whistleblower and hero and others said he was a traitor. He fled to Moscow and there have been several movies/documentaries about him.

Chelsea Manning, a US Army intelligence analyst assigned to an army unit in Iraq, leaked 750,000 documents to WikiLeaks in January 2010. The materials—army reports and diplomatic cables—showed there had been various air strikes against civilians in Iraq and Afghanistan and documented government corruption in many Mideast countries. Some of the released documents may have served as a catalyst for the Arab Spring. Manning was court martialed and sentenced to thirty-five years in prison. President Barack Obama commuted her sentence to seven years, and she was released in May 2017. After her sentencing, Manning, who was raised as a male, announced that she was a woman, had changed her name, and would begin hormone replacement therapy.

- *Only 25% of Americans supported the right of WikiLeaks to publish documents about the war in Afghanistan [7/10].*
- *Respondents had mixed opinions about Snowden, with 45% (42%, 14%) believing he did the right thing and 59% saying the Guardian and the Washington Post did the right thing in publishing the leaked information. In fact, only 37% supported the government's compiling of citizens' telephone logs and internet communication [6/13], and 51% said they were very concerned about government tapping internet communications. (Twenty-three percent were not concerned.) [10/13].*

Mass shootings continued. In January 2011, Congresswoman Gabby Giffords of Arizona was shot in the head by Jared Lee Loughner, who killed six others in the same attack; in July 2012, James Holmes killed twelve at a movie theater in Aurora Colorado; in September 2013, Aaron Alexis killed twelve at the Washington Navy Yard in D.C.; in December 2013, Adam Lanza, after first killing his mother, fatally shot twenty school children and six teachers at Sandy Hook Elementary School in Newtown, Connecticut;[21] in December 2015, Syed Rizwan Farook and Tashfeen Malik killed fourteen at San Bernardino Civic Center; in June 2016, Omar Mateen killed forty-nine at the Pulse nightclub in Orlando, Florida; in October 2017, Stephen Paddock killed fifty-eight people attending a concert in Las Vegas; in February 2018, seventeen were killed in a shooting at Marjory Stoneman Douglas High School in Parkland, Florida;[22] in October 2018, eleven people were killed in a shooting at the Tree of Life Synagogue in Pittsburg, Pennsylvania; and twenty-two were killed at a El Paso Walmart in August 2019.

- *Attitudes toward gun control remained at the same levels cited in the previous chapter covering the 2000s: in response to survey questions in this decade, 58% of Americans said they want to make gun laws stricter [12/12], but only 36% would ban assault rifles [10/16] and even less (25%)—handguns [12/12]. However, 83% supported required background checks for all gun sales [4/13].*

When asked about some specific shootings:

- *Fifty-five percent said problems with the mental health system carried a great deal of blame for the shooting of Giffords, while 43% said easy access to guns was to blame [1/11].*
- *Eighty-seven percent closely followed the shooting in Newtown and 52% said a similar school shooting could happen in their community [12/12].*
- *Sixty-two percent believed that stricter gun control laws would not have prevented the shooting in Las Vegas because the shooter would have found a way around the laws [11/17-Quinnipiac].*

One of the biggest changes in criminal justice policy was the movement to legalize marijuana. In November 1996, Californians approved Proposition 215 to allow marijuana to be used for medical purposes. Colorado became the first state to legalize marijuana for recreational purposes in January 2014. As of 2020, thirty-three states have legalized marijuana in some form (eleven for recreational use); however, the federal government still treats it as Schedule I drug, that is, having a high-abuse potential and no medical benefit. Obama stopped the Justice Department from prosecuting most marijuana cases, and in April 2016 he pardoned all arrested for nonviolent drug offenses.

- *In November 2012, 48% of survey respondents favored the legalization of marijuana. This had increased to 60% in October 2016 and 66% by October 2019. By July 2017, 45% said they had tried marijuana and 12% said they used it.*

Immigration was another major issue through the decade. Following the Republican loss in the 2012 presidential election, many Republicans believed that, given demographic changes, they would continue to lose if they did not stop alienating the Hispanic population. A bipartisan immigration bill passed the Senate 68-32 (fourteen Republicans voted yes) in June 2013. The bill provided a path to citizenship for many undocumented immigrants already living in the United States, expanded the employment verification system, and made more of an effort to bring in immigrants with advanced technical skills. However, conservatives in the House killed the bill claiming that it amounted to amnesty.

Obama's policies on immigration were mixed. On the one hand, he deported more undocumented immigrants in eight years than any of his predecessors (2.8 million). On the other hand, in March 2014 he announced the Deferred Action for Childhood Arrivals program (DACA) that would protect 800,000 illegal immigrants who were brought to the United States as children. He later announced that this would expand protection to four million others who were related to DACA children. This second policy was ruled unconstitutional by the Supreme Court in June 2016. Obama also admitted over 12,000 refugees from war-torn Syria.

Many Republicans claimed that immigrants were taking jobs away from those born in the United States, were security risks, and cost the taxpayer too much money. These sentiments were represented in the extreme when Donald Trump, in his first campaign event in June 2016, said (in reference to Mexicans), "They're bringing drugs. They're bringing crime. They're rapists." One of Trump's signature promises was to build a wall along the border with Mexico, which Mexico would pay for. Furthermore, he was against admitting many refugees from Syria, claiming that many of them could be terrorists, and advocated a general ban on Muslims entering the country. Three weeks after his inauguration Trump signed an executive order banning travel from seven predominately Muslim countries. Massive protests erupted, and different courts ruled the order unconstitutional for discriminating against a religious group. In June 2017, the Supreme Court reinstated most of the ban.

- *Only 47% (52%, 1%) supported the ban restricting travel from the seven predominately Muslim countries [2/17-Pew], and even fewer (36%) agreed with Trump's suspending the Syrian refugee program [1/17].*

In December 2018, the US government started a thirty-five-day government shutdown, arising from a dispute over funding for Trump's proposed US–Mexico border wall. The shutdown was the longest government shutdown in US history. Legislation eventually passed that did NOT include funding for the wall. In February 2019, Trump declared a national emergency and eventually the Supreme Court allowed him to divert around $6 billion from military construction projects to build parts of the wall.

In September 2017, Trump announced that he would end the DACA (Deferred Action for Childhood Arrivals) program in March 2018. They were protected from deportation because of a June 2020, 5-4 Supreme Court decision (*Department of Homeland Security et al. v. Regents of the University of California et al.*). One of Biden's first acts as president was to extend the protection for DACAs.

- *Americans were generally supportive of immigrants.*[23] *Fifty-nine percent said that immigrants were generally good for America [6/11] and 58% said they would support allowing illegal immigrants to apply for citizenship and only 14% wanted them deported [6/16-Chicago].*
- *Less than half (48%) favored building Trump's proposed wall [6/16-Chicago].*[24]
- *A large majority of Americans—84%—favored having DACA children remain [2/18-Politico/Harvard Public Health].*

Most Americans opposed Trump's policies on immigration and the wall. However, Trump believed it was more important to appeal to his base on these issues.

Issues concerning public education became increasingly politicized. Many of those who were not satisfied with public education supported public charter schools, which are publicly financed but semi-independent of the state school system. Opponents of charter schools argued that they took resources away from more traditional schools and did not provide a better education. By 2014, 5% of American primary and secondary school students were in charter schools. Some conservatives wanted to go further and advocated issuing vouchers to allow students to attend private schools, many of which are religious. Betsy DeVos, a strong supporter of school vouchers, became secretary of education under Trump in February 2017.[25] When possible, she diverted monies to private schools (e.g., $500 million of coronavirus relief funds from the CARES Act). Another point of contention concerned Common Core standards.[26] In June 2010, benchmarks were released specifying what students should know at the end of every grade level in math and English language arts. The standards were written under the supervision of the National Governors Association and the Council of Chief State School Officers and were quickly adopted by forty-five states and the District of Columbia. Some conservatives opposed the Common Core on the grounds that it eroded states' rights and local control of schools. Some liberals opposed it because they felt the standards were not properly tested and teachers were being unfairly evaluated based on the test.

- *Americans had a mixed opinion about the state of public education. Fifty percent gave their local schools an A or B rating, but only 17% gave US schools overall a grade of A or B [5/14].*[27]
- *On the Common Core, only 33% (60%, 7%; not asked of the 19% who had never heard of it) favored using the Common Core, and only 45% (54%, 1%) said standardized tests were helpful to teachers [5/14].*
- *Charter schools were supported by 70% of respondents but only 37% wanted to use public funds to send students to private schools [5/14].*

One of the most important events affecting political inequality was the 2010 Supreme Court case *Citizens United v. FEC*. In a 5-4 vote, the Court ruled that the government could not restrict political expenditures by non-profit or for-profit corporations or by labor unions. A nominal ban on some payment to political parties remained. An important element concerning political expenditures is that most of these can be made anonymously, which means that the public often has no idea who is funding political campaigns. OpenSecrets.org, a nonpartisan research group, estimates that outside spending in the 2008 election cycle was around $330 million. This increased to $1 billion in 2012 and to $1.4 billion in 2016.

- *At the time of the Supreme Court ruling on Citizens United, only 17% of respondents (68%, 15%) favored the decision [2/10-Pew].*
- *Americans were divided on some of these issues: 47% believed that individual citizens should not be limited in the amount that they contribute to political campaigns, compared to 37% in favor of no limits for corporations. Furthermore, 76%*

believed that contributions should be publicly disclosed and 82% said that contributions had a direct impact on decisions made by elected officials [11/15—AP/NORC].

RACE

The Black Lives Matter (BLM) movement started in 2013 following the acquittal of George Zimmerman in the shooting death of Trayvon Martin in Florida. Other prominent deaths of blacks included: the shooting of Michael Brown (2014) in Ferguson, Missouri, by a police officer; the chokehold death of Eric Garner (2014) by four New York City police officers following his arrest for selling loose cigarettes; the Cleveland Ohio shooting of Tamir Rice (2014), twelve years old, who had a toy gun; the death of Freddie Gray (2015) while in police custody in Baltimore, Maryland; the shooting of Walter Scott in the back (2015) while he was running away from a police officer in South Carolina; Laquan McDonald (2014), who was shot sixteen times by police officers as he was walking away in Chicago; and Philando Castile (2016), who was shot sixteen times by a police officer in Minnesota after being pulled over for a traffic stop. The shooting was live-streamed to Facebook by his girlfriend.

- *BLM was very successful in raising consciousness around these and many other deaths related to police brutality and systemic racism in the criminal justice system and in the economy. Thirty-nine percent (45%, 16%) of whites and 77% (16%, 7%) of blacks had a favorable opinion of BLM [9/16-CNN]. The relatively low approval rate for BLM among whites will be discussed in the next chapter on 2020.*
- *When George Zimmerman was found not guilty by a Florida jury for the murder of Trayvon Martin, 43% said that was the right decision (54% of whites and 7% of blacks) [7/13].*
- *When a grand jury refused to indict police officers for the choke hold death of Eric Garner, 22% said the right decision was made (30% of whites and 3% of blacks) [12/14-Pew].*
- *Regarding Freddie Gray, 65% said the State's Attorney did the right thing in bringing charges against the police officers [5/15-Pew], and 64% said the not guilty verdict gave them less faith in the criminal justice system [7/16-AP-NORC].*

With the election of Donald Trump, racists have become increasingly emboldened. Several hundred white nationalists marched on August 12, 2017, carrying torches, through Charlottesville, Virginia, shouting racist chants as well as anti-Jewish slogans such as "Jews will not replace us." The following day, one of the neo-Nazi demonstrators drove his car into a group of counter-protesters, killing one.[28] Trump was severely criticized for not immediately condemning the neo-Nazis and for making statements that equated the neo-Nazis with the counter-demonstrators ("very fine people on both sides").

- *Fifty-two percent said the white supremacists were at fault for the violence in Charlottesville, while 17% blamed the counter-protesters and 22% blamed both groups or neither [8/17-Fox]. With regard to Trump's comments, 60% said the media was fair in how they were reported [8/17-AP/NORC]; 35% approved of his response [8/17-Fox]; and 42% believed he was putting neo-Nazis on equal footing with the demonstrators [8/17-ABC/W Post].*
- *Whites and blacks continued to have very different opinions of race relations. At the end of Obama's tenure, 34% of whites and 73% of blacks thought race discrimination was a very serious problem, and 48% of whites and 74% of blacks said the criminal justice system favored whites [9/16-CNN]. On the other hand, only 3% of whites and 12% of blacks said most of the local police were prejudiced against blacks. The racial resentment that had such a large impact on Trump's victory can be seen in 58% of whites and 39% of blacks saying race relations had gotten worse since the election of Obama [9/16-CNN].*
- *On another racial issue: 87% of respondents now approved of interracial marriages [8/11].*

SEX AND GENDER

It was expected that Hillary Clinton would be the first woman president of the United States. Obviously, this did not happen, and there is some discussion that she might have lost some votes because of her gender (Kinder, Reynolds, and Burns (2020)).

In October 2017, Harvey Weinstein, a very successful film producer, was accused by dozens of women for sexual harassment and rape and was eventually forced to resign from the company he founded. The Me Too Movement (MTM), which encouraged women to come forward with their own stories of sexual misconduct, exploded on social media and other public platforms. It spread in Hollywood as well as in business, politics, sports, music, and the media. Some of the more prominent men who were accused included: Bill Cosby (actor), Garrison Keillor (author, *A Prairie Home Companion*), James Franco (actor), Tavis Smiley (PBS), Mario Batali (chef), James Levine (opera conductor), Matt Lauer (NBC's *Today Show*), Charlie Rose (CBS), Russell Simmons (Def Dog), Al Franken (senator), Roy Moore (Senate candidate from Alabama), Louis C.K. (comedian), Dustin Hoffman (actor), Kevin Spacey (actor), Mark Halperin (NBC News), George H. W. Bush (president), and Donald Trump (president).

MTM expanded beyond elites with the formation of Time's Up. Many in the entertainment industry donated $20 million to create an organization and legal defense fund to help low-income women fight sexual harassment in the hotel industry, farms, restaurants, and so on.

- *A survey for USA Today found that 59% of respondents believed the accusers, 5% believed the men, and the rest were undecided [12/17].*

- *Furthermore, 56% said the accusations served a useful role, compared to 36% who said they went too far [12/17-NBC/WSJ].*
- *Thirty percent had a positive opinion of MTM, 15% a negative opinion, and 55% either had no opinion or had not heard of MTM [12/17-NBC/WSJ].*
- *Respondents were asked how serious a problem they thought sexual misconduct was in different settings (extremely or very): Hollywood and the entertainment industry (74%), colleges and universities (67%), the federal government (61%), the US military (61%), high schools (57%), workplaces or business in general (56%), news media organizations (56%), your state government (51%), and your workplace (32%) [12/17-NORC].*[29]

Donald Trump was able to appoint three conservatives to the Supreme Court. In Obama's last year as president, Antonin Scalia died, and Obama nominated Merrick Garland as his replacement. Senate majority leader Mitch McConnell refused to allow a vote on this appointment claiming it was too close to the presidential election,[30] so the vacancy went to Trump to fill. He nominated Neil Gorsuch, who was confirmed in April 2017. In July 2018, Trump nominated Brett Kavanaugh to replace Anthony Kennedy. The confirmation became very controversial after Kavanaugh was accused of a participating in sexual assault when he was in high school by Christine Blasey Ford; other women accused him as well of sexual assaults when he was in college. His confirmation hearings were very contentious, and he was confirmed by a Senate vote of 50-48. Trump's third appointment was also controversial. Ruth Bader Ginsburg died 38 days before the 2020 election. Mitch McConnell was able to rush through the confirmation of Amy Coney Barrett despite the fact that he refused to consider the earlier nomination of Merrick Garland, claiming it was too close to the election (237 days!).

- *Ford was very credible in her testimony. Forty-five percent of respondents believed her compared to the 33% who believed Kavanaugh [10/18-Marist] and in the same survey only 40% wanted Kavanaugh confirmed.*
- *In an October 2020 Suffolk University survey 46% (49%, 5%) said the Senate should vote on the Amy Coney Barrett nomination before the election.*

There was a continued effort at the federal as well as the state level to erode a woman's right to choose an abortion. In 2015, the House of Representatives voted to defund Planned Parenthood and several states passed legislation requiring abortion clinics to follow rules that would have put them out of business (i.e., requiring doctors to have admitting privileges at hospitals that would not grant such privileges). In *Whole Woman's Health v. Hellerstedt (2016)*, the Supreme Court ruled that these restrictions placed an undue burden on a woman's right to abortion.

- *Only 30% of respondents wanted the Supreme Court to make it harder for a woman to obtain an abortion [8/18-ABC Wpost].*
- *Furthermore, only 29% wanted states to stop funding Planned Parenthood [4/19-SSRS].*

It was another extraordinary decade for gay rights. The House and Senate passed legislation that was signed by Obama in December 2010 allowing gays, lesbians, and bisexuals to openly serve in the US military. In 2015, the Supreme Court ruled (5-4) in *Obergefell v. Hodges* that the right to marriage was guaranteed to same-sex couples.

- *Support for the rights of the LGBTQ community continued to rise. Prior to Obergefell [11/12], most Americans believed that health insurance and other employee benefits should be provided to same-sex domestic partners or spouses (77%); that domestic partners or spouses should be able to inherit (78%); that gays and lesbians should be able to adopt children (61%); and that same-sex marriages should be legally recognized (53%). By May 2017, support for gay marriage had increased to 64% and 57% even thought it was a good thing [2/18-Pew].*
- *On other issues relevant to the LGBTQ community: 42% believed that the Boy Scouts should allow openly gay adults to serve as leaders [11/12]; 67% said they would vote for a person nominated by their party running for president if that person happened to be gay [6/11]; 70% approved of gays serving in the military [5/10]; and 63% believed discrimination against gays and lesbians was a serious problem [11/12].*

The battle for LGBTQ equality is not over, as Trump announced in July 2017 that transgender individuals could not serve in the military. Several courts ruled that this position was illegal; nonetheless, in March 2018, the Trump administration said any individual who underwent gender transition would be disqualified from serving in the military.[31] The battle over transgender rights moved into the bathrooms. In March 2016, North Carolina approved legislation requiring people to use the bathroom of the birth gender and not their gender identity. This became a national controversy when several national organizations began to boycott North Carolina. Most prominently, the NCAA disqualified North Carolina from hosting NCAA tournaments. A compromise was reached in January 2017 and part of the legislation was rolled back.

- *More than two-thirds of respondents (68%) thought transgender people should be able to serve in the military [7/17-Quinnipiac].*
- *Americans were split on the issue of transgender people using public bathrooms, with 48% believing that transgender individuals should be required to use the bathroom that corresponds with their birth gender and 47% stating they should be allowed to use the bathroom corresponding with their gender identity [5/17].*

THE ECONOMY

As discussed in the previous chapter, in his first year as president, Obama had to deal with the immediate fallout from the Great Recession. In particular, this entailed bailing out the automobile companies and the banks and passing a stimulus package.

Starting in 2010, he was able to turn his attention to more long-term issues such as regulating banks and Wall Street, changing the tax system, and health care.

The economy began to improve. In October 2009, the unemployment rate was 10.0%. At the time Obama left office it had dropped to 4.8%. The recovery was uneven, though. Stock prices rose, but wages barely budged.

- *Although the official end of the recession occurred in June 2009,[32] 82% believed in 2010 that the United States was still in a recession [8/10]. In December 2012, only 34% said the economy was growing. This increased to 57% two years later [12/14-Bloomberg].*

One of the major causes of the Great Recession was risky practices by banks and other financial institutions. In July 2010, the Dodd-Frank bill was passed that required these institutions to limit their risky investments and to have more financial reserves, created new government agencies to supervise them, and created the Consumer Financial Protection Bureau to protect consumers. The public was divided on the extent to which the government should further regulate financial institutions.

- *A plurality (46%, 43%, 12%) favored Congress passing a bill giving new powers to the government to regulate large banks and financial institutions. Similarly, 50% (36%, 15%) favored giving the government more power to regulate Wall Street [4/10]. After Dodd-Frank was passed, 61% favored the Congressional legislation that increased regulations on banks and financial institutions [8/10].*

Democrats and Republicans fought over taxes. Republicans wanted to keep the Bush tax cuts (2001 and 2003) which, among other provisions, cut the amount that wealthy people paid from 39.6% to 35%. Obama wanted to keep the tax cuts only for those earning less than $250,000 per year. A compromise in 2012 kept the tax cuts for those earning under $400,000 per year.[33]

- *Americans were somewhat conflicted over the Bush-era tax cuts: 37% wanted to keep the cuts for all, 44% wanted to end it for those earning over $250,000 per year, and 15% wanted to end them for everyone [8/10].*
- *Regarding other economic proposals by Obama, there was general support for: cutting taxes on small businesses that hired more workers (85%); more funds to hire teachers, firefighters, and police officers (75%); extending unemployment insurance benefits (56%); providing funds for infrastructure projects (72%); increasing taxes on families earning more than $250,000 per year (66%); and eliminating some tax breaks for corporations (70%) [9/11].*
- *Furthermore, 58% wanted the government to be more involved in preventing foreclosures [1/12].*
- *Americans were somewhat more likely to blame Bush rather than Obama for the economic problems. For example, In June 2016, 50% blamed Obama a great deal or a moderate amount compared to 64% blaming Bush. In contrast, a year into*

the Trump Presidency, 56% said Obama deserved a great or moderate amount of credit for improvements in the economy compared to 49% saying the same for Trump (1/18).

The debate over the Affordable Care Act (Obamacare), which was passed in March 2010, was extraordinarily acrimonious.[34] It was the most significant change in health care since the passage of Medicare and Medicaid in 1965. The system of Medicaid, Medicare, and employee-based health care were maintained. The Act required that insurers charge all individuals the same rate regardless of pre-existing conditions or gender; children could stay on their parents' policy until they were twenty-six years of age; all policies cover a minimal list of benefits; policies for people with low incomes be somewhat subsidized; states expand Medicaid (mostly paid by the federal government); and everyone buy a health insurance policy or pay a penalty. In addition, various policies were created that would lower health insurance costs.

The ACA survived a Supreme Court vote in June 2012, although the Court eliminated the requirement that states expand Medicaid. Republicans were nonstop in their criticism of the ACA. Its initial rollout in October 2013 was notably botched because the software did not work. However, the technical bugs were eventually worked out and by the end of the Obama presidency the percentage of those under the age of sixty-five who were uninsured decreased from 15.4% in 2012 to 10% in 2016 (with about twenty million people becoming insured).

Controversy about the ACA remained high. Republicans claimed the legislation set up so-called death panels were destroying the economy, took away people's liberty, increased the deficit, and made people sicker. The Republican House voted over fifty times to repeal the ACA. In fact, in October 2013, the government was essentially shut down for sixteen days after Republicans refused to pass a budget without repealing the ACA. Repealing and replacing Obamacare became one of the rallying cries of the Tea Party and candidate Donald Trump.

- *When the shutdown first started, 21% said it was a crisis and 49% said it was a major problem. Only 24% said it was only a minor problem or no problem at all. Fifty-eight percent said the shutdown made them feel more negative toward democratic leaders in Congress, 61% said it made them feel negative toward the Republicans, and 57% toward Obama [10/13].*

After Trump became president, the House voted in May 2017 (217-213) to repeal and replace the ACA. Republicans in the Senate were unable to come up with the fifty votes needed to repeal and replace or just to repeal. Republicans introduced different versions of the bill and the Congressional Budget Office (CBO) estimated that, if the ACA were repealed, between 22 and 32 million would lose health coverage. As discussed below, a majority of American turned against repeal and replace, large protests occurred at the local level, and in the final vote three Republicans voted against what became known as the "skinny" bill (Susan Collins of Maine, Lisa Murkowski of Alaska, and John McCain of Arizona).

- *Just prior to Congress passing the ACA in March 2010, 45% (48%, 7%) said they would recommend their representative in Congress to vote for the legislation [3/10]. Immediately following Obama signing the bill, 42% said the bill would make health care better, 45% worse, 11% no difference; 65% said it expanded the role of government too much; and 64% said it would cost too much. On the other hand, 52% wanted it to include the public option,[35] and 51% said it did not go far enough in regulating health care [3/10]. Support for the ACA remained below 50% through the end of Obama's presidency [48%—11/12; 44%—6/13; 43%—4/14; 47%—5/16].[36]*
- *After Trump became president and Republicans put forth their own alternative to the ACA, support for the ACA grew to 53% in July 2017. In fact, only 30% supported repeal and replace while 23% said keep the ACA as it is and 44% wanted to keep the ACA, but reform it. The ambivalence to Obamacare is best seen in a July 2017 AP-NORC survey. Fifty-one percent supported the program, 33% opposed it, and 16% neither supported it or opposed it.[37] Nevertheless, in 2018 the Democrats successfully used Republican opposition to Obamacare as one of their main campaign issues in regaining control of the House.*

On December 22, 2017, Trump signed into law his new tax plan. The plan cut the corporate tax rate from 35% to 21%, lowered individual taxes (the wealthy gained the most), doubled the estate tax exemption to $22 million for couples, repealed the tax on those who do not have health insurance, and limited the amount that people could deduct for state and local taxes. It was estimated that the new law will increase the deficit by about $1 trillion over ten years.

- *Just prior to the vote, only 29% (56%, 16%) favored the proposed tax bill [12/17]. Two months after the vote, approval was still low (39%, 48%, 13%) [2/18]. The reason why many Americans disapproved of the plan was that only 37% believed it was a good thing for the country and 60% said the tax law favored the rich [1/18-ABC/W Post].*

Labor unions continued their slow decline. Labor union membership declined from 20.1% of the workforce in 1980 to 11.3% in 2013. Many Republicans wanted to further decimate the unions because they were a major source of campaign contributions and support for Democrats. In 2011, Republican Governor Scott Walker got the Wisconsin state legislature to approve a bill that took away the collective bargaining rights of most public employee unions and required employees to pay more for health care and pensions. Membership in these unions was cut by over 50%.

- *Although 52% of Americans said they favored labor unions, 41% wanted them to have less influence (29% more, 25% the same) [8/12].*
- *As to the 2011 bill restricting the collective bargaining rights of Wisconsin public employees, only 33% favored this bill [2/11].*

- *In another related topic, 71% favored "open-shop" laws, which mandate that workers do not have to join unions that represented the workers [8/14].*

Trump ran in 2016 as an economic populist. He claimed he would "drain the swamp," and there was an underlying critique of economic elitism in much of his rhetoric.

- *Two years before Trump's election, 54% of Americans said most members of Congress were corrupt and 69% said they were focused on the needs of special interests [9/14].*
- *Americans were increasingly likely to believe that the economy was unfair. In April 2015, only 31% believed that the distribution of wealth and income was fair. In fact, 52% believed the government should "redistribute wealth by heavy taxes on the rich."*

Trump also campaigned against the North American Free Trade Agreement (NAFTA) claiming it was "the worst trade deal ever made." The effects of NAFTA are complicated to assess. Critics argue that many manufacturing jobs were lost, and threats of companies moving to Mexico resulted in lowering of wages. Proponents argue that 200,000 other export-related jobs were created and consumers benefited from lowered costs. Trump also railed against the Trans-Pacific Partnership Agreement (TPP) negotiated by Obama with eleven other countries. He essentially withdrew from the agreement upon becoming president.

Trump favored increasing tariffs on imports of goods and services coming from abroad. In May 2018 he said, "Trade wars are good, and easy to win." He then announced tariffs on steel (25%) and aluminum products (10%), mostly targeting Europe. He soon initiated four rounds of tariff increases on Chinese imports as well as products ranging from French wines to Italian cheeses. Even though he had railed against NAFTA in his campaign, he signed a new agreement with Canada and Mexico (USMCA) in January 2020, which included some minor improvements over the original NAFTA.

- *In a July 2018 [CCGA] survey, Americans were divided on NAFTA, with 52% saying it was good for the United States (42%, 6%). In a related question, 72% saw trade as an opportunity for the United States, while only 23% saw it as a threat [2/17].*
- *On the TPP, 27% agreed with Trump's withdrawal, 30% were opposed, and 43% had no opinion [3/17].*

SCIENCE, TECHNOLOGY, AND THE ENVIRONMENT

In July 2012, CERN announced the discovery of a new particle that supported the theory behind the Higgs boson. In August of that year, the rover Curiosity successfully landed on Mars. It was supposed to last for two years, but at the time of this writing is still chugging away. Commercial space ventures continued to grow, the most prominent of which was Space X, controlled by Elon Musk (who also controls Tesla). In December 2015, Space X was able to recover the first stage of its orbital rocket, allowing for a large reduction in the cost of future flights. These commercial space companies have become the major contractor of resupplying the International Space Station and launching satellites. In May 2020, for the first time, Space X sent two astronauts to the International Space Station.

- *Seventy-two percent of Americans believed that the Rover landing on Mars was a major accomplishment [8/12-CNN/ORC].*
- *Furthermore, 56% (34%, 10%) said that the 1960s space program to land on the moon had long-lasting benefits, and 51% (43%, 6%) believed that increased spending on the space program today would be a good investment for the country [12/14-Monmouth].*

The environment took a lot of "hits" in this decade. In April 2010, the Deepwater Horizon oil drilling platform in the Gulf of Mexico exploded, killing eleven workers. It took almost three months to cap the oil spill, by which time 4.9 million barrels of oil had been released. The ecological disaster had a major impact on marine life, tourism, and fishing. British Petroleum (BP) had chartered the rig and was found ultimately responsible for the disaster. The US government found that Transocean (the rig operator) and Halliburton (the main contractor) were also at fault. The three companies had cut corners, used flawed cement, and employed an ineffective safety system. Ultimately, BP had to pay over $60 billion in fines.

- *When asked who was to blame for the Deepwater oil spill, respondents said they placed a great deal of blame on British Petroleum (75%), and on federal agencies that regulate oil drilling (44%) [6/10]. BP's response was rated as very poor (39%) or poor (34%), The federal government also received a poor grade with 21% saying its response was very poor, and 39% saying poor [5/10].*
- *In March 2011 [Pew], 57% wanted to continue drilling for oil and gas in US coastal waters.*

There was tremendous debate about fracking, the injection of liquids into subterranean rocks at high pressure to open fissures and release more oil and gas. Proponents argue that it reduces the cost of oil and gas, and, by increasing the availability of natural gas (substituting for coal), reduces global warming. Critics argue that it contaminates ground water, creates earthquakes, and releases methane which is an even worse contributor to global warming than CO_2.

- *Only a minority favored fracking, with 39% supporting it, 58% opposing, and 2% not having an opinion [3/18-Pew].*

In September 2015, Volkswagen was accused of cheating on emissions tests for its diesel cars. Software was used to control emissions only when the cars were tested; but when cars were not being tested, the emissions control system was shut off, resulting in forty times more emissions of nitrous oxides. This affected 600,000 vehicles in the United States and eleven million worldwide. Volkswagen had to pay $17 billion in civil settlements and $4.3 billion to settle criminal charges.[38]

It became increasingly clear that global warming, caused primarily by the burning of fossil fuels, was threatening the habitation of the planet. In December 2015, 196 parties in Paris agreed to steps to reduce global warming. The Paris Accord called for policies that would hold the global increase in temperature to below 2 °C. However, scientists now believe that it is more likely that the temperature rise by the end of the century will be 4 °C or even as high as 8 °C. This would lead to sea level rises of close to 3 meters by the end of the century, acidification of the oceans, and a collapse of agriculture. In June 2017, Donald Trump withdrew the United States from the Paris Accord.[39]

In January 2019, Jair Bolsonaro became president of Brazil. He believed global warming was a hoax and Brazil needed to develop the Amazon Basin. Millions of trees have been cut down or burned to clear land for mines and agriculture. Massive wildfires occurred in the summer of 2019 and there is now worry that the Amazon Basin could essentially dry out and become prairie, which would result in millions of species dying out, as well as an enormous loss of forests, which are essential for removing CO_2 from the atmosphere.

Other massive and prolonged wildfires started in Australian in late 2019, covering an area the size of West Virginia, killing hundreds of millions of animals, and destroying over 2,500 homes. This is global warming in real time, not twenty years in the future. The fires were caused by unprecedented heat (2–3 degrees above normal) and drought. The fires also tripled the amount of carbon output that Australia typically emitted in a year.

The United States also had disastrous forest fires. The Camp Fire ignited in Butte County, California, in November 2018, and became California's deadliest and most destructive wildfire, with 88 deaths and 18,804 buildings destroyed.

- *Sixty-seven percent of respondents said they were closely following the Australian wildfires and 54% of these respondents believed the fires were related to climate change [1/20-Politico-Harvard].*
- *As to the 2018 California fires, 31% believed climate change made the fires a lot worse, 13% moderately worse, 6% a little worse, 24% said climate change had no effect, and 25% did not know [11/18-Ipsos]. Many Americans were not convinced that climate change led to worse fires and hurricanes.*

Trump's appointments to head the Environmental Protection Agency (Scott Pruitt), the Department of the Interior (Ryan Zinke), and Department of Energy (Rick Perry) did their utmost to roll back environmental protection standards developed in previous years and promoted fossil fuel development over alternative energy.

Although all three resigned, their successors (respectively, Andrew Wheeler, David Bernhardt, and Dan Brouillette) were all former lobbyists for the fossil fuel industry and were even more successful at rolling back these standards.

On the other hand, there has been a tremendous international upsurge in the environmental movement. Greta Thunberg from Sweden initiated a school strike in 2018 when she was fifteen, and soon after became inspiration for environmental activism worldwide. *Time Magazine* named her Person of the Year in September 2019. She was one person among many, though, as millions of people around the globe began or continued to demand the immediate reduction in the use of fossil fuels.

- *Of the 60% of respondents who had heard of Greta Thunberg, 66% said they trusted her as a source of information on global warming [11/19-Ipsos].*
- *Beginning in 1984, Gallup asked whether "protection of the environment" should be given priority "even at the risk of curbing economic growth." There has been substantial fluctuation in support of the environmental position: 61% (9/84), 71% (4/90), 62% (4/95), 67% (4/00), 53% (3/05), 42% (3/09), 50% (3/10), 50% (3/14), 65% (3/10), and 60% (3/20). Over 70% took the environmental position in 1990; support fell to 42% with the advent of the Great Recession in 2009; and rose to above 60% starting in 2019.*
- *A similar pattern occurred for whether global warming has "already begun to happen": 48% (11/97), 54% (3/01), 54% (3/05), 61% (3/08), 53% (3/09), 49% (3/11), 55% (3/15), 62% (3/17), 61% (3/20). Belief that global warming had already begun dropped with the Great Recession and has been growing in recent years. However, the 61% who believe this in 2020 is the same as in 2008.*[40]
- *Only 32% agreed with Trump's decision to withdraw from the Paris Accord [5/17-Quinnipiac].*

Public health was also problematic in this decade. An outbreak of Ebola that peaked in 2014 resulted in over 11,000 deaths that occurred mostly in Liberia, Sierra Leone, and Guinea. A fatality rate approaching 70% in conjunction with how easily the disease could spread resulted in panic throughout West Africa as well as among some people in the United States. Several aid workers from the United States contracted Ebola and there were calls for not allowing them to return to the United States and for travel bans for other people who were in the region. Ebola returned to Kivu Congo in 2018 and the death toll exceeded 1,000. Several Ebola vaccines are now being deployed. However, some aid workers were murdered when they went out to inoculate the local population.

- *Sixty-one percent of Americans said they had confidence that the US government could handle Ebola if there was an outbreak in the United States [10/14].*

POPULAR TRENDS

Some of the top movies of the decade included: *The Hunger Games* (2012); Marvel's *The Avengers* (2012); *Frozen* (2013); *Twelve Years a Slave* (2013); *Finding Dory* (2016);

Wonder Woman (2017); *The Shape of Water* (2017); *Black Panther* (2018); and *Parasite* (2019).

Nontraditional networks had an increasing influence on new television shows, including: *Homeland* (2011-Showtime); *Game of Thrones* (2011-HBO); *Veep* (2012-HBO); *House of Cards* (2013-Netflix); *Orange is the New Black* (2013-Netflix); *Stranger Things* (2017-Netflix); and *The Handmaid's Tale* (2017-Hulu).

New books published included: Michael Lewis' *The Big Short* (2010); Kathryn Stockett's *The Help* (2010); Jodi Picoult's *House Rules* (2010); Walter Isaacson's *Steve Jobs* (2011); Cheryl Stayed's *Wild* (2012); Ta-Nehisi Coates' *Between the World and Me* (2015); Bruce Springsteen's *Born to Run* (2016); J. D. Vance's *Hillbilly Elegy* (2016); and Bob Woodward's *Rage* (2020).

Digital music distributors continued to expand, the big players being: Spotify, iTunes, YouTube, and Amazon. Some of the musicians who ruled in this decade were: Nicki Minaj, Drake, Adele, Kanye West, Kendrick Lamar, Justin Bieber, Taylor Swift, Rihanna, and Katy Perry.

The internet continued to have a massive impact on different elements of popular culture. The sale of electronic books grew so rapidly that by 2010 Amazon announced they had sold 140 e-books for every 100 hardcover books; e-books were outselling paperbacks. However, in 2012 it was estimated that e-books accounted for only 8.5% of total book sales and by 2015 sales of e-books began to decline.

However, people increasingly used the internet ("to Google" was now an established verb) to obtain information. In 2012, the Encyclopedia Britannica discontinued its print edition after 246 years.

- *By January 2011, 43% of survey respondents said they had a Facebook page and 60% said they used Google at least once a week. Further, 44% had seen a movie streamed over the internet [12/12]; 87% used the internet at home or at work [10/13]; 53% were likely to shop for Christmas presents on the internet [10/13]; and 73% were using text messaging [9/14].*
- *As for what Americans owned: MP3 music player (45%); desktop computer (57%); laptop computer (64%); wireless internet access, or Wi-Fi, in your home (73%); a video game system, such as X-Box or PlayStation (41%); an internet streaming service like Hulu, Netflix, or Roku that brings you TV shows over your television or computer (39%); a smartphone, that is, a cellular phone that has built-in applications and internet access, such as an iPhone or Android (62%); a tablet computer, that is, a small hand-held computer, such as an iPad or Kindle Fire (38%); an e-reader, such as a Kindle or Nook (26%); cable TV (68%); satellite TV (34%): a Video Cassette Recorder (58%); and a DVD player or Blu-Ray player 80% [12/13].*
- *American use of media underwent a profound change. In 1956, 82% read a daily newspaper. This declined to 66% in 1987 and 49% in 2012 [5/12-Pew]. Similarly, the percent of Americans who were currently reading a book dropped from 43% in 1978 to 35% in 2012.*[41] *On the other hand, in the same Pew survey, 34% said they were getting news online.*

The internet's effect on the news media was massive. The total weekday circulation of newspapers declined from sixty-two million in 1990 to forty million in 2014. The decline of local newspapers was particularly intense. By 2017, 93% of Americans got at least some of their news online. The 2016 election was a watershed, as Donald Trump forced members of the news media to stand in holding pens at his campaign rallies and then denounced them. Any news reports that were critical of him became "fake news." People increasingly only read from sources they agreed with.

- *In September 2014, faith in the accuracy of the media was fairly low (10% had a great deal, 30% had a fair amount, 36% had not much, and 24% had no faith at all in the accuracy of media reporting).*[42]
- *After Trump became president, only 36% thought that news organizations got their "facts straight" and 62% believed the media favored one political party over another [3/17]. On the other hand, 72% said they trust the national news a lot or some [3/17-Pew] and only 27% thought the national news organizations regularly published fake news [3/17-Monmouth].*
- *Americans were fans of many sports: baseball (48%); professional basketball (33%); professional ice hockey (33%); college football (49%); college basketball (37%); auto-racing (24%); professional soccer (19%); and Olympic Sports (69%) [12/12].*

The decade had its share of sports scandals, starting with a fall from grace for the almost universally admired Lance Armstrong. He had won the Tour de France seven consecutive times beginning in 1999, an achievement that was seen as even greater given that he was diagnosed with metastatic testicular cancer in 1996, and his foundation had sold over $325 million in Livestrong bracelets to fund cancer research. However, in 2012 he was banned from cycling and his medals were taken away because of long-term doping.

- *In July 2005, 41% of respondents said that Lance Armstrong was the greatest male athlete in sports today.*[43] *In 2013, after the doping scandal broke, 30% still wanted Armstrong to get credit for the races he won [1/13-ABC/W Post].*

Another sports scandal involved Jerry Sandusky, assistant football coach under Joe Paterno for Penn State. The scandal surfaced in November 2011 when Sandusky was indicted on fifty-two counts of child sexual abuse and others were charged with perjury and obstruction of justice. Sandusky was convicted in June 2012 of forty-five counts of child sexual abuse. Furthermore, Paterno and others were fired by Penn State for not reporting accusations of abuse, and the NCAA sanctioned the football program by putting the program on a 5-year probation, removing 111 wins from its records, and fining them $60 million.

A third sports scandal enveloped women's gymnastics. Larry Nassar, a doctor for the national team was accused of sexual assault by over 300 girls (including Aly Raisman and Simone Biles) over a 14-year time span. In 2017, he was sentenced to prison essentially for life following a highly publicized sentencing hearing. Many felt that Michigan State University, where Nassar worked, as well as US gymnastics should have faced greater penalties.

- *Of the 58% who had heard of the Sandusky scandal, 14% wanted Penn State to cancel or forfeit the rest of the season, and 68% approved of the firing of Paterno [11/11].*
- *Over three-quarters, 78% wanted others at Michigan State University and US gymnastics to face criminal charges for the sexual assaults in women's gymnastics [1/18—Monmouth].*

CONCLUDING COMMENTS

A lot happened in this decade: ISIS, the election of Donald Trump, gay marriage becomes legal, police violence against blacks, and polarization.

The horrific consequences of Bush's invasion of Iraq became apparent. Destabilizing Iraq led to the growth of ISIS and its ability to take over large parts of Syria and Iraq and instability and armed conflict (terrorism) in Nigeria, Mozambique, Mali, Libya, Egypt, Somalia, the Philippines, and many other countries. Terrorist acts multiplied worldwide. The US struggle against ISIS was inconsistent: for example, sending in troops and advisors and later withdrawing them (as was done in Somalia), or helping those fighting ISIS but then later abandoning them (as was done with the Kurds in Syria). In other international events, a nuclear deal was signed with Iran by Obama and rescinded by Trump; North Korea continued acquiring nuclear weapons and ballistic missiles regardless of who the US president was; Russia continued its foreign policy of destabilization, ranging from an invasion of Ukraine and related disinformation campaign to interference in US elections. Britain left the European Union. Instability is perhaps the best one-word description of this decade.

Most Americans did not want to intervene in Iraq/Syria, stay in Afghanistan, or send weapons to Ukraine. Most also supported actions that would decrease international tensions, for example, the Iran nuclear deal or resolving conflict with North Korea through diplomacy.

The election of Donald Trump was the decade's most momentous event affecting domestic politics. Issuing directly from Trump himself and from officials of his administration, lies, misinformation, and attempts to subvert American democratic traditions became the norm. His actions led to two successful impeachment votes in the House. Other domestic developments included the rise of right-wing groups (e.g., the Tea Party) and contrasting liberal protest (e.g., the Women's March), an increase in mass shootings, attacks on immigration, increased influence of money (much of it secret) on politics, and the continued growth of legalized marijuana.

Polarization reached levels unprecedented since the civil war. Trump was historically unpopular; however, the public was split on whether he should be impeached. Although most Americans supported expanded background checks for gun purchases, most opposed bans on assault weapons. Most opposed Trump's restrictions on refugees or DACA children as well as his attempt to build a wall with Mexico.

Police violence against blacks became more apparent with many of these attacks now being captured on smart phones and bodycams. With the election of Trump, racists became more emboldened, as exemplified by hundreds of white nationalists holding a rally in Charlottesville in 2017. Whites and blacks continued to have different perceptions of police violence (George Floyd will be discussed in the next chapter), while at the same time there was widespread (but not universal) denunciation of neo-Nazi actions.

Scandals surrounding Harvey Weinstein, Jeffrey Epstein, and others gave rise to the Me Too Movement and the fight against sexual misconduct in the workplace and elsewhere. In contrast, Brett Kavanaugh was confirmed on a seat to the Supreme Court despite serious allegations that he had been involved in at least one sexual assault. In 2010, Congress passed legislation to allow gays, lesbians, and bisexuals to openly serve in the military and in 2015 the right to same-sex marriage was guaranteed by the Supreme Court.

Most Americans believed the stories of sexual misconduct in the workplace were real and, unlike reactions to the accusation of Anita Hill against Clarence Thomas in 1991, most believed in the accusations against Kavanaugh. In a striking transformation, the majority of Americans now supported same-sex marriages.

The aftereffects of the Great Recession dominated the early years of the decade. The economy improved and laws were passed under Obama to strengthen regulations protecting consumers and limiting risky practices of financial institutions. However, the improvement was uneven in that the wealthy did far better than others. This would play a large factor in Trump's election in 2016 (his claim to be a populist—"Drain the Swamp"). One of Obama's major legislative achievements was the passing the Affordable Care Act in 2010.

The public was divided on many of the financial reforms as well as whether the Bush-era tax cuts for the wealthy should be rescinded. Attitudes toward the ACA were mixed. Its passage would initially lead to electoral losses for the Democrats. However, in a somewhat surprising turn-of-events, the threat of it being repealed led to Democratic victories in 2018.

Highlights in science and technology included CRISPR, Space X, and rover landings on Mars. Amazon continued to increase its domination of internet commerce and the related decline of bricks-and-mortars stores. The rising influence of social media became starkly apparent when it was seen how Russia, Facebook, and Twitter affected the 2016 election. Ecological devastation became even more apparent with the Deepwater spill in the Gulf of Mexico in 2010, forest fires and heat waves in Australia, the West Coast, and elsewhere, and the growing intensity of hurricanes and other weather phenomena. Yet, in the face of many incontrovertible disasters linked to climate change, Trump withdrew from the 2016 Paris Accord on climate change, appointed anti-environmentalists to environmental posts, and signed a number of executive orders to open drilling, reduce improvements in gas mileage of cars, and undermine efforts to control the leaking of methane.

These events and actions contributed to an upsurge of the international environmental movement. There was increasing recognition that global warming was linked to forest fires and other extreme weather events. Americans were more likely to believe that pro-environmental policies needed to be enacted.

[The reader can find relevant crosstabs and discussion in the online appendix located at https://rowman.com/ISBN/9781793653505/US-Public-Opinion-since-the-1930s-Galluping-through-History.]

NOTES

1. In August 2011, the Obama administration wanted to keep 3,000–5,000 US advisors in Iraq.
2. A reminder to readers, the numbers in parentheses mean that 43% did not believe that this Iraq could limit attacks and 4% had no opinion.
3. In August 2013, the Syrian government used chemical weapons (sarin nerve gas) on civilians. Obama, having said in 2012 that if this occurred it would be crossing a red line, was under tremendous pressure to react. However, a September 2013 Quinnipiac survey found only 41% (49%, 10%) favored using cruise missiles to attack targets in Syria in response to the chemical attack. Russia helped to arrange the dismantling of most of these weapons. However, chemical weapons were again used in April 2017 and Trump had the US military launch fifty-nine cruise missiles in response (approved by 62% [4/17—NBC/*WSJ*]). Chemical weapons were again used since then, though, with little response from the US.
4. As much as I would like to analyze these questions in the crosstabs, the raw data from NBC/*WSJ* and Fox are not available. Unfortunately, the lack of raw data is a far-too-frequent occurrence in this decade.
5. It would take many paragraphs (or pages) to more fully explain the divisions within Syria.
6. Forty-two percent said they followed the killing very closely [5/11].
7. Trump's decision to withdraw support from the Kurds was widely condemned by many military officials for being a betrayal, leading to massacres of our former allies, and diminishing our credibility. See, for example, Denne and Gardiner (2019).
8. The reader should be extra cautious in interpreting these results. Respondents might believe that a policy would be effective, but still oppose it.
9. I was unable to find any survey data on the war in Yemen or questions about US arm sales to Saudi Arabia.
10. President Trump at a September 2018 rally in West Virginia said, "He [Kim] wrote me beautiful letters, and they're great letters. We fell in love."
11. Bob Woodward in his 2020 book, *Fear*, has an extraordinary account about the relationship between Trump and Kim Jong Un. Woodward was given twenty-seven letters between the two, twenty-five reported for the first time by Woodward.
12. This history is very complex. Essentially, Russia did not want any potential enemies on its borders. Flipping Ukraine from pro-Russian to pro-Western was unacceptable. A potential compromise, making Ukraine a neutral party, was not examined. Furthermore, Yanukovych was democratically elected, and some of his opponents were tied to Ukrainian fascist organizations.
13. I have not found any question by any survey organization on the Rohingya.

14. I have not found any questions by any survey organization on Trump's decision to potentially deport most of the Haitians who came to the United States following the 2010 earthquake.

15. As with any presidency, Obama's approval ratings fluctuated. For example, in February 2014 it was at 40%. At the time he left office it was at 59%. However, Michelle Obama's ratings were consistently high. In February 2014, hers was at 66%.

16. Although all US intelligence agencies agreed that it was Russia behind the stolen emails, only 29% (54%, 16%) believed that Russia stole the email to help Trump [7/16-Fox]. Unfortunately, no survey organization asked questions about this issue in the two months before the election.

17. Nate Silver of 538.com, probably the best compiler of election survey data, says it is likely that the Comey letter cost Clinton the election (Silver, 2017).

18. Unfortunately, this is another example where the raw data are not available.

19. Trump pardoned Flynn, Manafort, and Stone.

20. A brouhaha developed over the crowd size of Trump's inauguration as compared to the Women's March on the next day or to Obama's inauguration eight years before. Trump's press secretary, Sean Spicer, claimed, despite all evidence to the contrary, that more people attended Trump's inauguration than the other two events; however, the New York Times estimated that three times more people attended the Women's March in DC (Wallace and Parlapiano, 2017).

21. Alex Jones of Infowars made the outrageous conspiracy theory claim in September 2014 that the Newton shooting never occurred and the victims were child actors. Jones is a well-known friend and supporter of Donald Trump. In December 2019, Jones was ordered by a Texas Judge to pay one of the Sandy Hook families $100,000 as well as attorney fees in a defamation suit. Other suits are still pending.

22. The shooting at Majority Stoneham Douglas High School resulted in March for Our Lives demonstrations in 900 cities. It is estimated that over 250,000 people attended the main demonstration in Washington, D.C., in March 2018.

23. For a nuanced view of attitudes of immigrants and attitudes toward immigrants, see Schildkraut (2010). One finding is that whites who feel discriminated against are more likely to oppose immigration.

24. Question phraseology and mode of interview can have a dramatic effect. In June 2016, Gallup, in a telephone survey, found only 33% favored "Building a wall along the entire US-Mexico border," while the Chicago Council on Global Affairs in a web-based survey in the very same month found 48% supported "a wall expanding the 700 miles of border wall and fencing with Mexico to reduce illegal immigration into the United States."

25. Many believe that in her confirmation hearing in January 2017 Devos exhibited an appalling lack of knowledge about education policy. Her confirmation vote required Vice President Pence to break a 50-50 tie.

26. The debate goes back to 2002 when Congress passed legislation proposed by George W. Bush titled No Child Left Behind (NCLB) which required states to test all children grades 3–8 and if students were not proficient, sanctions would be imposed. Many teachers opposed NCLB as it required teachers to "teach to a test" that many felt was not relevant. In 2015, Congress stripped away the national requirements of NCLB.

27. Smith (1998) found that respondents rated the quality of local conditions far higher than how things were on the national level in areas such as crime, air quality, politicians, and so on.

28. The defendant was convicted of first-degree murder in July 2019.

29. Archer and Kam (2020) report that levels of sexism have barely changed between 2004 and 2018 and there is a strong correlation between sexism and recognition of sexual misconduct.

30. Sixty-seven percent wanted the Senate to hold confirmation hearing for Garland [4/16-ORC].

31. NBC News describes the current Pentagon policy as "Any currently serving troops diagnosed after that date must serve according to their sex as assigned at birth and are prohibited from seeking transition-related care. Prospective recruits who have received a gender dysphoria diagnosis are barred from enlisting or enrolling in military academies" (Moreau, 2020). Biden reversed this policy in February 2021.

32. The National Bureau of Economic Research has been the unofficial arbiter of dating when recessions and depressions begin and end.

33. For an excellent discussion of how tax policies affect income inequality, see Saez and Zucman (2019).

34. When Obama was addressing a joint session of Congress on health care reform, Representative Joe Wilson of South Carolina shouted out "you lie" twice.

35. The public option would have created a government health insurance agency that would have competed with private insurance companies. It was withdrawn from the ACA after Joe Lieberman (I-CT) threatened a filibuster.

36. One aspect of the debate over the ACA was whether employees should be required to cover contraception costs or whether an employee could opt out for religious reasons. Forty-eight percent agreed with Obama that coverage should be required (45%, 8%). The Supreme Court ruled in a 2014, 5-4 decision (*Burwell v. Hobby Lobby*) that privately held corporations were not required to pay for contraception coverage.

37. The AP-NORC question shows the wisdom of sometimes stating in the question phraseology that respondents did not have to choose between support or oppose. The Gallup version had 3% without an opinion compared to 16% for the AP-NORC version.

38. I was unable to find any survey question on this issue.

39. In the Summer of 2017, three of the most destructive hurricanes in US history occurred: Irma, Maria, and Harvey. Forty-six people were also killed in devastating wildfires in California. Most climate scientists believe the hurricanes and fires were exacerbated by global warming.

40. The question on whether global warming has already begun is subject to the effect of question phraseology. When Pew asked a similar question in March 2018, only 48% said the earth was getting warmer because of human activity compared to 60% when asked by Gallup. The Pew version gave respondents an additional choice: "There is no solid evidence that the Earth is getting warmer."

41. On whom does not read books see Perrin (2019).

42. The corresponding figures in 1997 were: 10%, 43%, 31%, and 15%. Trust had dropped.

43. The next highest ranked was Tiger Woods (10%).

10
2020

Covid-19, the Killing of George Floyd and Protests, an Attempt to Overthrow an Election

Many would prefer to forget the year 2020. It became a bad meme with the pandemic, protests following the deaths of George Floyd and others at the hands of police, devastating hurricanes and forest fires,[1] and a uniquely fraught and contentious presidential election. The previous chapters have covered entire decades, however, for many reasons it makes sense for 2020 to have its own chapter. Too much happened in the year to fold into the previous chapter, and 2020 became a fitting epilogue for the book on its own. The enormity and effects of 2020 events continued into the first month of 2021 with the violent disorders at the Capitol on January 6.[2] Therefore, this last chapter will end with the second impeachment trial of Donald Trump and the inauguration of Joe Biden and Kamala Harris. This chapter also has a different format than the previous chapters. I cover only three events: the Covid-19 pandemic, the killing of George Floyd and the subsequent protests, and the attempt to overturn the 2020 election.

COVID-19

Covid-19 (also called SARS-Cov-2) was first identified in Wuhan, China, in December 2019 and the first case in the United States was detected one month later. As most of us have now learned, Covid-19 is a coronavirus that is mostly airborne. It is related to two other deadly coronaviruses—SARS and MERS. SARS was first reported in Asia in 2003 and had a death rate of around 10% (774 total deaths). MERS was first reported in Saudi Arabia in 2012 and had a death rate of 33% (866 total deaths). Covid-19's death rate was far lower—approximately 1%. However, it was more dangerous because it was more easily spread since people could infect other people before they showed any symptoms. By the end of 2020, over two million people had died worldwide including about 350,000 in the United States.[3] The average life expectancy for people in the United States had dropped a full year in the United States, but the life expectancy for black Americans decreased by 2.7 years.

In September 2020, in one of a series of interviews with Bob Woodward, Trump revealed that he had found out in February that the virus was airborne, saying "this is deadly stuff," adding that it might be five times more lethal than the flu. He also revealed that his national security advisor, Robert O'Brien, had told him in January, "[t]his will be the biggest national security threat you face in your presidency." In that same month, there had been fifteen identified cases in the United States; Trump claimed cases would soon be at zero and that the disease would probably go away with warmer weather. However, speaking with Woodward later in the year, Trump excused his minimizing of the threat, saying he did not want people to panic.

The move to start shutting down parts of the economy jump-started on March 11, when the National Basketball Association suspended its season for thirty days and the World Health Organization declared Covid-19 a pandemic. The reaction of the NBA quickly spread to other professional sports.[4] Soon airplane travel between the United States and many other countries was suspended and Trump publicly supported CDC guidelines encouraging social distancing, asking people to avoid going to restaurants for fifteen days and to avoid unnecessary trips. One problem was the lack of national standards (or even suggestions) on what to shut down. Some states went into full lockdown while others essentially ignored Trump's limited suggestions. Another failure of national leadership was the unwillingness of the federal government to centralize the purchase and distribution of personal protection equipment (PPE) such as masks, gloves, and gowns, which led to states and hospitals bidding against each other.

The $2.2 trillion CARES Act was signed into law in late March.[5] The Act gave $1,200 cash payments to most Americans, extended unemployment insurance, provided forgivable loans to small businesses, loans to larger corporations, and payments to state and local governments. Over time the government established a renter eviction moratorium, federal relief for student loans, and help for those falling behind in their mortgage payments. In early May, the US government announced the establishment of Operation Warp Speed—a $10 billion public-private partnership to develop Covid-19 vaccines.

The economy took a big hit. Approximately eight million more people slipped into poverty, and it was projected that the total cost to the economy would be $16 trillion, with estimates of the number of people who were unemployed ranging from 10 to 20 million.[6] The economic effects were not evenly distributed. Billionaires as a class increased their wealth by $1 trillion (Elon Musk's wealth increased by $132 billion and Jeff Bezos by $70 billion; Ingraham, 2021). Nevertheless, the CARES Act was successful in limiting the economic carnage.

However, in March and April, procedures to avoid and treat Covid-19 became politicized. After the CDC advised the public to start using face masks, Trump said wearing them was voluntary and he would not do it. He touted the use of a drug used to treat malaria (hydroxychloroquine) and suggested injecting disinfectants as a treatment. States began deciding how to implement public health policies—such as

Table 10.1 Covid-19 Cases and Deaths

	New Cases (Seven-day Average)	Deaths (Seven-day Average)	Deaths (Cumulative)
March 1, 2020	2	0	1
April 1, 2020	18,769	503	4,519
May 1, 2020	28,051	1,973	64,310
June 1, 2020	20,111	985	105,195
July 1, 2020	43,869	891	128,097
August 1, 2020	62,793	1,147	154,162
September 1, 2020	42,689	897	184.254
October 1, 2020	42,033	706	207,416
November 1, 2020	91,303	825	230,468
December 1, 2020	163,303	1,545	269,915
January 1, 2021	191,538	2,489	347,333
February 1, 2021	143,612	3,090	442,128

Source: The CDC's Covid Data Tracker, https://covid.cdc.gov/covid-data-tracker/#trends_dailytrendscases

whether to require the wearing of masks or whether to reopen or keep open schools, bars, restaurants, and gyms—based more on ideology than science.

Covid-19 cases soon exploded in the country (see table 10.1). By August 1, 2020, there were over 60,000 new cases a day and over 1,000 deaths per day. These numbers flattened out over the summer but mushroomed again in the fall—partly due to people being exposed during summer travel and then spreading the disease upon their return home, and partly due to the hyper-politicization that developed over Covid-19. Many Trump supporters began to call the disease a hoax and therefore did not observe precautions, notably at Trump's election rallies and meetings where people did not socially distance or wear masks. By the end of the year, almost 200,000 new cases a day were reported, and by February 1, 2021, over 3,000 people a day were dying from the disease.

Covid-19 cases began to subside with the end of the election season. President-elect Biden provided an example by wearing a mask and social distancing, and people in general were taking greater precautions. In December, the FDA gave emergency authorization to two vaccines (Pfizer-BioNTech and Moderna). Hope was on the horizon. However, there is still concern about new variants of Covid-19 and whether vaccinations would keep up.[7]

- *Axios/Ipsos data displayed in table 10.2 show the extent to which people were affected by and what they felt about Covid-19.[8] For the twelve months for which we have data, the percent of respondents who said they were not concerned about Covid-19 never exceeded 20%. In the course of the year, the percent who knew someone who died from Covid-19 increased from 12% to 34% and the percent of people who worked remotely started at 45% when the lockdown started, and then after July averaged 36%. Trust in the information provided by the federal government dropped from 53% in March to 35% in July after it became obvious that some debates about Covid-19 had become politicized.*

Table 10.2 Attitudes toward Covid

	Not Concerned	Working Remotely	Small Risk Friends/ Family	All Times Wear Mask	Soon Get Vaccinated or Already	Trust Fed Govt with Info	Know Anyone Who Died from Covid
March	20					53	
April	8	45	18	30		53	12
May	13	42	31	50			12
June	17	43	42	50			15
July	16	37	33	62		35	16
August	16	57	34	65		37	19
September	20	35	39	68	13	36	21
October	17	32	38	68		35	22
November	17	35	28	69		39	24
December	14	36	27	72	27	41	30
January	16	35	25	74	49	40	34
February	19	34	31	73	50	50	34

Source: Axios/Ipsos

- *The majority of people took the pandemic seriously.* Only about one-third thought there was a small risk in attending gatherings of friends and families outside of one's household; the percent who said they always wore a mask outside their house increased from 30% in April to over 70% by the end of the year; and the percent who said they would be vaccinated as soon as they could, increased from 27% in December to 50% a month later.[9] Quinnipiac survey data in December showed that most people favored tightening restrictions in gyms (54%), bars (60%), and restaurants (53%). In fact, only 28% believed that orders to wear masks were a threat to basic freedoms [7/20-Norc].
- *Although conspiracy theories about Covid-19 were prevalent, they were held by a minority.* Of the 71% who had heard that powerful people had purposely created the coronavirus outbreak, 36% (51%, 13%; [Pew-6/20]) thought it was true; and 22% believed that the virus was intentionally planned by China [9/20-Ipsos]. On other misinformation, only 19% agreed that "Chloroquine is a safe and effective way to treat COVID-19" [9/20-Ipsos].
- *Respondents wanted the government to be involved.* A Fox survey in April indicated that 39% approved of the $2 trillion CARES relief bill and 39% wanted to spend even more (10% wanted to spend less and 12% did not know). When another bill was passed in December, Fox showed similar agreement levels (35%, 33%, 19%, and 13%).

RACIAL PROTESTS

On May 25, 2020, four Minneapolis police officers arrested George Floyd for allegedly passing a counterfeit $20 bill at a convenience station to buy cigarettes.

Officer Derek Chauvin, who is white, was filmed kneeling on Mr. Floyd's neck for over nine minutes. Floyd was slowly murdered while he told Chauvin he could not breathe, pled for his life, and asked for help. All four officers were immediately fired and eventually charged with murder or aiding and abetting a murder. The video is arguably the most disturbing video ever made of police misconduct in the United States. On April 21, 2021, Chauvin was found guilty on all charges.

Other incidents of deaths of black civilians at the hands of the police soon surfaced.[10] Most prominently, Breonna Taylor, a twenty-six-year-old black woman who was an ER technician, was fatally shot two months earlier on March 13 in Louisville, Kentucky. Three white plainclothes police officers raided the wrong apartment in a drug investigation. Her boyfriend, not knowing they were police, fired a warning shot when they burst through the door, which was returned by thirty-two rounds by the police officers. Taylor was struck five or six times. Although there were local protests right after the killing, the incident became nationally prominent following the death of George Floyd.

The reaction of people who saw the George Floyd video was visceral. Riots immediately broke out in Minneapolis and protests ensued in many cities and towns across the country. Outrage at police misconduct and racism linked the murder of Floyd to the murder of Taylor and other black civilians (some discussed in the previous chapter). Protests continued throughout the summer. One of the demands of the protesters was that Confederate flags and monuments needed to be taken down from public spaces. This was done in dozens of locations.

Given the graphic nature of the Floyd video, there was a sustained negative reaction toward police violence as well as sustained support for the protests among both blacks and whites. Protesters called for an end to police brutality and systemic racism. Polling data suggests that between 15 million and 25 million people participated in one of the protests (Buchanan, Bui, and Patel, 2020). The vast majority of protesters were peaceful. However, some looting and vandalism did occur and approximately 200 cities called for a curfew at some point.

- *Pew asked respondents on four different occasions whether they supported the Black Lives Matter Movement. The total level of support was 60% (2/16); 55% (8/17); 67% (6/20);[11] and 55% (9/20).[12] Although there was an increase in support after the killing of George Floyd, support had reverted by September.*
- *The events surrounding George Floyd led to an increased awareness of the effects of racial discrimination. Gallup polls have asked about job opportunities for blacks since 1963.[13] In 1999, 79% of whites believed that blacks had as good a chance as whites to get a job for which they are qualified. This increased to 82% by 2009 (soon after Obama was elected), declined to 67% in 2018 (the middle of Trump's term), and fell to 62% in June 2020 (right after Floyd's murder). Among blacks, the corresponding figures were 40% (1999), 49% (2009), 30% (2018), and 31% (2020). Black assessment of job opportunities also fell after 1999, but there was no additional drop with the murder of Floyd.*

Table 10.3   Attitudes toward Police and Police Use of Force

	White	Black
How serious is police violence against civilians (extreme)	16	53
Require police officers to wear video cameras (strong favor)	71	83
Prosecute police officers who use excessive force (strong favor)	63	80
Reduce funding for law enforcement (favor)	22	43
Penalize police supervisors for racially biased policing of subordinates (strong favor)	37	60
Require reporting of misconduct of peers (strong favor)	65	78
Require more racial bias training (strong favor)	56	80
Recent protests are change for the better (yes)	41	72
Recent protests police used excessive force (yes)	37	70
Did I participate in recent protest(s) (yes)	6	14
Have I ever been treated unfair by police because of race (yes)	6	51

Source: NORC, June 2020

- After the shooting of George Floyd, blacks were more likely than whites to believe that the criminal justice system favored whites over blacks (88% v. 63%) [6/20-CNN].[14] Awareness increased among both blacks and whites as compared to September 2016 (78% v. 48%.).
- In June 2020, NORC (see table 10.3) asked a comprehensive set of questions on the protests and attitudes toward the police. There were four questions in which the difference between the opinions of blacks and whites exceeded thirty points: had they been treated unfairly because of their race (51% v. 6%); how serious was police violence against civilians (53% v. 16%); did police use excessive force in recent protests (70% v 37%); and would recent protests create change for the better (72% v. 41%). The poll showed a consensus that police should be required to wear video cameras, that police should be required to report misconduct by their peers, and that police officers who use excessive force should be prosecuted. Fourteen percent of blacks reported having attended a recent protest compared to 6% of whites. Interestingly, less than half of both black and white respondents wanted to reduce spending for law enforcement.[15]
- A July 2020, Quinnipiac survey found that most Americans believed that the Confederate flag was a symbol of racism, rather than Southern pride (56%, 35%, 10%).

2020 ELECTION, CONSPIRACY THEORIES, AND INSURRECTION

On November 3, Joe Biden defeated Donald Trump in the 2020 presidential election (51.3% v. 46.9%). Although these results were not unusual or unexpected, the reaction was. To comprehend what occurred after the election it is important to understand two preceding factors: the psychology of Donald Trump and the growth of conspiracy theories and far-right organizations.

Glen Kessler, who heads a fact-checker team at the *Washington Post*, recorded over 30,000 lies by Trump in the four years of his presidency. In addition, his niece

Mary Trump—a clinical psychologist who diagnosed her uncle with narcissism and antisocial personality disorder in a 2020 book—predicted immediately after the election that Trump would never concede.[16] His inability to accept losing combined with his penchant for lying made it almost inevitable that he would claim the election was stolen.

With the advent of Trump, a variety of right-wing conspiracy-oriented groups formed. The most well know was QAnon. Q was supposedly a high-government official who claimed that Democratic politicians (in particular, Hillary Clinton), George Soros, and Hollywood elites were Satan-worshippers who ran a sex-trafficking ring (and even drank the blood of babies). Furthermore, Trump was supposedly working with Q to stop a coup d'état planned by these pedophiles. A related right-wing group was the Proud Boys, who were self-styled proud "Western chauvinists," who were not afraid of participating in violent activities and were often associated with racist events. Other groups included the Oath Keepers (a far-right, antigovernment organization whose members were mostly exmilitary and police) and the Three Percenters (who were pro-gun rights and antigovernment).

Voting experts knew that Biden supporters were more likely than Trump supporters to vote early and vote by mail. Some states did not allow mail ballots to be counted until election day, which meant that it would take days to count all the ballots. As predicted, Trump was ahead in some swing states when the polls first closed. However, also as predicted, his lead dissipated as the mail ballots were counted. Trump claimed the election was stolen because he claimed this "overnight" shift was not possible, and that he had really won by millions of ballots. Over time, the pro-Trump claims expanded as voting irregularities were now alleged in all close states that Biden won (Pennsylvania, Michigan, Wisconsin, Arizona, Georgia, and Nevada). These allegations included counting ballots of dead people, rigged voting machines, fraud by those counting votes by hand, ballot stuffing, counting ballots that came in late, non-citizens voting, and missing ballots. It was also claimed that mail-in ballots were illegal in general, and all should be discarded. Of the sixty lawsuits filed by the Trump campaign, fifty-nine were lost and many of which were decided by Trump-appointed judges.[17] These losses were sustained in the appellate courts and the Supreme Court. Nonetheless, the constant barrage of claims that the election was stolen resonated among many of Trump's supporters. He spent the seventy-seven days (and more) between the election and the inauguration trying to subvert the results. His false assertion that the election was "stolen" was echoed by several Republican leaders in Congress. The riot that occurred on January 6, 2021 would not have been possible without these false claims.

On December 11, 2020, Biden's win was certified in all fifty states and the ceremonial counting of the ballots in Congress was scheduled for January 6. The vice-president's role in this process is merely to report the results. However, Trump and many of his supporters falsely claimed Vice President Pence could officially reject the results.

A variety of organizations called for a "March to Save America" rally on January 6. Trump asked his supporters to attend the rally in Washington, saying it would be "wild." At noon on the day of the rally, he gave an hour-long address, telling his supporters "to walk down to the Capitol," that he would go with them, that he would never concede the election, to "fight like hell," to demand that Congress "do the right thing" and only count the lawful electors (i.e., Trump supporters), and that he hoped Mike Pence would also "do the right thing."

Thousands attended the rally at the Capitol. Many waved flags (American, Trump 2020, Confederate, Stop the Steal) and one group erected gallows on the Capitol grounds. Around 1 p.m., hundreds of rioters, led by Proud Boys, Oath Keepers, and QAnon supporters, stormed the Capitol.[18] Some rioters were prepared for physical confrontation: wearing military helmets and having brought with them handcuffs, poles that could be used as weapons, stun guns, metal pipes, bear spray, and so on. The rioters charged the police lines. One police officer was killed during the riot, two later committed suicide, and 140 were otherwise injured. In addition, one of the rioters was shot to death, one was trampled to death, and two died from a heart attack or stroke.

Approximately 800 rioters entered the Capitol and began searching for members of Congress and for the Vice President. Some chanted "hang Mike Pence" and came within 100 feet of him. Members of Congress had to evacuate the chambers that were soon occupied by rioters. The videos of the insurrection show that it was due to luck as well as to the bravery of many police officers that members of Congress and Pence were not captured or seriously hurt.[19]

An ongoing question about the riot is why the Capitol police were unprepared and why reinforcements and the National Guard were not called in earlier. Nevertheless, at around 5 p.m.—about four hours after police lines were first breached—the Pentagon finally gave the approval to mobilize the D.C. National Guard (over three hours after requested). Additional reinforcements came from law enforcement and National Guard elements from Maryland and Virginia as well as hundreds more D.C. police officers. It took three hours to clear the Capitol.

The rioters had interrupted the electoral vote count. The count is ceremonial in nature and typically takes under an hour. However, many Republicans in Congress challenged the vote, going along with Trump's false assertion that the election was stolen. After the rioters were cleared, the debate and vote continued until late in the morning of January 7. Eventually, eight senators (led by Ted Cruz and Josh Hawley) and 139 House members (all Republican) voted to reject the electors from at least one state.

In the aftermath of the insurrection, over five hundred rioters were arrested. In addition, many called for the immediate impeachment of Trump. It was claimed that he fomented the riot by asking his supporters to come to D.C. and further incited them in his speech on the morning of January 6. In addition, and perhaps most damning, it became evident that he had made no attempt to stop the riot after it began. During the attack on the Capitol, Mitch McConnell, Lindsay Graham, Kevin McCarthy, and other Republicans had tried to reach Trump, his children, or his chief of staff to ask that he call out the National Guard and tell his supporters to leave the Capitol. It was not until after 4 p.m. that Trump made his first public statement. Even then, the statement was mostly a claim about the election being stolen; he mentioned almost in passing that it was time to "go home." Later Trump tweeted that he loved the rioters and that they should "remember this day forever!"

Speaker of the House Nancy Pelosi asked Mike Pence to have the Cabinet invoke the 25th Amendment, which would have removed Trump from office. When it became apparent that this was not going to happen, the House voted for the second impeachment of Trump on January 13, one week after the insurrection. All 222 Democrats voted for impeachment as well as 10 Republicans. The Senate trial was relatively short but the videos that were shown were riveting. Nonetheless, Trump was acquitted on February 13 when the Senate fell ten votes short of the necessary two-thirds majority required for conviction. Seven Republican senators voted for Trump's impeachment.

Joe Biden and Kamala Harris were sworn in on January 20. By that time, almost 20,000 National Guard troops were stationed in Washington, D.C., a seven-foot fence topped with barbwire surrounded the entire Capitol grounds, and other fences surrounded the mall and most federal buildings. In a break from long-standing tradition, no spectators were allowed to watch the inauguration from the National Mall. Thus, began the 46th United States presidency.[20]

- *In assessing the level of support for QAnon, the glass can be considered either half-empty or half-filled. In one view, a less than significant minority—only 17% of survey respondents—believed that "a group of Satan-worshipping elites who run a child sex ring are trying to control our politics and media" (12/20 [NPR/Ipsos]). In an opposing view, the responses of almost 1/5 of those surveyed shows that a significant number of people believe this conspiracy-laden statement, which is compounded by the 37% who said they did not know (i.e., thought it was possible). An even higher percentage (29%) believed that there was a "deep state" that tried to undermine Trump (34%, 37%), and 30% believed that "Donald Trump has been secretly fighting a group of child sex traffickers that include prominent Democrats and Hollywood elites" (36%, 36% [1/21 Ipsos]). When NBC [1/21] asked respondents what they thought of Q, 2% had a positive opinion, 11% were neutral, 42% had a negative opinion, and 45% did not know. Pew [8/20] respondents displayed a more favorable opinion of QAnon: 20% said its followers were a good thing for this country.*[21]
- *Less than one-third (29%, 52%, 20%) believed that there was a widespread fraud in the 2020 election [1/21-Ipsos]; or that voter fraud helped Biden win (33%, 53%, 14%) (12/20 [NPR/Ipsos]), and 61% (35%, 4%) believed that Biden won legitimately ([1/21-NBC]).*[22]
- *Depending upon how the question was phrased, there was some support for the actions of the rioters. A USA Today survey [1/21] asked respondents to assess those who stormed the Capitol: 70% thought they were criminals, 24% thought they had a point but went too far, and 2% said they acted appropriately. NBC [1/21] found that 57% (40%, 3%) saw it as an act of terrorism. In another survey, a*

large minority of 30% (36%, 33%) falsely believed that Antifa was responsible for the violence that occurred on January 6 [1/21-Ipsos]. And in the same survey, 48% (36%, 16%) said that Trump "encouraged his supporters to break into the United States Capitol." A Marist survey [1/21] found that 58% believed that Trump was to blame for what happened. In another survey, 25% thought that Trump did all that he could to stop the insurrection (68%, 7% [1/21 Quinnipiac]).

- An ABC survey found that one week after the House vote to impeach Trump, 52% (45%, 3% [1/21]) favored the vote; one week before the Senate vote, 56% favored conviction; and the day after the vote, 58% said the Senate should have convicted.[23]

CONCLUDING COMMENTS

The year 2020 was a horrible year. Many felt they were gut-punched by the cascading crises: the epidemic, killings by police officers, and a violent riot (attempted coup, insurrection?) at the Capitol. The glass could be half-full given that most reacted to Covid-19 appropriately (wearing masks, wanting to get vaccinated, supporting economic measures to avoid depression), were appalled by the murder of George Floyd, supported the integrity of the election, and showed disdain for those who rioted at the Capitol. On the other hand, the glass is half-empty when a large minority believe in conspiracy theories about the epidemic and refuse to be vaccinated, are unlikely to support accountability for most acts of police violence, and believe in outlandish claims that the 2020 election was stolen. Polarization between blacks and whites and between Democrats and Republicans grew.

[The reader can find relevant crosstabs and discussion in the online appendix located at https://rowman.com/ISBN/9781793653505/US-Public-Opinion-since-the-1930s-Galluping-through-History.]

NOTES

1. Wildfires in 2020 set records in California and elsewhere. There were over 9,000 fires in California and 4% of the state had burned. The 2020 Atlantic hurricane season was the most active on record with thirty named storms. Seven hurricane names were retired, also a record.

2. There was a fascinating discussion at Wikipedia among its editors on whether the events of January 6 should be called an attempted coup, an insurrection, or a riot (Kelly, 2021).

3. At the time of this writing (6/2021), deaths in the United States topped 600,000.

4. The *New York Times* had a fascinating one-year retrospective on what happened when sports shut down. https://www.nytimes.com/interactive/2021/03/06/sports/coronavirus-canceled-sports.html.

5. A second relief bill was signed into law on December 27, 2020, and a third bill was signed by Biden on March 11, 2021.

6. On the poverty estimates, see Parolin, Matsudaira, Waldfogel, and Wilmer (2019); on the total cost of the economy, see Rockeman (2020); for a fascinating discussion of the difficulty of measuring unemployment during Covid-19, see Long (2021).

7. At the time this manuscript was being finalized, the Delta variant was becoming the predominant Covid-19 strand in the United States. It was far more transmittable and deadly than previous variants. Scientists were predicting even worse variants would soon emerge.

8. I rely upon the Axios/Ipsos data because they conducted surveys every two weeks and they made their raw data available at Roper. The panelists for their web-based surveys were recruited by using a probability sample.

9. Jo Craven McGinty (2021) had a fascinating article in the *Wall Street Journal* on how question wording had a large effect on measuring whether people wanted to get vaccinated—ranging from 20% to 63%.

10. Lett, Asabor, Corbin, and Boatright (2020), utilizing a *Washington Post* longitudinal study, found that fatal police shootings of people of color was constant from 2015 to 2020.

11. At the time of this writing, the Pew raw data that was released for the 6/20 and 9/20 surveys do not include the data on attitudes toward Black Lives Matter. The same omission occurs for a 7/20 ABC survey. Pew's press release on the 6/20 survey notes that 86% of blacks and 60% of whites said they supported BLM.

12. The level of support in 2016 should be viewed with some caution. Unlike in other years, in 2016 Pew first asked if respondents had heard of BLM. Only the 73% who had heard of BLM were asked the subsequent question. Another issue was that the 2016 and 2017 surveys were from telephone surveys while the 2020 surveys were web surveys. For more on the fluctuations in polling data on Black Lives Matter, see Barron-Lopez (2020) and Samuels and Mejia (2021).

13. "In general, do you think that Black people have as good a chance as White people in your community to get any kind of job for which they are qualified, or don't you think they have as good a chance?"

14. Unfortunately, at the time of this writing the raw data for the June 2020 CNN survey are not available.

15. "Defund the police" became a rallying cry for many of the demonstrators. Most argued this meant redirecting monies from the police to other agencies that could reduce the need for a police presence. Nonetheless, Republicans used this slogan during the 2020 election campaign to argue that Democrats were anti-police. Some moderate and conservative Democrats argued that this led to Democrats losing some seats that should have been won.

16. https://www.theguardian.com/us-news/2020/nov/08/mary-trump-on-the-end-of-uncle-donald-all-he-has-now-is-breaking-things

17. Rutenberg, Corasaniti, and Feuer (2020). The one victory concerned a deadline in Pennsylvania and affected a small number of votes.

18. More than a dozen groups were involved in the riot (Farivar, 2021). Many of these were neo-Nazi or neo-Confederate. The sight of a large Confederate battle flag being carried through the Capitol was one of the more disturbing sights.

19. The *New York Times* put together a 40-minute video compilation of the riot/insurrection. It is very disturbing and well done (Khavin, 2021).

20. Although this book was supposed to stop with the inauguration of Biden and Harris, I would be negligent in not mentioning the growth in misinformation about the election and the January 6 riot. Some of the more bizarre conspiracy theories put forth about the election not discussed in the main text was that ballots in Arizona were flown in from China and Italian military contractors used military satellites to switch votes from Trump to Biden. In a similar vein, it has been purported that the January 6 riot was organized by Antifa and/or the FBI; the rioters were simply tourists, and none of them carried weapons. Unfortunately, many have now accepted the myth that the election was stolen. A May 2021 Ipsos/Reuters survey

found 56% of Republicans believe the election was rigged or stolen and 53% thought Trump was the "true president."

21. On why it so hard to gauge support for QAnon, see Rogers (2021).

22. A December 2020 Quinnipiac survey found that 60% believed that Biden's win was legitimate. However, only 23% of Republicans held this view!

23. At the time of this writing, only the ABC data are available in raw form. However, a Gallup survey conducted immediately after the House vote showed an identical percentage in favor of the vote to impeach—52%.

Conclusion

In the previous chapters, I was looking at public opinion on specific historical issues. In this short final chapter, I look at some of the trends that span the decades as well as some of the problems with the availability of the data.

It is remarkable how public opinion has changed in the eighty years since Gallup and others began collecting data. This is especially evident in the areas of civil liberties, race, and gender/sexuality, while questions in other areas, such as foreign affairs, economic policy, crime, and science, have fluctuated or remained fairly constant. Unfortunately, many questions were not asked consistently over time and cannot be analyzed.

WORLD EVENTS

Several questions relevant to foreign policy have been asked with some consistency, in particular regarding defense spending and whether the United States should be involved in world affairs. Over the decades there have been sharp fluctuations on support for increased defense spending: 1966 (72%), 1969 (8%), 1980 (62%), 1990 (11%), 2004 (34%), and 2016 (38%). Attitudes on specific foreign policy issues are typically subject to rapid change given the success or failure of the policy, and in the above example of defense spending, the years of weak support reflect reactions to US involvement in Vietnam and in Iraq while the years showing strong support likely relate to the rise in nationalism as reflected in the election of Ronald Reagan.

Gallup began asking in 1944 whether it would be best for the future of this country if we took an active part in world affairs. This question was also asked by NORC and Knowledge Networks (GfK) beginning in 1973. Except for three years, all surveys showed between 60% and 70% of respondents agreeing it would be best if the United States were actively involved in foreign affairs. The number was 73% in 1944, a year when there was a pressing need for US involvement abroad, and 79% in 1965, at the height of the belief that this was the American century (just before the Vietnam War turned ugly). In only one year was the figure below 60%; in 2014 it was 58%, which was when the United States was in some danger of losing Iraq and Syria to ISIS. According to public opinion polls, there has been, since the 1940s, a clear consensus that the United States should be actively involved in world affairs.

Public opinion has often constrained the actions of policy-makers vis-à-vis foreign policy. At the outset of World War II, the American public was split on supporting France and Britain. Before the fall of France, only 32% favored changing the law so that these countries could borrow money from the US government. Even after the fall of France, only 44% favored lending money to England. This truly limited what FDR could do to support England and France. It took considerable effort by FDR to start turning around public opinion such that Lend Lease (the program that provided military aid to countries whose defense was critical to US interests) could become law in March 1941. By October of that year, only 27% of Americans said the most important thing for the United States to do was stay out of the war compared to 66% who said it was important to help England. Furthermore, 58% now favored using American ships to send war materials to England.[1]

In two other instances, after each of the World Wars, public opinion directly affected US foreign policy. In 1936, only 26% of Americans wanted the United States to join the League of Nations. In contrast, in 1945, 66% wanted the US Senate to vote to join the United Nations. This difference helps explain why one treaty was not ratified and the other was successful.

It is also clear, as discussed in greater detail in this book, that the growing public opposition to the wars in Vietnam and Iraq helped lead to US withdrawals from these conflicts. Similarly, opposition to potential US involvement in El Salvador and Nicaragua limited intervention by the Reagan administration.

US POLITICS

I will concentrate on six areas of public attitudes relevant to US politics.

Civil Liberties

Displayed in table 11.1 is a set of survey questions and responses on civil rights that was replicated with some frequency and over a significant span of time. The questions focus on the rights of certain groups to give speeches in public or teach in colleges and universities, to wit: atheists[2] (people who are "against all churches and religion"); communists and socialists (people who "favor government ownership of all railroads and all big industries"); homosexuals; and racists (people who "believe that blacks are genetically inferior"). These surveys show, over the course of six decades, a tremendous increase in tolerance for virtually all groups. From 1954 to 2016, support for

Table 11.1 Support for Civil Liberties

	1954 (%)	1972 (%)	1976 (%)	2016 (%)
Allow atheist give a speech	37	65	64	79
Allow atheist teach in a college	12	40	41	65
Allow communist give a speech	27	52	55	69
Not fire communist teaching at a college		32	41	64
Allow socialist give a speech	59	77		
Allow socialist teach at a college	33	56		
Allow admitted homosexual give a speech			55	88
Allow admitted homosexual teach in a college			52	87
Allow racist give a speech			61	60
Allow racist teach in a college			41%	48%

Source: These data are derived from NORC and/or Gallup.

atheists to be allowed to give a speech increased from 37% to 79%, and to be allowed to teach in college, from 12% to 65%. Over the same period, support for the right of communists to give a speech increased from 27% to 69%.[3]

On other relevant questions about communists, the results of a 1947 survey showed that 61% of Americans wanted to forbid membership in the Communist Party; and in 1948, 76% of those polled favored a law requiring all communists to register with the Justice Department. These responses underscore a political climate of the late 1940s that seemed comfortable with curtailing civil rights when it came to political affiliations. The last question I could find on this issue was in a 1965 survey that asked about the Supreme Court ruling that found it unconstitutional to require communists to register with the government (*Albertson v. Subversive Activities Control Board*). Only 29% (59%, 15%) approved this decision.[4]

Trust in Government

The public's trust in the government—the belief that Washington would do what is right all or most of the time—has been on a long-term decline since the ANES (American National Election Studies) first asked this question (1958: 76%; 1970: 55%; 1980: 26%; 1990: 28%; 2012: 23%, 2016: 12%). This troubling trend underscores the extent to which the public now distrusts the government and has very disconcerting implications for the future.

The Press

Long-term distrust of the media has also been growing. In 1973, 15% said they had hardly any confidence in the press. In subsequent years this has increased: (1980: 18%; 1990: 25%; 2000: 42%; 2010: 44%; and 2016: 50%).[5] With an incumbent (now ex) president stating that the media are "the enemy of the people," are "dangerous and sick," are purveyors of "fake news," and forcing members of the press to sit in holding pens at his rallies and then encouraging his supporters to verbally abuse them—this distrust in the media is a trend that is somewhat frightening.

Polarization

The gap between how Democrats and Republicans view the president has also widened (see table 11.2).[6] The average gap in approval ratings between Democrats and Republicans was fifty-eight points during FDR's presidency, which reflects the fact that Roosevelt presented a very different perspective on the role of government compared to the Republicans. In the time between the Truman and Carter administrations, however, there was a consensus that FDR's vision would not be radically challenged and hence the approval gap essentially stayed under forty points. Then, in the 1980s, with Reagan radically attacking the role of government, the average gap widened to fifty-two points. Starting with Clinton the average gap grew with each presidency. In the last year of his presidency, the average gap under Trump exceeded eighty points.[7] As discussed in the 2010s chapter, Trump's approval rating has also been historically low compared to other presidents.

Religion

Another long-term trend has been the gradual decline of religion. In 1937, 75% of Americans were members of a church. The percent who were members of a church, synagogue, or mosque in 2014 was 49%. Similarly, the percent who believed that

Table 11.2 Democrat/Republican Gap—Presidential Approval

President	Democrat	Republican	Gap
FDR	84	26	58
Truman	54	22	32
Eisenhower	49	88	39
Kennedy	84	49	35
Nixon	34	75	41
Ford	37	68	31
Carter	57	30	27
Reagan	31	83	52
Bush 1	44	82	38
Clinton	82	27	55
Bush 2	23	84	61
Obama	83	13	70
Trump	7	90	83

Source: Gallup Survey Data (Seltzer and Smith, 2015; Gallup.org; Pew-2017).

Note: FDR/Truman data—whites only. For FDR and Truman, how the respondent voted is sometimes substituted for political party.

the Bible was the "literal word of God" declined from 65% in 1963 to 38% in 1976, and fell further to 24% in 2017. Using another way to measure this drop in religiosity: 47% attended church weekly in 1954 compared to 29% in 2019.

Crime and Guns

Using capital punishment as a gauge of attitudes toward crime and punishment, attitudes toward the death penalty were consistent except for one decade. Gallup first posed questions on capital punishment in 1937. In that year, support for the death penalty for murder was 59%.[8] It was at 47% in 1965, but then surged to 80% in 1995. In 2019 it had receded to 56%. Given the strong fluctuations in attitudes toward capital punishment, it is surprising the level of stability about whether respondents were afraid to walk in their neighborhood at night according to the NORC-GSS (1973: 41%, 1984: 42%, 1994: 47%, 2004: 32%, 2018: 33%).

Americans have generally been supportive of gun control. When the question was first asked by NORC-GSS in 1972, 72% favored requiring Americans to obtain a police permit before purchasing a gun.[9] This reached a high of 84% in 1998 and has slowly declined back to 72% as of 2016. Gallup's first question on this issue asked if the laws concerning the sale of firearms should be made stricter was asked in 1989: 70% wanted stricter gun laws and a similar percentage in 2018 (67%).

RACE

Responses to early survey questions on race reflect a level of racism that would be unfathomable today. During World War II, only 40% of Americans thought that Negro and white soldiers should serve together, and in 1946, less than half of Americans—49%—thought that Negroes should have as good a chance as white people to get a job.[10] In a similar vein, a 1948 survey showed that only 32% of respondents believed the federal government should "require employers to hire people without regard to their race, religion, color, or nationality," and 42% thought that Negroes should sit in the back of buses or trains when traveling between states. In the ensuing years, attitudes and policy have changed such that these questions have not been asked for decades.

One question on race that has been asked in many surveys over the years is whether the respondent would vote for a black person as president. Only 37% said they would in 1958, but this had increased to 92% by 2007. The election of Barack Obama as president would have been unthinkable in earlier years.

One other long-term question concerned interracial marriage. In 1963, 37% said there should be laws against such marriages (Niemi, Mueller, and Smith, 1989), but this had declined to 10% in 2002 (NORC-GSS). Similarly, in 1958, only 4% approved of "marriages between white and colored people," but this had increased to 48% by 1991 and 94% by 2021.

One last long-term question to examine is whether white respondents said it would make a difference to them if a black with the same income and education moved onto their block. Sixty-two percent said it would in 1946; 36% in 1963; and 14% in 1972 (Niemi, Mueller, and Smith, 1989).

Since the brutal and sadistic seen-on-video killing of George Floyd in Minneapolis in May 2020, attitudes changed drastically in a very short period of time. Support for Black Lives Matter increased from 38% in 2017 to 52% a few weeks after protests began.[11] Similarly, support for the police dropped eleven points in a week to 61% (Morin, 2020). However, as discussed in the 2020 chapter (chapter 10), attitudes toward BLM soon reverted to pre-Floyd levels.

This is not to say that racial problems have disappeared (on race and incarceration, see Alexander, 2020).[12] In September 2016, according to a NORC/CNN survey, 77% of whites and 88% of blacks said racial discrimination against blacks was serious. Immediately after Floyd's killing, the corresponding percentages according to a Quinnipiac survey were 62% and 95% [06/20]. The gap had grown.

Sometimes public opinion does not hold sway in the policy arena. Perhaps the best example of a president who defied public opinion was Harry Truman's signing of Executive Order 9981 (abolishing racial discrimination in the armed forces). Two months before his signing, only 26% of Americans wanted Negro and white troops living and working together. His signing EO 9981 in July 1948, four months before the election, took true courage. It also had a major impact on reducing racial inequality in the United States.

SEX AND GENDER

Some early survey responses present stark reminders of past views on women. For example, in 1945, only 34% of Americans approved of women wearing slacks in public, and in 1953, 53% objected to women drinking alcohol in bars and restaurants. I could not find comparable questions to these in recent years, but again, social norms have changed, making the questions themselves irrelevant.

Very similar to the upward trend in racial tolerance, the surveys indicate an enormous change in the public's attitude toward women in the political arena. Only 33% of respondents said in a 1937 survey that they "would vote for a woman for president if she was qualified"; this had increased to 95% by 2015. Another big change is seen regarding women working. Seventy-two percent of respondents said in 1939 they would favor a bill "prohibiting married women from working in business or industry if their husbands earn more than $1,600 a year" ($28,000 in today's dollars). Contrast that with a 2018 poll in which 78% said it was a positive development that more women are working and having a career while they are raising children.

Not surprisingly, the surveys also trace a clear inclination over the decades toward more liberal opinions on marriage and sexuality. In 1969, 68% said sex before marriage was wrong; only 26% took this position in 2016. In 1948, only 9% thought the divorce laws were too strict, in an era when in most states one had to prove cruelty, abandonment, adultery, or mental illness; however, by 2017, 73% said divorce was morally acceptable.

Notably, the first national survey question on homosexuality was not asked until 1965, when 70% said homosexuals were, in the words of the survey question, "mostly harmful to society." By 1977, a slightly more tolerant view emerged in the survey results, with 43% saying they believed that homosexual relations between two adults should be legal, and this increased to 69% by 2015. Moreover, during the past two decades, support for gay marriage has more than doubled, increasing from 27% in 1996 to 67% in 2020.

Attitudes toward abortion have varied. In 1962, 55% said a woman should be able to have an abortion if the baby might be born deformed (Niemi, Mueller, and Smith, 1989). When NORC-GSS began asking a similar question in 1972, 75% said abortion should be allowed if there was a strong chance of a serious birth defect. This increased to 86% in 1977, and then slowly declined back to 75% in 2016. In a related question, in 1972, 44% said a woman should be able to have an abortion if she was married and did not want any more children. This percentage was identical in 2016. Regarding *Roe v. Wade*, 33% wanted to overturn this decision in 1989, but that number fell to 28% in 2018.

THE ECONOMY

Since Gallup began polling, Americans have been distrustful of public assistance. In 1939, 90% believed in government pensions, but 72% wanted to limit it to those who "are in need." In the depth of the Great Depression, 53% wanted to reduce relief expenditures. In 1994, 68% said that most people on welfare do not genuinely need help but are trying to take advantage of the system. Furthermore, in 1996, 71% wanted to eliminate welfare payments to people after two years.

A very different position is held on income inequality. Only 31% of Americans in 2015 thought that the distribution of income in the United States was fair; this finding is identical to that when Gallup first asked this question in 1984. How this affects policy is that in 2016, 58% favored increasing the minimum wage from $7.25 to $15 an hour. Compare this to 1946, when 65% wanted to increase the minimum wage from 40 cents to 60 cents an hour.

On the other hand, support for fiscal policy has been uneven. In 1936, only 34% thought the government "should start spending again to help get business out of its present slump." Support for increased government spending was much higher during the Great Recession, with 83% of respondents in 2009 supporting government programs to create jobs. At that same time, though, only 41% wanted to help the auto companies avoid bankruptcy.

Public opinion has often affected economic policy. FDR could not implement all his desired reforms given the constraints of public opinion. In 1936, 70% wanted to reduce the national debt and only 41% were in support of policies that would fix the price of farm products. More recently, President Obama had difficulty passing parts of his economic program even in the worst months of the Great Recession, for example, when only 41% of the public wanted to help the auto companies who were facing bankruptcy and only 28% thought his economic programs would work.

SCIENCE, TECHNOLOGY, AND THE ENVIRONMENT

Changes in technology have been rapid; here are some highlights:

- Radio: In 1937, 83% of Americans had a radio in their home and 70% said they depended on the radio for their daily news.
- Television: In December 1945, only 9% of Americans had ever seen a TV. As the decade ended, 6% of the population owned television and 54% thought TV would take the place of radio in the home within the next seven years. By 1965, an impressive 97% of Americans had at least one TV in their house.
- Computers: In 1982, 2% of Americans had a computer at home. In 2013, 62% owned a smart phone and 73% had Wi-Fi in their home. Contrast this with 1943 when only half of the population had access to a telephone.

Trust in scientists has been stable. In 1973, 41% said they had a great deal of confidence in the scientific community (NORC-GSS). This barely fluctuated over the years and was 44% in 2018. In that same survey, the scientific community was the second highest rated institution, the highest rated was the military (61%), and the lowest was Congress (6%).

When Gallup asked its first question about global warming in 1990, 57% said they worried about it a great deal or a fair amount. This increased slightly to 63% by 2018. However, partisan differences affected this belief, with only 36% of Republicans being concerned about climate change compared to 90% of Democrats. In 1997, Gallup first asked whether the seriousness of global warming was exaggerated in the news: 31% said it was exaggerated, 34% said it was reported correctly, and 27% said it was underestimated. By 2020 the corresponding figures were: 37%, 25%, and 38%. Furthermore, Pew reported that in June 2020, 72% of Democrats agreed that human activity contributed "a great deal" to climate change compared to 22% of Republicans. Although there has been growing recognition of the seriousness of global warming, attitudes on a scientific topic have become politicized and have not grown as fast as reality warranted.[13]

There is a history of science being politicized, for example, Darwinian evolution. However, the polarization over global warming is greater and far more troublesome as it is beginning to show an erosion of support for basic scientific findings.[14]

POPULAR TRENDS

How Americans choose to spend their free time has certainly changed over the decades.

Good comparative data on book readership is hard to find. Weisman (2014) reports that in 1978 there were few Americans—8%—who had not read a single book, but in 2014 the number had increased to 23%.

In 1941, Roper asked respondents how many hours per day they listened to the radio: less than an hour per day (11%), 2–3 hours per day (40%), 4–5 hours per day (19%), and six or more hours per day (16%). Pew asked a similar question in 2006. Thirty percent did not listen to the radio at all, and 41% listened two or fewer hours per day.

Movie attendance has also been in decline (Cowden, 2015). In 1930, 65% of survey respondents went to the movies on a weekly basis. This slowly declined until 1964, at which point it leveled out at around 10%. In the 1940s, the number of movie tickets sold per capita per year was around thirty. In more current years it is around three.

In 1964, NORC asked how many hours a person watched TV in a typical day: less than an hour (16%), 1–2 hours (49%), 3–4 hours (26%), five or more hours (9%). In 2018, the corresponding figures were: less than an hour (9%), 1–2 hours (50%), 3–4 hours (26%), and five or more hours (15%). Collectively, we watch a lot of TV.

It is no great surprise that the use of social media has skyrocketed. Pew found 5% of American adults used at least one social media site in 2005. In 2018, it reached 69%. The most widely used site was Facebook (76%) and 74% of those users said they visited this site at least daily.

In 1937, Gallup asked respondents what their favorite sport was to watch. The top four were: baseball (34%), football (23%), basketball (8%), and horseracing (5%). When the question was asked in 2018 the top choices were: football (38%), baseball (12%), basketball (10%), and soccer (9%). The biggest changes affected baseball and soccer.

PROBLEMS IN ANALYSIS

In closing, it is important to remind the reader of problems in the data. Particularly in the early years of survey research, sampling was far from rigorous. As noted in the introduction, there were five Gallup surveys with samples of less than 1% of black respondents. Poorly written questions and questions that were asked inconsistently over time are also problematic. Many topics lacked coverage from any survey organization or were taken up at a relatively late date. For example, racial issues were mostly ignored in the 1930s, and the first survey question on abortion was posed in 1962. Only a limited number of questions were asked about artists, movies, or books at any time, and few questions were asked about the Third World unless the United States was at war at the time (e.g., Vietnam, Iraq). I could find only two questions about Africa in the 1960s and they were not relevant.

To name a few specific omissions: there were no questions about Khrushchev's visit to the United States in 1959; no survey organization in the 1960s asked any question about the Beatles, the Rolling Stones, Bob Dylan, or Woodstock. There was no question about Jackie Robinson in the 1940s or about pornography in the 1950s, or Muhammed Ali in the 1960s, and none about the shootings at Kent State and Jackson State in the 1970s. The first question referencing Mahatma Gandhi was in 1983, and that was about whether the movie *Gandhi* should win an Oscar for Best Picture. As for more recent history, no survey covered Volkswagen's cheating on emission tests in 2015 or Trump's decision to deport the Haitians who had arrived following the 2010 earthquake, and no questions were asked about the Rohingya crisis in 2017.

On the other hand, there were many questions that were not expected, and ended up being very illuminating: from the propriety of women wearing slacks to the use of tactical nuclear weapons in Iraq.

CONCLUDING COMMENTS

In the introduction, I mentioned one of the perennial debates among those who study public opinion—is the public rational? There is not just one public. Some members of the public are relatively rational, others not so much. This is a continuum and people can also move from one group to another.

A great concern is how the public now consumes news. Pew reported that in March 2000, 18% reported that they got most of their news on social media. Furthermore, a Pew survey from August 2020 found that 23% often got news from Facebook, Twitter, or Instagram and another 30% said sometimes. Only 32% said they often or sometimes got their news from print sources.

The local print media is dying and there is an increasing concentration of all media in the hands of a few (Noam, 2009). Darr (2021) reported that from 2000 to 2018 weekday newspaper circulation fell from 55.8 million to 28.6 million. An in-depth article in the *Wall Street Journal* by Hagey, Albert, and Serkez (2019) noted that nearly 1,800 newspapers closed between 2004 and 2018 leaving 200 counties with no newspapers. Newspapers that remain are increasingly owned by hedge funds that often slash jobs (O'Connell and Brown, 2019) or have a political agenda. Less local news result in a public that is uninformed and polarized. Furthermore, Lyons, Guess, Nyhan, and Reifler (2021) report that most Americans are over-confident in identifying fake news and over-confident in their ability to sniff out fake news.

Essentially, people are increasingly getting their news from social media, in which trolls and bots often spread misinformation (Stanley-Becker, 2020); conservatives increasingly rule online (Scott, 2020); and many only follow or watch those they agree with.

As discussed elsewhere, polarization is increasing. It has intensified even more with the presidencies of Obama and Trump—to the point that opponents actively despise each other. In a February 2021 CBS/YouGov survey, 57% of Republicans viewed Democrats as enemies and not just opponents. Correspondingly, 41% of Democrats viewed Republicans as enemies.[15]

Demsas (2020) correctly predicted before the January 6 riots that Trump's false tweets attacking the legitimacy of the election would not affect the outcome of the election, but it would negatively sway American's trust in democracy.[16] Increasingly, the GOP has come to subvert democracy.

In an opinion column in the *Washington Post*, Michael Gerson (2021), George W. Bush's chief speechwriter for over five years, noted that elected Republicans know the election was not stolen and knowingly lie when they say otherwise. With elected officials and some media commentators repeating the big lie, voters increasingly distrust elections and democracy. One result is more laws have been passed which suppress voting (Jim Crow democracy) and, even more dangerously, sets up the future possibility of the actual subversion of elections. Essentially, the power to count the vote is placed in the hands of partisan election officials (democracy with an asterisk). Beauchamp (2021) fears the move toward competitive authoritarianism as seen in Hungary and Turkey.

To stop this from occurring requires a knowledgeable electorate and a public that is willing to accept the results of an election, regardless of the perceived threat that would occur by the victory of one's opponents. Allowing one side to increasingly subvert the norms of democracy (mutual tolerance—realizing that one's opponents are legitimate and restraint on the exercise of power) must stop (Levitsky and Ziblatt, 2018).

The loss of democracy is not a foregone conclusion. The public does not always conform to the attitudes of elites in their political party (Bullock, 2016). Furthermore, most Americans are not accepting misinformation about either the pandemic or the 2020 election. As mentioned in the 2020 chapter, two-thirds thought the 2020 election was free of fraud and Biden won legitimately. However, the concern is warranted when according to a Quinnipiac survey, less than one-quarter of Republicans believe that Biden won legitimately. Public opinion matters.

NOTES

1. Support for the US involvement in world affairs was high after the success of World War II. In 1945, 74% said they "[w]ould be willing to continue to put up with present shortages of butter, sugar, meat, and other rationed food products in order to give food to people who need it in Europe." In fact, 85% favored keeping our troops in Germany and stationed in other defeated nations. Contrast that with a 2017 survey showing that only 30% opposed a decrease in foreign aid, and 2016 survey results reflecting that only 40% wanted to send ground troops to Syria to fight ISIS.

2. Atheists, socialists, and racists are defined within the surveys.

3. For more on how attitudes on free speech have changed over time, see Chong and Levy (2018).

4. I could not find recent questions on whether communists should be outlawed, etc. However, I could not imagine much support for these policies.

5. Hanitzsch, Dalen, and Steindl (2017), using the World Values survey, note that the decline in trust for the media is not a worldwide trend. It is most pronounced in the United States.

6. The term "polarization" has become a derogatory term. However, Klein (2020) notes that it can be helpful in sorting us. In the 1940s and 1950s, Democrats and Republicans were less divided in part because Southern Democrats (Dixiecrats) created divisions on race among Democrats that was greater than between Democrats and Republicans. The subjugation of blacks shows there are worse things than polarization.

7. Iyengar and Westwood (2015) show another pernicious effect of partisan polarization. In their experiment with 1,021 respondents in an SSI sample on awarding of scholarships—people are much more likely to take into account an applicant's political party over either their race or ability.

8. Thirty-nine percent of respondents in 1937 wanted to restore the whipping post.

9. A similarly worded question by Gallup in 1959 found 75% favoring this position.

10. In the only time this question had been asked in the NORC-GSS, 96% said as "good a chance" in 1972.

11. https://civiqs.com/results/black_lives_matter

12. As this book is about to go into production, a new way to deny the existence of racism surfaced with attacks on Critical Race Theory (CRT). CRT is an academic framework that argues that racism is inherent in the legal structure and other institutions. Some conservatives warped this arguing that CRT also says all whites are racists and this is taught in the public schools. This wedge has been used to attack Democrats and to pass laws that essentially outlaw teaching the history of racism in public schools (Meyer, Severns, and McGraw, 2021).

13. One of the best books on global warming and the battle to discredit the science is written by Michael Mann and Tom Toles (2016). Also see Mann (2021). For a good review on attitudes toward climate change, see Egan and Mullin (2017). Pew had an excellent discussion of their questions on the environment: for overall trendline changes as well as how different groups (age, political party, and so on) changed over time, see Funk and Kennedy (2020).

14. When I first wrote this chapter, there was a partisan battle over wearing of face masks during the Covid-19 epidemic. Pew reported in a June 2020 survey that 53% of Republicans and 76% of Democrats wore masks when they went to the store. As this book is about to go into production, the partisan battle has moved to vaccinations. Civiq [06/21] reported that 95% of Democrats have been vaccinated or want to be vaccinated compared to just 50% of Republicans.

15. Klein's book on polarization (2020) is excellent. Among his many observations, he notes that today it is politically incorrect to express negative opinion based on race and gender. However, it is perfectly acceptable to do so on political identity.

16. Berlinski et al. (2020), using experimental data in a YouGov survey following the 2018 elections, show that exposure to unsubstantiated claims of voter fraud reduces confidence in the integrity of elections.

Appendix 1

Preamble to Gallup History

Note to Reader: Logically, this chapter/appendix should be the first chapter in the book—events that occurred before the 1930s. However, there is little survey research discussed in this chapter. This chapter is meant for those whose knowledge of US history is rusty. However, I believe that even those with a substantial background in the twentieth century US history will find it of value.

Obviously, history did not begin in 1936, when the first Gallup survey was released. In order to understand the world in 1936, and therefore the context for the questions Gallup asked in his first surveys, it is important to look at some of the preceding significant social and political events and trends that occurred from around the turn of the century up until and the years directly preceding that year.[1] I use the same categories here as in the following "decade" chapters that are connected to contemporaneous Gallup (and other) survey results.

WORLD EVENTS

The Age of Imperialism

Many historians characterize the years from 1870 to 1914 as the era of "New Imperialism." This term distinguishes the period from early colonialism that resulted in European powers talking over most of North and South America, India, and the Dutch East Indies (modern-day Indonesia). The New Imperialism resulted in the partitioning of Africa, the French takeover of parts of Indochina (Vietnam and Cambodia), and the effective takeover of much of China. In 1870, only 10% of Africa was under the control of European powers. This had increased to 90% by 1914. The United States was also involved in this scramble. The United States' successful war against Spain in 1898 resulted in the United States acquiring Puerto Rico, Guam, and the Philippines.

This imperialist process is important to understand because it led to two major historical events. First, the struggle among European countries for control of the conquered areas was one of the major factors leading to World War I. Second, the conquered areas eventually revolted, which had a major impact on later wars in Vietnam, the Mideast, and elsewhere.

World War I

Prior to World War I, a series of international alliances had been established in which participating countries agreed to go to war if one of their allies was attacked (MacMillan, 2013). On June 28, 1941, Archduke Franz Ferdinand of Austria was assassinated by a Serbian nationalist. Consequently, Austria-Hungary declared war on Serbia, and Russia mobilized in support of Serbia, triggering a cascade of declarations of wars as alliances were invoked. Germany, the Austria-Hungary Empire, and the Ottoman Empire (the Central Powers) then lined up against Russia, the British Empire, and France (the allies). Germany's invasion of Belgium and France almost resulted in the capture of Paris. Strong defensive systems, spurred by the use of machine guns, barbed wire, and artillery, made offensive operations very costly in terms of casualties, and trench warfare resulted.

In April 1917, the United States abandoned its position of neutrality and entered the war on behalf of the allies. The US decision came after Germany had resumed unrestricted submarine warfare (i.e., attacks on nonmilitary ships), and was compounded by intelligence[2] revealing that the German Foreign Minister had promised Mexico the return of lands it lost during the Mexican-American War if Mexico declared war on the United States. The war ended in August 1918 with the collapse of the German military. This collapse occurred as Germany's 1918 offensive failed, American troop strength increased, the German economy was faltering, and German troops were revolting.

Over nine million combatants[3] and seven million civilians died in the war,[4] which also resulted in widespread famine and economic ruin. The political consequences were stark: the disintegration of the Austrian-Hungarian Empire, the failure of the Ottoman Empire and resulting takeover of Middle Eastern countries by France and Britain, the creation of Poland, and the success of the communist revolution led by Vladimir Lenin in October 1917 and the concomitant collapse of the Russian Empire.

The Treaty of Versailles of 1919 formally ended World War I. It took away German lands, restricted the size of the German military, and required Germany to compensate the allies with massive financial reparations. In 1920, the influential British economist John Maynard Keynes said the treaty was too harsh and would lead to economic disaster.[5]

By 1921, hyperinflation in Germany had risen to the point where 263 German Marks were needed to buy an American dollar, more than 20 times what was needed in 1919. But that was just the beginning. Over the following two years that rate increased to absurd levels: in August 1923 it was 4.6 million Marks to the Dollar, and in November of that year 4.2 trillion Marks to the Dollar. In addition to economic calamity, war reparations led to political instability. In 1923, Belgium and France occupied the Ruhr area of Germany to force reparation payments. German reaction to the occupation helped lead in later years to support for the ultra-nationalism of the Nazi Party.

The horrors of World War I led to another kind of backlash in the United States. The success in the United States of the German novel *All Quiet on the Western Front*, which depicted the dehumanization of war and the disillusionment experienced by returning soldiers, was indicative of how the war was being perceived. The American-made movie adaptation of the novel won the Academy Award for Best Picture in 1930. There was a growth in the pacifist movement, and war profiteers were widely condemned and often blamed for World War I (see, e.g., the Nye Committee Hearings of 1935). The United States retreated into isolationism, best exemplified by the refusal of the Senate in 1920 to ratify the treaty to join the League of Nations.[6]

The Rise of Fascism

Coincidentally, in the same year that the US Senate voted not to ratify the League of Nations, Adolf Hitler made his first political speech in Austria; in the next year (1921), he became Führer of the Nazi Party. His future ally, Benito Mussolini of the National Fascist Party of Italy, came to power in 1922 with his March on Rome.

Increasing Involvement of the United States in World Affairs

The United States always had competing tendencies between involvement in world affairs and maintaining an isolationist position; however, the early years of the twentieth century saw increased international involvement. In 1898, the United States had engaged in and won a major conflict on foreign soil—the Spanish-American war. In 1905, President Theodore Roosevelt negotiated the treaty between foreign powers—victorious Japan and Russia—ending their war. Then, with the developments of World War I, US leaders felt the United States had little choice but to become even more involved with world events.

The Soviet Union

As discussed above, the horrors of World War I led to the collapse of the Russian Empire and the coming to power of the Communist Party. A five-year civil war ensued with the "Whites" fighting the "Red" army. The whites were a loose coalition of landowners, monarchists, army generals, and non-Bolshevik socialists. They were helped by the intervention of eight foreign countries including the United States (approximately 8,000 troops), Britain, and France. Vladimir Lenin, the first leader of what was to become the USSR, headed up the revolutionary forces. In 1918,

Lenin was shot in an assassination attempt and badly injured. (The shooting led to a series of strokes and eventually to Lenin's death in 1924.) In 1922, Joseph Stalin was appointed general secretary of the Central Committee of the Soviet Communist Party, and later that year the Union of Soviet Socialist Republics (USSR) was formed.

An estimated 7–12 million casualties resulted from the Russian Civil War. Famine alone caused approximately six million deaths in 1921. This famine was the combined result of drought, the collapse of the railroad system due to damages wrought in the World War, and a decreased food supply arising from the civil war (both sides had requisitioned food, and peasants reduced the planting of crops believing they would just be taken away).

US POLITICS

The period after World War I was not a time of tolerance in the United States. There was a lot of political fear given the success of the Russian Revolution and the growth of a radical union movement in the United States. The Palmer Raids under Attorney General A. Mitchell Palmer targeted union organizers, anarchists, communists, and other radicals and resulted in approximately 10,000 people being arrested and 500 deported. These raids were in some ways similar to the anticommunist fervor of McCarthyism that occurred following World War II.

In 1919, the 18th Amendment to the US Constitution banning alcoholic beverages was ratified; it stayed in effect until 1933. One of the primary consequences of prohibition was the rise in organized crime, as the Mafia and others began making large sums of money by importing, distilling, and distributing alcoholic products. As gangs fought over the spoils of bootlegging, the murder rate rose throughout the United States and gangsters such as Al Capone became household names. The rise in crime and corruption, the loss of tax revenue from liquor sales, the obvious hypocrisy of seeing prominent people drinking, and pressure from agricultural interests were all factors that contributed to the eventual repeal of prohibition (Okrent, 2010).

In 1924, J. Edgar Hoover was appointed head of the Bureau of Investigation. Before his appointment, Hoover had made his mark by carrying out the antiradicals Palmer Raids. Partially because criminal gangs could get away from local police by going over state lines (as the famous bank robber John Dillinger did), many crimes—whether related to prohibition or not—became federal offenses, allowing the Bureau to follow criminals into different states. Thus, the name of the agency was changed in 1935 to the Federal Bureau of Investigation.[7]

In 1928, the Democrats nominated Al Smith of New York for the presidential nomination. In a time of strong anti-Catholic prejudice, he was the first Catholic nominated by a major political party. He was defeated in his bid by the Republican nominee Herbert Hoover (58.2% v. 40.8%).

RACE

Following the civil war, there was severe resistance, often violent, to equal rights for blacks in the South. This was somewhat ameliorated with the election of Ulysses S. Grant in 1868 and the initiation of strong reconstruction policies. Among many other policies, this included using federal troops to combat the Ku Klux Klan and ensuring voting rights for blacks. The true end of reconstruction was in 1877 with the election of Rutherford Hayes, who became the president after a compromise in which he promised withdrawing federal troops from the South. An era of terror began. Thousands of blacks (and many of their white Republican allies) were killed. The result was that the vast majority of blacks could no longer vote, hold political office (it is estimated that during reconstruction, 15% of officeholders in the South were black), attend public schools, and so on.

Beginning in 1890, the eleven former Confederate states began to pass laws (known as Jim Crow laws) disenfranchising the rights of blacks to vote, use public facilities (restrooms, restaurants, etc.) or have access to quality education.[8] The popular official position among whites in the US south was that the races would be "separate" but would be treated "equally." This policy was clearly a façade. The use of poll taxes, literacy tests, and intimidation resulted in the virtual elimination of blacks in the South from voting, holding public office, and serving on juries. Schools and other public facilities designated for use by blacks were far inferior to those used by whites. The ability of whites to control the social, political, and economic system in turn allowed white landowners and factory owners to control black sharecroppers and other workers.

This segregation was enforced by systematic violence. A resurgence of the Ku Klux Klan (its "second era") began in 1915, but even before then white terrorists and the power of the state enforced the disenfranchisement of blacks. Lynching was the most extreme element of the terror. The Equal Justice Initiative, in 2015, found that 3,959 racial terror lynchings were carried out in 12 southern states between 1877 and 1950. This number did not include the tens of thousands of other race-motivated crimes against black people—murders, beatings, and rapes—that were also perpetrated during this time. Race riots were a factor in these numbers. For example, in July 1917, a race riot in East St. Louis, Illinois, resulted in 250 deaths.

The Ku Klux Klan reached its height of popularity in 1925 when it had an estimated 5 million members and held a march of 40,000 supporters down Pennsylvania Avenue in Washington, D.C. At the time, it was the largest fraternal organization in the country. Future President Harry Truman and future Associate Justice of the United States Supreme Court Hugo Black were members for a time.

Resistance to segregation and racial violence was present throughout this period; however, opposition became more institutionalized in 1909 with the formation of the NAACP and in 1914 when Marcus Garvey founded the Universal Negro Improvement Association, advocating the return of blacks to Africa.

Appendix 1

SEX AND GENDER

Prior to the 1920s, most women were denied the right to vote, birth control was illegal in most jurisdictions due to the Comstock laws (1873), and employment and education opportunities were denied to most women.

In October 1916, Margaret Sanger (Chesler, 2007) opened the first US birth control clinic (which eventually gave rise to Planned Parenthood). Sanger was arrested and her clinic was shut down, but attitudes began changing in part because venereal diseases contracted by US servicemen during World War I were described as a public health issue (not just a moral issue) by the US government. Seven-million-person days were lost by the US army because of venereal diseases. Sanger was able to reopen her clinic in 1923.

The 1920s also saw a broad loosening of sexual and other social mores, giving women some increased freedoms. Flappers received a lot of publicity during the Roaring Twenties. These were women who smoked, drank, had casual sex, listened to jazz, and flaunted traditional mores.[9]

In the nineteenth century women had been for the most part excluded from participation in political activities. Women were often condemned for publicly speaking out against slavery; in fact, the American Anti-Slavery Society split in 1839 when women were allowed to serve on committees. Following the civil war, women such as Susan Anthony and Elizabeth Cady Stanton helped organize the suffrage movement. In the early twentieth century, support for women's suffrage increased based on several factors, including the role of women in World War I, women getting the vote in other countries, and active protest by women's groups in the United States. The 19th Amendment to the US Constitution, which gave women the right to vote, was ratified in 1920.[10] It was also in that year that the League of Women Voters was founded.

Technological changes discussed later in this chapter were beginning to have a profound effect on women's lives. Gordon (2016)[11] reminds us that before these changes, housewives (or servants) made over ten trips a day hauling water, wood, and coal. The development of modern water and sewage systems resulted in a huge reduction in the number of hours women spent hauling water into the house and carrying liquid refuse out. Washing machines were also a major time saver, because they obviated the need for water to be hauled and heated, and for clothes to be scrubbed by hand on a washboard.

Women were increasingly able to enter the labor force: they made up 12% of the workforce in 1870, and 26% around 1900.[12] In a development ironically contrary to the goals of gender equality, women were encouraged to join the workforce by employers who believed they could pay them less and they were less likely to become unionized.

THE ECONOMY

The years following the civil war gave rise to large industrial corporations. In 1901 the first great Texas gusher of oil came in and US Steel was incorporated by J. P. Morgan. In 1908, The Hoover Company began manufacturing vacuum cleaners, and Henry

Ford produced his first Model T automobile in 1913. The Model T was important because it was initially priced at $825 and created a market aimed at the middle class. Eventually, over sixteen million Model T's were sold. Perhaps of equal importance, Ford was the first to introduce the moving assembly line in 1913.

Chain stores came to fruition in the 1920s and 1930s with A&P, Walgreens, and Woolworths all having created national retail empires. Department stores and mail order businesses like the Sears catalog led to important changes in everyday life, such as freeing consumers from the very labor-intensive process of producing one's own clothes. Similarly, the growth of supermarkets meant that consumers did not have to spend much of the day going from the butcher to the baker to the vegetable vendor, since most purchases could now be made at one location with one source of payment.

In 1910, 468,000 automobiles were registered; that number swelled to 23 million by 1929. The growth of car ownership led to the development of suburbs as people no longer had to live within a few miles of their workplace, and in rural areas people were becoming less socially isolated because cars, made it far easier to get to schools and to visit friends. Automobiles grew in tandem with paved roads and the entire highway system was developing apace.

Expansion of consumer credit, which had begun with the sale of sewing machines in the 1850s, spurred the sale of automobiles, refrigerators, washing machines, and other goods. By 1924, 75% of automobiles were bought on credit. Also, in the 1920s second and third mortgages were developed as financial products, leading to more homeownership and of course an attendant increase in consumer goods purchases.

The 1920s was also a time of large infrastructure projects. What was later named the Hoover Dam was approved by the US Congress in 1928. In 1927 the Holland Tunnel, under the Hudson River, opened between New Jersey and Manhattan. At 1.5 miles, it was the longest tunnel in the world at the time.

The birth of industrial corporations also gave rise to labor strife. Many of the strikes in the nineteenth century had centered around mining (e.g., the Leadville Silver Miners' Strike of 1896 and the Anthracite Coal Strike of 1902) and railroads (e.g., the Pullman Strike of 1894). At the beginning of the twentieth century strikes spread to textiles (the Lawrence Textile Strike of 1912), steel (1919), and trucking (the Teamsters strike of 1934).

Commercial aviation was taking off. In 1902, Orville Wright flew the first aircraft at Kitty Hawk, North Carolina, and only a quarter of a century later in 1927, Charles Lindbergh made the first solo nonstop airplane trip from New York City to Paris. That same year the first flight of Pan American Airways occurred between Key West Florida and Havana, Cuba.

During what is called the Progressive Era in the United States (spanning from the 1890s to the 1920s), the state took on a greater regulatory role in the economy. In 1906, *The Jungle* was published, Upton Sinclair's muckraking exposé of the meatpacking industry that led to the Federal Meat Inspection Act being passed. A raft of other safety laws was also passed during this period pertaining to railroads, mines, and factories. The Sherman Antitrust Act, enacted in 1890, prohibited actions that were deemed anticompetitive, with one of its major consequences being the 1911 breakup of Standard Oil into thirty-four companies. And, in 1913, the 16th Amendment to the US Constitution was ratified, allowing the federal government the authority to collect income taxes.

SCIENCE, TECHNOLOGY, AND THE ENVIRONMENT

The first two decades of the twentieth century saw the emergence of profound developments in physics. In 1900, Max Planck announced the discovery of black body radiation, initiating the birth of quantum physics. Then, in 1905, Albert Einstein had his "miracle year" when he published four seminal papers—one of which presented the Special Theory of Relativity (what happens as one approaches the speed of light), while another introduced his famous equation $E = mc^2$.[13] A third paper, which used Planck's quantum hypothesis to explain the photoelectric effect, won him the Nobel Prize in Physics in 1921. In 1911 Einstein published his first paper on the General Theory of Relativity (i.e., the theory that gravity warps space).[14]

In the few decades directly before the 1930s, a variety of technological changes set the stage for historical developments discussed in the following chapters of this book in conjunction with Gallup's surveys. As Gordon (2016) notes the great inventions of the last half of the nineteenth century were the steamship, the railroad, and the telegraph. The early twentieth century began the era of electrification; by 1940, 94% of urban households had electricity. A somewhat unappreciated but highly significant development in terms of public health and the general quality of life was the growth of clean piped water and flush toilets. Again by 1940, 80% of the US population had interior flush toilets and 94% had sewage pipes.

These changes had a massive impact on the economy as well as on everyday life. They led to rapid growth in productivity and a sharp decline in the number of hours worked per person.

With refrigeration, people could move away from salted and smoked pork and have the ability to store meats as well as fruits and vegetables. Coupled with food and drug regulations that began in 1906, the food supply was made much safer. The development of processed foods had corn flakes and citrus fruits replace mush and pork for breakfast. The growth in frozen foods (pioneered by Clarence Birdseye) also led to greater diversity in foods. Central heating meant that coal and wood no longer needed to be hauled into the home. By 1940, almost half of US households had washing machines and refrigerators. In 1893, 17 years after Alexander Graham Bell filed a patent for his invention, there were 250,000 telephones in the country; by 1907 that number had grown to 6 million.[15]

Life expectancy began a rapid ascent after 1890. This trend was in part induced by the evolution of separate water and sewage systems, systematic chlorination and filtration of water, a greater understanding of germ theory and the dangers of insects, the invention of the window screen, and the ever-increasing use of automobiles (which resulted in the eventual elimination of horse dung from urban areas). As noted above, improvements in food safety followed the 1906 publication of Upton Sinclair's book—*The Jungle*—which detailed travesties of slaughterhouses in Chicago and launched a political movement to enact reforms.

A number of changes affected medical care. Medical doctors had become a regulated profession that required licensing,[16] and medical schools were being more closely monitored following the Flexner report of 1910.[17] Hospitals became more than dumping grounds for those likely to die, and at the same time antiseptics, the use of gloves, and x-rays were introduced. The antibiotic Penicillin was discovered by Alexander Fleming in 1928 and was to be widely available by World War II. Medical insurance became more widespread with the establishment of sickness funds by unions, fraternal organizations, and some employers.

Despite all these advances, science was not universally upheld. This was exemplified by the Scopes ("Monkey") Trial in 1925 in Dayton Tennessee where John Scopes was arrested and found guilty of teaching Charles Darwin's theory of evolution. He was fined $100.

In 1924, Edward Hubble announced that the Milky Way was just one of many galaxies.

POPULAR TRENDS

The first modern World Series occurred in 1903 when the Boston Red Sox defeated the Pittsburg Pirates. In 1920, Babe Ruth was traded by the Boston Red Sox to the New York Yankees for the largest sum ever paid for a player at that time—$125,000. Blacks were excluded from playing in the major leagues. In the same year, Ruth was traded to the Yankees, the Negro National League had its first game.

Boxing was probably the most popular sport during this time. In 1908, Jack Johnson, who was African American, became the world heavyweight boxing champion. Two years later, Johnson beat James Jeffries, The Great White Hope, setting off race riots. Johnson was an advocate for racial equality and very controversial. He married three white women during a time when interracial marriages were outlawed in thirty-eight states (Pascoe, 2010). At the time, Johnson was probably the most famous black person in the world. Other sports also emerged as commercial ventures; in 1924, the National Hockey League added the first US team to its roster—the Boston Bruins.

This was also the era in which movie-going became immensely popular and movie making became an established industry. In 1915, the first full-length film, *Birth of a Nation*, which denigrated blacks and made the Ku Klux Klan out to be heroic, was released. It met both with commercial success and with a number of protests that were organized by the NAACP. (Of course, films, like any other technology, can be used for multiple purposes.) Walt Disney Studios opened in 1923; the first Mickey Mouse cartoon—*Steamboat Willie*—premiered in 1928, and the first Academy Award was given in 1929 (*Wings*, a silent film on World War I, won Best Picture).

The mid-1920s saw the beginning of sound films—the talkies. Soon after, weekly motion picture attendance among Americans was above 60%, a trend that continued for almost every year until the advent of television.

Film and radio grew up together. Five years after *Birth of a Nation* came out, the first commercial radio station began to broadcast in Detroit and the first radio sets built with vacuum tube technology that had first been developed in 1907 and produced by Westinghouse were sold in stores for 10 dollars ($272 in 2017 dollars). The next year, 1921, the first baseball game was broadcast live on the radio. Within twenty years, over 80% of Americans had access to a radio. With radio, people could follow events in real time.

Newspapers and magazines were very popular. In 1922 *Reader's Digest* was first published, followed by *Time Magazine* in 1923, and *The New Yorker* in 1925.

Phonographs had appeared by the 1890s, which led to the promotion of new forms of music and dance and allowed anyone with records and a phonograph to listen to music any time. Music was also transforming with the advent of popular jazz. Louis Armstrong made his first recording in 1923. In 1927, the first of the great musical plays opened—Kern and Hammerstein's *Show Boat*.

Television was also beginning its ascent. In December 1923, Vladamir Zworykin filed a patent for a television system, and in 1928 the first regularly scheduled television programming began in Schenectady, New York, by G.E. Station W2XB.

Modern art was becoming popular. For example, the Museum of Modern Art opened in New York City in 1929.

The sinking of the Titanic in 1912 with the loss of 1,517 lives brought together many of the above trends. The Titanic could only be built because of the development of modern steel was believed to be unsinkable, and the hubris of that belief translated into a fatal decision—not provide enough lifeboats to accommodate all of the passengers and crew. The 710 survivors were saved because of radio distress calls picked up by the ship Carpathia. The class structure of the early twentieth century meant that third-class passengers (and the crew) were left to fend for themselves, while a much greater percentage of the first-class passengers survived. The disaster also highlights the role of newspapers in that era, as the story was popularized and sensationalized by the press.

NOTES

1. For the most part, unless Gallup asked specifically about a historical event that occurred before 1930, the relevant Gallup questions will be discussed in other chapters.

2. Deciphered by the British, the January 1917 "Zimmerman telegram," sent from the German Foreign Office, offered US territory to Mexico in return for joining the German side in the war.

3. In the Battle of the Somme in 1916, over one million soldiers were killed.

4. Another 50–100 million people died in the flu epidemic of 1918 and 1919.

5. The results of Gallup's 1936 survey showed that of those who had an opinion, 57% thought the treaty was too severe [7/37], and only 46% said the war debts should be cancelled or reduced [12/36].

Appendix 1 235

6. According to the 1936–1937 Gallup survey, only 26% of Americans wanted the United States to join the League of Nations and only 28% of Americans thought it had *not* been a mistake for the United States to "Enter the World War." Gallup aggregated many questions asked in 1936 and 1937 into one combined response.

7. In January 1939, a Gallup poll indicated that 34% of Americans thought Hoover was doing an excellent job; 47% said he was doing a good job; and 8% said he was doing a fair or poor job.

8. For a full understanding of Jim Crow, see Woodward (2002). Jim Crow coincided with the origin of the myth of the "Lost Cause." Proponents argued that the civil war had little to do with slavery. Confederates wanted to preserve their unique way of life and states' rights. Furthermore, they argued that most slaves were happy under slavery. The Lost Cause mythology was prominent in most history textbooks and also resulted in the construction of hundreds of statues celebrating the leaders of the confederacy.

9. On the other hand, in 1921 the first Miss America Pageant was held in Atlantic City.

10. Prior to the passage of the 19th Amendment, women had full voting rights in fifteen states and could vote for president in twelve other states.

11. I am very indebted to Gordon's (2016) book on American economic growth since the civil war for much of the discussion on technology in this chapter and elsewhere.

12. The percentage of the workforce that was female increased to 30% in 1950 and 47% by 2000.

13. In classes that I teach, over 90% of my political science students know this equation. What is equally fascinating is that less than 10% can state any other equation in physics or chemistry.

14. In August 1945, Gallup survey respondents were asked to identify American public figures: Einstein: theoretical physicist [45%], Capone: gangster [80%], Tommy Dorsey: musician [76%], Fiorella LaGuardia: Mayor of New York [74%], and Upton Sinclair: novelist [37%]. Einstein, although not a "rock-star," was very well known. In fact, in June 1955, 63% of respondents could name Einstein in an open-ended question as the person associated with the Theory of Relativity.

15. Long distance calls were expensive long after phones were commonplace. In 1940, a three-minute phone call from San Francisco to New York cost the equivalent of $46 in 2005 dollars.

16. The FDA began in 1938 to require that only doctors could prescribe certain drugs.

17. The Flexner report, written under the aegis of the Carnegie Foundation, mandated that medical schools adhere to strict scientific protocols in teaching and research. Following the report, half of the medical schools in the country were forced to close or merge.

References

Achen, C., Bartels, L., Achen, C. H., & Bartels, L. M. (2017). *Democracy for Realists*. Princeton University Press.
Aleksievich, S. (1992). *Zinky Boys: Soviet Voices from a Forgotten War*. Random House (UK).
Alexander, Michelle. (2020). *The New Jim Crow: Mass Incarceration in the Age of Colorblindness*. The New Press.
Alperovitz, G. (2010). *The Decision to Use the Atomic Bomb*. Vintage.
Archer, A. M., & Kam, C. D. (2020). Modern Sexism in Modern Times Public Opinion in the# Metoo Era. *Public Opinion Quarterly, 84*(4), 813–837.
Bailey, M. (1965, June). How Contraception Transformed the American Family, *The Atlantic*.
Baker, R. (2020). Technology. In Smith, T. W. (Ed.), *A Meeting Place and More…: A History of the American Association for Public Opinion Research*. American Association for Public Opinion Research.
Bardes, B. A., & Oldendick, R. W. (2012). *Public Opinion: Measuring the American Mind*. Rowman & Littlefield Publishers.
Berelson, B. R., Lazarsfeld, P. F., & McPhee, W. N. (1986). *Voting: A Study of Opinion Formation in a Presidential Campaign*. University of Chicago Press.
Berinsky, A. J. (2006). American Public Opinion in the 1930s and 1940s: The Analysis of Quota-Controlled Sample Survey Data. *International Journal of Public Opinion Quarterly, 70*(4), 499–529.
Berinsky, A. J. (2009). *In Time of War: Understanding American Public Opinion from World War II to Iraq*. University of Chicago Press.
Berinsky, A. J. (Ed.). (2020). *New Directions in Public Opinion*. Routledge.
Berlinski, N., Doyle, M., Guess, A. M., Levy, G., Lyons, B., Montgomery, J. M., … & Reifler, J. (2020). The Effects of Unsubstantiated Claims of Voter Fraud on Confidence in Elections. *Journal of Experimental Political Science*, 1–16. doi:10.1017/XPS.2021.18.
Black, E. (2003). *War Against the Weak: Eugenics and America's Campaign to Create A Master Race*. Dialog Press.

Bullock, J. G. (2011). Elite Influence on Public Opinion in an Informed Electorate. *American Political Science Review, 105*(3), 496–515.

Burstein, P. (2003). The Impact of Public Opinion on Public Policy: A Review and an Agenda. *Political Research Quarterly, 56*(1), 29–40.

Campbell, W. J. (2020). *Lost in a Gallup: Polling Failure in U.S. Presidential Elections.* University of California Press.

Carpini, M. X. D., & Keeter, S. (1996). *What Americans Know About Politics and why it Matters.* Yale University Press.

Chesler, E. (2007). *Woman of Valor: Margaret Sanger and the Birth Control Movement in America.* Simon and Schuster.

Chong, D., & Levy, M. (2018). Competing Norms of Free Expression and Political Tolerance. *Social Research: An International Quarterly, 85*(1), 197–227.

Clawson, R. A., & Oxley, Z. M. (2016). *Public Opinion: Democratic Ideals, Democratic Practice.* CQ Press.

Coates, Ta-Nehisi. (2014). The Case for Reparations. *The Atlantic, 313*(5): 54–71.

Converse, J. M. (2011). *Survey Research in the United States: Roots and Emergence 1890–1960.* Transaction Publishers.

Converse, P. E. (2006). The Nature of Belief Systems in Mass Publics (1964). *Critical Review, 18*(1–3), 1–74.

Crespi, I. (1988). *Pre-Election Polling: Sources of Accuracy and Error.* Russell Sage Foundation.

Curtin, R., Presser, S., & Singer, E. (2005). Changes in Telephone Survey Nonresponse over the Past Quarter Century. *Public Opinion Quarterly, 69*(1), 87–98.

Draper, R. (2020). *To Start a War: How the Bush Administration Took America Into War.* Penguin.

Driscoll, D. (2019). Assessing Sociodemographic Predictors of Climate Change Concern, 1994–2016. *Social Science Quarterly, 100*(5), 1699–1708.

Egan, T. (2006). *The Worst Hard Time: The Untold Story of Those Who Survived the Great American Dust Bowl.* Houghton Mifflin Harcourt.

Egan, P. J., & Mullin, M. (2017). Climate Change: US Public Opinion. *Annual Review of Political Science, 20,* 209–227.

Eichenberg, R. C. (2007). Citizen Opinion on Foreign Policy and World Politics. In Russell J. Dalton and Hans-Dieter Klingemann (Ed.), *The Oxford Handbook of Political Behavior.* DOI: 10.1093/oxfordhb/9780199270125.003.0020.

Eichenberg, R. C. (2016). Public Opinion on Foreign Policy Issues. In Motta, M. P., and Fowler, E. F. (Ed.), *Oxford Research Encyclopedia of Politics.*

Equal Justice Initiative. (2015). *Lynching in America: Confronting the Legacy of Racial Terror.* https://eji.org/wp-content/uploads/2005/11/lynching-in-america-3d-ed-052421.pdf.

Erikson, R. S., & Tedin, K. L. (2015). *American Public Opinion: Its Origins, Content and Impact.* Routledge.

Finer, L. B. (2007). Trends in Premarital Sex in the United States, 1954–2003. *Public Health Reports, 122*(1), 73–78.

Frank, T. (2007). *What's the Matter with Kansas?: How Conservatives Won the Heart of America.* Metropolitan Books.

Geer, J. G. (2004). *Public Opinion and Polling around the World: A Historical Encyclopedia.* Abc-Clio.

Gilens, M. (1995). Racial Attitudes and Opposition to Welfare. *The Journal of Politics, 57*(4), 994–1014.

Gilens, M. (2019). Citizen Competence and Democratic Governance. In Berinsky, A. J. (Ed.), *New Directions in Public Opinion*, 41–72. Routledge.
Glynn, C. J., et al. (2016). *Public Opinion*, 3rd Edition. Westview Press, Boulder.
Gordon, R. J. (2016). *The Rise and Fall of American Growth: The US Standard of Living Since the Civil War*. Princeton University Press.
Groves, R. M., Couper, M. P., Presser, S., Singer, E., Tourangeau, R., Acosta, G. P., & Nelson, L. (2006). Experiments in Producing Nonresponse Bias. *International Journal of Public Opinion Quarterly*, 70(5), 720–736.
Hanitzsch, T., Van Dalen, A., & Steindl, N. (2018). Caught in the Nexus: A Comparative and Longitudinal Analysis of Public Trust in the Press. *The International Journal of Press/Politics*, 23(1), 3–23.
Harrington, M. (1997). *The Other America*. Simon and Schuster.
Herman, E. S., & Chomsky, N. (2010). *Manufacturing Consent: The Political Economy of the Mass Media*. Random House.
Hillygus, D. S. (2020). The Practice of Survey Research: Changes and Challenges. In *New Directions in Public Opinion* (pp. 22–40). Routledge.
Hofstadter, R. (2012). *The Paranoid Style in American Politics*. Vintage.
Holsti, O. R. (2004). *Public Opinion and American Foreign Policy*. University of Michigan Press.
HUD-Treasury Task Force on Predatory Lending. (2000). *Curbing Predatory Home Mortgage Lending*. https://www.huduser.gov/portal/publications/hsgfin/curbing.html.
Igo, S. E. (2006). "A Gold Mine and a Tool for Democracy": George Gallup, Elmo Roper, and the Business of Scientific Polling, 1935–1955. *Journal of the History of the Behavioral Sciences*, 42(2), 109–134.
Iyengar, S., & Westwood, S. J. (2015). Fear and Loathing Across Party Lines: New Evidence on Group Polarization. *American Journal of Political Science*, 59(3), 690–707.
Johnson, S. (2016). *Wonderland: How Play Made the Modern World*. Pan Macmillan.
Jones, H. (2017). *Descent into Darkness: The My Lai Massacre and Its Legacy*. Oxford University Press.
Keynes, J. M. (2013). *The Economic Consequences of the Peace*. Courier Corporation.
Kinder, D. R., & Sears, D. O. (1981). Prejudice and Politics: Symbolic Racism versus Racial Threats to the Good Life. *Journal of Personality and Social Psychology*, 40(3), 414.
Kinder, D., Reynolds, M. E., & Burns, N. (2020). Categorical Politics in Action. In Berinsky, A. J. (Ed.), *New Directions in Public Opinion*. Routledge.
Klein, E. (2020). *Why We're Polarized*. Avid Reader Press.
Krosnick, J. A. (1990). Government Policy and Citizen Passion: A Study of Issue Publics in Contemporary America. *Political Behavior*, 12(1), 59–92.
Lanouette, W. (2013). *Genius in the Shadows: A Biography of Leo Szilard, the Man Behind the Bomb*. Skyhorse.
Lazri, A. M., & Konisky, D. M. (2019). Environmental Attitudes Across Race and Ethnicity. *Social Science Quarterly*, 100(4), 1039–1055.
Leeper, T. J. (2019). Where Have the Respondents Gone? Perhaps We Ate Them All. *Public Opinion Quarterly*, 83(S1), 280–288.
Lett, E., Asabor, E. N., Corbin, T., & Boatright, D. (2020). Racial Inequity in Fatal US Police Shootings, 2015–2020. *Journal of Epidemiology and Community Health*. 75(4), 394–397.
Levitsky, S., & Ziblatt, D. (2018). *How Democracies Die*. Broadway Books.
Lewis, R. (1935). *It Can't Happen Here*. Doubleday.
Lhamon, W. T., & Crow, J. (2003). *Jump Jim Crow: Lost Plays, Lyrics, and Street Prose of The First Atlantic Popular Culture*. Harvard University Press.

Lusinchi, D. (2012). 'President Landon' and the 1936 Literary Digest Poll: Were Automobiles and Telephone Owners to Blame? *Social Science History, 36*(1), 23–54.

Lusinchi, D. (2018). 'The Great Fiasco' of the 1948 Presidential Election Polls: Status Recognition and Norms Conflict in Social Science. *Annals of Science, 75*(2), 120–144.

Iyengar, S., Lelkes, Y., Levendusky, M., Malhotra, N., & Westwood, S. J. (2019). The Origins and Consequences of Affective Polarization in the United States. *Annual Review of Political Science, 22*, 129–146.

Lyons, B. A., Montgomery, J. M., Guess, A. M., Nyhan, B., & Reifler, J. (2021). Overconfidence in News Judgments is Associated with False News Susceptibility. *Proceedings of the National Academy of Sciences, 118*(23). https://doi.org/10.1073/pnas.2019527118.

Macmillan, M. (2013). *The War That Ended Peace: The Road to 1914*. Penguin Canada.

Maddow, R. (2019). *Blowout: Corrupted Democracy, Rogue State Russia, and the Richest, Most Destructive Industry on Earth*. Crown Publishers.

Mann, M. E., & Toles, T. (2016). *The Madhouse Effect: How Climate Change Denial is Threatening our Planet, Destroying our Politics, and Driving Us Crazy*. Columbia University Press.

Mann, M. E. (2021). *The New Climate War: The Fight to Take Back our Planet*. Public Affairs.

Mcwhorter, D. (2001). *Carry Me Home: Birmingham, Alabama: The Climactic Battle of the Civil Rights Revolution*. Simon and Schuster.

Moore, D. W. (1992). *The Superpollsters: How They Measure and Manipulate Public Opinion in America*. Four Walls Eight Windows.

Niemi, R. G., Mueller, J., & Smith, T. W. (1989). *Trends in Public Opinion: A Compendium of Survey Data*. Greenwood Press.

Noam, E. (2009). *Media Ownership and Concentration in America*. Oxford University Press on Demand.

Norrander, B., & Wilcox, C. (Eds.). (2009). *Understanding Public Opinion*. SAGE.

Okrent, D. (2010). *Last Call: The Rise and Fall of Prohibition*. Simon and Schuster.

Oshinsky, D. M. (2005). *Polio: An American Story*. Oxford University Press.

Page, B. I., & Shapiro, R. Y. (1983). Effects of Public Opinion on Policy. *The American Political Science Review, 75*(4), 175–190.

Page, B. I., & Shapiro, R. Y. (2010). *The Rational Public: Fifty Years of Trends in Americans' Policy Preferences*. University of Chicago Press.

Parolin, Z., Curran, M., Matsudaira, J., Waldfogel, J., & Wimer, C. (2020). Monthly Poverty Rates in the United States during the COVID-19 Pandemic. *Poverty and Social Policy Working Paper*. Center on Poverty & Social Policy.

Pascoe, P. (2010). *What Comes Naturally: Miscegenation Law and the Making of Race in the United States*. Oxford University Press.

Phillips, M. (2012). The Long Story of US Debt, from 1790 to 2011, in 1 Little Chart. *The Atlantic, 13*. https://www.theatlantic.com/business/archive/2012/11/the-long-story-of-us-debt-from-1790-to-2011-in-1-little-chart/265185/ .

Piketty, T. (2017). *Capital in the Twenty-First Century*. Harvard University Press.

Robinson, D. J. (1999). *The Measure of Democracy: Polling, Market Research, and Public Life, 1930–1945*. University of Toronto Press.

Rothstein, R. (2017). *The Color of Law: A Forgotten History of How our Government Segregated America*. Liveright Publishing.

Saez, E., & Zucman, G. (2019). *The Triumph of Injustice: How the Rich Dodge Taxes and How to Make Them Pay*. WW Norton & Company.

Schildkraut, D. J. (2010). *Americanism in the Twenty-First Century: Public Opinion in the Age of Immigration*. Cambridge University Press.
Seltzer, R. A., Newman, J., & Leighton, M. V. (1997*). Sex as a Political Variable: Women as Candidates and Voters in US Elections*. Lynne Rienner Publishers.
Schuman, H., & Presser, S. (1996). *Questions and Answers in Attitude Surveys: Experiments on Question Form, Wording, and Context*. SAGE.
Schuman, H., et al. (1997). *Racial Attitudes in America: Trends and Interpretations*. Harvard University Press.
Shilts, R. (2011). *And the Band Played On: Politics, People, and the AIDS Epidemic*. Souvenir Press.
Simon, R. J. (1974). *Public Opinion in America, 1936–1970*. Rand Mcnally.
Smith, T. W. (1998). Why Our Neck of the Woods is Better than the Forest. *The Public Perspective, 9*, 50–53.
Smith, R. C., & Seltzer, R. (2000). *Contemporary Controversies and the American Racial Divide*. Lynne Rienner Publishers.
Smith, R. C., & Seltzer, R. (2007). The Deck is the Sea: The African America Vote in the Presidential Elections of 2000 and 2004. *National Political Science Review, 11*, 253–269.
Smith, R. C., & Seltzer, R. (2015). *Polarization and the Presidency: From FDR to Barack Obama*. Lynne Rienner Publishers.
Sudman, S., & Bradburn, N. M. (1987). The Organizational Growth of Public Opinion Research in the United States. *The Public Opinion Quarterly, 51*, S67–S78.
Trump, M. L. (2020). *Too Much and Never Enough: How My Family Created the World's Most Dangerous Man*. Simon and Schuster.
US Dept. of Health, Education, and Welfare. (1964*). Smoking and Health: Report of the Advisory Committee to the Surgeon General of the Public Health Service*. US GPO, Washington, DC.
Wasow, O. (2020). Agenda Seeding: How 1960s Black Protests Moved Elites, Public Opinion and Voting. *American Political Science Review, 114*(3), 638–659.
Wilson, W. J. (2012). *The Truly Disadvantaged: The Inner City, the Underclass, and Public Policy*. University of Chicago Press.
Woodward, B. (2020). *Rage*. Simon and Shuster.
Zaller, J. R. (1992). *The Nature and Origins of Mass Opinion*. Cambridge University Press.

ELECTRONIC REFERENCES

Barron-Lopez, L. (2020, September 2). Trump Attacks Take a Toll on Black Lives Matter Ssupport. *Politico*. Retrieved from https://www.politico.com/news/2020/09/02/trump-black-lives-matter-poll-407227
Beauchamp, Z. (2021, June 15). Call it Authoritarianism. *Vox*. Retrieved from https://www.vox.com/policy-and-politics/2021/6/15/22522504/republicans-authoritarianism-trump-competitive
Blinder, A., & Drape, J. (2021, March 6). When the Clock Stopped: The Three Days last March that Changed Sports. *New York Times*. Retrieved from https://www.nytimes.com/interactive/2021/03/06/sports/coronavirus-canceled-sports.html
Buchanan, L., Bui, Q., & Patel, J. K. (2020, June 3). Black Lives Matter May Be the Largest Movement in U.S. History. *New York Times*. Retrieved from https://www.nytimes.com/interactive/2020/07/03/us/george-floyd-protests-crowd-size.html

CNN. (2007, June 26). *CNN Opinion Research.* Retrieved from http://i.a.cnn.net/cnn/2007/images/06/26/rel7c.pdf

Darr, J. (2021, June 2). Local News Coverage Is Declining — And That Could Be Bad for American Politics. *FiveThirtyEight.* Retrieved from https://fivethirtyeight.com/features/local-news-coverage-is-declining-and-that-could-be-bad-for-american-politics/

Demsas, J. (2020, November 11). Study: Trump's Tweets Can Lead Republicans to Lose Faith in Elections. *Vox.* Retrieved from https://www.vox.com/2020/11/11/21558781/trump-tweet-election-rigged-republicans-violence-results-joe-biden-voting

Denne, L., & Gardiner, C. (2019, November 17). Former U.S. Officials Criticize Trump's Decision to 'Abandon' Kurds. *NBC News*, Retrieved from https://www.nbcnews.com/news/world/former-u-s-officials-criticize-trump-s-decision-abandon-kurds-n1084156

Farivar, J. (2021, January 16). Researchers: More Than a Dozen Extremist Groups Took Part in Capitol Riots. *VOANews.* Retrieved from https://www.voanews.com/2020-usa-votes/researchers-more-dozen-extremist-groups-took-part-capitol-riots

Funk, C., & Kennedy, B. (2020, April 21). How Americans See Climate Change and the Environment in 7 Charts. *Pew Research Center.* Retrieved from https://www.pewresearch.org/fact-tank/2020/04/21/how-americans-see-climate-change-and-the-environment-in-7-charts/

Gerson, M. (2021, May 3). Elected Republicans are Lying with Open Eyes. Their Excuses are Disgraceful. *Washington Post.* Retrieved from https://www.washingtonpost.com/opinions/2021/05/03/trump-republicans-big-lie/

Hagey, K, Albert, L. I., & Serkez, Y. (2019, May 4). In News Industry, a Stark Divide Between Haves and Have-Nots. *Wall Street Journal.* Retrieved from https://www.wsj.com/graphics/local-newspapers-stark-divide/

Harney, K. R. (2006, June 17). Study Finds Bias in Mortgage Process. *Washington Post.* Retrieved from https://www.washingtonpost.com/archive/realestate/2006/06/17/study-finds-bias-in-mortgage-process/c5b821f9-83ef-4a70-b284-3d6db7d3b95e/

Ingraham, C. (2021, January 1). World's Richest Men Added Billions to their Fortunes Last Year as Others Struggled. *Washington Post.* Retrieved from https://www.washingtonpost.com/business/2021/01/01/bezos-musk-wealth-pandemic/

Kelly, H. (2021, January 15). On its 20th Birthday, Wikipedia Might Be the Safest Place Online. *Washington Post.* Retrieved from https://www.washingtonpost.com/technology/2021/01/15/wikipedia-20-year-anniversary/

Khavin, D., et al. (2021, June 30). Day of Rage: An In-depth Look at How a Mob Stormed the Capitol. *New York Times.* Retrieved from https://www.nytimes.com/video/us/politics/100000007606996/capitol-riot-trump-supporters.html

Long, H. (2021, February 19). How Many Americans are Unemployed? It's Likely a Lot More than 10 Million. *Washington Post.* Retrieved from https://www.washingtonpost.com/business/2021/02/19/how-many-americans-unemployed/

McGinty, J. C. (2021, February 26). In Covid-19 Vaccine Surveys, the Wording Affects the Results. *Wall Street Journal.* Retrieved from https://www.wsj.com/articles/in-covid-19-vaccine-surveys-the-wording-affects-the-results-11614335402

Moreau, J. (2020, April 11). Years After Trans Military Ban, Legal Battle Rages on. *NBC News.* Retrieved from https://www.nbcnews.com/feature/nbc-out/year-after-trans-military-ban-legal-battle-rages-n1181906.

Morin, R. (2020, June 6). Americans' Perceptions of Police Drop Significantly in One Week as Protests Continue, Survey Finds. *USA Today.* June 6, 2020. Retrieved from https://www.usatoday.com/story/news/politics/2020/06/06/americans-views-police-drop-significantly-amid-protests-survey/3159072001/

Myers, T, Severns, M., & McGraw, M. (2021, June 23). 'The Tea Party to the 10th Power': Trumpworld Bets Big on Critical Race Theory. *Politico*. Retrieved from https://www.politico.com/news/2021/06/23/trumpworld-critical-race-theory-495712

O'Connell, J., & Brown, E. (2019, February 11). A Hedge Fund's 'Mercenary' Strategy: Buy Newspapers, Slash Jobs, Sell the Buildings. *Washington Post*. Retrieved from https://www.washingtonpost.com/business/economy/a-hedge-funds-mercenary-strategy-buy-newspapers-slash-jobs-sell-the-buildings/2019/02/11/f2c0c78a-1f59-11e9-8e21-59a09ff1e2a1_story.html

Perrin, A. (2019, September 26). Who Doesn't Read Books in America? Pew Research Center. Retrieved from https://www.pewresearch.org/fact-tank/2019/09/26/who-doesnt-read-books-in-america/

Rockeman, O. (2020, October 12). Summers Says Covid-19 Will End Up Costing U.S. $16 Trillion. *Bloomberg.com*. Retrieved from https://www.bloomberg.com/news/articles/2020-10-12/summers-says-covid-19-will-end-up-costing-u-s-16-trillion

Rogers, K. (2021, June 11). Why It's So Hard to Gauge Support for QAnon. *FiveThirtyEight.com*. Retrieved from https://fivethirtyeight.com/features/why-its-so-hard-to-gauge-support-for-qanon/

Rutenberg, J., Corasaniti, J., & Feuer, A. (2020). Trump's Fraud Claims Died in Court, but the Myth of Stolen Elections Lives On. *New York Times*. Retrieved from https://www.nytimes.com/2020/12/26/us/politics/republicans-voter-fraud.html

Samuels, A., & Mejia, E. (2021, April 13). How Views On Black Lives Matter Have Changed — And Why That Makes Police Reform So Hard. *FiveThirtyEight.com*. Retrieved from https://fivethirtyeight.com/features/how-views-on-black-lives-matter-have-changed-and-why-that-makes-police-reform-so-hard/

Scott, J. (2020, October 26). Despite Cries of Censorship, Conservatives Dominate Social Media. *Politico*. Retrieved from https://www.politico.com/news/2020/10/26/censorship-conservatives-social-media-432643

Silver, N. (2017, May 3). The Comey Letter Probably Cost Clinton the Election. *FiveThirtyEight.com*. Retrieved from https://fivethirtyeight.com/features/the-comey-letter-probably-cost-clinton-the-election/

Skelly, G. (2019, September 13). What's Going on With Trump's Approval Rating? *FiveThirtyEight.com*. Retrieved from https://fivethirtyeight.com/features/whats-going-on-with-trumps-approval-rating/

Stanley-Becker, I. (2020, September 15). Pro-Trump Youth Group Enlists Teens in Secretive Campaign Likened to a 'Troll Farm,' Prompting Rebuke by Facebook and Twitter. *Washington Post*. Retrieved from https://www.washingtonpost.com/politics/turning-point-teens-disinformation-trump/2020/09/15/c84091ae-f20a-11ea-b796-2dd09962649c_story.html

Wallace, T., & Parlapiano, A. (2017, January 22). Crowd Scientists Say Women's March in Washington Had 3 Times as Many People as Trump's Inauguration. *New York Times*. Retrieved from https://www.nytimes.com/interactive/2017/01/22/us/politics/womens-march-trump-crowd-estimates.html

Index

Note: Page locators in italics refer to tables.

AAA. *See* Agricultural Adjust Administration (AAA)
AAPOR. *See* American Association for Public Opinion Research (AAPOR)
ABC, 10n14, 85, 113, 210, 211n11, 212n23
ABC/*Washington Post*, 85
ACA. *See* Affordable Care Act (ACA) (Obamacare)
Adult Use of Tobacco Surveys, 65, 83n2
Affordable Care Act (ACA) (Obamacare), 188–89, 197, 200nn34–37
African Americans, 11; in crosstabular analysis, 4; in Gallup surveys' features and limitations, 2–3. *See also* race, 1930s
Agnew, Spiro, 89
Agricultural Adjust Administration (AAA), 21–22
Ali, Muhammed, 81, 84nn30–31
Alperovitz, G., 47n3
American Association for Public Opinion Research (AAPOR), 29
American Institute of Public Opinion, 9n3
American National Election Survey (ANES), 8, 215
American public ignorance, 8–9, 10n22
ANES. *See* American National Election Survey (ANES)
anti-bomb movement, 43

AP-NORC, 183, 189, 200n37
Archer, A. M., 200n29
Armstrong, Lance, 195, 200n43
Asabor, E. N., 211n10
atheists, 47n11, 175, 214–15, *215*
atomic bomb, 32, 33, 43, 47n3, 47n20
automation, 133, 143n23
automobiles, 23, 77, 99, 157, 232–33; in economy, 230–31

Baker, R., 85
Beatles, 80
Beauchamp, Z., 223
Berinsky, A. J., 9n4, 10n9, 10n17, 47n2
Berlin Wall, 105, 117n5
Biden, Joe, 177, 200n31, 203; Trump, D., *vs.*, 206–9, 211n17, 211n20, 212n22
Bin Laden, Osama, 123, 145–47, 170, 198n6
birth control, 20, 26, 27n15, 75, 230
birther movement, 176
Black, E., 27n12
Black Lives Matter, 183, 205, 211nn11–13, 218
Boatright, D., 211n10
Bosnia, 120
Brown v. Board of Education, 55–56, 62
Bush, George H. W., 122, 127, 165n4, *216*

245

Bush, George W., 148, 152, 153, 165n3, *216*, 223; Gore against, 149–51, 155nn11–12; Kerry against, 151

Campbell, W. J., 9n2, 9n5
capital punishment, 17, 217, 224nn8–9
Capitol riot, 208–9, 211nn18–20
Carter, Jimmy, 94, *216*
cartoons, 44
categories, 6
CBS, 65, 85, 145
CBS/*New York Times*, 85
Central Intelligence Agency, 37
Chamberlain, Neville, 12
Charles (prince), 140
Charlottesville, VA riot, 183–84, 197, 199n28
Cheney, Richard (Dick), 151, 165n3
Chicago Seven, 89–90
China, 15, 37, 50, 63nn3–4, 86, 99n2, 106
Chunnel, 121
Citizens United v. FEC, 7
civil liberties, 16–18, 71, 151–52; in US politics, 214–15, *215*, 223nn2–4
Civiq, 224n15
Clinton, Bill, 120, 123, 126–27, 134, *216*
Clinton, Hillary, 126, 134; elections and, 151, 176, 184, 199n17, 199nn16–17
Cold War, 51–52, 61–62, 67
Comey, James, 176, 199n17
Common Core standards, 182, 199n26
communism, 17–18, 215, *215*, 223n4; in US politics, 1940s, 38–39, 47nn9–12; in US politics, 1950s, 53–54, 62, 63nn8–9
Confederate flags, 154, 205, 206
conspiracy theories, 83n12, 128, 141, 199n21; about presidential election 2020, 206–10, 211nn18–20, 212nn22–23
Constitution, 26th Amendment, 83n14
consumer protection, 77, 84n27
consumer technology, 23–24
Converse, P. E., 9
Corbin, T., 211n10
Coughlin, Father, 19
countercultural movement, 78–79, 84n28

Covid-19, 210n4; attitudes about, 203, *204*, 211nn8–9, 224n15; Biden and, 203; deaths from, 201–2, 203, *203*, 210n3; economy and, 202, 204, 210nn5–6; politization of, 202–3; Trump, D., and, 202, 203; vaccines for, 203, 211n7, 211n9, 224n15
Crimea, 47n5, 173–74
Critical Race Theory, 224n13
Crossley, Archibald, 11
crosstabular analysis, 6, 10n7; differences in, 5, 10n10; education in, 4, 10n9; political party in, 4; questions in, 4, 10n8; regional differences in, 4; sample sizes in, 5
Cuba, 51, 66–67, 103, 149
Czechoslovakia, 105

DADT. *See* Don't Ask Don't Tell (DADT)
Dalen, A. Van, 223n5
data loading, 6, 10n19
data problems, 6, 10nn16–18
Demsas, J., 223
Department of Health, Education, and Welfare, US, 83n2
DeVos, Betsy, 182, 199n25
Diallo, Amadou, 130, 141, 142n16
Diana (princess), 140
Dodd-Frank bill, 187
Don't Ask Don't Tell (DADT), 132, 141, 142n19
drugs, 78–80, 107–8, 116, 117n7, 163

economy: automobiles in, 230–31; consumer credit in, 231; Covid-19 and, 202, 204, 210nn5–6; safety laws in, 231–32; strikes in, 231
economy, 1930s: AAA in, 21–22; FDR for, 21–23, 27n19, 219; Keynes on, 21, 27nn17; New Deals for, 21–22, 26; Social Security in, 22–23, 27nn18
economy, 1940s, 46; industrial milestones in, 41–42; socialism in, 42, 47n18; tariffs in, 42; taxes in, 43, 47n19
economy, 1950s: franchises in, 57; government in, 58; interstate highways in, 57–58, 62; Korean War and, 58

economy, 1960s, 82–83; consumer protection in, 77, 84n27; poverty in, 76–77; railroads bankrupt in, 77; taxes in, 77; Vietnam War costs in, 77, 84n26

economy, 1970s, 95, 99; balanced budget in, 94; energy crisis in, 94; government responsibility in, 93–94; stagflation in, 93–94

economy, 1980s, 117n6; advances for, 111–12, 117; deregulation in, 111; Reaganomics in, 110–12; recession in, 110–11; savings and loan crisis in, 111; welfare in, 111, 116–17

economy, 1990s, 141, 219; automation and, 133, 142n23; expansion in, 132, 142nn20–21; fraud in, 132–33; health care defeat in, 134, 142n24; inequality in, 133; NAFTA for, 133; welfare in, 133–34

economy, 2000s, 219; deficits in, 156; energy prices in, 158–59; fraud related to, 157–58; Great Recession in, 156–57; Lehman Brothers' bankruptcy in, 157; mortgages and, 156, 157, 166n19; Social Security in, 156; stimulus bill for, 157

economy, 2010s: ACA in, 188–89, 197, 200nn34–37; AP-NORC in, 189, 200n37; blame for, 187–88; Dodd-Frank bill in, 187; government shutdown in, 188; Great Recession fallout in, 186; labor unions in, 189–90; NAFTA and TPP in, 190; NAFTA in, 190; recovery in, 187, 200n32; taxes in, 187, 189; unemployment rate in, 187

education, 2, 4, 9n4, 10n9, 40, 57, 83n2; *Brown* in, 55–56, 62; in US politics, 1950s, 55–56; in US politics, 2010s, 182, 199n25–27

EEC. *See* European Economic Community (EEC)

Egypt, 53, 87, 168

Einstein, Albert, 232, 235nn13–14

election, conspiracy theories, insurrection, 2020: Biden *vs.* Trump, D., in, 206–9, 211n17, 211n20, 212n22; Capitol riot in, 208–9, 211nn18–20; false claims in, 207–9, 211n20; impeachment related to, 209, 210, 212n23; QAnon in, 209, 210

electricity, 23, 42, 232

energy crisis, 94

energy prices, 158–59

England, 29–31, 46n1, 214

EU. *See* European Union (EU)

eugenics movement, 19–20, 27n9

European Economic Community (EEC), 121

European Union (EU), 121

fascism, 26, 227

FDR. *See* Roosevelt, Franklin D.

fires, 192, 200n39, 201, 210n1

Floyd, George, 204–5, 218

Ford, Gerald, 89, *216*

France, 29–30, 50–51

Frank, T., 117n6

fraud, 132–33, 157–58

Freedom Rides, 72

Gallup, George, 2, 11

Gallup History Preamble, 234n1; economy in, 230–32; fascism in, 227; imperialism in, 224–25; popular trends in, 233–34; race in, 229, 233, 235n8; science, technology, environment in, 232–33, 235nn13–17; sex and gender in, 230, 235nn9–12; Soviet Union in, 227–28; US politics in, 228, 235n7; world events in, 225–28, 234nn2–5, 235nn6–7; world involvement increase in, 227; World War I in, 226–27, 234nn2–5, 235n6

Gallup surveys, 9nn2–3, 49, 65, 85, 213–14; African Americans in, 2–3; history and, 1; reliability and, 1–2; US presidential election 1936 and, 2

Gallup surveys' features and limitations, 4; phraseology in, 3; quota samples in, 2–3, 9n4; reliability in, 3; taboos in, 3

Gandhi, Mahatma, 35, 47n6

Garland, Merrick, 185, 200n30

gay rights, 93, 100n12, 110, 117, 131–32

Germany, 29, 120, 226–27, 234nn2–5; Hitler in, 11–13, 27nn4–5, 47n4; Soviet Union and, 30, 31, 34, 47n4

Gerson, Michael, 223
Gingrich, Newt, 125
González, Elián, 149
Gorbachev, Mikhail, 104–5, 119, 120
Gordon, R. J., 230, 232
Gore, Al, 149–51, 155nn11–12, 162
government research, 65, 83n2
Great Recession, 154–57, 166n17, 186
Grenada invasion, 103
gun control, 54, 153, 217, 224n9; in US politics, 2010s, 179–80, 199nn21–22

Haiti, 103, 124, 175, 199n14
Hanitzsch, T., 223n5
Harney, K. R., 154
Harris, Louis, 65, 83n1
health, 232–33, 235nn16–17
health care defeat, 134, 142n24
Herman, E. S., 7
Herzegovina, 120
highways, interstate, 57–58
Hindus, 35
"hippies," 78–79, 84n28
history, 1. *See also specific topics*
Hitler, Adolf, 11–13, 27nn4–5, 34, 47n4
Hollywood Ten, 38, 39, 47n10
Holsti, O. R., 10n22
Hoover, Herbert, 83n8, 235n7
Humphrey, Hubert, 83n9, 83n11
hurricanes, 152–53, 200n39, 201, 210n1
Hussein, Saddam, 102

impeachment, 177–78, 196, 209, 210, 212n23
imperialism, 224–25
India, 35–36, 47n6, 124–25
Indians, 40, 90
intercontinental ballistic missile, 173
International Space Station, 159
internet, 194–95, 200n42
Inter-University Consortium for Political Research, 65
inventions, 232
Iowa, 10n11
IPOLL, 5, 6
Iran, 87, 149, 172
Iran-Contra affair, 104
Iranian hostage crisis, 101–2, 116

Iraq, 102, 167–68, 198nn1–2
Iraq invasion, 146–47, 165nn3–4, 165nn5–7, 166n5
Islamic State of Iraq and the Levant (ISIS or ISIL), 169–71, 196, 198n5, 198n7
Israel, 36, 53, 68, 82, 104, 124, 150; in world events, 1970s, 86–87; in world events, 2010s, 171–72
Italy, 12
Iyengar, S., 224n7

Jackson, Jesse, 108, 117
Jackson, Michael, 163–64
January 6 riot, 201, 210n2, 211nn18–20
Japan, 14–15, 175; atomic bomb and, 32, 33, 43, 47n3, 47n20; in World War II, 30–33, 47n3
Japanese, 33, 38, 47n8
Jews, 12, 20, 26, 27nn11–12, 83, 93, 170; Coughlin against, 19; extermination of, 30, 34; as refugees, 19, 36; voting for, 27n13, 69, 175; white nationalists against, 183
Johnson, Jack, 233
Johnson, Lyndon B., 69–70, 82
Jones, Alex, 199n21

Kam, C. D., 200n29
Kennedy, John F., 69, 82, 83n8, *216*
Kennedy, Robert, 69, 83n9
Kerry, John, 151
Keynes, John Maynard, 21, 27nn17
Killing Fields, 99n2
Kim Jong-un, 173, 198nn10–11
Kinder, D. R., 118n8
King, Martin Luther, Jr., 55, 72, 73, 83n18
Kinsey, Alfred, 41, 47n16
Klein, E., 224n6
Korea, 49–50, 58, 62n2; North, 68–69, 149, 173, 196, 198nn10–11
Korean War, 58
Kristallnacht, 12
Ku Klux Klan, 40, 46, 72, 91, 92, 99n6, 229, 233

labor unions, 39, 47n13, 54–55, 108, 189–90; in US politics, 1930s, 16–17
LD. *See Literary Digest* (LD)

League of Nations, 15, 27n6, 35, 214, 227, 235n6
Lehman Brothers' bankruptcy, 157
Lend-Lease, 30, 31, 35, 45
Lett, E., 211n10
Lewinsky, Monica, 127
Libby, Lewis (Scooter), 165n3
Lindbergh, Charles, 30–31
Literary Digest (LD), 2, 9n2
literature, 25, 60, 97, 114, 138, 162, 194; in popular trends, 1940s, 44–45; in popular trends, 1960s, 79–80
Lusinchi, D., 9n2
lynching, 18, 27n10, 40, 229

Maastricht Treaty of 1991, 121
MacArthur, Douglas, 49–50
Manchuria, 15
Mandela, Nelson, 122
Manufactured Consent, 7
March on Washington, 72, 82
mass shootings and gun control, 153
McCarthy, Eugene, 69, 83n9
McCarthy, Joseph, 53–54
McCarthyism, 38
medical care, 233, 235nn16–17
Medicare, 70
Minnesota, 10n11
Miranda v. Arizona (1966), 71
Mitofsky, Warren, 65
Monroe, Marilyn, 56
Montgomery Bus Boycott, 55
mortgages, 156, 157, 166n19
movies, 44, 59, 79, 96, 114, 138, 162; in Gallup History Preamble, 233–34; in popular trends, 1930s, 24–25, 27n22; in popular trends, 2010s, 193–94
Mueller, J., 8
music, 45, 97, 115, 139, 162, 194, 234; in popular trends, 1930s, 25, 27n23; in popular trends, 1950s, 60–61; in popular trends, 1960s, 80–81, 84n29
Muslims, 35
My Lai massacre, 83n5

NAFTA. *See* North American Free Trade Agreement; North American Free Trade Association (NAFTA)

National Bureau of Economic Research, 200n32
National Opinion Research Center (NORC), 29, 49, 213–14, 218, 224n10
national surveys, 5, 10n11
NATO. *See* North Atlantic Treaty Organization (NATO)
Nazis, 11–13, 34, 183
NBC/*Wall Street Journal*, 85, 112
New Deals, 21–22, 26
news media, 194–95, 200n42
newspapers, 116
Newton shooting, 199n21
New York Times v. Sullivan (1964), 71
Niemi, R. G., 8
9/11, 145–46, 165n2
1930s, 11–26; conclusion on, 26; economy in, 20–23, 27nn17–19; popular trends of, 24–25, 27nn20–23; race in, 18–20, 26, 27nn10–12; science, technology, environment in, 23–24, 220; sex and gender in, 20, 27nn14–16, 218; US politics in, 15–18; world events in, 11–15, 26n3, 27nn4–5. *See also* Gallup History Preamble
1940s, 29–47; conclusion on, 45–46; economy in, 41–43, 46, 47nn18–19; popular trends in, 44–45; race in, 33, 38–40, 46, 47n8, 47nn14–15; science, technology, environment in, 43, 47n20; sex and gender in, 40–41, 46, 47nn16–17, 218; US politics, 38–39, 46, 47nn8–13; world events in, 29–37, 45–46, 46n1, 47nn2–6, 214, 223n1
1950s, 49–63; conclusion on, 61–62; economy in, 57–58, 62; popular trends in, 59–61; race in, 55–56, 62, 214–15, *215*; science, technology, environment in, 58–59, 63n11; sex and gender in, 56–57, 62, 63nn9–10, *215*, 218; US politics in, 53–55, 62, 63nn7–8; world events in, 49–53, 62, 62n2, 63nn3–6
1960s, 65–84; conclusion on, 81–83; economy in, 76–77, 82–83, 84nn26–27; popular trends in, 78–79, 84nn28–31; race in, 69, 71–75, 82, 83nn15–19, 84nn20–21; science, technology, environment in, 78, 220; sex and gender

in, 69, 75–76, 82, 84nn20–21, 84nn23–25, 219; US politics in, 65, 69–71, 82, 83nn8–14; world events in, 65–69, 81–82, 83nn3–7
1970s, 85–100, *215*; conclusion on, 98–99; economy in, 93–95, 99; popular trends in, 96–98; race in, 91–92, 98–99, 99nn5–7, 100n9; science, technology, environment in, 95–96, 99, 100nn13–14, 220; sex and gender in, 92–93, 99, 100nn11–12, 219; telephone surveys in, 85, 99n1; US politics in, 88–91, 98, 215; world events in, 85–88, 98
1980s, 101–18; conclusion on, 116–17; economy in, 110–12, 116–17, 117n6; popular trends in, 114–16; race in, 108–9, 116nn7–8; science, technology, environment in, 112–14, 117, 118n12; sex and gender in, 109–10, 118n9; US politics in, 106–8, 116, 117n7, 215; world events, 101–6, 117n2–5
1990s, 119–43; conclusion on, 140–41; economy in, 132–34, 141, 142nn20–22, 143nn23–24; popular trends in, 138–40, 142n14, 143n27–28; race in, 129–30, 141; science, technology, environment in, 134–37, 143n25–26, 220; sex and gender in, 130–32, 141, 142nn10–12; telephone surveys in, 119, 141n1; US politics in, 125–29, 140–41, 142n10, 215; world events in, 119–25, 140, 141nn2–5, 142n6, 142nn7–9
Nixon, Richard, 69, 83n11, 86, *216*; cover-up by, 88–89
NORC. *See* National Opinion Research Center (NORC)
NORC-GSS response rate of, 10n16
North American Free Trade Agreement (NAFTA), 133, 190
North Atlantic Treaty Organization (NATO), 36, 37, 46, 51, 119, 120, 146
North Korea, 68–69, 149, 173, 196, 198nn10–11
nuclear weapons, 149

Obama, Barack, 176, 199n17, 200n34, 219–20; approval ratings of, 168, 199n15, *216*; election of, 151, 154, 166n15

Obama, Michelle, 199n15
Obamacare. *See* Affordable Care Act
objectivity, 7
O'Connor, Sandra Day, 110
Office of Public Research-Harry Cantril, 29

Page, B. I., 8, 9
Palestine. *See* Israel
Pearl Harbor to World War II end, 32–35, 47nn2–5, 214
Pershing, General, 46n1
Pew, 200n40, 205, 211nn11–12, 220–22, 224n14
phraseology, 3, 7, 11, 27nn4–5, 199n24, 200n37, 200n40
Plame, Valerie, 165n3
polarization, 216, *216*, 224n6, 224nn6–7
pollution, 78, 95, 137, 143n26
popular trends, 233–34
popular trends, 1930s: literature in, 25; movies in, 24–25, 27n22; music in, 25, 27n23; radio in, 24; sports in, 24, 27nn20–21
popular trends, 1940s: cartoons in, 44; literature in, 44–45; movies in, 44; music in, 45; sports in, 45; television in, 44
popular trends, 1950s: literature in, 60; magazines in, 60; movies in, 59; music in, 60–61; sports in, 61; television in, 59–60; toys in, 61
popular trends, 1960s, 84nn30–31; countercultural movement in, 78–79, 84n28; literature in, 79–80; movies in, 79; music in, 80–81, 84n29; sports in, 81; Super Bowl in, 81; television in, 79
popular trends, 1970s: comic strips in, 98; legalized gambling in, 98; literature in, 97; movies in, 96; music in, 97; sports and fitness in, 97; television in, 96–97
popular trends, 1980s: literature in, 114; media distrust in, 116; movies in, 114; music in, 115; newspapers in, 116; sports in, 115–16; television in, 114
popular trends, 1990s, 142n14; boxer in, 139, 143n27; figure skater in, 139, 143n28; literature in, 138; movies in, 138; music in, 139; Prince Charles and

Princess Diana in, 140; sports in, 139, 143n28; television in, 138
popular trends, 2000s: Jackson, M., in, 163–64; literature in, 162; movies in, 162; music in, 162; steroids in sports in, 162–63; television in, 162
popular trends, 2010s: internet in, 194–95, 200n42; literature in, 194; movies in, 193–94; music in, 194; news media in, 194–95, 200n42; sports scandals in, 195–96; television in, 194
population, 78
pre-election surveys, 9n5
press distrust, 215–16, 222, 223n5
probability samples, 49, 62n1
public opinion, 9. *See also specific topics*
Putin, Vladimir, 148–49

QAnon, 209, 210
Quinnipiac surveys, 198n3, 204, 206, 210, 212n22, 218
quota sample, 9n4

Rabin, Yitzhak, 124, 142n9
race, 229, 230, 233, 235n8. *See also* Jews
race, 1930s, 26; Coughlin and, 19; eugenics movement and, 19–20, 27n9; lynching in, 18, 27n10; in sample, 19; Scottsboro Boys in, 18
race, 1940s, 224n10–11; housing and, 47n15, 218; Japanese in, 33, 38, 47n8; lynching and, 40; in military, 39–40, 46, 47n14, 217
race, 1950s, 214–15, *215*; *Brown* in, 55–56, 62; marriage related to, 56; Montgomery Bus Boycott in, 55; states' rights and, 56
race, 1960s, 69, 218; Freedom Rides in, 72; integration in, 72–75, 83n17; interracial marriage in, 73, 84n20; March on Washington in, 72, 82; militant groups in, 72, 73; mixed opinions about, 74–75; protests in, 71–74; racial integration of universities in, 72, 83n17; riots in, 73; state rights in, 74–75; violence in, 73, 84n19; voter registration campaigns in, 72, 83n16
race, 1970s, 99, 218; busing in, 91–92; interracial marriage in, 98, 100n9; Ku Klux Klan in, 91, 92, 99n6; presidential election and, 92, 99n7; Tuskegee study in, 91, 99n5
race, 1980s: Jackson, J., in, 108, 117; racial equality in, 109, 116n8
race, 1990s: Diallo killing in, 130, 141, 142n16; Million Man March in, 130; Rodney King beating in, 129–30, 142n15; Simpson trial in, 130, 142nn17–18
race, 2000s, 164; Confederate flags in, 154; Great Recession and, 154–55, 166n17; Obama, B., election in, 151, 154, 166n15
race, 2010s: Black Lives Matter in, 183; in Charlottesville, VA riot, 183–84, 197, 199n28
racial protests, 2020, 211n10; attitude toward police in, 206, *206*, 211nn14–15; Black Lives Matter in, 205, 211nn11–13, 218; Confederate flag in, 205, 206; Floyd and, 204–5, 218; Taylor and, 205
radio, 24, 44, 58, 234
readings, additional, 7
Reagan, Ronald, 47n8, 94, 101, 103–5, *216*; assassination attempt on, 107; election of, 106, 213
Reaganomics, 110–12
redundancy avoidance, 6–7
religion, 35, 71, 83n8, 134–35, 216–17. *See also* Jews
response rates, 6, 10n16
Ride, Sally, 110, 119n10
Robinson, Claude, 65
Robinson, D. J., 9n4
Robinson, Jackie, 39–40, 47n14
Rohingya, 198n13
Roosevelt, Franklin D. (FDR), 2, 9n2, 11, 13, 214, *216*; for economy, 1930s, 21–23, 27n19, 219; Lend-Lease from, 30, 31, 35, 45; Supreme Court and, 15–16; World War II and, 30–32, 38, 46n2, 47n8
Roper, Elmo, 11, 29, 49
Roper Center for Public Opinion Research (Roper Center), 5, 9n5, 10nn12–13, 65, 85, 145

Roper questions' historical analysis, 5, 10n11
Rosie the Riveter, 41
Russia. *See* Soviet Union
Rwanda, 121, 141n4

safety laws, 231–32
samples, 9n4, 83n2
Sandy Hook Elementary School, 179, 199n21
Saudi Arabia, 122
savings and loan crisis, 111
science, technology, environment, 232–33, 235nn13–17
science, technology, environment, 1930s, 220; communications in, 23–24; nuclear weapons in, 23
science, technology, environment, 1940s: atomic bomb in, 43, 47n20; calculating machines in, 43; health advances in, 43
science, technology, environment, 1950s: fluoridated water in, 59; littering in, 59; polio epidemic in, 58–59, 63n11; transistor radios in, 58; vaccines in, 59; window air conditioners in, 58
science, technology, environment, 1960s, 220; pollution in, 78; smoking in, 78; space program in, 78
science, technology, environment, 1970s, 99, 220; economy related to, 95; Environmental Protection Agency in, 95; metric system in, 96, 100n14; modern molecular biology in, 96; smallpox in, 96; technological innovation in, 95, 100n13; Three Mile Island nuclear accident, 95
science, technology, environment, 1980s: Chernobyl meltdown in, 113; computers in, 112; environment support in, 113, 118n12; Exxon supertanker spill in, 113–14, 117; global warming in, 113; ozone layer depletion in, 112–13, 117; solar power in, 118n12; space shuttle Challenger disaster in, 112
science, technology, environment, 1990s, 220; AIDS in, 136; antismoking policies in, 135; cloning in, 134, 143n25; creationism in, 135; HIV in, 136;

Microsoft in, 136; pollution in, 137, 143n26; religion and, 134–35; space science in, 135; World Wide Web in, 136; Y2K in, 136–37
science, technology, environment, 2000s, 165; diseases in, 160–61, 166n23; DNA evidence in, 160, 166n22; global warming in, 161–62, 166n24; internet and economy in, 159–60; internet security in, 160; politicization of, 160, 161; space programs in, 159; tsunamis and earthquake in, 160; Twitter in, 159, 166n21; vaccinations and anti-vaxxers in, 161
science, technology, environment, 2010s, 197–98, 220; Amazon Basin in, 192; Deepwater Horizon oil spill in, 191; Ebola in, 193; emissions in, 192; fracking in, 191; global warming in, 192–93, 200nn39–40; Paris Accord, 192, 200n39; rover Curiosity in, 190–91; Space X in, 191; Thunberg for, 193; Trump, D., appointments for, 192–93; wildfires in, 192
Scopes ("Monkey") Trial (1925), 233
Scottsboro Boys, 18
Sears, D. O., 117, 118n8
Serbia, 120–21
sex and gender, 230, 235nn9–12
sex and gender, 1930s, 218; birth control in, 20, 26, 27n15; shirtless men in, 20, 27n16; working women in, 20, 27n14
sex and gender, 1940s, 218; divorce laws and, 41, 47n17; Kinsey study on, 41, 47n16; nylon stockings in, 40; working women in, 41, 46
sex and gender, 1950s, 62, *215*, 218; clothing in, 57, 63n10; Monroe in, 56; pornography in, 56, 63n9; professions in, 57; sex education in, 57
sex and gender, 1960s, 69; abortion in, 75, 219; birth control in, 75; pornography in, 75–76; pre-marriage sexuality in, 75; Stonewall riots in, 76, 84n25; Women's Rights Movement in, 76, 84nn23–24
sex and gender, 1970s, 99; abortion in, 92, 219; ERA in, 92; gay rights in, 93,

100n12; presidential elections and, 93, 100n11
sex and gender, 1980s: AIDS in, 109–10, 117, 118n9; gay rights in, 110, 117; Moral Majority in, 109, 110; O'Connor in, 110; Ride in, 110, 118n10; sports teams and, 110
sex and gender, 1990s, 127–28, 141, 142nn10–12; abortion in, 130–31; DADT in, 132, 142n19; gay rights in, 131–32; pre-marital sex in, 132; women in combat jobs in, 131
sex and gender, 2000s, 164–65; liberalization of, 155; military and, 155; same-sex marriages in, 155; women's rights and, 155
sex and gender, 2010s, 200n30, 218; abortion in, 185, 219; bathrooms in, 186; Boy Scouts and, 186; Me Too Movement in, 184–85, 197, 200n29; in military, 186, 200n31; same-sex marriages in, 186
Shapiro, R. Y., 8, 9
Silver, Nate, 145, 199n17
Simon, Rita, 8
Smith, Al, 83n8
Smith, T. W., 8, 199n27
Snowden, Edward, 179
socialism, 42, 47n18
Social Science Research Council (SSRC), 9n5, 49
social security, 22–23, 27nn18, 156
Soviet Union, 37, 55, 67, 68, 227–28; Germany and, 30, 31, 33, 34, 47n4; Japan and, 14–15, 47n3; in world events, 1950s, 51–52, 63n5; in world events, 1980s, 104–5; in world events, 1990s, 119–21, 141n2
space program, 78, 159
Spanish Civil War (1936), 13–14
sports, 45, 61, 81, 97, 110, 139, 233; Covid-19 and, 202, 210n4; in popular trends, 1930s, 24, 27nn20–21; in popular trends, 1980s, 115–16; in popular trends, 2000s, 162–63; in popular trends, 2010s, 195–96
SSRC. *See* Social Science Research Council (SSRC)

stagflation, 93–94
state rights, 56, 74–75
Steindl, N., 223n5
Super Bowl, 81
Supreme Court, 15–16, 71, 185, 188, 197, 200n30
survey data sources, 5–6, 10nn12–14
survey organizations, 5–6
survey research inception, 1–2
Szilard, Leo, 43, 47n20

taboos, 3
Taft-Hartley Act, 39
tariffs, 42
taxes, 43, 47n19, 77, 187, 189
Taylor, Breonna, 205
telephones, 220, 232, 235n15
telephone surveys, 85, 99n1, 101, 119, 141n1
television, 44, 79, 114, 138, 162, 234; in popular trends, 1950s, 59–60; in popular trends, 1970s, 96–97; in popular trends, 2010s, 194
theoretical questions, 7–8
Thomas, Clarence, 127, 142n11, 142nn11–12
Thunberg, Greta, 193
Titanic, sinking of, 234
Trans-Pacific Partnership Agreement (TPP), 190
Treaty of Rome, 121
trendlines, 9
Truman, Harry, 43, *216*, 218, 229; CIA from, 37; election of, 29; FDR and, 38; against military racial segregation, 40; Taft-Hartley Act and, 39; Truman Doctrine from, 36
Trump, Donald, 192–93, 197, 216, *216*; Biden *vs.*, 206–9, 211n17, 211n20, 212n22; Covid-19 and, 202, 203; financial difficulties of, 142n20; on Haitians, 199n14; impeachment proceedings against, 177–78, 196, 209, 210, 212n23; inauguration crowd size for, 199n20; Iran and, 172; Israel and, 172; against Obama, B., 176; pardons by, 199n19; Russia and emails related to, 177, 199n16; Saudi Arabia

and, 172–73; Supreme Court of, 185, 200n30; Syria and, 170; *Washington Post* on, 206–7, 233. *See also* conspiracy theories; election, conspiracy theories, insurrection

Trump, Mary, 206–7

2000s, 145–66; conclusion on, 164–65; economy in, 156–59, 165, 166n19; popular trends in, 162–64; race in, 154–55, 164, 166n15, 166n17; science, technology, environment in, 159–62, 165; sex and gender in, 155, 164–65; US politics in, 150–53, 160, 161, 164, 198nn11–13, 215; world events in, 145–50, 164, 198nn1–10

2010s, 167–200, *215*; conclusion on, 196–98; economy in, 186–90, 197, 200nn32–37; popular trends in, 193–96, 200nn42–43; race in, 183–84, 197, 199n28; science, technology, environment in, 190–93, 197–98, 200n38–40, 220; sex and gender in, 184–86, 197, 200n29, 200nn30–31, 218–19; US politics in, 15–27nn, 175–83, 196–97, 215; world events in, 167–75, 196, 198nn1–14

2020, 220, 224n14; conclusion on, 210; Covid-19 in, 201–4, *203*, *204*, 210nn2–6, 211n7; election, conspiracy theories, insurrection in, 206–10, 211nn17–21, 212nn22–23, 222–23, 224nn16–17; racial protests in, 204–6, *206*, 211nn11–14, 224n13

Ukraine, 119
unemployment rate, 187
United Nations, 35, 37, 49, 53, 214
US-Mexico border wall, 181, 199n24
US politics, *216*, 216–17, 223n5, 224nn6–9; civil liberties in, 214–15, *215*, 223nn2–4
US politics, 1930s: Bonus Army in, 16, 27n8; civil liberties in, 17–18; communism in, 17–18; crime in, 17, 27n9; labor unions in, 16–17; Prohibition in, 17; Supreme Court in, 15–16

US politics, 1940s, 46; communism in, 38–39, 47nn9–12; labor unions in, 39, 47n13; McCarthyism in, 38, 47n10; racism in, 39, 47n8

US politics, 1950s, 215; communism in, 53–54, 62, 63nn8–9; death penalty in, 54, 63n8; education in, 55–56; Eisenhower in, 53; gun control in, 54; labor unions in, 54–55

US politics, 1960s, 65, 82; civil liberties in, 71; poverty in, 70, 83n13; prayer in public schools in, 71; presidential elections in, 69, 83n8, 83nn8–12; student protest movement in, 70–71, 83n14

US politics, 1970s, 98, 215; American Indian Movement in, 90; Chicago Seven trial, 89–90; crime rates in, 91; Pentagon Papers in, 90–91; Watergate scandal in, 88–89

US politics, 1980s, 215; illegal immigrants' amnesty in, 108; labor unions in, 108; Moral Majority in, 107; Reagan vs. Carter in, 106; "war on drugs" in, 107–8, 116, 117n7

US politics, 1990s, 140–41, 215; abortion clinic attacks in, 129; Branch Davidians siege in, 128; Clinton, B., investment scandal in, 126; Clinton, B., sex scandal in, 125–27, 142n10; Columbine High-School Massacre in, 129; Oklahoma City bombing in, 128; Ruby Ridge siege in, 128, 142n13; Thomas in, 127, 142nn11–12; Unabomber in, 129, 142n13; World Trade Center bomb in, 128

US politics, 2000s, 160, 161, 164, 215; Arab citizens in, 152; Catholic priests and child sexual abuse in, 153, 166n13; child sexual abuse in, 153; Hurricane Katrina and, 152–53; mass shootings and gun control in, 153; presidential elections in, 150–51, 166n11–12; terrorism and civil liberties in, 151–52

US politics, 2010s, 196–97, 215; *Citizens United v. FEC* in, 182–83; immigration

Index 255

in, 23–24, 180–81, 199n; impeachment proceedings in, 177–78; information leaks in, 179; marijuana legalization in, 180; mass shootings and gun control in, 179–80, 199nn21–22; Occupy Wall Street in, 178; presidential election 2012, 175; presidential election 2016, 175–76, 199nn15–19; public education in, 182, 199nn25–27; Russia in, 176, 177, 199n16; Tea Party Movement in, 178; US-Mexico border wall in, 181, 199n24; Women's March in, 178, 199n20
US politics, 2020s. *See* 2020
US presidential election 2020. *See* election, conspiracy theories, insurrection

vaccines, 59; for Covid-19, 203, 211n7, 211n9, 224n14
Vietnam, 35, 51
Vietnam War, 77, 84n26, 85–86, 99n2; in world events, 1960s, 65–66, 81, 82, 83nn3–5

Wallace, George, 83n11, 83n17
Wallace, Henry, 38
Washington Post, 10n14, 89, 90, 172–73, 179, 211n10; on Trump, D., 206–7, 233
weapons of mass destruction (WMDs), 146, 165n3
web-based surveys, 145
weights, 10nn17–18
welfare, 83n2, 111, 116–17, 133–34
Westwood, S. J., 224n7
WikiLeaks, 176, 179
WMDs. *See* weapons of mass destruction (WMDs)
Women's March, 178, 199n20
Women's Rights Movement, 76, 84nn23–24
women's suffrage movement, 230, 235n10
Woods, Tiger, 163, 200n43
Woodstock Festival, 80
Woodward, Bob, 89, 198n11, 202
working women, 92–93, 131, 235n12; in sex and gender, 1930s, 20, 27n14; in sex and gender, 1940s, 41, 46

world events, 213–14
world events, 1930s, 27n6; Hitler in, 11–13, 27nn4–5; Japan and China in, 15; Soviet Union and Japan in, 14; Soviet Union and Poland in, 14–15; Spanish Civil War in, 13–14; World War II in, 12–13, 26n3, 27nn4–5
world events, 1940s, 45–46, 214, 223n1; India in, 35–36, 47n6; Marshall Plan in, 36–37; Pearl Harbor to World War II end in, 32–35, 47nn2–5, 214; post-World War II, 35–37, 47n6; before US in World War II, 29–32, 46n1, 47n2
world events, 1950s: anticolonialism in, 52–53, 63n6; China in, 50, 63nn3–4; Cold War in, 51–52, 61–62; Cuba in, 51; Hungary's revolution in, 52; Israeli invasion of Egypt in, 53; Korea in, 49–50, 62n2; Soviet Union in, 51–52, 63n5; Vietnam in, 50–51, 63n6
world events, 1960s: African colonialism in, 68, 83n7; Berlin in, 67, 68, 83n6; Cold War in, 67; Cuba in, 66–67; Dominican Republic in, 68–69; Israel in, 68, 82; North Korea in, 68–69; Peace Corps in, 68; Soviet Union in, 67, 68; Vietnam War in, 65–66, 81, 82, 83nn3–5
world events, 1970s, 98; Cambodia in, 99n2; China in, 86, 99n2; Egypt and Syria in, 87; Indo-Pakistani War in, 87; Iran in, 87; Israel in, 86–87; Northern Ireland in, 88; Vietnam War in, 85–86, 99n2
world events, 1980s: Berlin Wall collapse in, 105, 117n5; Caribbean and Central America, 103–4, 117n3; China's Tiananmen Square in, 106; Cuban refugees in, 103; El Salvador aid in, 103–4, 116; Falkland Islands war in, 106; Grenada invasion in, 103; Haiti in, 124; Iran-Contra affair in, 104; Iranian hostage crisis in, 101–2, 116; Iraq invasion of Iran in, 102; Mideast in, 105–6, 116; Moscow Olympics in, 102; nuclear weapons in, 124–25; Poland's solidarity in, 105, 117n4;

Soviet-Afghan War in, 102, 117n2; Soviet Union and Eastern Europe in, 104–5

world events, 1990s, 140, 142nn7–9; Afghanistan in, 123–24; Battle of Mogadishu in, 123, 142n8; EU in, 121; Gulf War in, 122, 142n7; Kuwait in, 122; Mideast in, 124–25; Panama in, 123; Rwanda in, 121, 141n4; Somalia in, 123, 142n8; South Africa in, 122, 141n5, 142n6; Soviet Union and Europe in, 119–21, 141n2; Yugoslavia in, 120–21, 141n3

world events, 2000s, 164; Afghanistan in, 147; Cuba in, 149; Darfur in, 150, 166n10; Iran in, 149; Iraq invasion in, 146–47, 165nn3–4, 165nn5–7, 166nn5–7; Israel and Lebanon in, 150; 9/11 in, 145–46, 165n2; North Korea in, 149; prisoner mistreatment in, 147–48, 166n8; Russia in, 148–49; terrorism in, 145–46; WMDs in, 146, 147, 165n3, 166n6

world events, 2010s, 196, 223n1; Arab Spring in, 168, 198n3; Brexit in, 174; Clinton, H., on Libya in, 168–69, 198n4; Egypt in, 168; Fukushima nuclear power plant in, 175; Haitians in, 175, 199n14; Iran in, 172; Iraq in, 167–68, 198nn1–2; ISIS in, 169–71, 196, 198n7, 198n5; Israel in, 171–72; Libya in, 168–69, 198n4; North Korea in, 173, 196, 198n10–11; Rohingya in, 174, 198n13; Russia in, 173–74, 198n12; Saudi Arabia in, 172–73, 198n9; Syria in, 168, 198n3

World Trade Center, 95, 145, 165n2

World War I, 226–27, 234nn2–5, 235n6

World War II. *See* world events, 1940s

Yankelovich, Skelly, and White, 85

Yugoslavia, 120–21

About the Author

Richard Seltzer is professor of political science at Howard University. His most recent book, coauthored with Robert Smith, is *Polarization and the Presidency: From FDR to Barack Obama.*

www.ingramcontent.com/pod-product-compliance
Lightning Source LLC
Chambersburg PA
CBHW020114010526
44115CB00008B/823